ANCIENT
PEOPLE
OF THE **ANDES**

ANCIENT PEOPLE OF THE ANDES

MICHAEL A. MALPASS

CORNELL UNIVERSITY PRESS
Ithaca and London

First published 2016 by Cornell University Press

First printing, Cornell Paperbacks, 2016
Printed in the United States of America

Library of Congress Cataloging-in-Publication Data

Names: Malpass, Michael Andrew, author.
Title: Ancient people of the Andes / Michael A. Malpass.
Description: Ithaca ; London : Cornell University Press, 2016. | ©2016 |
    Includes bibliographical references and index.
Identifiers: LCCN 2015037596 | ISBN 9781501703218 (cloth : alk.
    paper) | ISBN 9781501700002 (pbk. : alk. paper)
Subjects: LCSH: Indigenous peoples—Andes Region. | Indians of South
    America—Andes Region.
Classification: LCC GN564.A53 M35 2016 | DDC 980/.01—dc23
LC record available at http://lccn.loc.gov/2015037596

Cornell University Press strives to use environmentally responsible suppliers and materials to the fullest extent possible in the publishing of its books. Such materials include vegetable-based, low-VOC inks and acid-free papers that are recycled, totally chlorine-free, or partly composed of nonwood fibers. For further information, visit our website at www.cornellpress.cornell.edu.

Cloth printing   10 9 8 7 6 5 4 3 2 1

Paperback printing   10 9 8 7 6 5 4 3 2 1

This book is dedicated to
Soren Kessemeier Malpass,
without whose unflagging support,
assistance, and encouragement it
would never have been completed

CONTENTS

PREFACE

As an instructor of college undergraduates since 1984, and as a person who spends quite a bit of time giving volunteer lectures on Andean cultures to local middle and high school classes, I have tried to be observant about what students like and do not like. Moreover, like most conscientious instructors, I work at determining what excites students about a class in prehistory. There are certain obvious things; for example, students today are much more visually oriented than my generation was. They like PowerPoint slides, websites, and videos more than reading. They are worried about how expensive books are, especially ones they might be selling at the end of the semester.

This book differs from others that are on the market in several ways that bear on these issues of what students like. First, a recurrent criticism that I have noticed on student evaluations is that there is too much emphasis on pottery and site plans, and not enough on the *people* who were responsible for them. Thus, I have tried to reduce the number of the former while increasing my discussion of the latter. Ample resources are given in the bibliography for the instructor to find more of whatever she or he wants to include, to flesh out the information in the book.

A book such as this obviously relies on the research of others and, even more so, on the published information available. The volume of information available on western South America is impressive and expands each year. As such, I have relied on particular sources of information for a lot of the basic research for this book. If one or two books served this purpose for given time periods, I have given them due credit at the beginning of the references cited. As usual, any interpretations of this information that are at variance with the authors' views are my responsibility. Finally, a book such as this can obviously take a long time to write. As such, any author has to make a decision about when to stop adding new information. For me, this was 2011, although if there was some important fact that could be added or changed with little bearing on the main point of the chapter, I used more recent information. Also, if the reviewers thought some important information or book that should be included in the bibliography had been overlooked, I also included that.

This book also reflects my personal interests in the prehistory of western South America and my own research foci. These include the early occupations and adaptations of people traditionally viewed as hunters and gatherers, the origins of cultural complexity and social inequalities, the Middle Horizon Wari culture, and the Inkas. As such, the information on these topics in chapters 3, 4, 5, 8, and 10 is perhaps more comprehensive than in other books.

A second factor influencing the coverage here, one not peculiar to this book, is the relative amount of research that has been conducted on the various cultures. The Moche have received an enormous amount of archaeological attention, especially in the past twenty years, so a great deal of information is available about them. Likewise, the Tiwanaku and antecedent cultures of the Lake Titicaca region have been the focus of several large-scale projects, and we have a wealth of material about them. The Wari too were a topic of major research in the 1970s and 1980s, and have been again more recently. Finally, the Inkas have been a topic of both archaeological and ethnohistorical investigations for longer than any other of these cultures. In contrast, some regions are necessarily covered less comprehensively, for example, the northern highlands of Cajamarca and the eastern lowlands. Nevertheless, I have tried to include as much current information about the state of our knowledge of these regions as I could. I am sure that I have overlooked some investigations that are worthy of inclusion.

This book also reflects a passion that I try to impart to my students about facts that support viewpoints. As a scientist, I want students to learn to support their ideas with evidence. As such, I have included a lot of basic data about the cultural developments in South America that are meant to show where my own perspectives on the reasons for the developments come from. My discussions of issues such as why social inequalities developed can be gauged by the information I provide, and I hope this will be a means to open discussions between students and instructors about them. This is how I myself will use this book.

This book is meant to be used in conjunction with audiovisual materials and supplemental readings that can be drawn from the bibliography. In this respect, the book can be used flexibly, covering the basic developments of the regions but allowing the instructor to expand discussions on whatever aspects seem important. With the availability of images on the Internet, it is easy for an instructor or student to find pictures and maps of virtually any of the cultures discussed as well. Although I have included as many illustrations as my publisher would allow (to keep costs down!), others are obviously available and should be used. Also bear in mind that new documentaries and specials come out often, on both public television stations and other television venues, such as the Discovery, Science, and National Geographic channels.

Probably the most popular reference source for today's students is the Internet. Yet this source is problematic, as all instructors are aware. With no editorial oversight, anyone can post information, from accurate and cutting edge to fanciful and prejudiced. There are a host of Internet sites that are useful, but given the volatility of the Internet, providing websites in a book is not prudent because such sites may disappear even before the book is in print. Instructors are encouraged to keep a list of such sites available for students, and a list can be found on the long-lived website maintained by Patricia Knobloch at San Diego State University (http://quipu.sdsu.edu/index.shtml/).

One difference between this book and more traditional surveys is that I deliberately try to use a more conversational style of writing. Although a certain amount of technical terminology is unavoidable, it is not really necessary to write in a scientific way that, perhaps, takes some of the interest out of the topic. I have avoided jargon, and where uncommon terms are needed, I have provided definitions. I hope the style of writing will be more reader-friendly than many other books.

Two main themes run through this book and form a framework for description and analysis. The first is the emergence of cultural complexity. The Andean region is one of the many places in the world where the development of social inequalities occurred, an interesting topic in itself. It is also one of the handful of places where powerful state-level societies emerged out of less complex ones without the influence of an existing state. How and why these two developments happened are topics of interest to professionals and lay readers alike. The second theme is the role that climate and the environment have on cultural developments. In the past twenty years, there has been a virtual explosion of studies on climate change in the Andes, and many archaeologists have emphasized its role in cultural transformations. I review and assess whether climate change and other environmental factors influenced the course of cultural developments. From the outset, I question how significant environmental factors were as primary causes of cultural evolution. Although there do seem to be some examples of direct causation, we must remember that cultures are flexible and can adjust to new circumstances and that environmental changes, particularly climatic ones, are slow to happen and so allow time for cultures to make such adjustments.

In chapter 1, I provide background on the terms and concepts that are important to this book. The two sources of information that are most important to any archaeologist working in the Andes, ethnohistory and archaeology, are emphasized. In addition, certain key concepts are discussed because students may be unfamiliar with them, or with aspects of them, especially those related to the Andes. Many students who use this book may not have much, if any, exposure to archaeological terminology, so I have erred on the side of more rather than less description.

In chapter 2, I provide the geographical, environmental, and chronological information needed for the rest of the book. A section on data about climate change sets the groundwork for evaluating its role in cultural developments. In chapter 3, I provide a summary of the earliest occupation of the Andes, plus additional information about the peopling of the New World in general to contextualize the information. I also cover the domestication of plants and animals in South America and the diversity of cultural adaptations that emerged after the initial peopling of the region. By necessity, in chapter 3 I cover the initial occupation of all South America, but I narrow its focus to the central Andes after the

continent has been settled. In chapter 4, I present a critical period of prehistory, the Late Preceramic, when the first complex societies, those with identifiable differences in occupation and probably status, began to emerge. Many of the most exciting new discoveries that have transformed our understanding of subsequent cultural developments date to this period. In chapters 5–10, I cover the developments in the traditional periods used in Andean studies: the Initial Period, Early Horizon, Early Intermediate Period, Middle Horizon, Late Intermediate Period, and Late Horizon.

CONVENTIONS

The spelling of the terms in this book may seem odd to the casual reader. This reflects the trend in scholarly work in the Andes toward the use of the Quechua spellings of terms rather than the more traditional Hispanic ones. Quechua, the language of the Inkas, was an unwritten language but had certain phonetic principles that suggest alternatives to Spanish. Therefore, the letters "k" and "w" substitute for "c" and "hu," respectively, so that "Inca" becomes "Inka" and "Huari" becomes "Wari." Where geographical place names are used from maps, the traditional spellings are used, such as "Nazca" rather than "Nasca." The culture that lived in the Nazca Valley, however, is spelled "Nasca," following current conventions.

Another change from more typical conventions is the use of the B.C.E. and C.E. rather than B.C. and A.D. in dates. C.E. stands for the "Common Era," and B.C.E. stands for "Before the Common Era." These terms are now considered preferable to B.C. (Before Christ) and A.D. (*anno domini,* "in the Year of Our Lord") because they are not tied to Christianity.

ACKNOWLEDGMENTS

I have always found Andeanists a friendly and helpful group, and nowhere has this manifest itself better than in this book. Many colleagues generously shared illustrations, photographs, and maps. For assistance with literature, information and interpretations, illustrations, and free sharing of work, both published and forthcoming, I am profoundly grateful to Warren Church, John Janusek, Silvia Rodriguez Kembel, Cynthia Klink, Ron Lippi, Greg Maggard, Heather McInnis, Ann Peters, Dolores Piperno, Jack Rossen, Kary Stackelbeck, and Karen Stothert. A particular debt of gratitude is due to Silvia Rodriguez Kembel and John Rick for providing useful feedback on the Chavín de Huántar section of chapter 6, and to Kurt Rademaker, who provided the radiocarbon calibrations to make all the dates consistent and commented on parts of chapter 3.

I thank a variety of individuals and offices at Ithaca College. The Office of the Provost and the dean of the School of Humanities and Sciences, Leslie Lewis, provided teaching reductions and financial assistance for both writing and completing the book as well as for defraying the costs of some of the images. The maps and figures 2.4, 8.2, and 8.13 were drawn by Matt Gorney of Information Technology Services, and his work was excellent and timely. Amy Gruar and Randi Millman-Brown were helpful in making high resolution scans of images for production purposes. Emma Heath Bealo, Albert Iglesias, Meredith Knowles, and Jules Wolinski provided much needed assistance, including but not limited to checking references and offering advice on which illustrations would be most useful. Julia Yang provided logistical and budgetary help and general support.

I owe a debt of gratitude to my son, Soren, who read the entire manuscript to identify ambiguities in arguments and unclear information from a college student's perspective.

Finally, I acknowledge the help of the Cornell University Press staff, particularly Katherine Hue-Tsung Liu, Emily Powers, and Susan Specter, and the copyeditor, Julie Nemer, who helped put the book in a more readable form. All were patient with my multitude of questions and in solving problems. I also thank the four anonymous reviewers of the original manuscript for their useful comments.

Any residual fuzzy thinking, errors, and omissions are my responsibility.

ANCIENT PEOPLE
OF THE ANDES

1

LEARNING ABOUT THE PAST

When Francisco Pizarro arrived with 168 men on the southern coast of Ecuador in 1531, he had no way of knowing that he was confronting the largest pre-Hispanic empire that existed in the New World and one of the largest of any time period anywhere. At its height, the empire of Tawantinsuyu ("the four parts together," as the Inkas called it), spanned over 30 degrees of latitude and included millions of people. Although the exact timing of the Inka expansion is currently under review, it is clear that it developed in a relatively short time, possibly in as little as 100–150 years. How the Inkas conquered this vast area is the topic of chapter 10. Here, I address the issues of how scholars know about the Inkas and the groups that preceded them. The two main ways are ethnohistory, the study of a people's history and culture through the use of texts, and archaeology, a set of methods and techniques used to learn about the past through a people's material remains. A third way is by studying the way of life of the Andean people today and in the recent past, especially those living in rural areas.

Ethnohistory and archaeology form complementary means to knowledge. As an example of this, think about our own society. If all humans suddenly disappeared, could an alien visiting North America afterward figure out what life was like by studying the tools we used, the buildings we lived in, the food we ate, and the settlements we constructed? Could the alien understand the complexity of our society? In contrast, if such an alien had access to our writings, and figured out how to translate them, then the alien would know quite a lot more. Of course, what information the alien learned would be dependent on what sources he, she, or it found. The understanding of modern society would be quite different if the alien had copies of only the *Weekly World News* than if he, she, or it discovered an *Encyclopedia Britannica*. In addition, using ethnographic data can broaden our understanding of the past. Many rural communities live a life that appears much like what is either described ethnohistorically or interpreted archaeologically.

ETHNOHISTORY

No South American culture that lived prior to the arrival of Europeans developed a writing system. Therefore, the only way we know about most of the pre-Hispanic societies of the Andes is through archaeology. We know more about the later Andean societies from what the earliest Spaniards wrote about them. Even later, as descendants of the Inkas became literate, they too become a source of information. As a result of the Spanish conquest of the

Inkas, we know a great deal about their way of life, which scholars then use to interpret earlier cultures. A few words are therefore necessary about the Spanish sources that form such an important part of our understanding of ancient Andean societies.

The written documents about the Inkas and others contain information of variable quality and therefore require careful scrutiny. Some of the best are several reports about the Inka conquest by those who participated in it, including Francisco Pizarro. After the conquest, Spanish royal authorities and clerics of the Catholic Church also recorded information about the empire, for both religious and administrative purposes. As time went on, colonial litigation occurred between natives and the Spanish authorities that become an important source of information. All these sources are what we call *primary historical documents;* they were written by people who participated in or saw the events with their own eyes. In addition to these sources, other writers followed who drew on the primary sources as well as their own backgrounds to provide additional information. Such *secondary historical documents* may not be as reliable because the authors depended on what others wrote. Still, some later sources used primary documents that no longer exist and so can provide valuable information, if carefully assessed.

One major problem with the early documents is that many have been lost. Because writing and publishing were expensive activities in the sixteenth century, reports such as the ones mentioned were not often duplicated, so only one or, at best, a few copies existed. Important archives in Europe and Latin America house many valuable documents dating to the early historical era, but it is not easy to find the documents because the systems of cataloguing are not always the best and often the manuscripts are poorly preserved. The Spanish writers of the time also had their own personal ways of writing things down, and their handwriting is sometimes difficult to read, further adding to the problem of interpretation. Finally, Spanish writers often copied each other without reference to the original, and if a copied document was incorrect, subsequent ones duplicated the mistake.

A milestone in the study of these historical documents is John H. Rowe's "Inca Culture at the Time of the Spanish Conquest," written in 1946. He made a careful study of the early documents and indicated which were most trustworthy and which contained errors. More up-to-date sources include Catherine Julien's *Reading Inka History* (2000) and Terence D'Altroy's general book, *The Incas* (2003).

How do scholars determine whether a historical document is true or not? By *true,* I mean that what was written down is an actual account of something. There were no editors to check on the truth of written statements, as there are today. One way to determine whether a writer is telling the truth is to cross-check her or his story with other sources. This is very common, and by seeing how many early documents give the same account of an incident, we can determine what is most likely to be the true rendering of the event (bearing in mind the earlier caution about how writers copied each other). Another way is to check the information against the archaeological record, which is an independent means of evaluation. For example, a particular document may state that a valley was important to the Inkas because of its agricultural output. This can be verified archaeologically by studying the field systems in the valley and evaluating how much food could have been produced there.

A major drawback to historical documents about the Andes is that the Spaniards most often asked the Inkas about their own history and the history of their empire. Moreover, they asked only the surviving members of the Inka elite. These people had their own interpretation of what had happened, when, to whom, and why, and this is what was recorded. As I discuss in chapter 10, at the end of the Inka civil war, just prior to the arrival of the Spaniards, a large number of one of the kin groups in Cuzco were executed. Therefore, what we have is an official record of the ruling faction's view of their history. But is it true? Conquered people and even other factions of the Inka nobility might have had their own views of events, but these were seldom recorded.

A final note of caution must be given, which refers to a central issue in our interpretations of how the Inka Empire developed and who the key figures were in its emergence as an Andean power. The generally accepted version of Inka history is the one written in Rowe's 1946 article, in which the entire Inka Empire is said to have developed beginning in 1438, when a young Inka noble, who became known as Pachakuti Inka, turned back a siege of Cuzco, the Inka capital, and then began a series of conquests that were furthered by his son Thupa Inka Yupanki and then by his grandson Wayna Qhapaq. In this history, the entire empire emerged in the short span of 92 years. As Brian Bauer (1992, 38–39), one of a younger generation of Inka scholars, notes, Rowe accepted this account because he felt that one of the early Spanish chroniclers, Cabello Balboa, had made a reasonable calculation of the ages of the last four Inka kings. Bauer notes, however, that other Spanish chroniclers stated that the Inkas did not keep track of their ages as we do, so we do not know exactly how old the kings were or the dates when the purported events of their reigns really occurred. Therefore, it is possible that the events that were given to the Spaniards occurred earlier than estimated. There is also some archaeological support for this view.

Other, more recent writers, such as Tom Zuidema (1964, 1982) and Gary Urton (1990), go further and suggest the early Spanish documents really cannot be used as literal sources of historical events. They suggest that the Spanish writers did not have a good enough grasp of the abstract concepts of the Inka culture to accurately describe it and attempted to fit it into their own European system. In addition, they claim the Inkas themselves distorted history for their own purposes. This view is based on more recent assessments of the Spanish documents and the recognition that there are too many different versions of events given to accept only one (Bauer 1992, 8–9).

In regard to this central issue, I follow a middle course, giving the generally accepted version of Inka history but also indicating when more recent investigations call aspects of it into question. It is important to provide the traditional account because it is the one most widely disseminated in the literature; new alternatives are provided when they are important in modifying our views.

ARCHAEOLOGY

For South American cultures prior to 1532, we can rely only on archaeology to reconstruct their ways of life. Archaeology is a field of study that belongs to the larger discipline of anthropology. Anthropology is the study of all aspects of humanity, past and present. Archaeological anthropologists study the peoples and cultures of the past, from the most distant relatives that we can call human to those that lived much more recently. To understand how archaeology learns about the past, we need to know the terms that are common to archaeology.

Archaeological Terms and Techniques

Archaeologists study the past through an analysis of the *material culture* of ancient societies. The material culture is everything that a culture has left that can be found by the archaeologist. This definition requires some explanation about the limitations on what we can know about the past. First, no society leaves a complete record of its behavior because not every behavior leaves remains. Take as an example your daily routine. You get up in the morning, clean up and get dressed, have breakfast (or lunch!), go to work or school, relax or play in the afternoon, have dinner, relax or work some more, and go to bed. How much of that activity leaves some material remains? Now think about weekly, monthly, and yearly variations in that pattern. What is different on the weekends? During the summer? And how will your behavior change after you complete school, begin a career, get married, and retire? Finally, how different is the pattern for other individuals in your society?

We can say with confidence that not every behavior leaves a trace for archaeologists to find. Whereas work leaves all kinds of remains, such as tools, work spaces, and products, social interaction leaves less: What evidence is there that a couple has married? What evidence is there that a person has religious convictions? This, of course, points up the utility of historical documents, when available, because they often can fill in these kinds of gaps in our knowledge.

A second limitation on achieving a complete understanding of past cultures is that not every material trace survives the ravages of time. In a temperate or tropical environment, where there are moderate to high levels of rainfall and warm temperatures, objects of wood, cloth, bone, and even shell and adobe will rot and disintegrate. Only durable materials such as stone, glass, and pottery remain after centuries. Thinking about this limitation, which of the behaviors I have mentioned would be identifiable after five hundred years? This limitation is why so little is known about ancient clothing, food, or even housing in nonliterate societies. In certain environments, such as very cold ones or very dry ones, perishable objects often are preserved because they do not rot. In Peru, the coastal zone is an extremely arid desert, which has preserved clothing, wooden implements, and even reed sandals, some over 4,000 years old. At the tops of the highest peaks in the Andes, well above 20,000 feet, Inka mummies with clothing and feathers have been preserved by the cold. Unfortunately, such environments are few, but we are fortunate that both cold and dry areas exist in the Andean region.

The material culture is part of a larger set of information that is collectively called the *archaeological record*. Archaeologists organize the archaeological record into the categories artifacts and ecofacts, features, structures, sites, and settlement patterns. *Artifacts* are portable objects made or modified by humans. Tools, jewelry, clothing, personal computers, and toys are all artifacts. The portability criterion is needed to differentiate not just smaller objects from larger ones but also objects that can move or be moved from ones that cannot. *Ecofacts* are nonartifactual organic and environmental remains that have cultural relevance (Renfrew and Bahn 2004, 581). Ecofacts are nearly always plant and animal remains,

or sediments and building materials made from plants or animals. They are not artifacts because they were not made or modified by humans; they were grown, hunted, or collected. Ecofacts are a very important class of objects because they give direct evidence about the kinds of foods and building materials used by a culture.

Problems with these neat categories can be found. Is a simple tool or rock really made by humans? Does a gopher skeleton represent food for the inhabitants of the site or the remains of an animal that moved in after a site was abandoned? Was the pollen collected in a sample from a plant that was eaten, or did the pollen blow into the site from elsewhere?

Features are nonportable disturbances in the soil that are due to human activity. Any unusual change in the soil at a site can be called a feature. Hearths, or fireplaces, burials, storage pits, *postholes* (the holes where poles for a structure existed that have either rotted away or been removed), wall foundations, and roads are all examples of features. It is often difficult to decide whether a disturbance is cultural or natural. The disturbance is a feature only if it can be shown to be the product of human activities.

A *structure* is anything built that is meant to define or delineate a space for human use. *Built* usually means humans have constructed some kind of wall or walls to define the space, which might be the area enclosed within the walls or an area on top of a structure, such as a platform or temple. Structures can be very simple or enormously complex, ranging from a windbreak to a massive skyscraper.

The last two categories of the archaeological record are *sites* and *settlement patterns*. A site is the location of human activity, a place where humans did something that left a mark. A site exists only if there is some way of identifying that humans used that spot. A site may consist of a scatter of stone tools or a city of 15 million people. The evidence for human activity might be the presence of artifacts or ecofacts, features or structures, or combinations of all of these. The categories of data that define a site reflect different kinds of activities and behaviors, which, in turn, tell us what life was like for the ancient inhabitants.

Finally, a settlement pattern is the distribution of sites across the landscape. A settlement pattern is usually defined for a region. Where do the sites from a culture exist? The locations can give clues about the reasons for the locations of the sites. Some may be near rivers for transportation and trade. Others may be located near good farmland or near forests where hunting is good. Still others may be near particular resources, such as stone that is good for making tools or clay for pottery. The distribution of sites, and their relative sizes, can give clues about the level of complexity of a culture as well.

In addition to the study of the material culture of an ancient society, the study of ancient human remains, termed *bioarchaeology,* provides another means for expanding our knowledge of past societies (box 1.1).

BOX 1.1 Bioarchaeology

Traditional methods of archaeology involve studying the evidence left behind by people as they lived and died. Still other kinds of information can be gleaned from the study of the people themselves when human remains are found at sites. Studying the context in which the remains are found, plus making a detailed study of the remains themselves, allows the bioarchaeologist to learn a great deal more about the people. Basic demographic information concerning the ages, sexes, and general health of a group can be determined by bone measurements and pathological analyses of skeletons. Other information about specific practices such as sacrifice and rituals can also be determined, which, in turn, can suggest reasons for the practices. In addition, chemical analyses of the bones and teeth (see box 8.1) can provide important details about the diet and place of origin of the people.

A good example of what can be learned from skeletons and their contexts is the information obtained from the excavation of Plaza 3A at the Huaca de la Luna, a large temple of the Moche culture in the Moche Valley (see chapter 7). Here, archeologists found bodies splayed in unnatural positions in what had been pools of mud at the time of deposition. The archaeological evidence suggested that the individuals were probably sacrificed during torrential rains associated with a massive El Niño disturbance (see chapter 2). But it was only the analysis of the skeletons and the identification of knife marks on the cervical vertebrae that showed that slitting their throats was part of the ritual. Other evidence showed that the individuals were tortured prior to sacrifice. The individuals were all adult males, some of whom showed previous traumas from combat, which supported the idea that they had been warriors (Verano 2001). Finally, additional studies of the dental traits suggested the individuals were nonlocals, although the significance of this point has been contested (Sutter and Cortez 2005, including the comments and reply section).

Another important contribution that bioarchaeological studies provide is evidence of human movements. This can be done in a variety of ways, such as noting general morphological features that are shared by some populations more than others (Haun and Cock Carrasco 2010) or by noting ethnic ways of deforming the head (Blom 2005; see chapter 8). Susan Haun and Guillermo Cock Carrasco (2010) find that local coastal men living near Lima during the time of the Inkas took wives from the highland regions to the east. They determined this by comparing individuals with specific bioindicators of the populations in each area. In addition, that most of the women were weavers was suggested by the kinds of muscle attachments found on some of the skeletons, which are consistent with the attachments found on modern-day professional weavers. Supporting evidence was also found in the grave goods of the individuals. Deborah Blom (2005) notes the different kinds of head deformation that were found among different populations, which can be used to identify the movements of people during Tiwanaku times.

These kinds of studies have broadened the knowledge that we have concerning the ancient cultures discussed in this book. With the studies on DNA and mitochondrial DNA that are just beginning, archaeologists should be able to identify social relations among skeletal groups that will further our understanding of these societies as well.

Archaeological Cultures

As a cautionary note, a few words are necessary about how archaeologists define cultures from the material record. In this book, I refer to various cultures, such as the Moche or Tiwanaku. But are those cultures the same as what we refer to as a culture in the present? Did they share a language, marriage and residency rules, and moral values? What about the groups that occupied the South American continent early on? In the absence of written records, our understanding of past societies is compromised, and the less evidence we have of them from archaeology, the less we understand.

In this context, it is important to note how the study of ceramics in particular influences our interpretations of the people who made them and our definitions of archaeological cultures. Ceramics constitute the largest volume of artifacts at the sites where they are found. Because a pot can be designed, constructed, and decorated in infinite ways, ceramics become a means by which people can input their ideas about proper conventions. When shared, these conventions become a means for identifying cultures. As Helaine Silverman and Donald Proulx note:

> Pottery contains technological and symbolic elements, learned by enculturation and through conviction. Each society develops its own patterns of behavior, which are reflected in artifacts, including ceramics, and other aspects of material culture

such as housing. Refining this normative view of culture is knowledge that, at the same time, material culture can be deployed consciously, expressively, and "emblemically" by societies, groups within societies, and smaller divisions thereof down to the level of the family and individual. . . . Ethnic identity is multi-dimensional; it is shifting and subjective; it is situationally subject to negotiation. . . . All of this complicates the interpretation of style as a primary basis for the identification of group cohesiveness. (2002, 13)

Therefore, we must remember that stylistic variability may be due to an individual, a group, or a culture. We must be cautious about determining which of these is the source of the variability. Two examples of this are the Moche and the Nasca. For the former, an early overemphasis on the interpretations of Moche society drawn from the detailed scenes on the pottery led to conclusions about the homogeneity of the society from north to south. In addition, the failure to adequately differentiate among different pottery styles through time clouded the picture of differing political histories for some of the valleys of that culture. Indeed, the very concept of "Moche culture" has been redefined as a result of more careful analysis and identification of the ceramic styles in the region typically identified as Moche. In like fashion, the Nasca society has had a long history of interpretational problems that are still being worked out (see chapter 7).

The Importance of Interpretation

An important element of archaeological studies, and one that is seldom explicitly discussed, is the role of interpretation. Interpretation is an integral part of classifying data into the categories just defined for them. Think about it: a piece of rock does not just say, "I am a knife used for cutting up a deer." It has a particular shape and size that suggest such a use. A feature does not tell us that it was a hearth; we have to come to that conclusion by finding charcoal, ash, and perhaps burned pieces of food or artifacts in it. Sites and settlement patterns are unambiguous in regard to defining them, but when we try to determine how the site was used or the reasons for the settlement pattern, then interpretation plays a major role.

A key concept in archaeological interpretation is *context*. Context may be defined as the relationship between a piece of data and its surroundings. What we find associated with an artifact or what kinds of ecofacts we find in a structure give clues to how the artifact or structure was used. A pot found in a structure associated with a hearth and food remains suggests it was used for cooking. The same pot found carefully placed under a floor in a temple suggests a ritual use.

In each of these scenarios, the pot is the same, but how and for what purpose it was used are quite different. The only thing that allows us to interpret the way the pot was used is context. This is one reason why archaeologists excavate so carefully; it allows us to identify every piece of data that provides a context for interpretation.

ETHNOGRAPHY

The third way that we can try to understand the past is by carefully studying how modern, or recent, people live and comparing that to our information from the past. Traditional means of agriculture and pastoralism used today, particularly in rural areas, appear to be very similar to what has been documented from the past, although this situation is changing fast. There are also social customs that still exist, such as the division of communities into *moieties* (two complementary parts) and *ayllus* (traditional groups of related kin). Religious beliefs, such as the power of mountain spirits (or *wamanis*) and the importance of offering *coca* and alcohol to the Pachamama (earth goddess) appear to have ancient, pre-Hispanic roots. Thus, studying modern people can provide insights into aspects of ancient people that might not be readily apparent through either archaeology or ethnohistory.

Nevertheless, as with the other two sources of knowledge, ethnography must be used carefully. Although recent people appear to have customs similar to those recorded in documents, we must remember that indigenous people have experienced dramatic changes since the arrival of Europeans. For example, we know that in 1572 the Spanish government introduced a resettlement policy, known as the *reducción*, that dramatically changed where many Andean people lived. Small communities located in their field systems were resettled into larger villages, where they could be both taxed and evangelized better. Such changes, plus others throughout the colonial and modern periods, have transformed native ways of living. Thus, the investigator must be careful to assess what might be ancient as opposed to what is more recent. Still, by comparing modern ways of doing things with past ones we can often identify patterns that have survived.

DATING ISSUES

Chronological control over data is absolutely essential to archaeological work. It is my experience that students often are unaware of how archaeologists date sites and of the drawbacks that are inherent in the procedures.

The dating procedure used most frequently is radiocarbon dating, which measures the amount of radiocarbon or carbon-14 (^{14}C), which decays to nitrogen-14 (^{14}N) at a uniform rate. All organisms take in the ratio that is present in the environment when they are alive, and when they die, the ^{14}C begins to decay. It takes about 50,000 years for ^{14}C to completely convert to ^{14}N, which gives an upper limit to the dating technique.

Radiocarbon ages are always given as a single year with a margin of error: 1,445 + 55 B.P. (before present, which by convention is the year 1950). This margin of error is a statistical measure of the range of the true date, which has a 68 percent chance of being accurate. To give a date that has a 95 percent chance of being accurate, the error term after the plus/minus sign is doubled, in this example to ±110 years. Technically, what this date means is that the sample is 1,445 years old, give or take 55 or 110 years. This means the true date falls in the range of either 450–560 or 395–615 C.E.[1] So the best way to interpret a radiocarbon date is by saying the real date of the sample lies somewhere between 395 and 615 C.E.—there is *no* way of knowing where in that range the true date lies! This is quite different from saying that the sample dates to 505 C.E., which implies that we can actually pin the date down to a single year. To avoid confusion for the reader, however, the dates in this book are not given as the ranges; instead, I give them as a single mid-point date. The reader should keep this in mind. In cases in which the range of dates presents a concern regarding interpretations, I provide the range and a discussion.

Another problem with radiocarbon dating is that it was assumed until the 1960s that the amount of radiocarbon was constant through time. We now know that this is not the case; during certain time periods, the amount of ^{14}C was different. Hence, the actual radiocarbon dates can be different from calendar dates as well. Scientists have studied the variations and come up with *calibration graphs* to give more accurate ranges of the dates for a given sample (Renfrew and Bahn 2004, 143–146). For dates before about 3000 B.P., the calendar dates become progressively earlier until, by 10,000 B.P., the date might be almost 1,900 years earlier (Silverman and Isbell 2008, xix). For dates more recent than 3000 B.P., the calendar dates are actually slightly later.

Dates that have been corrected are often given with the designation cal for "calibrated" (e.g., 750–850 cal B.P.).

As more and more radiocarbon dates are being calibrated, the graphs are becoming more refined. This means that older published calibrated dates may be slightly different than newer ones. This makes using published dates, whether they are calibrated or not, challenging, and a uniform calibration graph has yet to be developed. To save the reader the problem of converting B.P. years to B.C.E. ones, I have calibrated and converted all the dates in chapters 3 and 4 to B.C.E. dates. I did this only for these chapters because the dates are so much different from the uncalibrated ones. It may take some who are used to noncalibrated dates some time to adjust to this, but we need to start using the calibrated dates. (The programs used for the calibrations are given in chapter 3, note 1.) Because the problem is not really significant after about 3000 B.P., I have chosen to simply use the standard dates from the literature, although if an author uses calibrated dates, they are noted. This issue is particularly significant in chapter 6.

Two final problems with radiocarbon dating are worth noting. First, a dependable date requires that the amount of radiocarbon not be affected by anything but normal decay. If older material (with less radiocarbon) has been mixed with younger material, or vice versa, a new amount is present that will give an incorrect date. Such contamination of samples can occur very easily; for example, modern roots can invade an old hearth or carbon from a bog deposit can seep into a later house. Second, a fairly large piece of dateable material is needed for this method. Because we never have pure radiocarbon in a sample, the larger the sample, or the purer the sample, the more likely there will be sufficient radiocarbon to date. Although theoretically any material that was alive at one time can be dated, in practice certain materials give more dependable dates than others. Wood charcoal is the best because it is fairly pure carbon, whereas marine shell is problematic. Still, we need a piece of charcoal the size of a standard gambling die for a reliable date.

An advance on traditional radiocarbon dating began to be used in the 1990s. This method, called accelerator mass spectrometry (AMS), works on a different principle than traditional radiocarbon dating. Rather than measuring the radioactive decay, the spectrometer actually counts the radiocarbon atoms directly. As a result, much smaller samples can be used for this method, an advantage over the traditional method. The method should be more accurate as well; however, when AMS dates were tested against other, more traditional methods, it was determined that AMS dates should also be evaluated in their context (Rossen, Dillehay, and Ugent 1996). In addition, the problem of contamination can be more serious, and such dates still need to be calibrated as well.

CULTURAL EVOLUTION IN THE ANDES

Anthropologists and archaeologists often describe societies in terms of how complex their cultural systems are. Complexity is a difficult concept to define and identify archaeologically. There is no generally agreed-on way of defining how complex a society is, although certain concepts—occupational specialization, categories of status, nature of the political system, economic mechanisms, and religious differentiation, to name a few—are often used.

One theme that runs through this book is the relationship between population size/density and complexity. There is a clear positive association between these variables, but whether the former is responsible for the latter is debated. What can be stated is that the larger a society becomes, and the more concentrated that population becomes in its environment, the more new institutions and other cultural features arise that can be used to define complexity.

One of these critical cultural features that is emphasized in this book is the shift from an egalitarian to a nonegalitarian society. In egalitarian societies, everyone is more or less equal, and differences in status are based on attributes such as gender, age, or what an individual has accomplished during his or her lifetime (which anthropologists call *achieved status*). As such, leadership or political roles are poorly developed, and whoever is the leader of the group leads only while her or his decisions are accepted as good for the group. The leader cannot force people to do anything; she or he leads by example.

A significant cultural threshold has been passed when leaders *can* tell other community members what to do and the society provides sanctions for them to do so. How this threshold is passed is one of the great questions of archaeology, and one that is discussed often in this book. And as leaders gain the authority to determine what other people in society should do, this authority—and the leadership roles through which it is manifested—often becomes hereditary. Anthropologists use the term *ascribed status* to describe this situation.

Nonegalitarian societies are thus often based on hereditary inequalities, ones present at birth. Social inequality based on heredity means that an individual's position in society is based on his or her family ties, not on individual achievement, and that an individual's social level is therefore inherited. This is not to say that an individual may not advance her or his position by achievement; rather, such achievements are attained within a social structure defined by heredity. As nonegalitarian societies become larger, the social groups also can become *ranked,* and the ranking develops based on principles that vary from culture to culture. One common principle, and one that was widespread in the Andes, is the importance of lineage, descent from certain common ancestors, especially the founding ancestors. Therefore, the social rank of a group depends on how directly the group members are related to the founding ancestor or ancestors of their society. As we see in chapter 10, the Inkas carried this concept to an extreme in which the former kings' social groups were considered the highest because each was descended from the original founder of the Inkas.

Leadership roles in nonegalitarian societies can become institutionalized and permanent as a result of hereditary factors. When leadership is maintained by a single lineage through time, as in the Inka case, the position becomes permanent. In Andean societies, such leaders were often called *kurakas,* and in more developed societies, they had the authority to order people to do things. This suggests a fundamentally different means of accomplishing tasks, in which individuals may be required to do work for others rather than being requested to work or offered reciprocal work to accomplish them. The authority to demand and use labor is an important development of nonegalitarian societies. Whether this development was present as the position of leader became inherited is unclear, both in the Andes and elsewhere.

Most archaeologists would agree that all human societies were generally egalitarian until around the end of the Pleistocene Epoch around 10,000 years ago, when conditions changed that led to the development of social inequalities. Still, many societies remained egalitarian throughout prehistory, and some remain that way even today because their ways of life are well adapted to their environments. Why cultures switched from one to the other is an important question because many of the inequalities in modern societies can be traced back to this fundamental shift. This question is addressed in chapter 4.

Another major development as cultures grow is the shift from an economy based on *reciprocity* to one that is redistributive. Reciprocity is the mutual sharing of resources and labor. Reciprocity is fundamental to hunting-and-gathering societies, in that food is shared among members of a community because not everyone may be successful in his or her search for food during a given day. Billie Jean Isbell (1978, 167) discusses reciprocity in Andean agricultural societies in terms of the private and public spheres. Private reciprocity is manifest in the concepts of *ayni* and *minka,* an obligatory exchange of labor between parties. A person might ask relatives and friends to help clear a new field for crops. The request for the labor is minka, and the requested parties are said to "lend ayni" by coming to work. When one of the relatives needs a new field cleared by minka, the person is obligated to help the relative but is also said to "lend ayni."

Mit'a and *faena* are public exchanges of labor that involve the community as a whole and some institution. Faena is work that the community does on a common project, such as building a road. Mit'a is rotating work that members of a community do in turns for another institution, such as a church or the state government.

An important aspect of both private and public labor exchanges in the Andes today is the provisioning of the laborers with food and drink, and sometimes coca, an Andean plant that is chewed to relieve physical discomfort, or cigarettes. It is the obligation of the person or institution asking for the help to provide these things, and if they are not provided, the workers can refuse to do the labor. In egalitarian societies, these obligations can be expensive, so the ability to provide the leadership shifts from one social group to another. The group sponsoring the work, however, gains status in the community by its willingness and ability to support the common project. Thus, wealth differentials are distributed from more affluent groups to less affluent ones. This means of completing community work often is called a *cargo system;* it contrasts with a kuraka system by rotating the means of supporting group work. In a kuraka system, the kuraka and her or his social group are in charge of the activities of the community.

Both of these forms of exchange, reciprocity and redistribution, are ancient, and groups such as the Inkas used mit'a principles to extract large amounts of labor from their conquered subjects. Nonetheless, they also provided for their laborers in a way that was typical of the reciprocal systems of their local communities.

In most of the Andean world the basic unit of kinship is the nuclear family, although extended families are common, as they are in the United States. In addition, there is another social group of importance in the Andes above the family, the ayllu. The term *ayllu* has several meanings in the Andes. Here, I define it as a group of families descended from a real or fictive ancestor that shares labor, often under informal leadership. Ayllu members are bound to lend ayni to each other and participate in faena and mit'a as a group. That being said, there can be marked differences in wealth between individual families and lineages in an ayllu, based on the success of the individuals in gaining wealth. As Michael Moseley (1992) notes, these basic wealth differences may have been the seeds out of which hereditary inequalities grew.

Ayllus in Inka times, and probably earlier, were grouped into two moieties: *Hanan,* or Upper moiety, and *Hurin,* or Lower moiety. The moiety distinction is an example of a broader Andean concept of duality, the pairing of concepts, often in opposition. For the Inkas, hanan members took precedence in leading the various ceremonies and in political activities. They even lived in the upper part of Cuzco and held the higher posts in the army, administrative, and religious hierarchies (D'Altroy 2003, 90).

Redistribution involves the collection of some of the products of the different segments of society and their use either for the good of the community or to increase the personal wealth of the leader and her or his family. Redistribution seldom replaces reciprocity; it provides an additional mechanism for the distribution of resources. The collected goods are used for trade with other groups to obtain materials needed or desired by its members, or the goods may be used in rituals or in activities that benefit the entire community, such as a harvest celebration. Redistribution provides the means by which the individuals in charge may increase their own wealth or prestige, either through the mechanisms described or by keeping some of the redistributed goods for their own use.

Another feature that appears as societies become larger is occupational specialization. In small communities, everyone can do the same things, and no one needs to specialize. When many people live together, certain positions become necessary, so individuals emerge to do those tasks. One of the first is a leadership role, which might be political, religious, or both. As society grows, other leadership roles may emerge as well. Sometimes religious positions may be separate from political ones, but this is more typical of very advanced societies. As populations

increase, craft specialization may also develop, although it is usually only part-time at first. While most people are still involved in food production, some may spend part of their time making pottery, weaving cloth, or manufacturing tools or other items. Food production itself may become more specialized, with herders becoming distinct from farmers and fisherfolk. It is the emergence of occupational specialization that leads to redistribution, probably as a more efficient means of assuring that everyone gets what he or she needs.

In more advanced societies, such as the Inkas, the economy may differentiate into staple finance and wealth finance (D'Altroy and Earle 1985). Staple finance refers to the production of essential materials such as food and housing supplies; wealth finance is the production of luxury items. These two systems may diverge in such a way that only the upper strata of society are involved in wealth finance, and its activities are restricted to those strata, while everyone participates in staple finance.

A final aspect of population increase that we need to discuss is the development of social levels. With the emergence of hereditary inequalities and occupational specialization, society begins to differentiate into higher-status and lower-status individuals and lineages. In this book, I call these the elites and the commoners. There are probably several pathways to the emergence of elites (Aldenderfer 2005; Hayden 1995). Such individuals usually also become the leaders of their communities, and these individuals and their families may begin to show material benefits because of their positions, such as accumulating luxury items, building larger houses, or having more impressive burials. With further differentiation, a middle level of status may also emerge, filled by individuals whose roles are intermediate in importance. What defines the levels may differ from society to society: in some, it may be based on wealth accumulation; in others, it may be kin relations. As populations continue to increase and social, economic, and political differentiation occurs, other integrative cultural mechanisms such as bureaucracies and formal religion may emerge.

A word of caution is necessary here with regard to the concept of increasing sociopolitical complexity. Different social theorists use different terms to describe the kinds of societies that manifest different suites of the traits just described. Probably the most widely used framework is the band-tribe-chiefdom-state system (e.g., Price and Feinman 2010). Whereas the term *band* as it is traditionally used is probably an accurate description of the earliest societies and *state* describes the latest ones I discuss in this book, the terms *tribe* and *chiefdom* are more problematic and I do not use them. Instead, I emphasize aspects of complexity such as the emergence of ascribed status, redistributive economies, craft specialization, and political differentiation.

The most problematic of the sociopolitical levels is the chiefdom, the level in which hereditary inequalities and leadership are said to emerge (Service 1975). Chiefs in classic chiefdoms, however, often had power that far exceeds the authority that appears in the archaeological record early on, when social inequalities first emerge. As Moseley (1992) notes, the ethnohistorical terms kuraka and *señorío* are probably better analogues for early sociopolitical institutions than chiefdom. Hayden (1995) coins the term *transegalitarian* to describe different kinds of inequalities that develop and become hereditary. It is these kinds of societies that are a focus of inquiry here, particularly at the critical point where inequalities begin to emerge.

One reason for this focus is that there is an emerging view in the studies of Andean societies that they did not follow the developmental trajectories associated with the band-tribe-chiefdom-state model (Moseley 1992). For example, in the traditional scheme the role of kinship diminishes as chiefdoms become states and bureaucracies replace lineage-based institutions of government; however, this did not occur in the Andes. There, traditional kin groups continued to play important roles even as societies and polities became larger and more complex by other criteria.

What is interesting to archaeologists is the question of *why* these different cultural features develop as a society becomes larger. Many theorists have their explanations, but no one theory has been proposed that explains why societies become more complex everywhere. Indeed, the conditions under which such complex societies emerged may be the most critical aspect to consider. I review the evidence and reasons for emerging complexity in different regions of the Andes throughout this book.

SUMMARY

In this chapter, I have discussed how historians and anthropologists study past peoples using documents and ethnography and some of the problems inherent in such studies, as well as how archaeologists study the past, and the basic concepts of the field. I have defined several terms that are important for understanding how archaeologists work and for reading the literature of the field. Also discussed was the concept of sociopolitical complexity and the importance of context in archaeology. We now can look more specifically at western South America and the prehistory of this fascinating region.

2

GEOGRAPHY OF THE CENTRAL AND SOUTH ANDES

Western South America is a land of stunning contrasts, ranging from arid coastal deserts at sea level to the highest peaks in the Western Hemisphere to lush, tropical rain forests. The contrasts have presented both opportunities and challenges to humans from their earliest arrival. Unique combinations of climate and geology have led to a wide variety of local environments. In this chapter, I look at the major regions in the area of western South America that are the focus of this book. It is important to review what the environmental conditions were for the inhabitants of these regions to understand the challenges that they faced. But the environment only provides or limits opportunities for humans; it does not determine the path of cultural development. Because of culture, humans have always had a variety of possible responses to environmental challenges: droughts may lead to migration to more favorable regions, to warfare for conquest, or to more intensive means of farming, such as irrigation.

This book is limited to discussing the cultural developments of the area between the Peruvian-Ecuadorian border in the north and northern Chile in the south, and the Pacific Ocean in the west and the eastern slopes of the Andes. The exceptions to this focus are in chapters 3 and 10, in which I discuss other regions in regard to the earliest and latest developments on the continent.

Although ecological variability is the hallmark of this area, there are three main kinds of environments: the Andes Mountains, the western coastal desert, and the tropical rain forest.

THE ANDES MOUNTAINS

The Andes run the entire length of South America, although they are generally lower in the northern and higher in the central and southern regions. There are between two and four major chains of the Andes, and all are oriented north-south. The Andes Mountains are the result of the collision of the east-moving Nazca Plate under the Pacific Ocean and the west-moving South American continental plate. Because the Nazca Plate is made of a denser material, it is forced under South America, which has the effect of pushing up the western part of South America. This upthrusting resulted in the Andes. Similar actions from the collisions of different plates caused the Himalayas and the mountain chains of the western United States and Mexico. These collisions also cause earthquakes and volcanoes.

As a result of the formation of the Andes, the typical mountain setting in the region is a deep valley surrounded on both sides by high mountain peaks

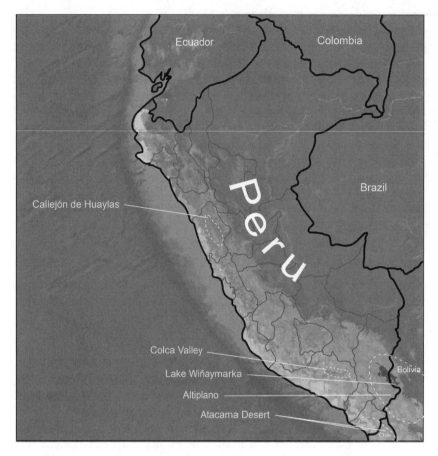

Figure 2.1. Locations of features mentioned in chapter 2. Map by Matt Gorney.

(figure 2.2). The vertical distance between the bottom of the valley and the adjacent peaks can be thousands of meters. The north-south trend of the valleys makes travel in that direction generally easier than east-west, for which one has to climb to the lowest pass between the peaks to cross into the next valley. In the north, in Ecuador, the Andes reach their narrowest, being only about 100–160 km wide, whereas in the south, near the Chilean-Peruvian border, they reach their widest, approximately 650 km wide.

A unique part of the Andes is the region around Lake Titicaca in southern Peru and northern Bolivia, the highest navigable lake in the world. This region is called the *Altiplano* ("high, flat land") (figure 2.3). It is called this because much of it is above 4,000 m

(13,000 ft) and is rolling to completely flat, with only some low hills to break the vistas. As we see in later chapters, this region saw important cultural developments that were unique in South America.

The climate of the Andes can be characterized as having two seasons, dry and wet, although there are also temperature differences, which become more marked the farther south one goes. The rainy season occurs in the Southern Hemisphere's summer, from December to February, whereas the dry season lasts from May to September, the austral winter. The rains come from Amazonia and the eastern regions, where warm air rises up against the Andes, loses its ability to carry water, and drops it as the rain. As a result, the Andes are considerably wetter in the east than in the west, especially in

Figure 2.2. The Callejón de Huaylas, a typical Andean valley. Photo by author.

Figure 2.3. The Altiplano. Photo by author.

the wider regions in the south. There is also a north-south gradient such that the northern Andes receive much higher amounts of rainfall than the southern Andes. There is a large yearly variation in rainfall amounts. It should also be noted that these trends are general ones and that the particular geographical setting of a valley determines whether it gets a lot of rain or a little.

The typical Andean setting of high peaks with a deep valley between leads to the development of vertical environmental zones. Rainfall increases and temperature decreases with increasing altitude. This combination of altitudinal variations in rainfall and temperature defines particular ecological zones, as can be seen in figure 2.4. The *yunga* zone is the region between about 500 and 2300 m above sea level. It is a warm arid zone of thorny plants, such as cactus and prickly trees. With irrigation, a wide variety of plants can be grown there (figure 2.5). The zone between 2300 and 3500 m is the *quechua* zone, one of moderate rainfall and temperatures. It is a highly productive zone today, where many kinds of economically important plants, such as maize, quinoa, potatoes and other tubers, squashes, and various fruits

grow (figure 2.6). Above the quechua zone is the *puna* zone, which is high-altitude grassland. This region, lying between 3500 m and the permanent snow line (which varies from region to region), is above the tree line, hence, only hardy grasses, notably *ichu,* and other cold-resistant plants exist there (figure 2.7). Even though much of the puna zone is near or above the limit of agriculture, hardy species of tubers, such as potatoes and *ullucu,* can be grown in the lower range. It is, however, a prime herding zone and was important prehistorically for this reason. It should be noted, of course, that these zones grade into each other, so it is difficult to define the borders between them.

Stephen Brush (1977), an anthropologist, discusses the ways that Andean people adapted their cultural systems to accommodate this vertical zonation of environmental zones. They adapted in different ways depending on the distribution of the three zones. In many areas, the yunga, quechua, and puna zones are located fairly close together, between a valley bottom and a mountain top. In such a situation, Andean people located their villages in the quechua zone to take advantage of the favorable conditions there. They

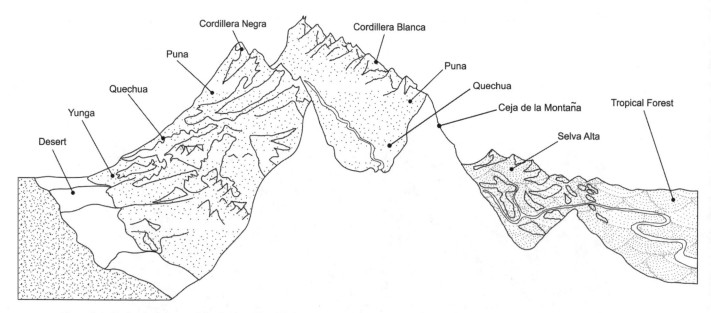

Figure 2.4. Ecological zones of the Andes. Drawing by Matt Gorney.

Figure 2.5. The yunga zone. Photo by author.

located their potato and tuber fields in the lower portion of the puna and also used it to pasture their herds of *camelids* (llamas and alpacas, two domesticated New World members of the camel family). Their fields were also placed in the yunga zone. Individuals would spend a few days or weeks in temporary shelters in the puna zone, planting and later harvesting tubers and pasturing their herds. In the yunga zone, they would spend short times gathering fruits and planting and harvesting low-altitude plants, such as *achira* and *yuca*. The fields were maintained in all these zones and were scattered about to avoid a major catastrophic loss of their food. In addition, many different varieties of beans, squash, maize, and potatoes were developed and used, which had different

resistances to pests, had different uses as food, and were adapted to particular altitudes. In this way, Andean people could minimize a disaster that would wipe out their food supply. This buffer system is still in use today.

In other regions, where all three ecological zones were not in proximity, Andean people developed other means for obtaining the resources in each zone. On the Altiplano, virtually the entire region is in the puna zone; hence, many of the major food crops cannot be grown. In such regions, villages would often send individuals on long caravans to trade puna resources (dried meat, potatoes, and wool) for those of the quechua and yunga zones. At each village along the route, the individuals would trade a consignment of highland resources for local ones. After reaching the coast, they would return, collecting their traded-for resources along the way. Sometimes these round trips would take two months. Such caravans still cross the Andes through regions such as the Colca Valley, where travelers can see the brightly colored ribbons tied to the llamas as they pass first going down valley to the coast and then back up (figure 2.8).

Finally, another pattern developed in which villages in the puna zone would send colonies to the lower zones; there the members of the puna village would live, growing the local resources and exchanging them with their home village. The advantage of such colonies was the greater assurance that the resources in other zones could be obtained because there was no exchange with people not from the village. The extreme version of this pattern was developed by the Inkas, if not others before them, in which the Inka state sent colonies of people to grow products in different ecological zones far from their native homes.

The preceding description of the mechanisms for gaining access to resource zones is based largely on cultures lacking any kind of centralized control or administration. John Murra (1972), an ethnohistorian, discusses the mechanisms by which political authorities could access such zones via colonies and control of trade as well. Maria Rostworowski de

Figure 2.6. The quechua zone. Photo by author.

Figure 2.7. The puna zone. Photo by author.

Figure 2.8. Llama caravan passing through the Colca Valley of southern Peru. Photo by author.

Diez Canseco (1977c) discusses an analogous mechanism along the coast, called horizontality, in which powerful lords controlled resource zones in different valleys to achieve the same result (discussed in Salomon 1985). In these cases, the resources could be geographical, such as farming and fishing, but could also include craft specialties and merchants.

THE WESTERN COAST

Between approximately the Peruvian-Ecuadorian border and central Chile, the region between the Pacific Ocean and the Andes is an arid desert. In fact, the Atacama Desert of northern Chile is the driest in the world (Lettau and Lettau 1978). A unique combination of the north-flowing, very cold Humboldt (or Peru) Current in the Pacific Ocean, the Andes, and a high-pressure system in the south Pacific Ocean leads to a situation in which rainfall

seldom occurs. This same climatic situation results in a constant upwelling of cold subsurface water that keeps the coast temperatures stable and cool. The aridity is such that there are no plants, not even cactus, except in certain sheltered areas. Along the coast, there are two seasons, the sunny summer and the foggy winter. During the latter, thick fogs, called *garuas,* settle over the coast, and rise and fall during the day. At no time, however, is there actual precipitation.

The coastal hyperaridity is broken in valleys where rivers flow down from the western slopes of the Andes, collecting the rainfall in the higher altitudes. In such valleys, agriculture is possible because the soils are quite rich. Still, the river valleys are widely spaced, occurring about every 40 km along the Peruvian coast but much more widely spaced in Chile.

Two other zones of economic importance exist along the coast. The first is the ocean itself, which is one of the richest biomes in the world. The same conditions that keep the coast dry lead to an upwelling of nutrients from deeper to shallower waters, feeding a food chain of microorganisms, small fish and invertebrates, and then larger fish, sea birds, and sea mammals. The coastline itself has many microenvironments, from sandy shores where clams and other burrowing organisms thrive, to rocky headlands, where mussels and rock-clinging species exist. The enormous abundance of the sea was a key element in the emergence of large-scale societies there (see chapter 4).

A final resource area along the coast is the *lomas,* or fog meadows. These are limited areas in which hills rise above about 400 m (1,300 ft) near the shore, high enough to catch the moisture-laden garuas in the winter. The fogs provide enough moisture to support a relatively simple ecosystem that was small to large in extent, depending on the local geographical conditions. Lomas formations were used during early times as a source of food and probably fiber for clothes and fishing lines, and later as pasture for domesticated herds. The lomas are relatively scarce in northern Peru, occurring in isolated zones where mountain outliers rise up from the sea. They gradually become more extensive and continuous in southern Peru and northern Chile, although modern overgrazing by cattle has largely depleted them in regions close to towns. During times of El Niño rainfall (see below), they can become quite widespread (plate 1A).

There is one important exception to this general condition of aridity. At times, the stable climatic conditions of the coast are disrupted by a southward flow of warm equatorial water that is known as an *ENSO* (El Niño/southern oscillation). ENSOs originate in the western Pacific as a pulse of warm water that flows eastward along the equator and then down the western South American coast. The warm water flows over the colder water, allowing rain clouds to form and torrential rains to fall on the arid coast. Such downpours, which can last for months in a severe ENSO, cause incredible destruction because there are no plants to stabilize the ground. Mudslides, called *huaycos* in Spanish, flow down the slopes and valleys, washing out irrigation canals, fields, and communities. In the ocean, the normal abundance of the sea is drastically reduced. Sea birds and marine life die by the millions. The only positive effect of an ENSO is a temporary increase in terrestrial plant life, which can then be used as pasture, although this dries up after a few years. A severe ENSO spreads its devastation from northern Peru to northern Chile, whereas a less severe one affects only Peru.

ENSOs are highly variable in both their occurrence and severity. Until the twentieth century, a major ENSO occurred only about twice each century. In the twentieth century, however, there were major events in 1925, 1982–1983, and 1998, with less severe ones also in the years between 1925 and 1992. As discussed in the section on Climate and Climate Change, there is some evidence that ENSOs are a recent development along the coast.

Like the vertical system of resource use described for the highlands, the different juxtapositions of the coast, river valley, and lomas zones in different regions led to different patterns of exploitation. Before the development of agriculture, a permanent village could be located where all three were found in close proximity. Where the zones were more widely spaced, a village would usually be located in the valley flood plain to take advantage of the availability of water, and seasonal or sporadic visits would be made to the other zones as needed. As agricultural societies developed, specialized fishing and farming communities emerged that exchanged their products for those in the other zones. At that time, the lomas lost much of their importance, except as temporary pasture for llamas and alpacas during ENSOs.

THE TROPICAL RAIN FOREST AND EASTERN LOWLANDS

All along the eastern flanks of the Andes, the mountains descend into lowlands that are thick tropical forest, seasonally soggy parklands, or more arid grasslands, depending on how far south one goes. We know much less about this region archeologically, so only a brief description is necessary.

The most important zone in this region is the Amazonian rain forest, lying east of the Andes in Ecuador, Peru, and northern Bolivia. It is a low-lying, hot, and humid region, much of it below 500 m above sea level. There is a rainy season during December to February, but the temperature variation is much less than in other regions, being generally warm year round. The resources of the tropical forest are widely scattered. A variety of plants that were domesticated have their probable origins in this zone, and it has always been important for its medicinal plants.

There is a transitional zone worth mentioning between the high Andes and the low tropical forest. This zone, called the *ceja de la montaña,* "eyebrow of the jungle," is characterized by its extremely thick vegetation and steep slopes. The region has one major plant of importance to Andean societies—coca. This plant today and in the ancient past was chewed with a small amount of ash, calcium carbonate, or other base to release the alkaloid agents that have the effect of numbing the mouth and reducing hunger and fatigue as long as the user continues to chew it. The effects are mild and non–habit forming. In an environment in which work is hard and the conditions can be severe, chewing coca was an indispensable means of coping. One species of coca is a ceja-zone plant, although a different species is grown in an analogous zone on the western flanks of the Andes, called the *chaupiyunga* (Jack Rossen, pers. comm. 2010). The chaupiyunga is a narrow zone above the desert but below the quechua zone, and it is the prime coca-growing region along the western flanks of the Andes.

The tropical lowlands to the east of the Andes are virtually unknown archaeologically because of the difficulty in conducting research there. Today, there are few roads or means of transportation, and the vegetation is so thick that it is hard to do either surveying or excavations. In addition, due to the high temperatures, high humidity, and thick vegetation, sites are buried rapidly. Along rivers and streams, sites are destroyed by meanders, floods, and deposition. Finally, the bugs, snakes, and generally inhospitable climate make it a less enjoyable place for archaeologists to work! This does not mean that the area was any less important; it simply means we know much less about what kinds of cultural developments occurred there.

ANDEAN CLIMATIC CHANGE

Identifying past climate change is not always easy. Some of the ways this can be done are by noting changes in plant or animal communities that indicate a different environment than the present one. Geological features can be indicative as well, such as the presence of moraines, piled up earth that are the result of the melting of glaciers. Lake cores can record changes in the pollen communities that indicate shifts in the plants of a region, and ice-core data can show subtle changes in the amount of snowfall over time. In the arid environment of the coast, evidence of massive flooding can be interpreted to be the result of ENSOs, and a long absence of flooding can indicate an absence of this kind of perturbation. Evidence from both the coast and highlands indicate that not only did the climate change dramatically at the end of the *Pleistocene* but that the *Holocene* climate has varied through time as well.

Thus, the present climate and the environmental zones that are influenced by it have not always been as they are today. During the last ice age, called the Pleistocene Epoch, global climates were generally cooler, which allowed for greater snowfall in the winter and less snowmelt in the summer. The result in the northern hemisphere was massive continent-wide glaciers that covered much of Canada, extending into the continental United States as far south as St. Louis. This ice was over a mile thick. Similar glaciers covered most of northern Europe and Asia. In the southern hemisphere, however, there were no continental glaciers due to the reduced amount of landmass. Glaciers did extend far down the slopes of the Andes, however.

Global temperatures were rising by 18,000 B.C.E.,[1] with several minor colder fluctuations, until modern temperatures were achieved around 9600 B.C.E. This marks the boundary between the Pleistocene and Holocene (the current geological epoch). Note, however, that global climates have fluctuated periodically throughout the Holocene, although temperatures have not decreased to Pleistocene levels.

The lowering of global temperatures and the growth of continental glaciers had two major effects of significance to humans. First, the environmental zones I have defined moved downslope, so the lower limit of each was at a lower altitude. One important effect of this was an expansion of the puna zone, making it more extensive and continuous (Lynch 1974). The temperature decrease had other effects on local environments (discussed in subsequent chapters). The second major effect of the Pleistocene conditions was a lowering of the sea level. As water was locked up in ice, the sea level dropped. Scientists have ascertained that the sea level had dropped by more than 100 m as late as 18,000 B.C.E. The significance of this drop is that any part of the continental shelf that was under less than 100 m of water became dry land. Although the shelf drops below this level within 10–16 km (6–10 miles) of the present coastline over much of Peru and Chile, in northern Peru, as much as 100 km (60 miles) of coast were added (Richardson 1981).

As the Pleistocene ended, global temperatures rose, the ice sheets melted, and sea level began to rise. The environmental zones rose to their current altitudes as well. This process took several thousand years, and the sea reached its current level only around 5,000 years ago. Therefore, any early archaeological site in that former coastal region is now underwater.

Regarding climate change along the coast during and after the Pleistocene, a distinction must be made between the regions north and south of 12° S. South of this latitude, the climate was hyperarid during the Pleistocene, a fact supported by several lines of research, including soil development (Noller 1993),

differences in lomas (Rundel and Dillon 1998), and preservation features (Sandweiss et al. 1997). For the early Holocene period, there is a growing body of evidence that indicates an increased aridity about 9600–5800 B.C.E., at least below about 12° S latitude. A marked drop in the number of archaeological sites along the coast in Chile and southern Peru, called the *Silencio Arqueológico* ("Archaeological Silence"), argues for a drop in the amount of water available in this region. The best explanation for the lack of water is increased coastal upwelling, which may have decreased coastal freshwater resources in this region (Fontugne et al. 1999). In addition, evidence for a drop in ENSOs is indicated by a lack of flood deposits during this time. Flood deposits before about 11,100 B.C.E. and after 6100 B.C.E. support there having been a climate more like today (Keefer et al. 1998; Fontugne et al. 1999).

In contrast, in the region north of 12° S, but especially north of 10° S, several lines of evidence support the view that this region had more rainfall until 3800 B.C.E., including evidence of warm-water species of clams and fish, and land animals that occupy only grassland environments (Richardson 1978; Rollins, Richardson, and Sandweiss 1986). Thus, the north coast of Peru was not only much more extensive, due to the lowered sea level, but also much better watered until about then. This set of environmental circumstances also suggests that ENSOs did not develop until after that time (Sandweiss et al. 1996). More recent data argue that ENSOs reached their current frequency only after 1200 B.C.E. There is little to suggest marked changes in the climate along the coast since then, although evidence for dramatic ENSO events is seen throughout this period (Dillehay and Kolata 2004).

Evidence for climate change in the highlands comes from ice cores taken from high mountain glaciers, along with cores from lakes or infilled lakes. Ice cores from Mt. Huascarán in central Peru indicate that the Pleistocene ended around 9600 B.C.E., with warmer conditions existing between 7500 and 4000 B.C.E. The period 5500–4000 B.C.E. marked the maximum warming phase for this period, with a gradual cooling of the temperature to current conditions afterward (Thompson et al. 1995). Multiple indicators support increased aridity during this same period (Chepstow-Lusty et al. 2003). Lake Titicaca dropped to as much as 100 m below its present level, and reached its current levels only after 1600 B.C.E. (Chepstow-Lusty et al. 2003; Wirrman, Mourguiart, and de Oliviera Almeida 1988). The warming and drying of the climate during this period in western South America is similar to evidence from elsewhere in the world where this warmer-than-usual period has been identified. In North America, this is called the Hypsithermal Period and in Europe the Atlantic Period.

Support for decreased rainfall in the adjacent highlands is found in the lower water levels in Lake Titicaca during this same period. Due to the extremely flat topography around the shores of much of Lake Titicaca, a drop of 1 m in the water level of the lake can result in a 5-km shift in the shoreline (Janusek 2008). Cores taken along the southern end of the lake by Mark Abbott et al. (1997) show dramatic fluctuations over the past 3,500 years (figure 2.9). Prior to around 1500 B.C.E., Lake Wiñaymarka, the southernmost basin of Lake Titicaca, was probably dry land due to the decreased rainfall. The lake rose rapidly to its modern levels over the next five centuries, only to drop again starting around 1000 B.C.E. After two centuries of low levels, the lake rose again, only to fall for another two centuries, between 450 and 250 B.C.E. The lake rapidly rose to levels above the present level by around 200 B.C.E. but dropped again significantly by 100 C.E. After 300 C.E., the lake rose and remained high until about 1100 C.E., when it dropped again, staying low until at least 1300 C.E. and perhaps until 1500 C.E., after which it rose to its present levels (see box 2.1).

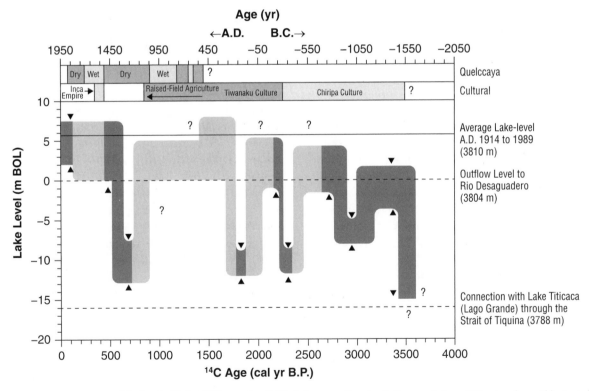

Figure 2.9. Fluctuations in lake level of Lake Wiñaymarka. BOL, below overflow level. By permission of Elsevier, from Abbott et al. 1997; permission conveyed through Copyright Clearance Center, Inc.

The drops in the lake level were clearly the result of decreased rainfall, and the rises corresponded to increases in rainfall. These rainfall changes are recorded in ice-core data from glaciers in the central Andes. Although several indicators suggest that conditions in the highlands have become gradually cooler and wetter since 3800 B.C.E., much shorter periods of precipitation change have been documented in the past 1,500 years. Ice-core data from the Quelccaya glacier in central Peru indicate there were several severe periods of drought, when rainfall was at least 20 percent lower than today, interspersed with periods of higher than normal rainfall (Thompson et al. 1985).

BOX 2.1 Periods of aridity and higher rainfall recorded in the Huascarán glacier, Peru, over the past 1,500 years

Periods of aridity (C.E.)	Periods of higher rainfall (C.E.)
540–560	
563–594★,†	610–650
636–645	760–1040
1245–1310★	
1500–1720★	

★ Periods in which rainfall is 20 percent lower than the mean.
† The original data published by Thompson et al. in 1985 gave dates for this episode of 570–610 C.E. These were corrected by Shimada et al. (1991) to the range given here. This reduction is also 30 percent lower than the mean, indicating a particularly severe drought.

A more recent pollen core taken from Lake Marcacocha, located in the eastern Andes near Cuzco, extends this sequence and suggests that there was a generally cooler and seasonally dry period there between 2200 and 750 B.C.E., followed by a dry episode from 700 B.C.E. to 100 C.E. (Chepstow-Lusty et al. 2003). A marked drop in agricultural pollens between 100 and 1100 C.E. is interpreted as indicating cooler temperatures, leading to depopulation, followed by a much drier period starting around 1100 C.E.

Note that there is a widespread acceptance of a relationship between severe ENSOs along the coast and periods of severe drought in the highlands. Smaller ENSOs, however, may not be correlated with drought and, in fact, are associated with normal or wetter conditions (Chepstow-Lusty et al. 2003).

The dates of the changes in lake level and these ice cores indicating extreme periods of aridity and rainfall often correlate with periods of cultural change, which suggests a cause-and-effect relationship. Nevertheless, most researchers studying this relationship argue that caution is needed when drawing conclusions due to the ability of cultural systems to respond to such changes (Dillehay and Kolata 2004; Erickson 1999; Shimada et al. 1991).

For the Amazonian region, current evidence supports a shrinking of the tropical forest into what is now the heart of Amazonia during the Pleistocene and the replacement of the rain forest by mixed forests (Lynch 1983, 99–103; Thompson et al. 1995). What effect that had on people traveling or living in this region is unclear. It has been suggested that the present ceja de la montaña zone was cooler and drier grassland, which might have facilitated travel along the eastern flanks of the Andes during the Pleistocene (Lynch 1974). Changes in this region during the Holocene have not been well documented.

All these climatic features had impacts on human occupation during these periods.

CHRONOLOGY OF ANDEAN DEVELOPMENTS

In this book, I cover approximately 14,000 years, from the earliest good evidence of human occupation to the arrival of the Spaniards in the early part of the sixteenth century C.E. Because of the length of time covered, it is necessary to divide time into more manageable units for purposes of discussion. Archaeologists use the appearance of distinctive cultural developments to mark changes in periods of time. The prehistory of the Andes is characterized by periods when cultural influences spread out from a center over a small to large area, followed by other periods when this integrating influence ceased and cultures followed their own developmental pathways. In archaeology, periods when an area is integrated by a single cultural influence over a relatively short period of time are called *horizons*. The last of these great influences was the Inkas, but others preceded them. Therefore, these influences form a convenient way to mark the beginning and end of time periods.

Different archaeologists define the time periods in different ways. The most common chronology used by North American archaeologists is the Rowe-Lanning system, originally defined by John Rowe in 1960 and then modified later by Edward Lanning and others. This system is used in this book. For convenience, the uncalibrated dates are given in the traditional B.C.E.-C.E. scale.

Preceramic Period (15,000[?]–1800 B.C.E.)

The time when humans first occupied South America until the appearance of pottery making. It is the period when animals and plants were domesticated and village life replaced nomadic hunting and gathering. This long span is divided into three subperiods: Early, Middle, and Late. The Early Preceramic begins with the appearance of humans in South America and ends with the beginning of the Holocene Epoch around 9600 cal B.C.E. The Middle Preceramic spans 9600–4,000 cal B.C.E., corresponding to the Early and part of the Middle Holocene in climate terms. This was a critical time when plants and animals were domesticated in several areas of South America. The Late Preceramic (4000–1800 B.C.E.) was marked by the first appearance of temples, large settlements, and social differentiation.

Initial Period (1800–900 B.C.E.)

This period saw the expansion of the settled way of life and the first appearance of pottery as well as an intensification of the processes of social differentiation, reflected in larger temples and other structures in some regions.

Early Horizon (900–200 B.C.E.)

The spread of the Chavín art style and its associated cult over northern and central Peru marks the first appearance of a widespread cultural influence.

Early Intermediate Period (200 B.C.E.– 600 C.E.)

This period saw the emergence of many local cultures that had exquisite art, such as the Moche, Nasca, and Recuay. Warfare increased during this time, and societies became even more complex in certain areas.

Middle Horizon (600–1000 C.E.)

This period marked the rise of two state-level societies, Wari and Tiwanaku, and the spread of their influence over much of the central and southern Andes, respectively.

Late Intermediate Period (1000–1438 C.E.)

This was the time after Wari and Tiwanaku influence waned, when regional conflicts between increasingly powerful local cultures are indicated, culminating in the emergence of the Inka in the region around Cuzco.

Late Horizon (1438–1532 C.E.)

This was the time when the Inkas brought much of western South America under their control. The period ends with the appearance of the Spaniards and their capture of the last Inka king, Atawallpa.

This chronology has a major disadvantage in that it was developed for the Central Andean region, where it works very well. But the farther from the Central Andes we go, such as into northern Peru and Ecuador, southern Peru, Chile, and Bolivia, the less well it describes the developments. This is because both the timing of the cultural markers and their presence/absence are different in other regions. For example, the Early Horizon is the time of Chavín influence in the Central Andes, yet this influence never reached farther south than the region around Ayacucho. Therefore, this cultural marker is nonexistent in southern Peru. In like fashion, the Initial Period is defined by the appearance of pottery, but this development occurs earlier in Ecuador and later in northern Chile, where it becomes common only around 1000 B.C.E. For this reason, other scholars use different terms for the time periods, such as the Formative, Regional Development, and Regional States instead of the Early and Late Intermediate Periods (Lumbreras 1974). The term *Formative* is particularly problematic because it is sometimes used chronologically, as in Lumbreras's and Peter Kaulicke's (1994) schemes, but other times is used as a level of cultural development, more or less corresponding to the Neolithic of the Old World.

Currently, there is no one accepted chronology for the cultural developments, and there have even been calls for avoiding defining periods altogether (Silverman 2004b). Still, I use the Rowe-Lanning chronology here whenever necessary because it is the one that is most familiar and the one used in the literature from which this book is drawn. I modify it, or avoid using it completely, when discussing the south-central Andes.

3

THE TIME BEFORE TEMPLES
The Early and Middle Preceramic Periods

We do not know with any confidence when people arrived in South America, but we know from a host of different kinds of evidence that their ancestors came from Asia. Subsequently, they spread southward through North and Central America, ultimately arriving in South America. The question of the arrival date in South America is obviously bound up with the larger question of when people arrived in North America. Unfortunately, we have little knowledge of when people came across from Asia. But we can discuss the evidence that is known and the environmental conditions that would have impeded, or assisted, the human occupation of the New World.

From evidence presented in this chapter, we know that people arrived in South America during the Pleistocene Epoch. As discussed in chapter 2, this was a time of globally cooler temperatures, when continental glaciers covered much of northern North America and Eurasia. Because sea level was as much as 100 m lower than it is today, the present-day Bering Straits, which separate Siberia from Alaska, were a 1,000-km-wide region of dry land, now known as Beringia. This allowed humans to walk into the new land without even knowing they were entering one. They followed game herds across into central Alaska, which, oddly enough, was unglaciated at the time. But then they faced the massive glaciers that impeded their migrations south.

There are two possible ways people were able to move south of the great glaciers covering Canada. One is along the Pacific coastline (Fladmark 1978). The Pleistocene coastline is now underwater, but we can suggest it was a very irregular region of glaciers entering the ocean from the Rocky Mountains to the east and of dry land and islands with isolated pockets of forest. Such a route would have required both boats of some kind and a *maritime* (sea-oriented) subsistence base. Because people had arrived in Australia much earlier than this (ca. 45,000 B.C.E.) using some kind of boat, the early inhabitants' having knowledge of watercraft is not unreasonable. If people had boats, then it is also likely they were aware of maritime resources and how to exploit them. Therefore, many scholars feel the early inhabitants moved down the Pacific coastline to occupy the continent south of the glaciers. Once groups arrived in present-day Washington State, they could easily have followed the Columbia River into the interior and spread out from there. Other people simply continued down the Pacific coast, perhaps as far as South America.

Alternatively, scholars have suggested a land route through the glaciers as the means of human entry into the rest of North America. Although the Pleistocene is characterized as being a colder time than the present, there were swings in temperature in which colder

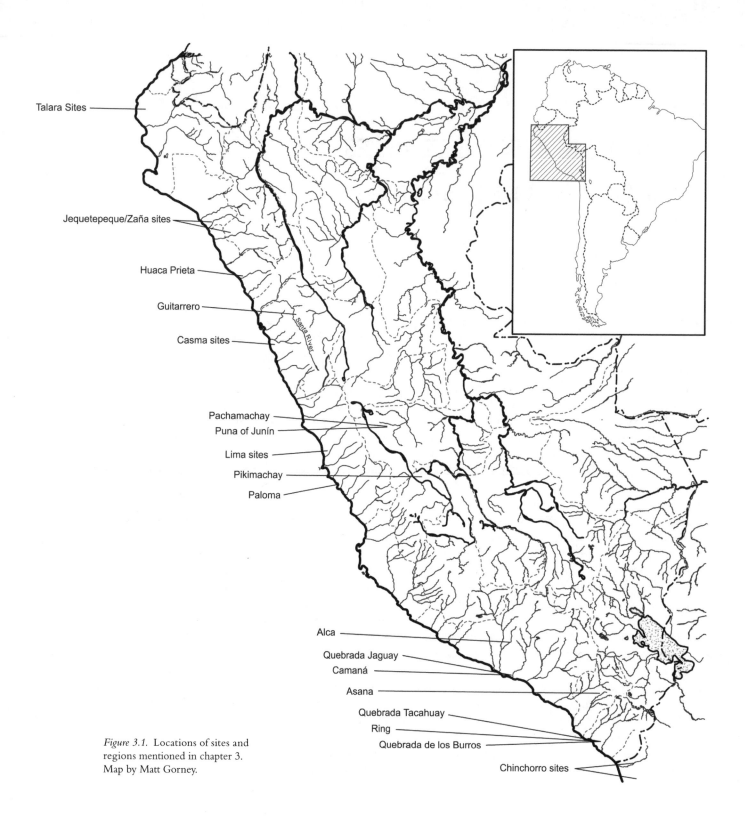

Figure 3.1. Locations of sites and regions mentioned in chapter 3. Map by Matt Gorney.

periods alternated with warmer ones. During the warmer periods, called *interstadials,* the glaciers would begin to recede and an *ice-free corridor* would open in present-day Edmonton, Canada, between the glacier that originated in the Rocky Mountains and another glacier that developed over the present-day Hudson Bay. Such a corridor would have been a harsh environment, with cold winds blowing through it, glacial lakes, and regions of permafrost. Still, game animals would have inhabited it, and so humans may have followed the animals into such a corridor and ultimately arrived south of the glaciers.

The question of when the ice-free corridor was completely open to allow travel southward is controversial. Many sources suggest it was not available for immigration into the continent south of the glaciers until around 12,000 B.C.E. Others argue for an earlier opening, perhaps by 13,500 B.C.E. This controversy need not concern us here; however, it does appear more and more likely that humans arrived south of the glaciers via the coastal route because we now have more dates for human occupation south of the glaciers in the twelfth millennium B.C.E.

Once south of the glaciers, humans would have found a land teeming with game and other resources. The kinds of animals present during the ice age were very different from those found today: mammoths and mastodons, relatives of modern elephants, would have ranged widely in small herds over grassland and forested habitats. Horses, bison, saber-tooth cats, bears, and ground sloths all were present, some as prey and some as predators. Small animals, birds, and plant resources also were consumed, perhaps even more than the large game.

It is likely that the human population expanded after its initial arrival south of the glaciers. A factor against population increase would have been the highly mobile and energetic lifestyle of these groups, which is one reason why modern hunter-gatherers have low fertility rates. In short, we do not know how rapidly the human population expanded. We must also remember that the occupation of the New World was a continuous process, with later groups following the earliest ones.

It is important to digress for a moment and talk about how human populations expand in general. *Homo sapiens* have been steadily expanding their range for at least 200,000 years, from a homeland in Africa to the southern tip of South America. This implies population growth. When birth rates exceed death rates, because of cultural factors that allow for an adequate diet, success in finding mates, and effective protection of the young so that they reach reproductive age, a group can increase in size. When a band of hunter-gatherers gets too large, it will *fission* (split apart) into two smaller groups. One group may stay in the original region while the other moves to an adjacent region. Alternatively, both may continue to move to new regions. Because humans need other humans for procreation, bands maintain knowledge of the locations of other bands where their members can find mates. Thus, human groups did not just move out of Africa and continue moving; they moved only far enough to procure resources while keeping in touch with other groups for reproductive purposes.

A question that we do not have the answer to is, how mobile were the early colonizers of the New World? Were the groups highly mobile, continuing to advance forward, or did some remain in certain regions, adapting to the resources of the recently occupied areas? The question is important for the speed of colonization. The model followed here is one in which humans filled in regions as they went, however sparsely, so that once an area was occupied it continued to be occupied by a group or groups. This does not imply that whole regions were filled up to their carrying capacity (the population that can be sustained by an environment) before humans moved on; rather, some groups stayed in a region while others did move forward into new regions. That the groups had to maintain contact for reproductive reasons seems logical because the alternative would require higher amounts of inbreeding that could have had deleterious genetic effects.

The peopling of the New World is the end result of the expansion of our species out of Africa, across Asia, and into northeastern Siberia. Humans then occupied

Alaska and the regions south of the glaciers. As a result of their successful adaptation to the new lands they found, their populations continued to rise and the human front expanded farther south until reaching Tierra del Fuego, at the southern tip of South America, by around 11,000 B.C.E. at the latest. This is not to say the human population expanded uniformly and into every region before moving on. The high Andean regions were probably occupied later than lower areas due to the difficulties in adapting to the low-oxygen environment at high altitudes.

PLEISTOCENE OCCUPATIONS: THE EARLY PRECERAMIC PERIOD (15,000?–9600 B.C.E.)

For humans to arrive in South America, they must have come through North and Central America first, so a brief discussion of the question of when they passed through those regions is important. Until recently, there were two views on when humans arrived in the regions south of the continental glaciers. The Clovis-first theory states that humans, called *Paleoindians,* arrived south of the continental glaciers around 11,100 B.C.E. and quickly spread across the continent. In contrast, the pre-Clovis theory argues that humans arrived earlier than the Paleoindians using simpler technologies and that the Paleoindian technology is one of several that developed from this earlier occupation.

The Clovis-first theory developed from the wealth of evidence for human occupations of North America starting around 11,100 B.C.E., a time known as the Paleoindian Period in North America (11,100–9900 B.C.E.). Paleoindian sites are recognized by the hallmark artifact of the period, large *fluted* (the name for a flake driven off the base of a shaped stone point to make attaching the point to a shaft more effective) projectile points called Clovis points, from the site where they were originally identified (figure 3.2). For many years, it was believed that Clovis represented the initial occupation of North America and that the spread of the lifestyle was due to its success. Sites dating earlier than 11,100

B.C.E. all had problems, either with the dates, the artifacts, or the association of the two.

This question of which theory is correct has largely been decided by the discovery of the site of Monte Verde, located in south central Chile (Dillehay 1989). The site has a range of dates that place its occupation at 12,300–12,000 B.C.E. (Dillehay et al. 2008).[1] This site was extraordinary in that it was covered by a peat bog after its use by humans, so many perishable remains were recovered, including a wide variety of plants. The bog preserved a series of house foundations constructed of logs tied together by bark strings and covered by pieces of mammoth hide. The plants recovered showed that the people ranged widely to find food, from the coastal region 40 km away to the more distant Andean foothills. Initially, the pre-Clovis age of the site was challenged, but the dates of the site were accepted as legitimate by a group of experts who visited the site, reviewed the evidence, and agreed that it was pre-Clovis (Meltzer et al. 1997).

Figure 3.2. Clovis projectile point. Photo courtesy of the Virginia Department of Historic Resources.

Although the dates for Monte Verde are not extremely early, they do indicate that people must have been in central Chile by 14,000 years ago. By extension, they must have traveled through North, Central, and northern South America earlier than that. How much earlier is now the controversy.

The earliest generally accepted dates from Alaska, at the point of entry of humans into the New World, come from the Nenana complex and are only around 11,800–11,000 B.C.E. In fact, the earliest dates for the human occupation of northeastern Siberia, from which humans must have arrived in Alaska, are only around 16,000 B.C.E. This evidence suggests that there must be earlier sites yet to be discovered in Alaska and Siberia or that humans arrived in Alaska via a coastal route, and that the sites are all now submerged by post-Pleistocene sea-level rise.

There are no sites that are as early as Monte Verde from elsewhere in South America, but many date to approximately 10,800 B.C.E. I refer the reader to Borrero 2008, Dillehay 2008, and Ranere and Cooke 2003 for thorough lists of early sites and discussions of the evidence from them. The site of Santa Julia on the central coast of Chile has a date of 11,000–10,000 B.C.E. and is notable for the clear association between artifacts and Pleistocene mammals (Jackson et al. 2007).

Excavations at the site of Huaca Prieta in the Chicama Valley of northern Peru have provided dates between 11,800 and 11,300 B.C.E. for an early maritime-based occupation (Dillehay et al. 2012).[2] At the Jaguay site near Camaná, Daniel Sandweiss and his colleagues (1998) found evidence of fishing and shellfish collecting with no evidence for terrestrial resources dating to 11,100–8500 B.C.E. At Quebrada Tacahuay, a contemporary site near the Chilean border, the exploitation of marine birds was found (Keefer et al. 1998). Finally, the Amotape Complex of Talara on the far north coast of Peru, has an uncalibrated date of 11,200 B.P. on mangrove mollusk.[3]

There are several caves in the central Andes, among them Pikimachay, Pachamachay, and Guitarrero, that have yielded problematic dates and stone tools in the 9000–7400 B.C.E. range, but the remains are so limited that little is known of these early occupants. Guitarrero Cave does have recently published AMS dates on cordage and wood artifacts in the 10,200–9800 B.C.E. range (Jolie et al. 2011). Kurt Rademaker (pers. comm. 2013) has twenty-three Terminal Pleistocene dates from Cuncaicha Cave between the Majes and Cotahuasi valleys in southern Peru. The site, located at 4,500 meters above sea level (masl), has a variety of stone tools. The dates for all these cave occupations do support the idea that the high cordillera of the Andes was occupied later than the lower regions around them. Finally, Anna Roosevelt and her colleagues (1996) have found evidence of a 11,200–10,800 B.C.E. occupation of Pedra Pintada Cave in Brazil. Significantly, this site is in eastern Brazil, suggesting a much earlier arrival for their ancestors to have crossed the Amazonia region or come along the northern coast of the continent.

Indirect evidence for the early arrival of humans in South America comes from projectile points; at least three distinct styles of points were being manufactured in different areas at the end of the Pleistocene or early Holocene. Large, stemmed points (figure 3.3A) are found along the Peruvian coast and in the Ecuadorian highlands, whereas bipointed, long, lanceolate points (figure 3.3B) were made at Monte Verde and Taima Taima (a site in Venezuela with controversial dates of 13,600–13,400 B.C.E.). A third style, the so-called fishtail-fluted point (figure 3.3C), which shares the fluting technology with Clovis, is found from the north coast of Peru to Tierra del Fuego, including regions where the other two are found. Finally, many sites along the western coast do not have stone projectile points at all, such as the Talara, Jaguay, and Tacahuay sites described earlier, suggesting adaptations that did not require such specialized weapons. A comparable unifacial Edge-Trimmed Tradition of toolmaking has been defined for eastern South America (Bryan and Gruhn 2003). These tool traditions emerged independently as early people moved into South America. If they all originated from a single migration, it would suggest, although not prove, an occupation of the continent much earlier than 14,000 years ago. By how much is not known.

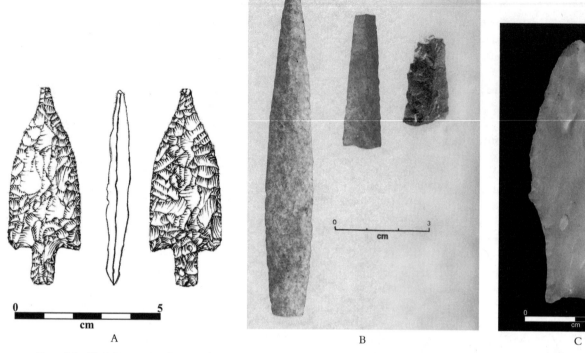

Figure 3.3. (A) Paiján projectile point from Quebrada del Batán, Perú. Courtesy of Greg Maggard; illustration by Iris Bracamonte. (B) Long, lanceolate projectile points. From Dillehay 1997, figure 14.17. Courtesy of Tom D. Dillehay. (C) Fishtail-fluted projectile point from Quebrada del Batán, Perú. Courtesy of Greg Maggard.

This smorgasbord of sites is mentioned just to indicate that humans were already fairly widespread across the continent by the end of the Pleistocene, about 11,500 years ago. The early dates from Monte Verde and Pedra Pintada, located a continent apart, indicate that humans began to spread out upon their arrival at the border of present-day Colombia and Panama. Whether the date of this arrival is 15,000 years ago or earlier remains to be resolved with future discoveries. By extension, this evidence argues for the coastal route of occupation for North America to allow groups to have arrived in South America by this early date.

Adaptations

What was life like for these earliest bands of people moving through the vast continent of South America? Although the evidence is scanty, it appears that very early on people began to diversify their diets,

taking advantage of the local resources that were available in different regions (Dillehay 2008). This is reflected in the different projectile-point styles and tool assemblages mentioned previously. The information suggests that the earliest occupants of the continent arrived as broad-spectrum hunter-gatherers, using a wide range of plants and both marine and terrestrial animals. The latter included extinct Pleistocene game as well as modern game such as *guanacos* (a wild relative of llamas) and deer. A wide variety of resources was used by the earliest inhabitants if the plant species identified from Monte Verde are any indication (Dillehay et al. 2008).

Monte Verde reflects adaptations to a largely terrestrial environment, although plant species from the shore were also found there. Other early sites indicate a different kind of adaptation, one to maritime resources. Evidence of both fishing and shellfish collecting at the end of the Pleistocene is found in southern Peru and northern Chile. Here, the continental shelf is much narrower, so the present coastline is much nearer to the Pleistocene coastline than in regions farther north. As previously mentioned, at Quebrada Jaguay and Quebrada Tacahuay, there is evidence for specialized economies based on maritime resources dating between 13,000 and 11,000 years ago, and Sandweiss et al. (1989) has identified a maritime focus that has a slightly later age at the Ring Site near the Moquegua Valley farther south. Finally, the Quebrada Las Conchas site in central Chile shows Early Holocene evidence of maritime resource use in the form of fish *otoliths* (ear bones) (Llagostera Martínez 1979). All these sites suggest that people may have adapted to maritime resources quite early, probably as a result of their hugging the Pacific coast as they expanded southward.

Along the north coast of Peru, a series of campsites overlooking a freshwater source in the Talara region shows the use of mangrove mollusks with one questionable date of 11,200 B.P. (Richardson 1978). Similar exploitation of mangroves is characteristic of the subsequent Siches culture of the same region. Farther north, on the Santa Elena peninsula of western Ecuador, Stothert (1988) notes that the Las Vegas culture (9200–5400 B.C.E.) subsisted on a mixture of terrestrial hunting, gathering, and shellfish collecting. The tools of Siches and Las Vegas are very similar, being unifacial and lacking bifacial projectile points. Such simple tools, and by extension the resources used, are found during the subsequent Middle Preceramic along the coast of Peru as far south as the central coast near Lima (Lanning 1967; Malpass 1983), although in these regions projectile points are also found.

A common description of the early inhabitants of western South America since the 1960s has been that they were hunters of Pleistocene megafauna. But actual evidence for such an adaptation is scarce. The site of Santa Julia in central Chile has good evidence for this exploitation, but the site is small and there are few remains (Jackson et al. 2007). Interestingly, this site is within 5 km of the current coastline, yet no marine resources have been recovered, suggesting a different subsistence focus than the ones just discussed. The contemporary sites of Quereo[4] and

Tagua Tagua, located in central Chile, also have evidence of humans and extinct megafauna (Montané 1968; Nuñez et al. 1987). Borrero (2008) notes that, although sites with Pleistocene megafauna are present, virtually all also include modern species, including a heavy emphasis on guanaco.

It is likely that the fishtail-fluted points were also made for hunting terrestrial game because the majority of sites where they are found are inland, although some examples are known from the west coast (Briceño 1995, 1999; Gálvez 1992). These points have the widest distribution, having been found from Ecuador to Argentina. They are found at the Tierra del Fuego sites excavated by Junius Bird, dating to around 10,800 B.C.E., and are associated with extinct species such as the horse. Due to the distinctive fluting technology of these points, many scholars see them as related to the Clovis of North America and, by extension, see the culture that used them as similar to the kind of Paleoindian adaptation seen with Clovis. As Gregory Maggard and Thomas Dillehay (2011) note, however, so little actual subsistence evidence has been recovered from fishtail-fluted sites anywhere that we do not know what their inhabitants' economic base was.

A distinct adaptation that existed during the Late Pleistocene and Early Holocene epochs along the north coast of Peru belongs to the Paiján culture. This culture is geographically restricted to the region between the Santa and the Jequetepeque rivers, although finds of this group have occasionally been recorded as far south as the Ica Valley. This complex dates to the end of the Pleistocene, during the time when this region had much more rainfall and a greater quantity and variety of terrestrial resources, including megafauna (Lemon and Churcher 1961). The distinctive artifact of this complex is the large, stemmed projectile point, often well over 10 cm in length, which tapers to a fine tip (figure 3.3A). The long tips make their functions hard to determine. Because these points are commonly found with fish remains, spearfishing has been suggested as the main activity conducted with these points (e.g., Moseley 2001, 94). The lack of barbs to keep the point in the fish and their general thickness, however, argue against this interpretation. Other tools found in the assemblage are more typical of broad-spectrum hunting, gathering, and maritime collecting, including scrapers, knives, boring tools, and denticulated tools (ones with jagged but irregular edges). Grinding equipment is found at some sites. Food remains include modern prey, despite several dates that suggest Late Pleistocene extinct fauna may have been exploited.

Recent work by Greg Maggard (2010) has greatly clarified our understanding of the Paijan complex (see also Dillehay et al. 2003, 2011a; Maggard and Dillehay 2011). He has found chronological differences between point styles, with Early Paijan (11,000–9400 B.C.E.) points having a straight stem but Late Paijan (9400–7800 B.C.E.) points being more variable but usually having contracting stems. He has found that the Early Paijan occupations were mainly located in the quebradas, where the Andean foothills flattened out into the coastal plain, affording the occupants easy access to a wide range of resource zones, both higher and lower in altitude. Subsistence remains include a range of terrestrial and marine resources, including fish and shellfish but also land snails (one of the most common food remains), lizards, and small mammals (Maggard 2010). Few structures have been found with Early Paijan sites, suggesting these were probably ephemeral camps rather than longer-term occupations.

Late Paijan represents a continuation of the earlier broad-spectrum resource use but is much more localized. Through the Late Paijan phase, residential sites go from short-term occupations to more continuous occupations with some evidence of the cultivation of squash (Maggard and Dillehay 2011). Broad-spectrum resource use continued through this time and laid the foundation for the early adoption of cultigens in the Zaña Valley to the east. Tools include the same general forms as during Early Paijan times, but the projectile-point forms diversify even further and grinding stones appear (Maggard and Dillehay 2011). The Late Paijan also evolved into Middle Preceramic complexes, such as Siches, Mongoncillo (Malpass

1983), and possibly Las Vegas after 8200 B.C.E. (Maggard 2010).

In the Casma Valley farther south, I found evidence that Paijan hunters occasionally visited the top of the first range of the Andes, probably to hunt deer and camelids (guanacos and *vicuñas*, the wild relatives of llamas and alpacas) (Malpass 1985). Because the point styles there are all contracting-stemmed varieties, this supports a Late Paijan date for these sites. The incorporation of the nearby highlands into the subsistence activities in this region began a behavior that continued into later periods.

As previously mentioned, several caves at mid-elevations in the central and south Andes have evidence of late Pleistocene habitations in their deepest levels. Unfortunately, most of the evidence consists of very small deposits, leaving little for the archaeologists to interpret. Still, what evidence has been found argues for a lifestyle based on the hunting and gathering of the available resources, mostly camelids and deer. The scarcity of remains suggests that people did not stay long in any one place, and this might be the result of the difficulty of living at such altitudes at the end of the Pleistocene. Resources in Andean valleys are highly seasonal, and it is likely that such deposits represent short-term visits by small groups that moved on to other areas after a few seasons (Rick 1980).

A final adaptation that seems to be distinct is a focus on tropical-forest resources, identified by Roosevelt and her colleagues (1996) along the Amazon flood plain in eastern Brazil. There, floral and faunal remains revealed a broad-spectrum economy based on forest collecting, fishing and freshwater shellfishing, and hunting of a wide variety of small game, but few large animals.

All this evidence supports the idea that humans dispersed in different directions relatively quickly after they arrived in northwestern Colombia. Some followed the coastline south, reaching Monte Verde by 14,600 years ago. These people and their descendants focused on maritime resources, as indicated by the evidence from coastal Peru and Chile. Others moved east along the Caribbean coast and spread down the rivers of northern Amazonia. These people ended up at sites such as Pedra Pintada.

An interesting question of human adaptability is the date that people moved into the high Andes, a place that would have been difficult due to both its colder temperatures and lack of oxygen. Early models of the peopling of the continent suggested that hunter-gatherers followed the valleys of the Cordillera Central of Colombia into the Andes and then expanded southward, following the spine of the mountains through highland Ecuador, Peru, and Chile (e.g., Lynch 1983). Current evidence from the South Andes suggests that the initial colonization of the Titicaca basin was from the Pacific coastal region (Aldenderfer 1998; Klink and Aldenderfer 2005). Work by Kurt Rademaker (2012) at Cuncaicha Cave also supports this contention. Because dates for occupations are consistently earlier along the coast than anywhere in the highlands, and the early projectile-point styles are similar in both regions, it seems likely that movement into the highlands came from the coast. Evidence for temporary movements into the highlands is also seen in the Casma Valley evidence, already discussed, where Paijan projectile points were found in caves at the top of the adjacent range of the Andes but not in the valley to the east.

It is worth mentioning that, although this characterization suggests relative independence among the groups moving in different directions, it is equally true that communication among the groups must have existed. The Quebrada Jaguay people obtained *obsidian,* a volcanic glass highly prized for its sharp edges, from a source high in the adjacent mountains, either by long-distance visits to the source or trade with groups that did have access to it (Sandweiss et al. 1998). The Monte Verde people also used resources from the foothills to the coast. In their forays to different zones, these people may have contacted others, sharing ideas and technologies, and probably even mates. As these groups all adapted to their respective environmental settings, they learned more about the particular resources of each, setting the stage for the developments of the early Holocene, when present-day climatic conditions were achieved. It is to these developments that we now turn.

MIDDLE PRECERAMIC PERIOD (9600–4000 B.C.E.)

This is the time when the *Archaic* lifestyle developed out of the earlier ones just described. This lifestyle is associated with groups becoming less migratory, often settling into a particular valley or basin. The groups developed a better familiarity with the modern plant and animal resources, enabling them to more effectively use them. New technologies, especially grinding implements, were developed or became more common to exploit these resources. In some regions, foraging behaviors persisted due to their appropriateness to local conditions. In others, the new information and technologies resulted in a move either toward sedentary occupations or the domestication of plants and animals, or both. The importance of this transition suggests this period is a critical one to understanding many of the later developments in the Andes—yet it is one of the least well-understood ones (Richardson 1994).

Domestication

First, what does *domestication* mean? Fundamentally, it means that humans genetically alter an organism through artificial selection such that it can be distinguished from its wild relatives (Piperno 2009). Domestication results from the manipulation of the genetic variability of the species to favor traits that are advantageous to humans. For example, maize (or corn) started out as a plant with very small cobs and only a few kernels, but through selection for larger cobs and more kernels, people have developed the very large ears that characterize modern races. Beans have become larger and more permeable, thus easier to cook and digest. Squash has become fleshier. Animals have been bred for specific purposes as well, for wool, meat, or milk production or as beasts of burden. By finding the animals that have the best qualities, then using them for breeding, humans can increase the incidence of desirable traits in the population.

Identifying domesticated versus wild species can be very difficult. If the process of domestication did not result in a change in any specific seed or fruit, bone, or horn, then it is difficult to determine whether an archaeological example is from a wild or domesticated type. Such can be the case with camelids. There are four different New World camelids, two wild and two domesticated versions (figure 3.4). Guanacos and vicuñas are wild; llamas and alpacas are domesticated. Llamas and guanacos are large; vicuñas and alpacas are small. Because there are both wild and domesticated large and small versions, bone size cannot be used to distinguish wild from domesticated camelids. In fact, although vicuñas are considered a different species, it is actually unclear whether the other three are different species or only different subspecies (Mengoni Goñalons 2008; Stahl 2008).

Guillermo Mengoni Goñalons (2008) discusses several ways that the different camelids can be identified archaeologically. Direct methods include tooth and bone morphology, such as the shape of the incisors or the enamel distribution, and indirect methods include the relative abundance of one form of camelid versus other forms and mortality curves (e.g., a large number of juvenile males is a good example of a herded mortality curve). Finally, contextual information such as the presence of corrals, which implies herding, can be used.

For plants, the situation can be analogous. The differences between modern domesticated versions of many plants and their ancient wild ancestors are obvious. For example, chili pepper fruits have a distinctive morphology when domesticated that allows their identification, as do other plants such as cotton. However, the changes from wild to domesticated forms were sufficiently gradual to make the process of domestication difficult to document through time in many species.

Over the past twenty years, there has been a significant increase in our understanding of the process of plant domestication due to advances in genetic and archaeobotanical studies, new theoretical models, and simply more data collected (Piperno 2009). For example, domesticated forms of plants can be identified through their *phytoliths*. Phytoliths are microscopic silica bodies that are formed by plants as part of their cell walls. Their shapes are distinctive, and because they are composed of silica, they resist deterioration in the soil. Domesticated and wild forms often have distinct phytoliths, which can be identified by an expert. Likewise, starch grains in plants can be used for identification. An analysis of starch grains from a Late Preceramic site in the Cotahuasi Valley of southern Peru allowed investigators to identify early maize and other plants there in the absence of any macrobotanical remains (Perry et al. 2006).

In South America, a wide variety of plants were domesticated, such as potato, sweet potato, achira, manioc, *oca,* and ulluco (all tubers); beans and squash of many varieties; quinoa, *tarwi,* and *kiwicha* (three high-protein grains); *lúcuma, pacay*, avocado, chili pepper, and tomato (all fruits); and cotton; gourd; and coca. The origins of maize, the most important crop to the Inkas and many earlier groups as well, appear to lie in Mexico, with its introduction into the Andes by the early Holocene. Although it is not clear where other plants originated, we do know that several were originally tropical forest species (Piperno and Pearsall 1998) (see box 3.1).

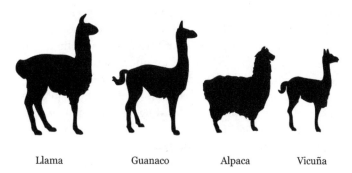

| Llama | Guanaco | Alpaca | Vicuña |

Figure 3.4. The four camelids. Drawing courtesy of Natalie Lazo.

BOX 3.1 Why agriculture?

Hunting and gathering was a highly successful way of life that allowed humans to expand across the globe and inhabit diverse ecosystems. Why people settled down and began to farm and herd rather than hunt and gather is therefore one of the important questions of archaeology in many regions of the world. Indeed, the fact that agriculture developed more or less simultaneously and independently in at least seven different regions requires explanation. A related question is, why did this shift begin only around 12,000 years ago and not earlier?

The answers to these questions are difficult to find, and indeed there may not be a single explanation that accounts for why it happened throughout the world at the beginning of the Holocene. However, as more and more data are discovered, and new means of analyzing and interpreting the data are developed, we get closer to understanding how and why this change occurred. For the Andes, Dolores Piperno (2009) reviews the evidence bearing on this question. It is now clear that there were multiple regions of domestication and that plants that later were grown together were not domesticated as a group. It is equally interesting that humans selected only certain plants to focus on rather than others. Moreover, it appears the seasonal tropical forest, those warm forests with prolonged dry seasons, were important in this process. It is also evident that cultivation was occurring almost as early as humans arrived, with several plants consistently found at occupations dating to the Early Holocene or even Late Pleistocene. The latest evidence supports the idea that humans actually brought the bottle gourd, *Lagenaria ciceraria*, with them as they occupied the continent (Erickson et al. 2005). The earliest crops included tubers (*leren* and arrowroot), tree fruit (pacay), and seed plants (three kinds of squash and peanuts).

As cultivation and domestication took hold, stone-tool technologies were adapted to process these new plants. Grinding stones and edge-ground cobbles appear and increase in frequency during the Middle Preceramic Period as the variety and quantity of plants increased. It is significant that there is no relationship between the appearance of domesticated plants and permanent settlements, as is the case for China and the Near East. Virtually all early sites with evidence of domesticated plants are seasonal, and permanence seems to be a result of the ultimate adoption of domesticates rather than a causal factor (see also Pringle 1998). It is likely that domestication was preceded by a long period of cultivation of plants that sometimes resulted in the genetic modifications we recognize as domestication and other times did not (Piperno and Pearsall 1998).

Implicit in this view is the idea that early cultivators were modifying the environment to favor the plants they were growing, by clearing forests, tilling the soil, and even practicing small-scale irrigation. Evidence from starch grains taken from the teeth of burials in the Zaña Valley shows a significant intake of cultigens. Root crops such as leren and arrowroot form a sizable proportion of the early Las Vegas plant inventory as well. Thus, many of the practices we typically associate with faming began during this incipient cultivation period. Given that hardly any of these early cultivators were permanent, the search for the earliest farmers in the Andes becomes an arbitrary activity: Where do we draw the line between cultivation and farming?

Regarding the "why" of this issue, Piperno (2009, 25) and Piperno and Deborah Pearsall (1998) use human behavioral ecology (HBE) as a theoretical framework to explain the shift from foraging to farming. They focus on optimal foraging theory, whose basic assumption is that "all things being equal, more efficient food procurement strategies should be favored by natural selection over those less efficient . . ." (Piperno 2009, 24). They note that there was a dramatic change in the climate, vegetation, and fauna with the onset of Holocene conditions. With increases in temperature, rainfall, and levels of carbon dioxide, there was an expansion in the seasonal tropical forest zone and a replacement of the large Pleistocene megafauna by smaller and more dispersed Holocene fauna in this zone. This led to a shift to a broader spectrum diet because lower-energy-level foods, such as plants and small animals, had to replace the larger game and other resources. With the energetic costs of foraging increasing, due to the dispersed nature of the fauna hunted and the increased costs of plant collecting and processing (which often required extensive manipulation to remove toxins), farming became a better choice. Piperno (2009, 27) notes that new studies of neotropical farming practices indicate that they actually have lower energy costs than full-time foraging, in contrast to previous studies.

In contrast to the HBE model, recent research, such as that by Dillehay et al. (2011b), suggests that the shift may have been a much more serendipitous process, one that some groups participated in while others, even those nearby, did not. Humans are creatures of both habit and whim, so we should not expect that all would do what seems the most efficient in terms of energy costs. As more detailed research is conducted, whether the HBE model is appropriate to all regions where agriculture developed will be better evaluated.

The Formative way of life, equivalent to the Neolithic of the Old World, is traditionally defined as permanent villages based predominantly on the farming of domesticated plants and herding of domesticated animals. Using this definition, the Formative way of life generally appeared around 4,000 years ago in the Andes, perhaps slightly earlier in some regions. But the transition to this way of life began much earlier, nearly as soon as people settled in different regions of South America. With the shift in climate and change in the kinds of resources available, early people began to identify and exploit a variety of plants. They developed new tools for using them and began to invest more time and energy in their care. This was done in the context of broad-spectrum hunting and gathering of other wild resources. We might expect that some of this shift might have been effected by changes in labor, such that gender and age groups might have been involved in the different subsistence activities. Through time, as plants responded to selection for their productive parts, they became more energetically efficient for humans to focus on, at the expense of hunting and gathering. It was only when such cultivation practices and selection reached a point where enough food could be grown and stored to last a family through an entire agricultural cycle that people could settle down. It appears that that threshold was passed at 4,000 years ago. Other pathways, however, allowed groups along the coast and on the Puna of Junín to settle into permanent communities in the absence of cultivated plants or tamed animals. As research continues in other regions of South America, it is likely other pathways will emerge as well.

Of greater significance than the variety of domesticated plants is their adaptive value to humans. Agriculture is practiced at higher elevations in the Andes than anywhere on Earth. Potatoes (several hundred varieties are known), oca, and ulluco are grown in the lower puna or upper quechua zones, at around 4,000 m. Corn, beans, squash, quinoa, tarwi, and other grains are best cultivated in the mid-elevation quechua zone. In the yunga zone, fruits and other vegetables, such as chili peppers, manioc, and achira are grown. This range of crops allowed the development of the verticality system described in chapter 2.

For animals, the most important Andean domesticates are the camelids (llamas and alpacas) and guinea pigs. Llamas and alpacas were originally domesticated as sources of meat, but later, and up to the present, the former were used as pack animals and the latter for their wool. Work by Jane Wheeler and her colleagues (1976, 1995) at caves on the Puna of Junín suggests that wild camelids went through a period of taming and semi-domestication between 4200 and 3000 B.C.E. Taming camelids and then getting them to breed must have been a time-intensive effort, one that took a long time to become stabilized. The evidence of increasing permanence at Pachamachay suggests the means by which this could have occurred. Based largely on mortality curves, Wheeler feels the llamas and alpacas were domesticated by 3200 B.C.E. on the Puna of Junín and perhaps independently on the Altiplano as well. The use of the domesticated species then spread to adjacent areas.

Citing more recent data from the Central Andes to Argentina, Mengoni Goñalons (2008, 65) states that populations in many regions of the Andes were intensifying their use of camelids starting earlier, around 7400 B.C.E. By 4800 B.C.E., he argues, llamas had been domesticated in the Central Andes, and perhaps an independent process led to their domestication in the southern Andean region between 3400 and 1100 B.C.E.

Guinea pigs, or cuys (*Cavia porcellus*), were domesticated as a source of meat and are still used today. Because of the relative lack of work on their wild ancestors, the process of their domestication has not been well defined (Stahl 2008). In addition, because of the small size of the bones, they may be underrepresented in archaeological work due to recovery procedures. That being said, the best archaeological evidence for domesticated guinea pigs comes from the Ayacucho region, dating to around 4400 B.C.E., although other evidence from the same region suggests possible penning as early as 6200 B.C.E. From the central Andes, domesticated guinea pigs gradually spread out, reaching the central coast and the north highlands by the second millennium B.P. (Stahl 2008).

One of the great questions of archaeology anywhere in the world is when and why people changed from being hunters and gatherers to food producers. This issue is discussed in box 3.1.

Archaic Lifestyles along the Pacific Coast

It is now apparent that the earliest domesticates in South America were the bottle gourd and the dog, which came over with the earliest inhabitants from Asia (Erickson et al. 2005). However, it is equally apparent that neither of these made a significance difference to the lifestyle of the early inhabitants. The shift to an Archaic lifestyle required more fundamental changes that were engendered by the use of multiple domesticates. South America is one of the world's primary centers of domestication, but exactly where people began the process is uncertain; it is likely there were multiple points of origin (Piperno 2009, 2011; Piperno and Pearsall 1998).

In 1950, Carl Sauer posited that the Neotropics of the New World would be a place where plant domestication was likely to have occurred. Recent evidence has borne out the wisdom of this prediction (Pearsall 2008; Piperno and Pearsall 1998; Piperno 2011). It now appears that plants were domesticated both in a wide variety of ecological settings and as early as the beginning of the Holocene. With the revolution in new analytical techniques, our understanding of this process has greatly expanded (Pringle 1998).

A broad-based subsistence is indicated by the Las Vegas culture of coastal Ecuador (Stothert 1988; Stothert, Piperno, and Andres 2003). Thirty-two sites of this culture have been found, including two larger sites with cemeteries, suggesting base camps from which people moved to the smaller camps nearby to find resources. Animal remains include both large and small mammals. Marine resources include an abundance of shellfish characteristic of mangrove swamps as well as sandy and rocky coastal microenvironments. Twenty-five kinds of fish have been identified, but all are of kinds that can be caught using simple technology from the shore.

Knowledge of plant resources from the Las Vegas sites were scarce until the application of phytolith analysis to the deposits (Piperno 1988). Abundant phytoliths from the 8200–8000 B.C.E. levels of the Las Vegas site showed the people were already cultivating squash, bottle gourds, and leren, along with collecting local plants (Stothert, Piperno, and Andres 2003). By 5800 B.C.E., more productive varieties of squash were being cultivated, and early maize was also being eaten, as witnessed by both phytoliths and starch grains identified in the teeth of these people. In addition, these later people intensified their fishing activities but reduced the hunting of small game. The excavator of these sites, Karen Stothert, argues this might reflect a shift in gender roles, in which women began to focus on horticultural practices rather than netting small game and harvesting wild plants while men continued to hunt and fish (Stothert, Piperno, and Andres 2003, 39).

The Las Vegas people also shifted their burial practices from individuals being interred in their own graves to large, secondary burials (in which the corpse is defleshed elsewhere and the bones collected and reinterred). This suggests shifting social behaviors and a greater emphasis on communal rituals that related to their changing way of life. In this respect, the food production and intensified fishing might have been responses to a need to share food, both to broaden social networks and as aspects of ceremonial behavior (see also Rossen 1991; Stothert, Piperno, and Andres 2003, 39).

It is likely that the Las Vegas people were fully sedentary, certainly by the end of their occupation. Although the structures are relatively simple (Malpass and Stothert 1992), the site of Las Vegas produced food remains representing all seasons. Tools were relatively simple, and no stone projectile points have been found. Whether this means that hunting with darts or spears was not carried out or that hunting was done without stone points is uncertain. But the Archaic way of life is evident in the successful use of marine and terrestrial resources, including cultivated plants. The use of some grinding stones during the occupation also reflects the increased use of plant resources. This certainly set the stage for the emergence of some of the earliest full-blown sedentary communities (discussed in the next chapter).

Other Archaic ways of life developed along the northern Peruvian coast, some that relied on domesticates and some that did not. The coastal plain in this region is very broad from the Sechura Desert to around the Chicama Valley. There is also a large region of foothills that is intermediate between the coastal plain and the high cordillera. The coast and foothills narrow considerably south of the Santa River. As discussed earlier, the earliest well-dated sites in this region are from the Paijan assemblage from the Chicama Valley, beginning around the end of the Pleistocene. Siches, the culture that evolved from the possibly earlier Amotape, was an adaptation to mangrove-swamp collecting and hunting (Richardson 1978). The basic way of life and the unifacial tools found are similar to those of the Las Vegas, and in excavations gourd and squash were identified in the remains dating to 10,800 B.C.E. (Piperno 2009).

As a result of research conducted in the Jequetepeque and Zaña valleys, we now better understand the relationship between the bifacial Paijan and fishtail complexes of this region and the unifacial ones such as Siches. In the Jequetepeque Valley, research by Greg Maggard (2010) and Kary Stackelbeck (2008) shows that the bifacial complexes are chronologically earlier and evolved into the later ones due to a shift in the kinds of resources exploited. This shift, in turn, was the result of the drying of the Holocene environment and the fewer large mammals that could be hunted by the inhabitants of this zone. Early Holocene occupations concentrated on land snails, lizards, foxes, and occasional deer, and there is little evidence of permanent settlements (Stackelbeck 2008; Stackelbeck and Dillehay 2011). This region is 30 km inland, and there is little evidence of other marine resources, other than some fish remains. However, because the sea level was still rising, if other sites were located along the coast, they are now underwater.

In the middle reaches of the Zaña Valley, roughly 500–1200 m above sea level but 90 km inland, evidence demonstrates that foragers began to settle down and cultivate plants (Dillehay 2011; Dillehay et al. 2004, 2007; Rossen 1991, 2011). During the Early Holocene, this zone was a region of tropical forest that gradually dried out through the mid-Holocene. Tropical forest plants and animals are found in the middens, and remnant patches of these forests still exist in the upper Nanchoc Valley, the name for the Zaña in this region. This distinct environment led to an early development of cultivation and permanent settlements.

During the Las Pircas phase (7800–5800 B.C.E.), people lived in groups of one or two round houses with furrowed garden plots and storage features nearby. Up to twenty-five of these clusters have been found on some of the alluvial fans in the quebradas leading down to the Nanchoc River. People used a set of unifacial stone tools that reflect plant use, had grinding stones, and probably used other implements of wood and bone. Squash, peanut, and quinoa-like remains have been recovered (Dillehay et al. 2007). Because none of these plants is native to this region, they represent transplanted species that the inhabitants were using to augment their diet of wild plants and hunted animals.

The Las Pircas people also hunted small mammals and collected wild plants in addition to their cultivation. Stackelbeck (2008) suggests these people may have been the same as those who used the adjacent lower-altitudinal zones of the Jequetepeque Valley where she worked, making occasional forays into that zone to take advantage of the specific resources there.

The discovery of exotic materials such as quartz crystals, stingray spines, malachite beads, and marine shells in the garden furrows suggests the possibility of household rituals, perhaps associated with the growing importance of cultivated plants (Dillehay et al. 1999). Male human remains cut into 1- to 4-inch lengths and stacked in piles at one site devoid of houses suggest ritual inhumation and the bones suggest possible cannibalism. Jack Rossen (2011; see also Verano and Rossen 2011a) has suggested that this evidence together argues for a process of ritualization whereby the increasing importance of plant resources generated new means to control the supernatural forces involved with agriculture. Whether the ritual cannibalism was part of this or some other means of honoring the dead is uncertain. It does suggest a new relationship between the dead and the living that might be related to agriculture or increasing sedentism. This relationship continued into later periods and by late pre-Hispanic times was associated with agricultural fertility.

During the subsequent Tierras Blancas phase (5800–3000 B.C.E.), the Nanchoc people moved down the lateral quebradas toward the valley floor and began to use small-scale irrigation canals to provide water to their fields. Fewer but larger sites and rectangular multiroomed houses reflect a greater commitment to permanence and agriculture. Cotton was added as a domesticate during this period, and quinoa became more common. An important development in this time was the construction of two mounds across the valley from the occupation zone that were used for producing lime. Lime, made by burning seashells or other sources of calcium carbonate, is commonly used with coca. It is the catalyst that releases the psychoactive ingredients. This suggests that the mounds had ritual significance for the communities that constructed them. Additional evidence of ritual is seen in the recovery of rock crystals from the mounds as well as from canals and fields. Rock crystal is a common ceremonial rock used by shamans even today in the Andes. Thus, the garden magic that began in the Las Pircas phase continued in this phase, possibly in a new form related to water control (Dillehay et al. 1999; Stackelbeck and Dillehay 2011).

Simple unifacial tool complexes such as those from Las Vegas and Siches are known from the Casma Valley all the way down to Lima, although none from the latter regions have been firmly dated. Oddly, these complexes are distinct from the Zaña ones, even though they are geographically closer. The differences in tools probably reflect the different resources used in each area. In the central and north-central coastal complexes, where the coast is closer to the cordillera, the inhabitants spent their year moving among the valley floodplain, nearby lomas, and the ocean to procure their subsistence needs for the year. The broad mid-altitude zone of tropical forest vegetation that is typical of the upper Zaña and Jequetepeque valleys is absent here. There is no good indication of seasonality for these movements. An interesting aspect of the Casma and Lima assemblages is the presence of bifacial projective points, an addition that I have suggested is due to the closer proximity of these sites to highland regions, where such points originated (Malpass 1983). It is therefore likely that occasional trips may have been made to the adjacent highlands for food and to find mates. This continued the pattern of highland movements begun with the earlier Paiján occupation. An alternative explanation is that the highland people occasionally made trips to this region to procure coastal resources or find mates. It is likely that the pattern of visits went both ways.

A distinctive Archaic adaptation has been identified at the site of Paloma, located south of modern Lima in the Chilca Valley. This site is somewhat unique in being located within a large lomas formation, yet only 4 km from the ocean and 8 km from the Chilca floodplain. Thus, it was within a one-hour walk of all three major resources zones. The site, occupied from around 6000–3500 B.C.E., shows evidence of permanent settlement, at least for extensive periods (Benfer 1986; Quilter 1989). Shallow circular houses of cane covered by thatch were excavated, and over two hundred burials of males, females, and children were excavated. Fires over the burials and salting of the corpses might have had ritual significance. Artifacts included a wide variety of fishing equipment, including nets and fish hooks as well as a limited number of projectile points. Food remains indicated a heavy reliance on marine resources, with lomas plants and rare domesticated foods, mostly squash, also included.

Extensive analysis of the skeletons indicated that the occupants of the site generally enjoyed good health, but with injuries typical of their lifestyle. Damage to the inner ear of males from swimming in cold water, probably to collect the shellfish found at the site; broken foot bones; and even evidence of shark attacks were all identified (Quilter 1989). Males seem to have enjoyed higher status, indicated by their placement in the center of the houses after death and the fewer grave goods found with women through time. However, a reduction in sexual dimorphism could be interpreted as reflecting a reduction in the sexual division of labor, such that both sexes were doing equivalent tasks. Evidence for female infanticide was also found, although the reasons for it are not clear.

Some of the more interesting results of this study reflect changing cultural patterns through time. Although the general health of the population was good, indicated by there being little evidence of malnutrition, analysis of the plant remains suggests a gradual overexploitation of the lomas plants, which might account for the abandonment of the site (Weir and Dering 1986). Such a pattern of lomas overexploitation has also been suggested for the region around Lima (Cohen 1977).

The results of the work at Paloma indicate that some populations could enjoy permanence along the coast if the resource zones were close together. A subsistence based on maritime resources was adequate for good health when combined with supplemental contributions from terrestrial sources. Similar villages with preliminary dates that are contemporary have been found in many valleys along the coast (Engel 1973), but few have received the extensive study that would verify similar adaptations.

Along the southern coast, from the Chilca Valley south, there are few sites that date to this period until the Camaná Valley in southern Peru is reached. Surveys along the coast by Frederik Engel (1957) identified many sites that probably date to this period, and testing provided Early and Middle Preceramic ages for some of them. A project conducted by Heather McInnis (2006) in the region to the west of the Quebrada Jaguay site found a pattern of lomas and marine exploitation to be present in this region throughout the period. It may have involved trips to the Alca obsidian source 130 km north in the highlands, although it is equally likely the inhabitants stayed locally on the coast and traded for the obsidian. Settlements appear to have been temporary, with occupations of the coast and inland lomas locations the rule. Early and Middle Preceramic sites have been identified in the lomas region east of Camaná as well (Malpass and de la Vera Cruz n.d.), suggesting the same kind of resource use in that region.

Farther south in the Quebrada de los Burros near the Chilean border, Danièle Lavalleé et al. (1999) found evidence of a possible year-round occupation of the zone, based on a broad use of both marine and terrestrial resources. The presence of deepwater fish species argues for the introduction of boats to the region by 8000 B.C.E. (in McInnis 2006, 521–522).

A unique adaptation during the Middle Preceramic Period was the Chinchorro culture of the coastal region of northern Chile and far southern Peru. This culture developed out of earlier groups that had occupied the region and used a combination of maritime and terrestrial resources. Owing to the great abundance of marine resources, plus the locally useful terrestrial ones in the river valleys and estuaries, the Chinchorro people were able to settle into a sedentary way of life by 5800 B.C.E. (Arriaza et al. 2008). The tools they used included fish hooks made of cactus spines, bone, and shell; fiber fishing line; stone sinkers; harpoons with stone tips; and *atlatls* (spear throwers). Nets and baskets of fibers were used for collecting shellfish, and prying tools of wood were used to remove the shellfish from rocks. Seaweed was also consumed.

Bone chemistry and skeletal analyses of the Chinchorro people indicate that they relied heavily on the ocean for their food and suffered a variety of health problems. Diving into cold water led to bony growths around their ear canals. Parasitic tapeworms have been found in their remains, and many people suffered from anemia from these parasites. In addition, both men and women suffered from back problems, although from different kinds of work. Violence has recently been identified among the Chinchorro people. Women often had fractures of their arms from trying to deflect blows to the head, whereas men suffered from broken noses and cranial fractures as a result of attacks (Standen and Arriaza 2000).

The most interesting aspect of the Chinchorro culture was the careful mummification of the dead (figure 3.5; Arriaza et al. 2008). Mummies were prepared in different ways, some painted black, others painted red, and still others just covered in mud or buried in the sand. It used to be thought that the differences reflected status distinctions, but careful dating of the different mummies indicates the differences are largely chronological, with the black mummies being the earliest, fol-

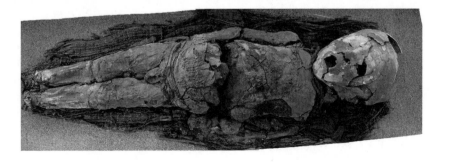

Figure 3.5. Chinchorro mummy of a child (Morro 1-T7-C5). From Standen, Arriaza, and Santoro 2014, figure 3.1b. Photo courtesy of Vivien G. Standen.

lowed by red mummies, and then natural ones (Arriaza et al. 2005). It was also thought that the dead were buried in families, but it is now clear that they were simply laid out in clusters, which might have any combination of adult and young males and females.

The mummification process for the earlier, black mummies involved placing the body in a location where the flesh could decompose, and then recovering it and cleaning the bones. The body was then reconstructed, using sticks to reinforce the skeleton and using clay to rebuild the form, including the sexual organs. The original skin of the head was then placed over the skull, and skin from animals was used to cover the rest of the body. A wig of human hair was put on the skull, and the whole body was painted black, giving these mummies their name. In later, red-mummy burials, the internal organs were removed right after death through incisions in the skin, and then the body was dried and rebuilt, again using sticks to reinforce the skeleton but stuffing the body cavity with feathers, earth, and camelid hair. A long wig made of human hair was attached, and the body was painted bright red. Naturally mummified bodies were simply interred in the sand, where the heat and dryness desiccated the bodies.

The dead were buried with only a few grave goods, often harpoons for males and fishing gear for females. Females also had reed brushes that were used for painting the mummies, suggesting they were the morticians. Bone necklaces and shells were also found, and fishing gear was common in burials of both sexes. All dead, regardless of sex or age, were buried in shrouds made of vegetal fibers skillfully woven by hand, although not on a loom.

The careful mummification of the dead required a great deal of effort and anatomical knowledge, again suggesting possibly early specialization among these foraging people. The care given to the corpses indicates a strong emotional and probably ritual attachment of the living to the dead. The Chinchorro were therefore the earliest people to display the links between the living and dead that sees its most elaborate manifestations in the later Chimú and Inka customs of ancestor veneration.

Archaic Lifestyles in the Northern and Central Highlands

In the central Andean highlands, there were at least two different ways by which the Archaic way of life developed. Using data from Guitarrero Cave in the Callejón de Huaylas, Thomas Lynch (1980) outlines the process by which domesticated plants may have been incorporated into the foraging diet, starting at a relatively early date. Fully domesticated chili peppers and what may be semi-domesticated lúcuma and pacay (two Andean fruits) appeared here in levels dating to 10,800–6200 B.C.E. Ulluco and oca (two tubers that later were domesticated but that may have been wild here) also appeared in the same levels. After 6400 B.C.E., maize and other species of beans were added. In the upper levels of the cave, a much greater variety of plants were used, suggesting a greater intensification of agricultural activities.

The Guitarrero Cave evidence indicates that the cave was never occupied year-round. It has been interpreted as a wet-season, summer camp, where the inhabitants collected wild plants, did some cultivation, and hunted deer and camelids. Where did they go during the winter dry season? Guitarrero Cave is located at 2580 m above sea level in the northern part of the Callejón de Huaylas, the basin through which the Santa River flows before it turns west and empties into the Pacific Ocean. Excavations at caves higher up in the southern part of the valley indicated that people spent the dry season there, mainly hunting (Lynch 1971). The dates and artifacts are the same as for Guitarrero, although the percentages of the tool types vary significantly, indicating that the same people occupied the two areas in different seasons.

This evidence can be interpreted as showing that the Middle Preceramic inhabitants of the Callejón de Huaylas learned that different resources were available in different parts of the valley during different seasons. During the wet season, they could live in lower elevations, such as Guitarrero Cave, and exploit the seasonally available plant resources while also hunting. When the plant resources became scarce at the start of the dry season, the people moved to the higher-elevation camps and spent the rest of the season there, predominantly hunting because few edible plant species live at that altitude. As the rains began, they probably moved down the valley again.

How did this result in the transition to village life? First, domesticated plants and animals were introduced into the valley from adjacent areas as the process of domestication occurred elsewhere. How did the inhabitants of Guitarrero Cave learn about them? As the band, or perhaps bands, that lived in this valley moved through their seasonal round of activities, they would have connected with other groups or made forays into adjacent valleys or even to the coast and met people there. They probably had relatives among the other groups, so social visits could have introduced them to domesticates. Such fluidity in group membership is very typical of small egalitarian societies of hunters and gatherers. Perhaps they began to clear small areas around the cave to plant the seeds neighbors had given them, or perhaps the seeds just grew there as a result of being deposited at the edges of the cave. With little extra effort, such cultivation would yield additional resources for the occupants. Perhaps each year more planting and cultivating occurred, with some accidental or deliberate selection for the better traits of the plants. Through time, more effort was expended at planting but more food was being produced to augment the collected varieties. During the dry season, the group continued to migrate to the high puna zones for hunting, perhaps storing the seeds in the cave for the next season. At some critical juncture, the productivity of the plants was sufficiently high that enough food could be stored to last through the entire year, thus making a move up the valley unnecessary. At this point, around 2400 B.C.E., the transition to settled village life was complete because it is at this date in the archaeological record that permanent villages appear in the Callejón de Huaylas.

A similar scenario for the development of the Archaic lifestyle has been defined for the Ayacucho Valley (MacNeish, Paterson, and Browman 1975). There, seasonal movements between high-altitude and lower-altitude cave sites is suggested as well, although the two zones are not spatially separated, as in the Callejón de Huaylas. The same process of the gradual increase in the use of domesticated plants until permanent villages could be supported is indicated. This process was likely to have been a general one, repeated in many regions of the central highlands as bands in the different valleys were contacted each other and shared information about subsistence. It is this generality of the process that makes it highly unlikely that we will ever be able to pinpoint one region where the domestication process first occurred.

A different Archaic lifestyle developed in the puna of central Peru, based on an environment that was quite distinct. The Puna of Junín, a large, high, windswept region east of Lima, was the focus of study for John Rick in the 1970s. He found that early hunter-gatherers learned to take advantage of a very abundant resource, vicuñas, and by selective hunting could stay in a single location, possibly for hundreds of years. As discussed in chapter 2, punas are high-altitude grasslands and have few edible plant resources. However, herds of deer, guanacos, and vicuñas lived there, and the size of the Puna of Junín made it an ideal location for hunting these animals. In particular, vicuñas live in small family groups in defined territories that are aggressively defended by the dominant male. The early hunters to arrive in the region occupied large caves such as Pachamachay, the site Rick (1980) investigated. They hunted the vicuña groups to local extinction, and when there were so few near the cave that the travel time to find them became significant, they abandoned the cave for other regions. After the vicuñas repopulated the zone, the people returned and did the same. However, through time, the humans learned that, if they selectively harvested only one or two members of each family group, then it was possible to stay at Pachamachay for extended periods. By 3800 B.C.E., Rick argues, a single group occupied the cave more or less permanently and probably for hundreds of years, reflecting a successful adaptation to the local environment. Starting around 2800 B.C.E., the cave was occupied much less often due to the greater emphasis on domesticated camelids and the reduced need for hunting.

In summary, after humans occupied the north and central Andean region, they settled into an Archaic lifestyle that involved reduced nomadism and seasonal movements within a single valley or part of a valley. In the different regions, the people learned through trial and error which plants and animals were edible and their reproductive behaviors. They began to cultivate the plants and tame the animals. Sedentism appeared in the Zaña Valley after 8000 B.C.E., based on the mix of domesticated plants and wild resources, although the evidence from that region suggests that not all groups shifted from foraging to farming. Some chose that pathway, whereas other groups chose other subsistence patterns (Dillehay 2011b). Thus, even in the same general area, the transition to farming was a gradual and sometimes local decision.

In areas further south along the coast, resources were dispersed and domesticates were not introduced, so local groups moved among the coast, lomas, and valley floodplain. In places such as Paloma, the juxtaposition of the three resources zones allowed permanent settlement.

In the highlands, as time passed, there was a shift from hunting and gathering to horticulture and pastoralism. As we can see from the time lines for this period, this process took thousands of years. Groups would not have perceived the changes in their subsistence, and their way of life probably seemed identical to that of their parents and grandparents. Although in some areas agriculture developed long before sedentism, in others, such as the Puna of Junín, the particular circumstances of that region allowed sedentism to predate agriculture. Either way, by around 2000 B.C.E., settled village life based on farming and herding was in place over much of the area.

Archaic Lifestyles in the South Central Highlands

This region is centered on the Altiplano, the large region around Lake Titicaca that lies in the puna zone. To the north, there are highland valleys more typical of the Central Andes; to the west, the land falls off into the dry valleys leading down to the Pacific coast. To the east lie the vast seasonally inundated grasslands of Paraguay and northwestern Argentina. Excavations at sites throughout the region suggest that small bands of hunter-gatherers moved into the area after the Pleistocene ended, when conditions were more favorable for human occupation, probably from the western coast (Aldenderfer 1998; Klink 2005). Paintings and geoglyphs in rock shelters show human and camelid figures, indicating the importance of these mammals to the subsistence activities of the early people. Subsistence was based on hunting camelids and deer and collecting the plants of the region. During the Middle Archaic (defined in this region as 7000–4800 B.C.E.), there was an increase in the number of sites, more focused on permanent water sources, perhaps due to increased aridity during this period.

One well-documented occupation is found at the open-air site of Asana, located in the upper reaches of the Osmore Valley in southern Peru. There, Mark Aldenderfer (1998) found evidence of a long occupation, spanning the entire Preceramic Period. He found an even rarer thing—architecture, indicated by a series of small shelters that were constructed at the site. Probably used seasonally, the site was a wet-season base camp for groups that exploited other zones during the dry winter months. A careful analysis of the food remains shows that intensification of deer, camelid, and certain plant remains occurred through time.

Little is known about plant and animal domestication in the region or about the process by which domesticated plants and animals were introduced from elsewhere. Although the Altiplano has been identified as a possible place where camelids were domesticated, due to their later importance and abundance, there is little evidence for it. Almost certainly, domesticated plants were introduced into this region from their places of origin farther north and east.

The earliest domesticated maize near this region comes from the Late Preceramic site of Alca in the Cotahuasi Valley, a tributary of the Ocoña River

(Perry et al. 2006). At an altitude of 3800 m, the site dates to approximately 1600 B.C.E., at the very end of the Late Preceramic Period. Here, domesticated maize, potatoes, and arrowroot were identified from their starch grains, found both on the floor of a partially excavated house and among fragments of grinding stones. The maize is from both coastal and highland races, and the arrowroot must have come from the tropical forest to the east. Arrowroot followed the same route that the obsidian from a source just above the site followed, but in the opposite direction. The presence of arrowroot, a tropical forest plant, indicates that the long-distance exchange of plants was a fairly early activity in the Andes.

SUMMARY

Small groups of hunters and gatherers began moving into South America late in the Pleistocene. It seems apparent from the existing evidence, spotty as it is, that from earliest times groups branched off into different regions. Some of these earliest groups moved down the western coast, where they used marine resources, reaching Monte Verde by 14,600 years ago. Others moved along the north coast of the continent and spread down the eastern side of the Andes and out into Amazonia. It seems likely that these first people used simple unifacial tools, wooden and bone implements, and other material culture as they adapted to the new lands. Bifacial projectile points were invented in at least two areas, Monte Verde and northern Peru or southern Ecuador, and used in hunting.

Later groups used bifacial projectile points with fluting, and by 13,000 years ago humans had occupied caves at Tierra del Fuego, the southernmost part of South America. Whether the fishtail-fluted points, which also occur in Panama, were a technological development that spread through the existing populations or due to an actual immigration of later people is unclear. Until we have more skeletal data to examine, it will be difficult to determine which of these ideas is correct. Recent research on dental

traits suggest that all the early occupants of South America came from a similar stock (Sutter 2009), but whether there were one, two, or more waves of immigrants is not certain.

Soon thereafter, groups began to move into the highlands, adapting to the resources and oxygen-poor environment of that region as the Pleistocene ended. This expansion must have been driven by population growth as well as curiosity about new regions. As people settled into different regions, they began to experiment with the control of local plant reproduction. Ultimately, this led to the domestication of these plants. Other plants, such as maize, were introduced from Central America. With the loss of the Pleistocene megafauna, humans focused their attention on modern animals and began the process of domesticating llamas, alpacas, and guinea pigs. There is a dramatic increase in the variety of projectile points during the period 9600–4800 B.C.E. all over the Andes, which archaeologists interpret as meaning different social groups were emerging. This, in turn, argues that populations were becoming less nomadic, staying in more restricted regions.

Along the coast and adjacent inlands, different adaptations also emerged during this period. In Ecuador and some areas of northern Peru, hunters and gatherers adopted cultigens and began to settle down into permanent or semi-permanent villages. In other coastal areas, groups using simple unifacial tools continued to practice a mixed terrestrial and maritime subsistence, using resources of the ocean, lomas, and valley floodplains. There is a tendency to assume that these groups had a seasonal round of activities, based on our modeling of ancient groups on modern hunter-gatherers. Yet there is nothing to prove that such was the case, especially as many of the resources used by these coastal people did not have a marked seasonality. Fish and shellfish could be obtained throughout the year, and terrestrial game, such as deer and rodents, has no marked seasonal behaviors either. Early interpretations stated that groups moved to local lomas to take advantage of the fog-season resources of this special zone, but given the relative lack of edible plants there, this seems less likely now. One of the main uses for lomas plants was probably for fiber, used in making nets and perhaps bags, prior to the appearance of cotton.

In some areas, such as the site of Paloma, the close proximity of the three resource zones—ocean, lomas, and valley floodplains—allowed groups to settle into permanent villages. At this time, we do not know how common this situation was.

One other zone that coastal groups probably used occasionally was the adjacent highlands. In the region north of the Santa River, the broad coastal plain meant that hunter-gatherers using maritime and flood-plain resources would have been far from the nearest mountains, where other resources could have been found. The latest evidence from the Paiján region indicates this seems to have been the case there. In addition, a wider mid-elevation zone of foothills is present, where the Nanchoc adaptations developed. In contrast, in the valleys south of the Santa River, where the continental shelf is steeper and therefore less coastline was lost to rising sea levels at the end of the Pleistocene, the westernmost cordillera of the Andes is much closer. Therefore, it would have provided a whole series of other resources that would have been available within a day's walk. The idea that groups practiced seasonal transhumance between these zones is an old one (Lynch 1971), but also one that has little evidence to support it. My research in the Casma Valley and adjacent highlands indicates that groups probably stayed in their respective coastal or highland valleys, although contacts were maintained to find mates. Reciprocal visits by highland groups to the coast are indicated by the occasional presence of projectile points made of stone from that region.

Farther south, the Chinchorro people developed a sedentary way of life based on maritime resources along the Chilean and south Peruvian coast. For reasons unknown to us now, these people developed elaborate mortuary rituals for preserving the dead, and these rituals persisted for over 3,000 years.

What was happening socially to the groups in this region during this time? There is nothing to suggest that anything but simple egalitarian societies were present, either at the coast or in the highlands. At sites that have large numbers of skeletal remains, such as Paloma, evidence suggests that households were the basic social unit. All burials were in close proximity to houses, and many were inside the houses. There is little to discern status differences among individuals, although males seem to have had higher status than females at the end of the occupation. The size and shape of the houses during this period suggest that households were the primary social unit and probably consisted of nuclear or small extended families (Malpass and Stothert 1992).

In the highland zones, the incomplete evidence we have argues for a gradual adoption of domesticates, both plant and animal, through time. On the Puna of Junín, groups settled in permanent locations based on productive camelid resources, and this ultimately led to the domestication of the llama and alpaca. In other regions of deep valleys and altitudinal variation, plant domestication took hold and spread, leading to the patterns of verticality seen today. The fact that many of the earliest cultigens in the Central Andes came from other regions argues that the process of domestication began quite early, probably at the end of the Pleistocene or beginning of the Holocene. The mixed farming and herding economy developed as the productivity of domesticates increased. Somewhere during this time, guinea pigs came under domestication as a supplemental meat source. Yet this process of settling down took thousands of years because there is little evidence of permanent occupations until around 4600–4200 B.C.E. Ideas, domesticates, and other resources such as obsidian crossed large areas, indicating communication among groups in different regions, despite the localized settlement patterns.

The scarce evidence we have suggests that the local use of resource zones was a successful way of life for thousands of years. Groups were able to obtain satisfactory amounts of food; mating partners, from groups either in adjacent valleys, on the nearby coast, or in the highlands; and other essentials of life to keep them functioning through time. There is little evidence of any significant population growth, although this is virtually impossible to identify due to the loss of possible sites to coastal processes, river erosion, and fluvial deposition.

Nonetheless, fundamental changes began to occur in some regions of the coast beginning around 4000 B.C.E. or even before, which manifest themselves more clearly over the next 1,000 years and culminate in the appearance of larger-scale villages and towns; nondomestic architecture, some of monumental size; and social evolution toward more complex forms. The precursors of these developments lay in the garden rituals associated with the emergence of farming in the Zaña Valley, in the mortuary rituals of the Las Vegas and Chinchorro people and those of Paloma, and even in the emergence of a ritual structure at the site of Asana. Changes in the relations between people in and among settlements, and between people and their environments, set the stage for the more significant changes that we see in the succeeding period.

4

SETTLING DOWN AND SETTLING IN
The Late Preceramic Period

Over most of western South America, this period (4000–1800 B.C.E.) is characterized by a continuation of the way of life that had been emerging throughout the Middle Preceramic Period. Societies continued to be egalitarian and focused at the local-group level, although interactions among groups were common for trade and mate exchange. In the highlands, agriculture became more and more important as domesticates became more productive. Hunting as an economic activity was greatly reduced as a result of the spread of domesticated camelids and guinea pigs. Wild-plant collecting continued to be practiced as a dietary supplement. The result of this shift to the use of domesticated plants and animals was the emergence of permanent villages by the end of this period. In contrast to the highlands, the coastal settlements were based on abundant maritime resources rather than terrestrial ones, although domesticated cotton and gourds became common. The importance of gourds and cotton was related to their use in the fishing industry: cotton for fishing nets and gourds for net floats. New research in the central coastal zone, however, shows that domesticated plant use for food had become more important there during this period than previously thought. Although permanent communities had appeared in some coastal regions earlier, they became

more widespread during this period because of the increased emphasis on maritime resources.

This period is important in the study of emerging cultural complexity because the first evidence of something more than small-group organization appeared. Along the central and northern coast of Peru, large-scale constructions were undertaken, marking the emergence of individuals who could coordinate the labor of a large number of people, either in a single large community or several communities. In the region between the Supe and Fortaleza valleys, evidence of inequalities in housing suggests that groups of individuals had gained greater social, political, or religious importance in ways that were new. Smaller community constructions were also found in the north central highlands, reflecting similar shifts in social patterns, although on a smaller scale.

One of the critical issues of this period is the nature of the new power structures that are reflected in these architectural developments. Virtually all the monumental constructions have been interpreted as religious structures, suggesting that the source of power was the control of rituals. In addition, the appearance of a distinct religion based on rituals involving burnt offerings in rooms (figure 4.2), called the

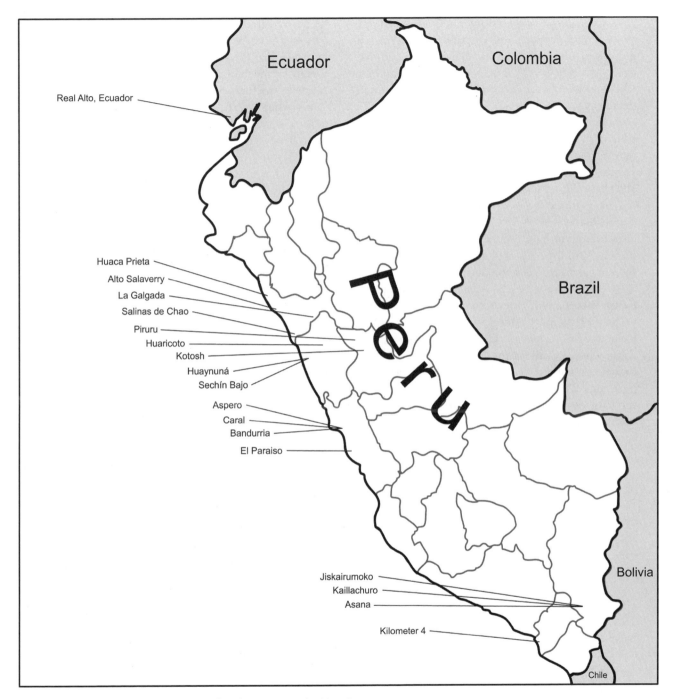

Figure 4.1. Locations of sites mentioned in chapter 4. Map by Matt Gorney.

Kotosh Religious Tradition (Burger and Salazar-Burger 1980, 1985), supports the emerging power of religious individuals at this time. That being said, Michael Moseley (1992) makes the cogent argument that it is likely that civic activities were also conducted as part of the actions at these monuments.

Some researchers, however, argue that it was control of the economy, particularly the exchange of marine resources for terrestrial ones, that was the key to the new power differentials in these societies and that religion was a way of justifying the emerging inequalities. Long-distance trade for resources between the coastal and highland communities is also thought to have been a factor. The mechanisms by which individuals could increase their status by these means have yet to be determined.

To avoid the problem of stating what kind of power these early higher-status individuals manifest, priestly or political, Moseley (1975) has coined the term *corporate authority*. Corporate authorities are those who can call on the labor of others for communal, or corporate, undertakings, such as public buildings. The term does not assume anything about the basis of the authority, whether religious or economic, hereditary or not. Such interpretations must

be derived from information at the sites. The emergence of a corporate authority at this time is clear evidence that the social fabric of these early societies was different than the previous ones. How different is one of the themes of this chapter.

Elsewhere in the Andes, societies based on agriculture continued to develop and spread, although in an irregular fashion. While evidence for domesticates is scarce in the southern Andes at this time, research has shown that social transformations were beginning there too. A precocious development of settled village life during this period, based on mixed agricultural and maritime resources with the addition of ceramics, has been found along the Ecuadorian coast and warrants a brief digression from our main region of interest.

COASTAL ECUADOR

At present, there is some uncertainty about the relationship between the Las Vegas culture of the Santa Elena Peninsula and its successor, the Valdivia culture. The old view that there was a 1,500-year temporal gap between the two (Stothert 1992) appears to have been superseded by the current view of an evolution of the one into the other (Zeidler 2008), although the transition cultures are yet to be identified.

Nonetheless, when the Valdivia culture appeared around 4400 B.C.E., its way of life was very different from that of the earlier Las Vegas culture. Settlements such as Real Alto were permanent villages of large oval houses, with special activity structures for feasting and ancestor reverence. These settlements represent long-term occupations of the region. Subsistence was based both on agriculture and hunting and gathering wild resources, plus significant maritime resource use. Early reports argued that Valdivia culture was based on maize agriculture, but few actual remains were identified at these sites. More recent research (Pearsall 1988; Perry et al. 2007) confirm the use of leren, achira, arrowroot, maize, manioc, jack bean, chili peppers, and cotton. Thus,

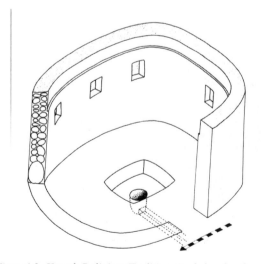

Figure 4.2. Kotosh Religious Tradition ritual chamber from La Galgada. From Grieder et al. 1988, figure 24. Courtesy of the University of Texas Press, copyright 1988.

it is now affirmed that a wide range of crops were grown, although the dietary percentage of these domesticates is unknown. James Zeidler describes the Valdivians as having "a mixed economy of floodplain horticultural production . . . hunting, fishing, and the gathering of wild plants and shellfish" (2008, 462).

Valdivia villages consisted of groups of houses surrounding a plaza area. At the well-excavated site of Real Alto, a Charnel House was located on one side of the plaza and a Fiesta House on the other (Zeidler 2008). The former is a structure where the secondary burials of bones were prepared, apparently continuing the tradition of secondary burials from the earlier Las Vegas culture. The Fiesta House gets its name from the quantities of serving vessels found there, suggesting community feasting was its main function, possibly associated with the rituals conducted for the dead at the Charnel House.

Valdivia is best known for its beautiful ceramics, which represent a level of skill that is surprising for pottery that is among the earliest in South America. The pots are thin walled and well constructed, with designs that show great skill in their production. All this argues for an origin of the ceramics elsewhere. Early investigators found superficial similarities between this pottery and that of the contemporary Jomon culture of Japan that were argued to reflect an actual introduction of this industry from Asia (Meggars, Evans, and Estrada 1965). More definitive analysis of the Valdivia evidence, however, supports an indigenous origin (Zeidler 2008).

In fact, Donald Lathrap and his colleagues (Lathrap 1977; Lathrap, Collier, and Chandra 1975) have suggested an origin in the tropical forest region of eastern Ecuador, based on several lines of evidence. First, the house form and shape, plus the village layout, is typical of many twentieth-century Amazonian tribes. In addition, the ceramics appear to be related in forms and decorative techniques to later groups from the Peruvian ceja. This suggests to Lathrap that the ultimate origins of the cultures in both of these areas will be found in the upper Amazon, from whence it spread west and south, up the tributaries of the Amazon. Using tropical forest societies as a model, he argues that Valdivians practiced horticulture in garden plots near their villages, including both food and medicinal plants. A problem with this interpretation is that no similar contemporary sites have been identified in the intervening highland region of Ecuador.

THE NORTH AND CENTRAL COAST OF PERU

It is interesting that this region, which saw the precocious development of agriculturally based communities in the Nanchoc Valley, is where the first steps toward social inequalities occurred, although in the regions south of Nanchoc. Several important changes appear during this period that set the stage for later developments. First, domesticated plants make their initial appearance in many regions, although both the quantity and variety are generally limited. The two most common plants are cotton and gourd, both nonedible; however, food plants also appear. The bottle gourd, as noted in chapter 3, had been present in the far-north region since around 7000 B.C.E. Second, a symbiotic relationship emerges between the littoral communities and inland ones in which the former provided marine resources to the latter in exchange for cultivated and wild plant resources. In addition, communal architecture makes its first appearance, along with some kind of authority figures associated with its construction (Dillehay 1992; Moseley 1975). All these developments mark a significant period of change from the earlier way of life.

One explanation for these changes, called the maritime foundations of Andean civilization (MFAC) hypothesis, was presented in 1975 by Michael Moseley based on work done along the central coast near Lima. He suggested that people began to exploit the rich resources of the ocean from permanent villages along the coast. To fish more effectively, cotton and gourds were grown for fishing nets and floats, thus introducing farming. Cultivation was done along the river valley, and the cotton and gourds were exchanged for fish and shellfish with the coastal people. The abundance and nutritional quality of the marine resources engendered a population increase that led to other plants being introduced from the neighboring highlands, this time for food—beans, squash, peanuts, achira, and other fruits and vegetables. Although more recent evidence indicates that the marine resource use has a much deeper time depth than this hypothesis initially assumes, its basic tenets are still reasonable. I assess this hypothesis later in the chapter, after I present newer evidence.

We now know that the apparent increase in marine resource use was a function of the stabilization of sea level by around 3800 B.C.E. and that this is simply the first time period for which we have widespread evidence preserved for its use; the earlier coastal settlements are now submerged. The evidence at hand does suggest that some communities in the valley flood plains began farming, mostly cotton and gourd, whereas others along the coast focused on fishing and shellfish collecting. An alternative explanation is that the same people occupied the two zones and moved between them, possibly seasonally. In the region called Norte Chico, the evidence argues for the permanent occupations of both zones. In many other areas, however, the evidence for this is not as strong.

What we do know is that some communities that were located at the mouths of rivers could successfully exploit the resources of both the ocean and valley floodplain. These sites grew to larger sizes than contemporary ones located along the coast (Moseley 1975; Feldman 1987). One such site is El Paraiso, located near the mouth of the Chillón River, near modern Lima. This site consists of the remains of nine architectural complexes on six mounds, arranged in a rough U-shape, with a large plaza between the two largest mounds of rubble. Excavations indicate that most of the mounds are large piles of construction debris, with groups of rooms filled in and built on by later occupants. Walls were constructed of *shicra,* which are cotton or reed bags filled with rock. Although some researchers argue that the use of shicra

reflects a way to count the labor of different groups helping to build the structures (e.g., Moseley 1992), its use could also reflect the special character of the structure because shicra is not used for residential architecture (Feldman 1987). It is estimated that 100,000 tons of rock were moved to build the entire site. The site was occupied from around 1800–1500 B.C.E. into the later Initial Period, however, so it is unclear how much of the site was built and occupied at any given time.

Food remains indicate subsistence based on marine resources, mostly small fish and shellfish, and wild plants probably collected in the river floodplain. Domesticated food plants included squash, chili peppers, achira, jícama, beans, and tree fruits such as guava, lúcuma, and pacae, although the tree fruits might not have been domesticated. In addition, gourds and cotton were grown for use in the fishing industry (Quilter et al. 1991).

One of the mounds has been excavated and reconstructed (figure 4.3). Of interest to our discussions of complexity, this mound had a series of rooms, including one with a sunken square area and four hearths at each corner. Whether this was a ritual structure used by the entire community is uncertain, although little evidence of domestic activity was found in the structure (Burger 1992).

Thus, El Paraiso represents a very large residential complex but one that may have been self-supporting. Although some researchers have suggested it was a political or economic center for the region, due to its large size and the quantity of fill moved (Moseley 1975), it is unclear if there was a residential authority that controlled the labor of the site or other sites around it. The residential mounds could have been the result of lineage or other social group activities.

A similar site has been found at Aspero at the mouth of the Supe River farther north. El Paraiso dates to around 1800 B.C.E., but it is now evident that Aspero was occupied much earlier. A series of radiocarbon dates from the tops of platform mounds there date to just after 3700 B.C.E.; therefore, the occupations at the bases of the mounds must be even earlier. How much earlier remains to be determined.

Figure 4.3. Reconstructed mound at El Paraiso. Photo by author.

The site is dominated by six small mounds built using shicra, as at El Paraiso. Unlike at El Paraiso, there is a large zone around the mounds that was used for residences but that were not concentrated into mounds of rubble through time. Also, the rooms on these mounds appear to have served ritual functions because excavations at the top of one of them recovered a unique set of figurines (Feldman 1987). There is restricted access to the ritual rooms at the tops of these mounds, which Robert Feldman has argued indicates the presence of a social hierarchy. Nevertheless, a cargo-type society could also have built such structures for the use of different ayllus or other social groups. The presence of six contemporary ritual mounds could argue against a centralized authority at the site.

A cautionary note is in order at this juncture. There is sometimes an assumption that the platform mounds that have been described were built either in one phase of construction or in several phases over a relatively short period of time. This implies a large labor force under the control of some corporate authority. But given the quite large range of dates for some of these monuments, spanning centuries in most cases, we must question how much labor was actually employed at any given time. For example, the large mounds at Aspero and El Paraiso were constructed by building a series of rooms out of shicra. When the rooms were no longer needed (for residences or rituals) or new rooms required, the old rooms were filled in and the new rooms constructed on top of them. Through time, the mounds grew. Only a small number of people, however, would have been required to do the actual construction at any given time. The fact that Aspero has six major mounds that were used at the same time indicates smaller groups within the community were probably responsible for each. For sites such as Caral and probably Salinas de Chao (discussed later in the chapter), the evidence is better for their requiring a much larger labor force because the main pyramids are much larger and constructed in a few stages over relatively short periods of time.

Looked at in another way, we can devise figures for the labor required to construct a pyramid, based on the amount of dirt and stone one person could move working a certain number of hours per day. Let us assume one person can fill, transport, and place 2 cubic meters of shicra in a six-hour day. The largest mound at Caral has 432,000 cubic meters of fill. To build such a mound would then require 216 people working 1,000 days each, or slightly less than three years. Thus, even large mounds could be built in a small number of years with a relatively small workforce.

Better evidence for a centralized authority has been identified at other sites in the Norte Chico, the region encompassing the Huaura, Supe, Patavilca, and Fortaleza valleys. This region has recently been shown to be the earliest along the coast to manifest complex societies, and one that might therefore have served as a source of cultural transformations for other regions in subsequent periods (Haas and Creamer 2004; Shady Solís et al. 2000; Shady Solís, Haas, and Creamer 2001).

Although the early dates for Aspero have been known for some time, its cultural relationship to other sites was identified more recently. The work by Ruth Shady Solís (1997, 2006a, 2009) and others at the site, located 25 km inland, has indicated that this site was a sizable community at a date that overlaps the occupation at Aspero (figures 4.4A and 4.4B). The central part of the valley comprises a capital zone and six other settlements that stretch along the Supe River for 7 km. The capital zone has seven major platform mounds, several smaller ones, two sunken circular courts (sometimes called plazas), and an array of residential and other structures (Shady Solís 2009). The Great Pyramid (Pirámide Mayor) is the largest mound, measuring 171 by 150 by 30 m (from which the total volume was derived for the earlier computations) (plate 1B). There is a

structure with a ventilated hearth, similar to Kotosh Religious Tradition sites elsewhere during this time. Shady Solís and her colleagues argue that the different mounds were associated with a ritual calendar that was linked to cosmic deities and a labor cycle.

In addition to Caral, there are seventeen other contemporary inland sites that also have mounds in the Supe Valley, and more recent work by Haas and Creamer (2004) has identified similar, although smaller, complexes in the Fortaleza and Patavilca valleys as well. Although the dates are few at present, some, such as Vinto Alto in the Patavilca Valley, are as early as Caral (ibid.).

The subsistence remains from Caral indicate that marine resources were the primary source of protein for the residents of the site and that wild and domesticated plants provided other parts of the diet. These included squash, sweet potatoes, beans, avocados, chili peppers, guavas, and pacaes (Shady Solís 2006a, table 2.4). Of these, guavas made up over 99 percent of the food plants. It is uncertain whether the guavas were cultivated or collected wild. Fifteen maize cobs, two husks, and one panicle of maize were also recovered, but all the corn was from ritual contexts, indicating it had more of a ceremonial than economic role (Shady Solís 2006b). Maize was also found in an offering on one of the mounds at Aspero. The economic system of Caral is described as an exchange of cultivated plants such as cotton, gourds, and perhaps guavas for marine resources with coastal communities such as Aspero and Bandurria, located slightly farther south.

What is important about Caral and these other inland sites is the labor required to build them. Like Aspero and El Paraiso, the main mounds at Caral were constructed in many phases (Shady Solís 2009). This suggests that many people may have been involved in the construction, but it could also reflect smaller groups working over longer periods. That being said, it is clear the workforce at Caral was larger than at the other sites nearby. The fact that there are many contemporary sites indicates that similar processes of cultural evolution were at work simultaneously in each region of the valley.

Shady Solís (2009) has made the case that Caral and the other settlements along the Supe Valley represent a pristine state, indeed, the earliest state in the New World. While noting that the different settlements appear to be self-sustaining with regard to basic subsistence, she suggests there was a hierarchy of settlements that reflects power relationships between them. The economic exchange of cotton for marine resources linked the inland and coastal settlements. What linked the inland settlements is less clear because most have public architecture. Shady Solís identifies Caral as the capital of the state by virtue of its size and internal complexity. She notes that there are four levels of residences that seem to reflect status differences by their size and proximity to major public buildings. She sees a conceptual distinction between the upper and lower parts of the settlement, which she interprets as indicating the presence of a moiety division. Two craft workshops suggest specialization of a kind not yet identified at other settlements of this date.

Finally, burial practices suggest status differences. She notes that the majority of the burials are of children, and the different objects buried with them denote status differences, which, due to their age, must be ascribed (Shady Solís 2009,117). The objects, however, are not discussed. She does describe in detail a burial of a young adult male in an infilled atrium on the Great Pyramid. The paleopathology of the skeleton suggests he was involved in hard labor consistent with that involved in building the monuments at Caral. She infers this burial was an offering representing a lower-class sacrifice, placed there presumably by the ruling class.

Although the complexity of the architectural remains at Caral do argue that someone had to be in charge of such projects, we do not know whether the means of control were via hereditary kurakas or powerful nonhereditary leaders in a cargo-like society. As at Aspero, the presence of multiple mounds used at the same time could argue for multiple social groups being involved. The association of different residence types with different mounds could reflect internal social groups of equal status rather than hi-erarchy. As discussed in chapter 5, a similar situation is seen in the Lurín Valley during the Initial Period, with different interpretations of the political authority provided. In addition, Shady Solís argues that the sheer size and number of the large monuments in the capital zone must have required labor from other settlements, yet the multiphase construction might have been done by the sizable population at the site itself. Finally, the burial evidence does appear to support status differences, but if the burials were offerings, not regular inhumations, then their special statuses might represent their importance to the gods, not their positions in society.

To me and others (Makowski 2008), the evidence is not sufficient to claim that a state-level society was present in the Supe Valley, but that disagreement rests on definitional arguments that are not so important. The significant point is that powerful leaders had emerged at these sites who could control labor and perhaps even exchange and who certainly could organize labor for large construction projects. Whether the leaders of Caral had power over other settlements is a point to be clarified with subsequent research. It is also unclear whether the leadership positions during this time were hereditary, although there is little evidence to support it.

What is the evidence from elsewhere in the Norte Chico? The site of Bandurria, located on the coast south of Huacho but very close to Caral as the condor flies, has three main mounds, one of which includes a circular sunken court in front of it (Chu Barrera 2008). The site has a similar economy to that of Caral, based on sardines, anchovies, and shellfish, and also includes mainly plant resources such as guavas. Cotton and gourds are common as industrial cultigens. Unlike Caral, the main mound there was built in a single phase late in the period. Alejandro Chu Barrera (2008) argues that an elite class had emerged in Bandurria to organize the labor of constructing the mounds, which he interprets as ceremonial. Yet no unequivocal evidence for such a class is presented. It seems likely that Bandurria, like Aspero, was part of the cultural network that supplied Caral with marine resources.

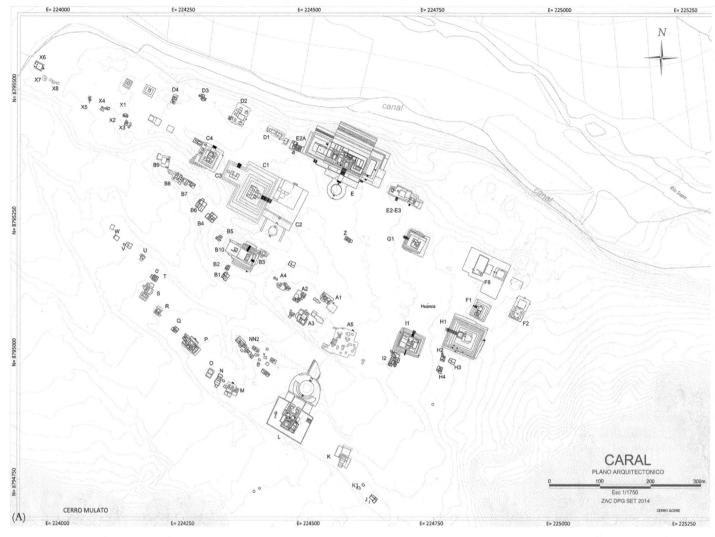

Figure 4.4. (A) Plan of the Sacred City of Caral. (B) Panoramic view of the central area of the Sacred City of Caral. Images courtesy of Zona Arqueológica Caral and Christopher Kleigehe.

On the coast farther north, littoral sites show evidence of intense use of marine resources, similar to those to the south. There are few large sites similar to Aspero or Caral, however. This is not to say that similar social processes were not as work. At Huaynuná in the Casma valley, a ventilated hearth structure was found that resembles those associated with the Kotosh Religious Tradition. Huaynuná has a series of four artificial platforms built on a hillside on which structures were found (Pozorski and Pozorski 1990).

Recent work at the site of Sechín Bajo in the Casma Valley has provided new evidence of ceremonial activity at least as early as that at Caral (Lorenz and Fuchs 2009). Under the Initial Period mound that dominates this site, German archaeologists and geophysicists identified four preexisting sunken circular courts that had slightly different main orienta-

(B)

tions from the later buildings. The main axis of these early structures pointed toward the summer solstice sunrise; in contrast, the later structures were oriented toward the winter solstice sunrise, indicating a shift in the importance of these two solar events over time.

The site of Salinas de Chao, located in the small Chao valley just to the north of where the Santa River flows into the Pacific Ocean, has two areas of architecture. One, located along an upraised beach, has a large mound with architecture on the top. Remote sensing on the mound, called Los Morteros, suggests it is entirely human-made, not just a stabilized sand dune with constructions on top (Sandweiss et al. 2010). If it

is an artificial mound, it ranks as one of the largest along the coast at this time, approximately 3500 B.C.E. Located about 1 km away is another set of architectural remains, these set on a hillside. Platforms with house remains face the flat plain leading to the other mound site. Two sunken circular courts are located in the desert in front of these. Moseley (2001) argues that the constructions in the Chao Valley are too large to have been built by the residents of the site, so must have been built with labor drawn from adjacent areas, much as Shady Solís argues for Caral and the large sites of Norte Chico. Because we do not know the time interval during which the mound was built, however, this remains conjectural, although likely. Where these adjacent settlements were is also unknown.

A similar, although smaller, sunken circular plaza with stairs leading down into it from two sides was also found by Sheila Pozorski and Thomas Pozorski (1979) in the Moche Valley at the site of Alto Salaverry. This site is considerably smaller than Salinas de Chao; nevertheless, the identification of the ceremonial plaza with a domestic occupation indicates similar social processes were at work there.

Finally, no survey of northern Late Preceramic sites would be complete without a description of Huaca Prieta, located at the mouth of the Chicama River. This large mound was originally excavated by Junius Bird in the 1940s. Although an earlier occupation has also been identified there (see chapter 3), radiocarbon dates from Bird's main excavations fall between 3350 B.C.E. and 17 C.E. (Dillehay et al. 2012). Bird identified small stone structures and a simple stone technology at the site. The economy was based on marine resources supplemented by incipient farming. Textiles and gourd carvings show a rich set of beliefs in deities had already developed among the occupants of the site (Bird 1963; Bird et al. 1985).

More recent work at Huaca Prieta by Dillehay et al. (2012) has shown the site also had a sunken circular plaza constructed at its summit, with a ramp added later, before the abandonment of the site. In contrast to contemporary sites, Huaca Prieta had many burials placed at the summit during its final phase of construction.

Much less is known about developments in the Late Preceramic Period along the coast of Peru south of Lima. Few sites have been identified or excavated. The Kilometer 4 site near Ilo in the Moquegua drainage shows a settlement still based on marine resources but with some evidence of agricultural activities (Wise 2000).

Maritime Foundations of Andean Civilization Hypothesis Revisited

What, then, can we make of the MFAC hypothesis? Even though maritime resources were an important staple in coastal communities long before this period, it is also now apparent that the emergence at this time of larger communities able to construct monumental structures was associated with an economy based on domesticated plants in addition to wild ones (Feldman 1992; Quilter 1991, 1992). This pertains to both the inland Norte Chico sites and the ones closer to the coast. Although the question of whether coastal groups were importing bulk domesticates from the adjacent highland regions in exchange for coastal goods has yet to be resolved, the lack of abundant remains at coastal sites argues for the relative unimportance of domesticated food plants along the coast. What remains an important conclusion of the MFAC hypothesis, then, is that maritime resources were of primary importance and domesticated food plants did not play a significant role in the appearance of complex societies in this region, in contrast to other parts of the world (Feldman 2009; Sandweiss 2009).

A different modification of the MFAC hypothesis has recently been suggested by Shelia Pozorski and Thomas Pozorski (2008). They note that several of the Late Preceramic sites with monumental architecture, such as El Paraiso and Salinas de Chao, actually have radiocarbon dates that are from the Initial Period (post-1800 B.C.E.) rather than earlier. The truly Preceramic coastal sites were smaller fishing villages, with the exception of Aspero. Significantly, with the discovery of the inland horticultural communities such as Caral, the idea that maritime resources underwrote the development of monumental architectural sites has been challenged. Nevertheless, given the relative prominence of maritime resources at the inland sites and the question of how important domesticated plants were there, we could still argue that the basic tenets of the MFAC hypothesis are relevant. Note that most researchers accept the Late Preceramic dates for the sites of El Paraiso, Salinas de Chao, and others.

A point of interest in the discussion of emerging complexity along the coast is why it was restricted to the zone north of modern Lima. South of this zone, Late Preceramic sites are scarce, and most of those known are not well reported. We know, for example, that along the far south coast near Ilo sites were small and widely dispersed (Owens 2009; Wise 1997, 1999). The valleys in this region are much more restricted and incised than those in the north, suggesting lower population densities were a factor; however, why maritime based settlements did not develop at the mouths of such rivers is not known. Sandweiss (2009) has explained that one reason for the growth in the size and complexity of settlements along the coast north of Lima is that this is where small schooling fish, such as anchovies and sardines, became more prevalent after 5,300 B.C.E. This, combined with the domestication of cotton, led to a technological advance in subsistence that engendered the population increases seen during this time. These increases, in turn, led to the emergence of the new social forms reflected in the monuments discussed here.

Of Monuments and Movements

Before discussing other regions of the western Andes, it is worth thinking about the kinds of monuments that were built during the Late Preceramic Period along the coast and in the highlands and what they represent. There are at least three kinds of monumental structures that appeared in the Late Preceramic Period: sunken circular courts; platform mounds, often stepped with rooms on top; and the Kotosh Religious Tradition use of small enclosed rooms with hearths (sometimes ventilated), benches, and niches inside, sometimes placed on platform mounds as well. Although many scholars, notably Moseley (2001), Richardson (1994), and Richard Burger (1992) see a U-shaped monumental structure emerging at the site of El Paraiso, I am uncertain that the U form of that site is intentional, unlike the sites that emerged in the succeeding Initial Period. Although there are two parallel mounds with a large plaza between them at El Paraiso, the flanking mounds are for residential structures, which is not the case at the later sites. In addition, the single mound thought to be at the base of the U is not connected to a flanking mound and is not centered between the arms. Finally, unlike most Initial Period U-shaped structures, the purported U complex does not face upstream.

Two kinds of information can be gleaned from these monumental structures. The first is the connections between valleys and regions. Where different communities are building similar kinds of ceremonial architecture, there must be a common belief system that is shared among them. This denotes information exchange among the people in charge of these structures. There are basic similarities in form in the sunken circular courts at different sites, although the size and the location of the structure may vary from site to site. The same is true of the Kotosh Religious Tradition sites. There is much more variation in the summit structures of the mounds, which suggests that local decisions were playing a major role in which specific rooms were necessary.

What is less obvious is the means of information exchange. Were emerging leaders sharing information or was the information part of a more generally accepted set of religious or social beliefs? Assuming, as we have, that someone was in charge of construction, the former seems more likely. What else was exchanged among these individuals? Was marriage exchange conducted to cement alliances or economic exchange? That similar architecture is seen in several valleys, and even along the coast and in the highlands, bespeaks of communication that was interregional. Perhaps ideas concerning leadership and authority were also exchanged.

The second kind of information provided by the early monumental architecture, which is sometimes lost in discussions about these monuments, is what it *represents*. First, they do represent a labor investment of the community for some special purpose. The purpose could be either secular or sacred, although most of the time the latter is assumed, sometimes with evidence, sometimes without. I am guilty of that myself! Recall that many of the Late Preceramic monumental structures were actually built by what is often called interment, the infilling of a room and the construction of another room or rooms on top of it. Through time, the structure rises above the level of the ground. The mounds at Aspero and El Paraiso were constructed in this fashion, and it now appears likely that even the large mounds at Caral were constructed in this way, although more formal modifications of the building shape might have been part of this practice there. As already discussed, this method of construction reduces the number of people required to construct the edifice.

It has been argued that the use of shicra bags for carrying mound fill reflects corporate control of the labor because it would be a means to identify who contributed to the building and how much. This is possible, but the use of shicra might also be a construction feature for special structures, a way of keeping unconsolidated earth and rock together in a wall. In addition, as Burger (1992, 41) notes, the amount of fill in each bag varied considerably, which would make determining comparable labor difficult.

As long ago as 1985, Donald Lathrap argued that the U-shaped temples of the Chavín culture (discussed in chapter 6) symbolically represent the jaws of a cayman deity. Although we can never know what gods were worshipped, we can attempt to interpret some meaning from the architecture. It is hard not to find significance in the fact that most mounds are elevated above the ground and the sunken courts are excavated into it. Andean people, both modern and ancient, had underground and sky deities, and it is most likely that these were worshipped in such ritual buildings. Moseley (2001) suggests the mounds might represent *apus*, powerful male mountain deities while sunken courts might be for the worship of the female earth deity, *Pachamama*. That the sunken courts are often associated with mounds suggests that the religious practices could be combined. Hearths are sometimes found in the center of the court, indicating that burned offerings were part of the rituals at some centers. Sunken courts nearly always have two opposing stairways by which an individual could enter and leave, and these stairways are oriented to the central staircase of associated mounds, when the latter are present. This suggests processions were an important part of the rituals associated with these structures.

The political and social aspects of these monuments are also important. The tops of most mounds usually include small rooms or complexes of rooms where the actual activities were carried out. The small size of these rooms argues that only part of the community could be involved at any one time. The idea of *restricted access,* meaning that only certain individuals are privileged by social convention to enter a space, is often an archaeological hallmark of social inequality. The nature of the privilege, however, is never certain. It is easy to assume that the leaders in charge of building the monument are the ones who had access to the rooms on top and who conducted the activities or rituals for the rest of the community. This is not an unreasonable suggestion, especially when there is a single public structure at a settlement. We must keep alternative possibilities in mind, however, such as that these structures might have been communal and that any group could have used them. Perhaps they were for male or female activities, such as are common in Amazonian tribes. When there is more than one monument at a site, the issue becomes more complicated because we need to consider why there are multiple structures, who would be using each, and what the relationship of these groups were to each other. When there is more than one kind of evidence supporting social inequalities, then it becomes easier to make the case that there were individuals who were in charge. Lacking other such lines of evidence, such as burials or wealth accumulation, we should be cautious about making arguments about hierarchical power relationships in a society based solely on the architectural evidence.

It is another common assumption that the individuals involved in conducting the rituals were also in some way directing economic activities. Again, this is not unreasonable, but we should be open to alternatives. There could be emerging ritual specialists at a settlement whose claims to authority were supernaturally based while other families had claims based on possessing the best land for resources or being the best traders or being best at resolving disputes.

To me, there are few sites along the north and north-central coast where it is unambiguous that a hierarchical society emerged during the Late Preceramic Period. It is clear that leaders were present in the planning and construction of these large monuments, but whether they had any power to control people's lives in other ways is not evident. At sites such as Caral, the residential evidence plus perhaps the burials could argue for more marked social differentiation. In most sites, however, there is little to support the idea of ascribed status or political power. Such evidence does appear in the subsequent time period.

What must have been happening during this period is the internal differentiation of society. In his thoughtful 1992 reassessment of the MFAC hypothesis, Moseley suggests that the large Late Preceramic mounds reflect the development of specialized construction tasks that were conducted by specific groups and that these groups had chains of command that directed them. That the mounds were continually rebuilt or added to argues that the chains of command were maintained through time, yet there is no evidence that they were hereditary. This suggests to Moseley that the work was done by some system that, perhaps, was the precursor to the more recent cargo system, in which important ritual and civic positions were held on a rotating basis by lineage heads with the support of their lineage. Such activities would be conducted for a period of time; then the position would rotate to someone else. The labor for doing the construction fell to the community, which worked for the particular head at the time. Economics played a role because the food and drink for the labor parties might well have been the responsibility of the person in charge.

This model works for settlements that have a single mound or multiple ones. We can envision competing lineages building their own mounds for ceremonial or civic reasons at Aspero, Caral, or other sites. Possibly, there was a kind of competition, for prestige if not for other reasons, among lineages. This kind of competition could have set the stage for the greater sociopolitical elaboration of architecture in the subsequent Initial Period.

South of the central coast of Peru, there are no major constructions nor any evidence that societies had evolved further than the egalitarian stage present earlier. These societies continued to practice a mixed maritime and terrestrial economy in small villages.

THE NORTH AND CENTRAL HIGHLANDS

In the highlands, the first temples appeared after 2400 B.C.E., about the same time that settled village life began in many regions. In the central highlands, the first temples are associated with the appearance of the set of religious beliefs called the Kotosh Religious Tradition. Richard Burger and Lucy Salazar-Burger (1980) define this tradition based on data from several sites located in the northern part of the central highlands. The tradition refers to a set of rituals conducted in small closed rooms that included the burning of offerings in a central hearth, followed by the covering over of the pit until the next burning. Offerings included chili peppers, marine shells, and other materials.

The religious tradition is named for the site of Kotosh, where the first evidence was uncovered. Kotosh is in the Huallaga River drainage near the modern city of Huánuco, at an elevation of 1950 m above sea level. The Japanese archaeologists who dug the site concentrated on the largest two mounds of building debris (Izumi and Sono 1963). They trenched the larger mound and found that it consists of a series of ten superimposed structures. The lowest two lack any pottery and so pertain to the Late Preceramic Period in this region.

Excavations at one of the lowest, therefore earliest, structures at Kotosh found a single room, roughly 9 m², which has a large hearth in the center. The hearth has two horizontal ventilation shafts that brought air to the base of the fire from outside the structure. Along the walls are *niches* (recessed areas), under which are crossed forearms made of modeled clay. This feature gives the temple its name, Templo de los Manos Cruzados (Temple of the Crossed

Hands). In the niches were found the remains of burned llama and guinea pig bones, probably offerings. The room itself is on top of an artificial platform approximately 8 m (26 ft) high, so it must have loomed above the surrounding village. Ten other chambers have been found at the site that date to this period, and many more are thought to exist. Farther down the Huallaga River from Kotosh are two other sites, Shillacoto and Waira-Jirca, that also have similar chambers that date to this period (Burger 1992).

A similar kind of ventilated hearth structure has been identified at the site of La Galgada in the Tablachaca River drainage, a tributary of the Santa, at an altitude of approximately 1,000 m above sea level (Grieder et al. 1988). Here, another pair of mounds was excavated, and a whole series of superimposed rooms with central hearths were uncovered (figure 4.2). As at Kotosh, some of these hearths have ventilation shafts that brought air from outside the room, under the floor, to the base of the hearth. This assured that the fire would continue to burn effectively, despite the enclosed nature of the room. The excavators found remains of chili peppers in the ash of the hearths, which must have provided a stinging smoke to the rooms and the activities within them. The acrid smoke may have been important to stimulate tears and coughing, to cause an altered state whereby communication with the gods became possible. The site dates to 2800–2100 B.C.E., making it one of the earliest in the region, although the dated excavations do not come from the lowest levels, which must be earlier. By the end of the Late Preceramic, the north mound might also have been one of the highest because earlier ritual chambers were entombed and others built on top of them. A large sunken circular court is located in front of the main mound at La Galgada, reflecting the presence of this religious tradition here, which was probably introduced from the coast.

Other square rooms with ventilated hearths that belong in the Kotosh Religious Tradition and help define it are found at Piruru in the Tantamayo drainage to the north and at Huaricoto in the Callejón de Huaylas. Their presence at these sites indicates that the beliefs associated with burned offerings were widespread. Similar hearths without the rooms are also found on the coast, indicating the tradition was widespread during this period. Note that the earliest ventilated hearth structure is actually at Caral in the Supe Valley, suggesting that this tradition may actually have its origins on the coast (Pozorski and Pozorski 2008).

The emergence of a corporate authority that directed the construction of these mounds and rooms marks a change from the kind of social organization that had existed earlier in the highlands. Feldman (1992) argues that these ritual structures were made for the private ceremonies of a smaller group than the mounds on the coast. At sites such as Kotosh and La Galgada, the principles may have been the same as discussed for the coast: someone was in charge and that person or those people were able to call on the labor of more than just their own family or ayllu. But the relatively smaller size of the mounds argues for smaller groups being involved. That this occurred after people had settled down in permanent communities reflects either the emerging need for a means to integrate a larger number of people or perhaps the development of individuals who were actively trying to increase their power and influence in the community. At sites such as Huaricoto, it seems as if a much smaller group was responsible for constructing the ventilated hearth structures, possibly a single lineage.

It is an interesting point that burned offerings in small rooms were conducted both on top of platform mounds and in isolated rooms without mounds. The presence of the ventilated hearth structures at the coastal sites also suggests the essential nature of the rituals could be separated from the presence of mounds. Small egalitarian communities could participate as well as larger ones.

The importance of the religious beliefs is also indicated by the entombment of the rooms at Kotosh and La Galgada. The earlier temple rooms were carefully filled in before new structures were constructed on top of them. This bespeaks a reverence for the room and its activities, and for the people buried in them (at least at La Galgada). The continued use of the mounds and rooms through time supports the idea that the religious tradition was an organizing force for the people involved for many centuries. It could also indicate a means by which the corporate authority maintained its power in the community—or by which power might have become hereditary.

In other areas of the central highlands, village life developed without the emergence of integrating religious beliefs. No evidence for any kind of formal rituals is known from other areas, such as Ayacucho or the Apurimac drainage. Still, as more excavations are conducted, the known sphere of influence of the Kotosh Religious Tradition may expand.

Evidence from the food remains at these sites indicate that a settled village way of life was operating, based on a wide variety of domesticated plants and the herding of llamas and caring for guinea pigs. The system of verticality mentioned in chapter 2 was no doubt fully developed, with the fields of a household spread across several zones to minimize the chance of catastrophic loss. Trade was developing between regions, with coastal products showing up in the highlands. These trade routes became the conduits for the exchange of religious ideas along with economic products. Such a situation has been common through history; witness how Christianity spread across Europe following the trade routes of the Roman Empire.

THE SOUTH-CENTRAL HIGHLANDS

Research by Cynthia Klink and Mark Aldenderfer (2005; see chapter 3) in the Huenque and Ilave river valleys of the western Altiplano indicates that there was generally a continuation of Middle Archaic patterns of occupation in these regions. For the Huenque drainage, groups moved often, locating near permanent water early in the period, but moved down toward Lake Titicaca as rainfall increased. In the adjacent Chila Valley, mobility was also high, and residents subsisted on hunting camelids and deer and trading for a species of Chenopodium (a plant family that includes quinoa and other domesticated grains) that grows only in the lower regions. The presence of obsidian from the Chivay source in the Colca Valley indicates another trade good coming in from a long distance (Aldenderfer 2005).

For the Ilave drainage, a pattern of decreasing mobility and larger settlements is associated with an increasing reliance on chenopods and tubers. At the site of Jiskairumoko, a group of small pithouses, interpreted as residences, surround a larger one that has special features, a large central hearth and benches around the perimeter. Aldenderfer (2005) argues that the central structure had ritual or public uses for the group. An important find at this site is a necklace made of hammered gold tubular beads and lapis lazuli, both of nonlocal origin (figure 4.5; Aldenderfer et al. 2008). This artifact is the earliest known use of gold in the Andes. At the nearby site of Kaillachuro, nine low mounds were found in domestic refuse areas that contained secondary burials. In a central mound, a five- to eight-year-old child's body was found colored with red ochre, a mineral pigment often used to symbolize blood, along with a small amount of obsidian debris (Aldenderfer 2005, 24).

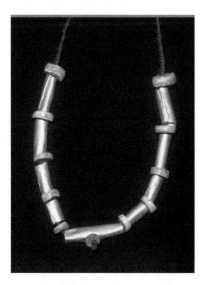

Figure 4.5. Gold necklace from Jiskairumoko. From Aldenderfer et al. 2008, figure 4. Photo courtesy of Mark Aldenderfer.

Finally, at the site of Asana in the upper Osmore valley, a ritual structure located in the central part of the site became progressively larger through time and, by the end of the period, had been enclosed and included a clay platform. The site was permanent; however, the subsistence was based on collecting and hunting, though domesticated camelids may have been used. During the final phase of the Archaic, the ceremonial structure disappeared and the site was a focus only of camelid pastoralism, part of a larger settlement pattern involving occupations elsewhere.

SUMMARY

The Late Preceramic Period marked the time when societies in some regions began to develop new social mechanisms for dealing with larger groups that were living together. In the highlands, these groups were agriculturally based, whereas on the coast, they were oriented to maritime resources. Exchanges between the highlands and coast are evident in the products of each zone found in the other. There can be little doubt that ideas about social integration followed food and resource exchange between the regions. In many areas of the Andes, however, life continued as it had previously, with mixed farming and collecting of wild resources. Egalitarian communities were probably still the norm in many regions of the central and south Andes as well as along the south coast.

In contrast to what many scholars working in the Andes think, I feel that there was very little actual social inequality during the Late Preceramic Period and that what social inequality was present was based on individual abilities, not heredity. There is not enough clear evidence of inequalities to say that some individuals were living better, more privileged lives than others. That being said, I cannot discount the idea that hereditary leaders might have existed and derived their authority from activities that benefited the community rather than themselves. The existence of effective leadership is obvious in the ability of some communities to construct large mounds, but this leadership could still be based on achieved status. I also believe that the basis of the emerging authority was the control of rituals rather than any economic advantage.

It is likely, however, that toward the end of this period some families had begun to claim political leadership as a right based on their direct descent from earlier rulers, such as the people responsible for the mounds. The development of such hereditary positions is the topic of the next chapter.

5

SOCIETAL GROWTH AND DIFFERENTIATION
The Initial Period

The Initial Period is defined as the time when pottery appears, loom weaving is invented, and a larger emphasis on the use of domesticated foods becomes apparent. But in fact, none of these traits was universally present across the Andes during this time period. The perception is that people during the Initial Period relied almost entirely on domesticates, especially in the highlands. One significant new fact about this period is that the use of domesticated plants was not as intensive as previously thought. This is a reflection of the greater amount of actual subsistence information that has been collected by investigators in recent years.

Starting around 2100 B.C.E., agriculture appears to have become a more important part of the diet of the people, although marine products still provided the bulk of the protein along the coast. A much wider variety of domesticated plants appear in the archaeological record and in much greater abundance. In contrast to other regions of the New World, maize was still not a major contributor to the diet at this time. Agriculture gradually spread southward through the Andean region, from its early appearance in Ecuador and northern Peru, to its appearance in the south highlands and coast in mid-second millennium B.C.E. The plants were probably introduced to the coast from the adjacent highlands, where agriculture had been practiced for thousands of years. In the coastal areas, the increased emphasis on agriculture engendered a shift in settlement patterns. Most of the large Initial Period communities were located inland, many kilometers from the sea. In addition, many of the Late Preceramic Period coastal communities were abandoned, leaving only a few to produce the marine resources needed for exchange.

This shift inland is typically interpreted as reflecting an increase in the importance of irrigation (Moseley 1975, 2001; Richardson 1994; Pozorski 1987). Irrigation requires a drop in altitude between the inlet of a canal and the fields that it waters. At sea level along the coastline, there is little altitudinal drop, making irrigation difficult. Inland, however, the land is steeper, allowing the necessary differential to be exploited. This might be the reason for the emergence of earlier sites such as Caral at their inland locations in the Norte Chico. During the Initial Period, this shift became more widespread. The power to control irrigation canals, specifically the places where the canals left the river, is seen as a new mechanism to explain sociopolitical differentiation. By controlling these key places, the amount of water reaching individuals' fields could also be controlled. Nevertheless, the precise means by which one group could control such locations is unclear. In fact, we could argue that irrigation might not have been as significant as has been suggested by many investigators.

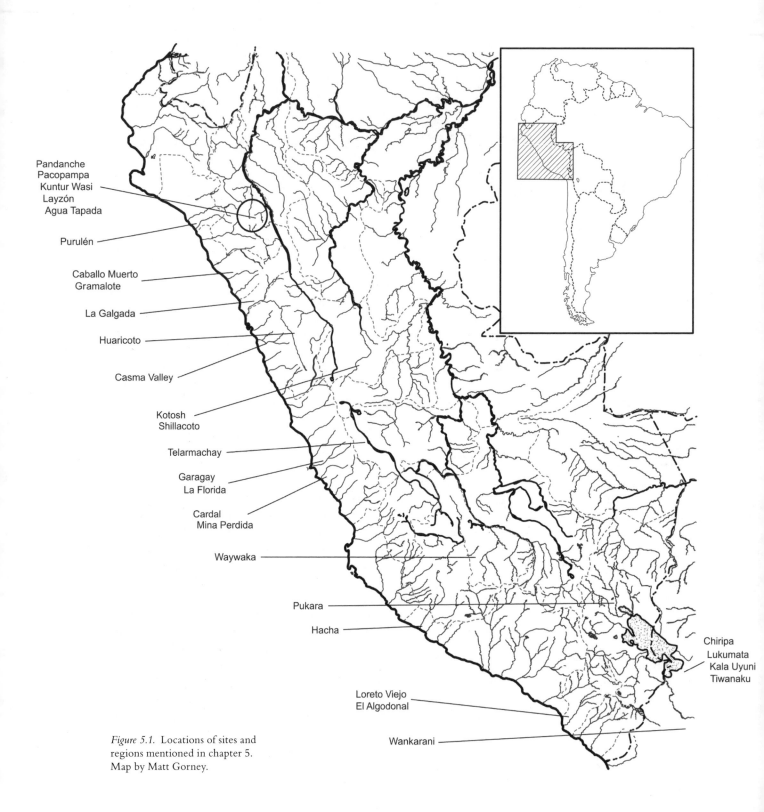

Pandanche
Pacopampa
Kuntur Wasi
Layzón
Agua Tapada

Purulén

Caballo Muerto
Gramalote

La Galgada

Huaricoto

Casma Valley

Kotosh
Shillacoto

Telarmachay

Garagay
La Florida

Cardal
Mina Perdida

Waywaka

Pukara

Hacha

Chiripa
Lukumata
Kala Uyuni
Tiwanaku

Loreto Viejo
El Algodonal

Wankarani

Figure 5.1. Locations of sites and
regions mentioned in chapter 5.
Map by Matt Gorney.

Associated with the greater importance of plants is an increase in the size of the communities and the architecture found at the coastal sites. Truly enormous temple structures appear in places such as the Casma Valley. In the highlands, smaller constructions reflect smaller aggregations of people. The processes that began in the Late Preceramic leading to social differentiation became both more widespread and more elaborated in the Initial Period. We see the first evidence of societal differentiation in the Altiplano region as well.

Two other technological innovations occurred during this period. The most obvious of these is pottery. Ceramics are known to have been in coastal Ecuador by around 4400 B.C.E., but the technology apparently did not spread south until later. The difference between early Ecuadorian pottery and that from coastal and highland Peru suggests either the independent invention of pottery in Peru or the spread of the idea of fired clay vessels, not the exact technology, forms, and decorative elements.

The rapid appearance of pottery along the coast and in the highlands, even as far as the Altiplano area, indicates how useful this new technology was. Pottery served several functions, and probably all were important to its successful incorporation into the cultural life of the people involved. The storage of seed against rot and vermin was one advantage; new means of preparing food and collecting water was another. Less obvious is the role ceramics might have played as a new medium for artistic and religious expression.

Pottery along the coast was largely modeled on the gourds that had long served as containers there. The two main forms are open bowls and globular closed ones called neckless *ollas* (figure 5.2). If decorated at all, they had incisions or simple paint. The earliest forms from the highlands, however, show a much wider range of forms and decorations. Similarities to Valdivia and later Machalilla pottery from Ecuador are evident in the pottery from the north highlands at Pandanche, and forms from the Initial Period occupation at Kotosh show relations to the tropical forest forms from farther east (Burger 1992). It is evident

that both original ideas and borrowed ones were present in different regions of the northern area. That the concept of pottery spread so quickly reflects the contacts that were present among people in different parts of the coast, highlands, and tropical forest.

A final innovation of the Initial Period was the appearance of the loom, probably a backstrap loom (figure 5.3). Previous to this invention, textiles were made by looping and knotting string together. Making a tight weave by such processes is difficult. A loom enables the textile worker to tightly bind the strings together, making a finer cloth, from either cotton or wool. Using different colored strings, designs can be woven into the cloth. We know that the loom was invented by this time along the coast because the arid environment has preserved the evidence. Less obvious is when the technology spread to the highlands. Textiles as a form of artistic expression predate the Initial Period, but it is safe to say that, with the introduction of the loom, this form of art greatly expanded, to the point that it was one of the most valued commodities in the Inka Empire (see chapter 10).

Although these new technologies and social behaviors mark significant changes during this period, in many regions of western South America the way of life changed little from the Late Preceramic. Along

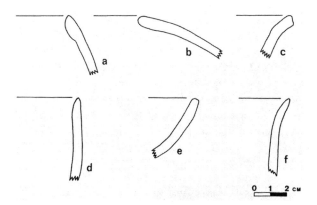

Figure 5.2. Initial Period pottery forms. Rim profiles of ceramic vessels from Pampa de las Llamas-Moxeke, including (a, b) neckless ollas, (c) a jar, (d, e) bowls, and (f) a bottle. From S. Pozorski and T. Pozorski 1987, figure 18. Image courtesy of Shelia and Thomas Pozorski.

Figure 5.3. Backstrap loom. Photo courtesy of Eleanor Kuhns.

the southern coast and in the highland regions south of the Puna of Junín, the way of life typical of previous times remained, although perhaps with an increasing emphasis on domesticated camelid herding in the latter region. The one area that showed other developments was the Altiplano, where corporate building activities began on a small scale.

THE NORTH AND CENTRAL COAST

The shift inland and abandonment of the coastal sites is typical of the central coast to the north coast during this period. There appears to have been an environmental boundary between the cultural developments of the regions south of the Lambayeque Valley and those north of it. This boundary corresponds to the Sechura Desert, a vast arid zone with no rivers that cross it, making it virtually uninhabitable. North of this zone, Initial Period settlements appeared, but they were small with no public architecture. The exception to this is only seen when we reach the Santa Elena Peninsula of Ecuador, with the Valdivia

and succeeding Machalilla cultures. Even there, however, the public architecture was small compared to the regions south of the Sechura Desert, although the villages could be quite sizable.

In a similar fashion, there are few significant Initial Period settlements found south of the Lurin Valley. One reason for this may be the less significant Late Preceramic occupations in this area and the less abundant maritime resources compared to those regions farther north (see chapter 4). Another reason may be that the valleys in this area are more deeply incised, with less agricultural land supporting only smaller communities. Still another reason might be that agriculture was late coming to this region. Three well-studied areas of the northern and central area are the Moche, Casma, and Rimac-Lurín valleys.

Moche Valley

In the Moche Valley, major sites were located inland near pockets of irrigable land. The most impressive of these sites is Caballo Muerto, a complex of eight pyramid mounds that spans the late Initial

Period and succeeding Early Horizon. Caballo Muerto, located 50 km inland, appears to have been a large settlement or series of settlements, with a resident population living near the main complexes, although this is uncertain (Pozorski 1975). The site received marine protein from the site of Gramalote, located along the coast, which probably received its cultivated plants from Caballo Muerto.

The best-preserved pyramid mound complex at Caballo Muerto is Huaca de los Reyes (figure 5.4), which was built in two major phases, although William Conklin (1985) suggests there were at least seven individual subphases within the two major ones. The earlier major phase consisted of a small temple structure on top that was dwarfed by the later phase, focused on the construction of a much greater, symmetric group of colonnaded rooms and courts. The site has an impressive symmetry, with progressively smaller plazas as one approaches the main pyramid mound. This mound itself has a series of courts of smaller size until one reaches the highest and oldest of these at the rear. Thomas Pozorski (1980) notes that both the linear and areal measurements used at the complex appear to have been based on the number twelve. The continuity in the use of this number over time argues for a stable corporate authority in charge of the construction over several centuries.

A series of larger-than-life clay figures and human heads have been found interposed with clay feline heads that share traits with the Chavín style of the Early Horizon (figure 5.5; see chapter 6). These figures were located along the façades facing the main plazas, where they would have been visible to the largest number of people. Other friezes of gods or perhaps ancestors were present in the upper rooms of the main mound (Pozorski 1980).

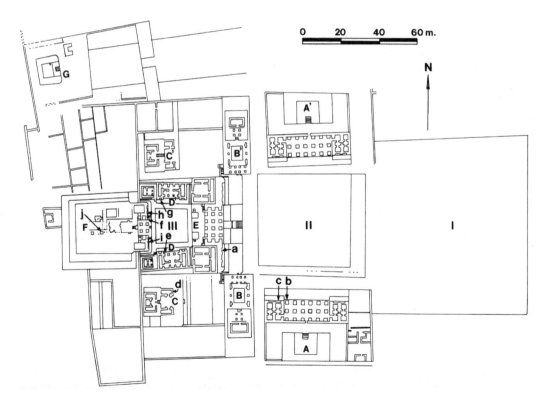

Figure 5.4. Map of Huaca de los Reyes. Roman numerals indicate plazas. Letters signify mounds, architectural wings, and locations of friezes. From T. Pozorski 1982, figure 10.2; see pp. 233–235 for descriptions. Drawing courtesy of Thomas Pozorski.

Figure 5.5. Clay figures and heads from Huaca de los Reyes. From T. Pozorski 1982, figure 10.4. Drawing courtesy of Thomas Pozorski.

Restricted access for privileged individuals is particularly marked at this site. Not only do the plazas progressively grow smaller as one travels from east to west, but the access to the upper levels of the flanking mounds as well as the main mound have narrow staircases that only a few individuals could use at a time. The west mound at the top of the complex would have been a place where only the most privileged individuals probably had access because it was entered by a single narrow staircase from the lower plaza. That being said, the dating of the other architectural complexes at Caballo Muerto is insufficient to rule out the possibility that more than one complex was used at the same time, implying contemporary but independent authorities.

The distinctive pottery of the north coast, from about the Virú to the Lambayeque valleys, is called Cupisnique after the dry quebrada where it was first encountered by Rafael Larco Hoyle in the early part of the twentieth century. Earlier pottery is known from this region; however, classic *Cupisnique* ceramics, which are black or gray with globular bodies and stirrup-shaped spouts, are a form that appears here and lasts throughout the pre-Hispanic sequence. As Burger (1992) notes, local contemporary styles in other valleys are now typically lumped together with the classic vessels under the term *Cupisnique* (plate 2A). The ceramics in general are well made and contrast markedly with the simpler early forms. A question I address in the next chapter is the relationship of these ceramics to the succeeding Chavín ones, to which they are related.

The evidence from the Moche Valley argues that during the Initial Period there were more people living inland for agricultural reasons than remained on the coast. The site of Alto Salaverry was abandoned, and the only known occupation along the coast at this time is Gramalote. The fact that the large mound complexes at Caballo Muerto were inland argues for the appearance of a corporate authority (or perhaps more than one, if more than one of the mounds were occupied at the same time) that could organize the labor to construct them. It also argues for a willingness of the people involved to work on such constructions. It is an interesting point that no burials or architecture have been discovered that tell us whether social inequalities were appearing.

On the coast farther north, only the site of Purulén in the Zaña Valley has an architectural complex with monumental architecture. This site has fifteen mounds scattered over a 3-km² area and surrounded by settlements (Burger 1992). None of the mounds is as large as Huaca de los Reyes, however. While civic-ceremonial sites are known in other valleys in this area, all are small, suggesting that the corporate authorities responsible for them were small as well. This mirrors the other information that argues against marked social differences between individuals in this area.

It is of some interest to later cultural events that the evidence reported suggests that these developments discussed were largely restricted to the coastal plain below around 200–300 masl. In the mid-valley regions above this, the little work that has been done on subsequent periods suggests that the groups occupying this zone had affiliations with highland groups from the adjacent Cajamarca region, rather than with the ones lower down, despite their proximity to the coastal zone (Burger 1992).

Casma Valley

In the Casma Valley, Thomas and Shelia Pozorski (see especially S. Pozorski and T. Pozorski 1987, 2002, 2008; T. Pozorski and S. Pozorski 1990, 2005) have provided the most detailed information about cultural developments during this important period. This valley seems to have experienced the most complex development of any valley during the Initial Period. Six major sites with monumental architecture are located there, with additional sites marking a sophisticated distribution network for the exchange of marine and agricultural foods. The Pozorskis defined two phases of developments, but I have combined these in this summary.

At the beginning of the period, the small Late Preceramic population developed into a complex society relatively rapidly. The site of Pampa de las Llamas-Moxeke (figure 5.6) consists of a main east-west axis bounded by two large structures, the Moxeke terraced pyramid mound and Huaca A,

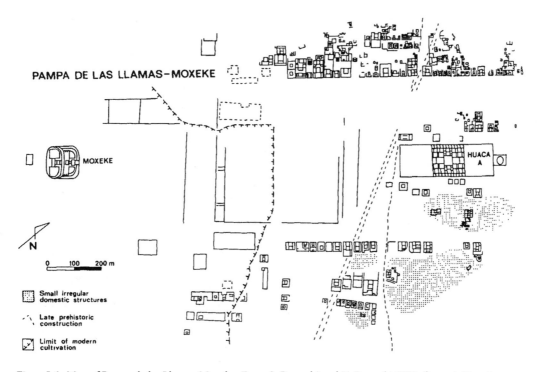

Figure 5.6. Map of Pampa de las Llamas-Moxeke. From S. Pozorski and T. Pozorski 1992, figure 4. Drawing courtesy of Shelia and Thomas Pozorski and *Antiquity*.

along with a series of smaller constructions along either side of the main axis. The Moxeke mound measures 160 by 170 by 30 m in height and formerly had friezes of robed figures in niches and large heads along the front of the third terrace. The figures were originally 3 m high and were painted black, to contrast with the white and pink paint of the niches in which they were found (Burger 1992).

At the east end of the main axis, more than a kilometer away, is the large Huaca A, a 140 by 140 by 9 m symmetrical storage complex of rooms with a sunken circular court behind it (figure 5.7). A series of open plazas separated this structure and the Moxeke mound.

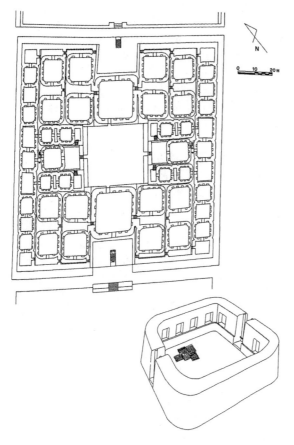

Figure 5.7. Huaca A and isometric drawing of a square room unit. From S. Pozorski and T. Pozorski 1992, figures 5 and 6. Drawings courtesy of Shelia and Thomas Pozorski and *Antiquity.*

The mound itself was composed of tiers of *square room units,* uniformly sized rooms with rounded corners and niches, with each tier having a bar closure, a wooden bar that could be drawn out from the wall to bar entrance to the rooms. Pollen samples from these rooms indicate they were used for the storage of foods (S. Pozorski and T. Pozorski 1987).

On both the north and south sides of the central axis of the site are room complexes built on low platform mounds consisting of groups of interconnected rooms. The main room in each was a square room unit. The Pozorskis call these "intermediate mounds" and interpret them as the residences and work areas of a middle-level elite whose jobs probably entailed directing the flow of goods and food from the producers elsewhere in the valley to Huaca A (Pozorski and Pozorski 1992). A large area of small, irregular structures to the south of Huaca A is interpreted as housing for lower-status individuals who probably did the work of moving and storing the goods and possibly cottage craft production (S. Pozorski and T. Pozorski 2002).

Marine resources were collected at the coastal sites of Huaynuná and Tortugas, and transshipped to Pampa de las Llamas-Moxeke through the site of Bahía Seca, located on the former coastline near the Port of Casma. The administrative function for Bahía Seca is supported by the presence of a square room unit and pottery similar to that of the main settlement. In fact, the Pozorskis have interpreted the square room unit as a formal administrative feature of the ruling elite of the valley (S. Pozorski and T. Pozorski 2011).

Another four contemporary monumental sites—Sechín Alto, Sechín Bajo, Cerro Sechín, and Taukachi-Konkán—are located along the Sechín branch of the Casma River. Collectively called the Sechín Alto Complex by the Pozorskis, they comprise an integrated series of temple and residential structures covering 10 km² (figure 5.8). It is likely that in the zone around these sites were residential complexes for the farming population that provided labor for the mounds. This complex is located only 4 km from Pampa de las Llamas-Moxeke.

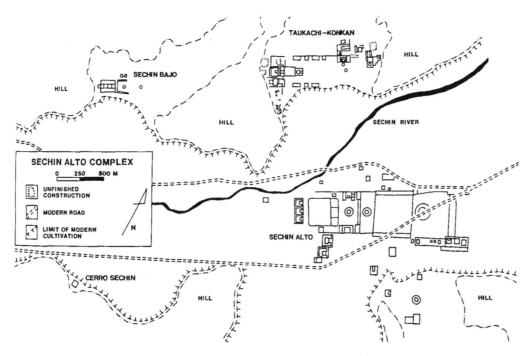

Figure 5.8. Map of Sechín Alto complex. From S. Pozorski and T. Pozorski 1992, figure 11. Drawing courtesy of Shelia and Thomas Pozorski and *Antiquity*.

The largest structure in the New World at this time was begun during the early phase at Sechín Alto, a massive mound measuring 300 by 250 m and still 40 m high. The whole structure is a U-shaped complex, with three large circular sunken courts in the plaza area in front. The length of the temple complex is over 1 km. Although later reoccupations and remodeling make the early layout difficult to discern, the Pozorskis have suggested that it had both administrative and religious functions.

Taukachi-Konkán is interpreted to have been a palace for the ruler of the Sechín Alto Complex that also had administrative functions reflected in the presence of square room units. Sechín Bajo is a smaller, poorly understood U-shaped complex that was the site of sunken circular courts during the Late Preceramic Period that were oriented toward the summer solstice sunrise. During the Moxeke Phase, this earlier structure was filled in and another, larger mound was constructed consisting of

several rooms and courts oriented to the winter solstice sunrise.

The final monumental site in the Sechín Alto Complex is Cerro Sechín, a small temple located up against a prominent hill only 1 km west of Sechín Alto. The site is known for its outer wall composed of a series of warrior figures with maces and other weapons, interspersed with other carvings of dismembered human bodies (figures 5.9A and 5.9B). Some investigators interpret the wall as an actual memorial to a battle fought, but between whom is not known. The Pozorskis suggest that it reflects the defeat of the Moxeke-Pampa de los Llamas group by those of the Sechín Alto Complex, based on the victims wearing clothes resembling the figures on the Moxeke temple (S. Pozorski and S. Pozorski 2005). Burger (1992) argues the battle is a mythical one, perhaps waged by the ancestors of the builders of the monument. He bases this on earlier friezes within the temple structure that seem to show similar themes.

Figure 5.9. (A) Victorious warrior figure on outer wall of Cerro Sechín temple. (B) Dismembered and decapitated figures on outer wall of Cerro Sechín temple. Photos by author.

In addition to the economic activities identified at the sites in Casma, ventilated hearth structures have been found both at Pampa de las Llamas and Bahía Seca, indicating some individuals at those sites participated in rituals related to the Kotosh Religious Tradition. The presence of circular sunken courts at several sites supports the use of these structures in rituals common to many sites at this time. The reorientation of the Sechín Bajo courts from the orientation of the Late Preceramic Period suggests a shift in religious belief by the authorities in charge of the rituals conducted there as well.

Located along the coast south of the main valley, Las Haldas has distinctive ceramics and an occupational history that sets it apart from the other sites. It was a major Preceramic village community that developed in parallel to the valley developments during the early phase. It appears to have been an autonomous political entity, reflected in distinctive architecture and ceramics (S. Pozorski and T. Pozorski 2006). Around 1400 B.C.E., they were able to exert their political influence over the Sechín Alto Complex elites, reflected in Las Haldas-style ceramics and architecture appearing on the Sechín Alto mound.

The Casma Valley evidence represents an impressive political development that emerged relatively rapidly at the beginning of the Initial Period. The Pozorskis argue that the Casma Valley polity might represent a pristine state-level society, the first in South America (excluding the suggestion that Caral was the first). The five tiers identified in the valley hierarchy (table 5.1), the presence of a controlling authority that maintained consistent rule over five centuries, the amount of labor required to construct the main buildings, and the presence of distinct administrative, religious, and elite residential functions at different sites, all argue for a well-differentiated society. The Pozorskis interpret the evidence as indicating the emergence in this valley of a powerful elite, probably a hereditary one, during the Initial Period (see box 5.1). Their authority probably stemmed from their control of ritual and irrigation. It is conceivable that the authorities in charge of the polity held sway over the populations of adjacent valleys, although this is hard to prove. However, others argue against the idea of a

Table 5.1. Casma Valley political hierarchy

Tier	Site
1st	Sechín Alto
2nd	Pampa de las Llamas/Moxeke, Taukachi-Konkán
3rd	Sechín Bajo, Cerro Sechín
4th	Bahía Seca
5th	Huaynuná, Tortugas and other farming and fishing communities throughout the valley

Source: Pozorski and Pozorski 2008.

state at this date because there is little evidence of marked differences in status other than in the architecture (much like the arguments against Caral having been a state) and little evidence of craft or other occupational specialization.

BOX 5.1 Why hereditary social inequalities?

Why do leadership positions emerge in a society? More important, when do such positions become hereditary and why? The shift from egalitarian to hereditary inequality is a difficult one to identify archaeologically. Following Brian Hayden (1995) and others, Aldenderfer (2005) notes that the conditions under which persistent leadership develops (as he calls the situation leading to hereditary inequality) are varied. He notes that there are two main pathways: prestige and dominance. In the prestige pathway, a leader convinces followers, both relatives and nonrelatives, to support him (or possibly her) through some perceived advantages he or she will provide. The advantages might be economic (gaining access to desired resources), social (gaining access to marriage partners or alliances of other kinds), or religious (gaining access to supernatural support for economic activities). In the dominance pathway, a leader uses the threat of force, but usually the threat is an external one and the leader is responding to that. In this situation, communities are often in conflict, usually over resources of some kind.

In either case, the conditions under which leadership becomes permanent in a lineage must persist over generations, and the individuals in charge must continue to provide the advantages to the community as a whole. This is probably why hereditary inequalities take a long time to develop; there must be persistent conditions as well as a lineage in which consistently effective leaders follow one another.

An important factor in the development of hereditary inequality appears to be resource abundance (Aldenderfer 2005,16; Hayden 1995). Environments that provide abundant food are ones in which leaders can generate the surpluses required for gaining power. This, however, is a necessary but not sufficient condition because there must be a reason for the accumulation of surpluses: for trade, for ritual activity, or for support of military operations. The relationship of population size and density to resource abundance comes into play at this point. When there is the possibility of food shortages, either because of a too large population, changed environmental conditions, or warfare, the conditions for someone to assert leadership become evident. It becomes necessary, then, to identify which combination of factors lead to hereditary inequality.

With regard to the evidence presented in this book, I suggest that both coastal and highland societies coped with the demands of larger populations through the intensification of religious activities. Given that the earliest monumental structures appear to be temples, based on the lack of food remains and the presence of special offerings, control of rituals and communication with supernatural powers would be seen as a primary source of power for these early leaders. To construct these monuments, there had to be a division of labor in these societies into the workers and the organizers. We can assume that the organizers were those who claimed they could communicate with supernatural powers and had the ability to discern what those powers wanted. Evidence for these two groups, leaders and commoners, is found at Caral, although it is less evident at other sites. The fact that the major structures at Caral are interpreted as temples supports the view that the authorities there had a religious nature. The evidence at Caral for larger houses that are more centrally located suggests that the emerging leaders warranted better places to live than the commoners.

Although Aldenderfer (2005) states that the emergence of conflicts between expanding populations in the southern highlands might have been a factor in the later development of social inequality in that region, there is little evidence to support such an explanation elsewhere, particularly in the littoral regions. Control of irrigation along the coast is often cited as a means by which one group could coerce others into doing its bidding. I feel this suggestion is unlikely at this stage of cultural development. If someone tried to control the irrigation canal intakes, others could resist or move to other areas to start new fields. Given that the social inequalities reflected in monumental architecture emerged while agriculture was still in an incipient stage, the connection to irrigation is still more tenuous. Moreover, what would these coercive individuals use their control for? Because there were no marked differences in wealth, it is hard to see how such power would benefit those in control. Perhaps more marriage partners and children were the benefit.

Quilter (1991) suggests an economic reason for the emergence of authorities along the littoral, the control of cotton production for exchange. Cotton became a major domesticate during the Late Preceramic Period, and it is possible that certain individuals were able to develop prestige through the control of cotton for exchange, both locally and with the highland communities. Given that marine products are also found in highland sites, the control of multiple resources for exchange can be postulated (ibid., 428–429). The unanswered question for this reason is, what would the emerging leaders in the highlands exchange cotton for?

Farther south, there are several Initial Period sites with monumental constructions in the Norte Chico region, although few have been described. Unlike the Casma and Moche valleys, these valleys seem to have had multiple polities similar to the situation in the Lurin Valley farther south.

Rimac-Lurín

Similarities in monumental architecture and ceramics in the region between Chancay Valley in the north and Lurín Valley in the south have led Burger and Salazar (2008, 2010) to formally define the populations living in this region as the Manchay culture. The ceramics vary in some traits from valley to valley, but it is the public architecture that sets this region off from the ones farther north. Carlos Williams (1985), the Peruvian architect, identified the salient traits of the architecture as terraced platform complexes in the shape of a U that are oriented to the northeast, asymmetric arms of the U with at least one not connected to the main mound, a central staircase rising up from a large rectangular plaza between the arms of the U, and unfired clay friezes. Burger and Salazar (2010) add the further traits of staircases up the backs of the main mounds and there usually having been several contemporary complexes operating at the same time, in contrast to the centers farther north. The distinctive iconography includes motifs of waves and a mountain, beings with hemispherical eyes with the pupils off-center, a spider figure, and arch-shaped mouths with the upper canines jutting over the lower lip (for other characteristics, see Burger and Salazar 2008, 88). All this bespeaks a different political, religious, and social situation in this region.

In the Rimac valley of the central coast, many of the Late Preceramic coastal settlements were abandoned and a large new site, La Florida, was constructed 11 km inland. The site of El Paraíso continued to be occupied, although its relationship to La Florida is unclear. La Florida was a true U-shaped construction with the arms of the U connected to the main mound and extending approximately 500 m from it. It represented approximately 6.7 million person-days of labor, not including the leveling of the ground or plastering of the outer surface (Patterson 1983). Although there is evidence of distinct construction phases at the site, it appears to have been built and abandoned within just a few centuries, arguing for a significantly larger labor pool involved in its construction than in the Late Preceramic monuments in the region.

Later in the Initial Period, an even larger U-shaped pyramid was built at Garagay, located just 3 km west of La Florida. The main Manchay culture temple here included different construction phases with distinctive friezes and offerings. One of the friezes consists of a spider deity, often associated with agricultural fertility along the coast. The use of San Pedro cactus spines on an offering figurine and in the adobes of the temple suggests that hallucinogens might have been a part of the rituals conducted in the recesses of the temple (Burger 1992). San Pedro cactus is a source of a mescaline-like psychoactive drug.

Unfortunately, both La Florida and Garagay are located in modern Lima, and so both are currently surrounded by urban developments, making an understanding of the relationships of these sites to their neighborhoods and hinterlands unknowable. Ceramics from settlements in the general region of modern Lima are found at La Florida, suggesting that it drew on a labor force from a large area. That these are the only large constructions in this region suggests that the authority there was highly centralized, similar to the situation in the Casma Valley.

The sites in the Lurín Valley, the next valley south of the Rimac, are relatively small, but during the Initial Period the valley had six temple complexes located along its lower section, all very close together. Work by Richard Burger and Lucy Salazar has shown that these complexes largely overlapped in time, and functioned independently. The largest of these sites, Mina Perdida, is located 11 km inland from the Pacific Ocean and covers an area of 30 ha. Like all Manchay centers along the central coast, it is in the form of a U facing upriver. The main mound rises to an altitude of 22 m, and at least twelve construction phases have been identified (Burger and Salazar 2010).

An interesting technological innovation found from this time in the Lurin Valley at Mina Perdida is copper working (Burger 1992). The thin sheets of beaten copper were located on one of the public structures there but were not formed into any kind of finished objects. Nonetheless, the appearance of copper reflects a new interest in materials other than stone and clay.

The second largest of these sites, Cardal (figure 5.10), is located 3 km inland from Mina Perdida, but it is contemporary with the it (Burger and Salazar 2008). Like most Manchay complexes, Cardal has one arm of the U attached to the main mound and the other arm separate. It has two rectangular plazas in front of the U and a larger rectangular plaza within the arms. A 6-m-wide staircase rose up the main mound to an atrium from which other staircases led to smaller rooms. The walls on either side of the door to the atrium had a frieze of a face with fangs. The interior layout of the main mound is very similar to that of Garagay (Burger 1992).

In addition to the main mound architecture, there are ten sunken circular courts, both within the U and behind or on its sides. These were all small, none larger than 13 m in diameter, and were probably for rituals conducted by segments of the society that also were involved in the primary rituals on the mound. Unlike the monumental centers of the north-central coast, these sunken circular plazas are not aligned along the central axis. This suggests the activities conducted in them were peripheral to the main use of the central mound.

A final site studied by Burger and Salazar (2008) was Manchay Bajo, located across the valley from Cardal at a distance of only 1.7 km. It has a main U-shaped mound 13 m high and appears to have been contemporary but lasting somewhat later because ceramics associated with the later Chavín culture are found in the uppermost levels (see chapter 6).

Summary of the North and Central Coast Evidence

All in all, the evidence from the north and central coast indicates marked changes in the way of life of their occupants during the Initial Period. Larger settlements, monumental architecture, settlement hierarchies, and elite residences suggest the emergence of social inequalities in some of these societies, although not in all. A significant increase in the use of agricultural products suggests how these developments were underwritten. The absence of sophisticated ceramics or other material culture and any evidence of burial

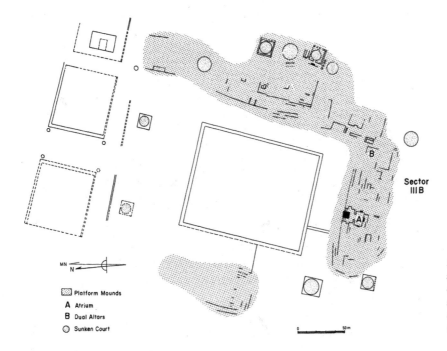

MN
N

▨ Platform Mounds
A Atrium
B Dual Altars
◯ Sunken Court

0   50 m

Sector III B

Figure 5.10. Plan of the public architecture of Cardal. By permission of Maney Publishing, from Burger and Salazar-Burger 1991; permission conveyed through Copyright Clearance Center, Inc.

distinctions suggest that these societies were not highly specialized and that there were not many social levels. It is not even clear whether the inequalities were hereditary or achieved, although the persistence of the authorities could argue for the former, at least in places such as the Casma and Moche valleys.

Why the Shift Inland?

The reason for the shift away from coastal resources to inland sites is generally regarded to be a function of the increasing importance of agriculture. As domesticated food plants became more important, people moved to places where irrigation was more effective. The question, then, might be, why did domesticated foods became more important at this time? Coastal communities had not seen any reason to change prior to this time, despite knowing about such crops from neighbors in the adjacent highlands.

In his MFAC hypothesis, Moseley argues that growing cotton and gourds for fishing pre-adapted the Late Preceramic communities to agriculture and that even some inland communities were specialized for this. Thus, it was a simple thing to start growing food crops as well because the technology and activities were already in place. With more emphasis placed on agriculture (possibly but not necessarily due to increased populations), people moved inland where irrigation could be practiced to increase yields.

Research in the Supe Valley at the Late Preceramic sites of Caral and Aspero (see chapter 4), however, suggests another reason for the shift from primary maritime resource use during that period to farming in the Initial Period. Sandweiss et al. (2009) note that there is evidence of a massive earthquake at Caral, indicated by damage to all the summit structures on the main pyramid (Pirámide Mayor) and a bulging outward of the lower wall. At the contemporaneous site of Aspero, there is also evidence of earthquake damage. The estimates of the severity of this earthquake, if the same one at both sites, range from magnitude 6.9 to 7.2 on the Richter scale.

The implications of such an earthquake, or quakes, are that they would have resulted in landslides along the Supe Valley, depositing large quantities of unconsolidated sediments along the river. With the onset of El Niño at this time or slightly before, the resulting torrential rains would have flushed the sediments into the river and down to the sea. As a consequence of this flooding, a massive beach ridge formed parallel to the coast that allowed the infilling of local bays and estuaries. As these infilled areas dried, massive amounts of sand became available and were driven inland by the steady winds blowing onshore. These created dunes moved inland and destroyed agricultural fields and wild plant resources along the Supe River. In fact, there is evidence of this at the site of Aspero, as well as evidence for people occupying the temple mounds as a result of it (Sandweiss et al. 2009). Significantly, this environmental shift also led to a decrease in the marine resources on which these complex societies had depended because the sediments formed beach ridges and choked off the existing shellfish beds. The double-edged sword of decreased marine resources and terrestrial plants led to the abandonment of the Late Preceramic sites in the region and also all along the north central coast. Note, however, that, although this explanation works for the Supe Valley, it remains to be supported by similar evidence from other valleys.

Another possibility is that the shift to an agriculturally based economy in these regions occurred as groups from the adjacent highlands moved into these zones after a period of environmental stabilization. Because the coast and highlands had always been linked by social relations, groups from the latter could have moved down into the lower zone during or after the environmental crises mentioned. Evidence for this movement is seen in the shift at this time in dental traits from the earlier form (sundadonty) seen in the original inhabitants of this region to a different form (sinodonty) in these and later populations. Sutter (2009) suggests this shift in dental traits is due to agricultural communities intermingling and absorbing coastal ones. This could have happened only if the agricultural communities were larger than the coastal ones, allowing for the replacement of dental forms. This would also support the explanation for the Late Preceramic abandonment of coastal sites suggested by the environmental evidence.

The Coast Farther South

South of the Lurin Valley, there are no sites with monumental architecture along the coast. The evidence identified to date suggests that the valleys in these regions were sparsely occupied. The site of Hacha in the Acarí Valley is perhaps the best known (Riddell and Valdéz 1988). Here, simple neckless ollas (e.g., figure 5.2) were found along with abundant stone hoes (from which the site gets its name, although they were not actually axes, as the Spanish name implies). A possible ceremonial room decorated with a frieze of camelids was found, along with evidence for domesticated plants. In contrast to sites in the north, hunting was a major activity here, reflected both in the large number of animal bones and projectile points. Marine resources were also found here by John Rowe (1963).

Work in the Osmore Valley (the name of the Moquegua Valley where the Moquegua River drains into the Pacific Ocean) of far southern Peru has resulted in a better understanding of the transition from an Archaic hunting and gathering lifestyle to a more settled one based, at least in part, on agriculture. Research in the lower part of the valley at two sites, Loreto Viejo and El Algodonal, located 12–15 km inland, has indicated that this shift occurred roughly at the same time as in the regions to the north (Owen 2009). The beginning of agriculture at Loreto Viejo dates to 1900–1600 B.C.E., with the appearance of beans, lima beans, cotton, gourds, and a tuber that is probably yuca. Shellfish are more prevalent than fish, but both appear to be more important than guinea pigs and camelids, which are found in limited amounts. The nature of the occupations whence these samples come suggests that they were permanent settlements, although whether the occupants were trading their agricultural produce for maritime resources or traveling to obtain them is not clear. Because maritime and agricultural activities were highly specialized by the Middle Horizon in this region, it is tempting to suggest these different specializations were already developing at this early date.

In contrast to other regions on the coast, pottery does not appear in the Osmore drainage until after 920–430 B.C.E., but before 20–220 C.E. (Owen 2009). This indicates a prolonged and increasing use of domesticates prior to the adoption of ceramic technology. Why this gap exists is unclear. Nonetheless, by the Early Ceramic Period, starting in the first century C.E., several new trends in subsistence appeared. There was an increase in the use of fish relative to shellfish in the diet; corn, a minor food during the Late Preceramic, became much more common, and other cultigens increased as well. These trends continued throughout the subsequent period in this region.

Bruce Owen (2009) suggests the adoption of agriculture occurred in the Osmore Valley at about the same time as in the central and northern regions (the Supe Valley excepted) and he suggests the need for a general phenomenon, or more than one, to explain it. He notes that there is evidence of a climatic amelioration in Africa and the eastern Mediterranean after a dramatic dry period in 2500–1600 and 2200–1900 B.C.E., respectively. If there were a comparable increase in rainfall in the Andes, it could have led to greater water resources along the coast that encouraged the adoption of agriculture. The research described in chapter 2, however, argues for generally drier conditions at this time, which contradicts this possibility.

NORTH AND CENTRAL HIGHLANDS

The appearance of pottery during the Initial Period in Peru did not change the basic way of life significantly for the groups living in the north and central highlands. Although pottery first appeared in coastal Ecuador by at least 4400 B.C.E., the forms and decorative techniques identified indicate it was not developed there; its origins lay elsewhere. In Peru, pottery appeared almost contemporaneously throughout the central and northern Andes around 2000 B.C.E. Similarities to the earlier ceramics found in coastal Ecuador (see chapter 4) and the Peruvian jungle to the east suggest that the idea of making pottery may have diffused southward. Initial Period Waira-Jirca ceramics, found at Kotosh and other sites, both in the highlands and in the jungle to the north of that site, have decorative elements that are indicative of tropical forest influence. No doubt the concept of making pottery spread rapidly because the utility to agriculturalists of fired clay vessels was readily apparent.

For the northern highlands, which includes the region south of the present Ecuadorian border to the Huamachuco basin, environmental conditions are much more temperate than in the regions farther south, both due to the proximity to the equator and the lower altitudes of the Andes. Rainfall is abundant in many of the regions. Initial Period sites here typically do not include camelids, but deer remains are quite common. There are few reports of actual domesticated plants, although agriculture must have been a significant activity of the residents.

Mound building began in some regions where it had not been present earlier and continued in regions where it had. The largest mounds at this time were built in the Cajamarca area, where the sites of Pacopampa (actually located north of the Cajamarca basin proper) and Kuntur Wasi are found. Both of these sites are similar in being hilltops that were artificially modified by terracing into stepped platforms with large central staircases (figure 5.11). They also had

Figure 5.11. Pacopampa. Image copyright Pacopampa Archaeological Project.

drainage systems, buildings, and courts at the tops of the mounds. Pacopampa was the main site that served a larger region of settlements, all in the quechua zone. Stone sculptures were found there, some said to bear similarities to later Chavín sculpture (see chapter 6), and the motifs on the ceramics of birds, snakes, and felines are also similar. That being said, Burger (1992) notes that the latter are widespread motifs reflecting commonly held ideas over a wide region of the northern Andes at this time.

Artifacts from Pacopampa reflect a wide region of interaction. Shellfish are very common in the excavations there, and Cupisnique-style seals are also present. Similarities to eastern forest sites are noted as well. The location of Pacopampa in the region where the Andes are near their lowest indicates why there is such evidence of east-west interaction. That being said, there must have been a sizable population to construct the terraces, and at least thirteen contemporary sites are known, scattered throughout the quechua zone. A possible residence of a religious specialist was excavated near Pacopampa, perhaps one of the people in charge of the construction there (Burger 1992).

Kuntur Wasi is located in the western part of the Cajamarca basin and, like Pacopampa, is a hilltop modified into a platform mound, this one with four terraces rather than the three at Pacopampa. Painted clay murals adorned the walls of a sunken rectangular court on the summit. Like Pacopampa, it had a series of stone sculptures that were both similar to ones at Chavín de Huantar and local in theme. The presence of ceramics reflects widespread exchange with Ecuador, the eastern lowlands, and the northern coast. A burial from a nearby site had an individual with exotic materials such as lapis lazuli and *Spondylus* (Terada and Onuki 1988), possibly reflecting some higher status, much like the religious specialist at Pacopampa.

In the Cajamarca basin proper, a series of sites were identified and excavated by a Japanese project in the 1980s (Terada 1985; Terada and Onuki 1982, 1985, 1988). Although the principal sites were located in the quechua zone, sites at higher and lower

altitudes were also noted, indicating an economic system encompassing the main ecological zones present. The earliest site with public architecture is Huacaloma; here the Japanese investigators found a rectangular room with a hearth in the center, which appears to be an example of the Kotosh Religious Tradition in this region. Later, this building was filled in and a much larger platform mound was constructed on top, complete with stone-lined canals and buildings, much like the contemporary centers of Layzón and Agua Tapada (discussed next). The flat land around the mound appears to have been occupied by the residents of the site (Burger 1992).

The two main sites of the region are Layzón and Agua Tapada. The two sites are located along a gorge and linked by two canals that split above the sites and join below them. Layzón was a stepped pyramid made by leveling the bedrock and constructing a terrace, and it had drainage system and summit constructions similar to the other major sites in this region. It is possible that smaller sites such as Huacaloma might have been linked to the larger centers through ritual or economic activities.

The Cumbemayo canal that feeds both these sites is part of a 9-km-long canal that is one of the unique features of this region. It is both carved out of the bedrock and dug out of earth, and sections of it have a series of right-angle turns that would not be necessary if its use was solely for irrigation. Petroglyphs along its length suggest ritual uses; archaeologists link them to carvings on the walls at Layzón (Burger 1992). Many scholars feel this canal must have been primarily built for rituals rather than irrigation, indicating a relationship between water and deities that reached its pinnacle in the waterworks of the Inkas 2,500 years later.

The next major area south where there are Initial Period settlements is the Callejón de Huaylas and upper Huallaga River drainage. These are the locations where the Kotosh Religious Tradition had its major centers, and they continued to thrive. In contrast, the region between the Callejón de Huaylas and Cajamarca shows few settlements for this period; for example, John and Theresa Topic (J. Topic 2009) have located only five tentative sites dating to this period in Huamachuco. This scarcity of sites suggests that the adoption of an agricultural lifestyle was not as uniform as many scholars think. It is intriguing to think that the reason for this absence has to do with the spread of agriculture up from the tropical forest of western Amazonia, although the similarities between the ceramics of the north highlands and the Valdivia region of coastal Ecuador suggest an alternative route.

Public architecture of a ritual nature has been found at La Galgada and Huaricoto, occupied during the previous period by Kotosh Religious Tradition devotees. Whereas the people at Huaricoto continued the tradition, those at La Galgada developed new institutions and means of showing their devotion. The ritual structures at Huaricoto remained small and were likely the results of small family groups working together. At La Galgada, however, the top of the main mound was transformed from a series of individual ritual rooms with hearths to a more unified summit structure (Grieder and Bueno Mendoza 1985; Grieder et al. 1988). A large court was built in the middle of the summit with a hearth in the center. This, in turn, was enclosed on three sides by a wall, which opened to the main staircase. A new burial feature at the site is the construction of long funerary galleries that replaced the burials within abandoned ritual chambers. These galleries were built along the walls of the mounds and were covered with large stone slabs. Textiles, shell jewelry, foreign ceramics, and other exotic goods indicate the individuals interred were important, and the galleries themselves, which included men, women and children, suggest family chambers. These are the most impressive grave goods found anywhere in the Initial Period, but whether they reflect hereditary rule or simply families with more wealth who could build such structures is yet unknown. The collapse of this center at the end of the Initial Period does indicate that whatever social structure existed there was unable to sustain itself through time.

Two other impressive tombs were found at the small site of Shillacoto, downstream from Kotosh (Izumi, Cuculiza, and Kano 1972). One was a free-standing tomb measuring 3.7 by 3.2 by 2 m tall that had been plastered and painted within. Although it had been disturbed, evidence found there indicated that several individuals had been interred there with a T-shaped stone ax, a jet mirror, and ceramics. The other was a subterranean tomb that was undisturbed and contained a single individual buried with ceramics, shell and bone artifacts, jet mirrors, and stone projectile points. Shillacoto is also known for its large Initial Period Kotosh Religious Tradition structure that dwarfs the earlier ones elsewhere.

One of the most exciting and controversial developments over the past decade or so is the evidence that part of the Early Horizon site of Chavín de Huántar, located in the Mosna Valley on the east side of the Cordillera Blanca, now dates to the Initial Period (Rick et al. 2009). In fact, a very large number of radiocarbon dates now suggest that the main temple structures there may be earlier than previous researchers have stated. (The implications of this information are discussed in chapter 6.)

Research in the major valleys and basins south of the Callejón de Huaylas indicate a very different kind of Initial Period way of life. The Puna of Junín, the place where early vicuña hunters had been able to settle down permanently based on the predictable nature of these camelids, continued to be dominated by pastoral groups. Much of this was probably due to the fact the puna is at the very upper margins of any kind of agriculture. Still, the evidence found at sites such as Telarmachay (Lavallee 1979) indicates that small groups of llama and alpaca herders occupied the caves of this region as part of a seasonal round that is likely to have included settlements elsewhere, either at lower elevations or along the margins of Lake Junín.

Farther south, the Mantaro region is a broad valley flanking the river of the same name that has its source south of the Callejón de Huaylas. This valley was the focus of later large-scale developments, but during the Initial Period, it apparently was sparsely occupied, if at all (Matos Mendieta 1978). Still farther south, in the Ayacucho Valley, a vertical system of settlements in the puna and quechua zones linked people together economically. Neither the Mantaro nor the Ayacucho region has sites with any kind of public architecture, although one small ceremonial structure is reported for the region of Ayacucho (MacNeish, Patterson, and Browman 1975). But the earliest site in the central Andes where goldworking is found is at the site of Waywaka in Andahuaylas (Grossman 1972). Like the evidence from Mina Perdida for copper, a small amount of gold was found hammered into thin sheets and placed with a burial (Burger 1992).

Summary of the North and Central Highland Evidence

Before moving on to the south highlands, let us review what is known about the north and central highland regions. First, economically, the settlements north of the Puna of Junín appear to have been largely based on agriculture supplemented by hunting more than herding because overwhelming evidence indicates deer were more prevalent than camelids at these sites. Although guinea pigs were often present, it is uncertain whether they were domesticated or not (see chapter 3). A wide variety of domesticated plants were used, but maize still did not play a major role in the diet of Andean people. The possible exception to this is the population in coastal Ecuador, who appear to have adopted corn as a major cultigen during Valdivia or later Machalilla times.

In contrast, groups living in the Junín, Mantaro, and Ayacucho regions were more heavily dependent on herding camelids, which appears to have been just as important, or more so, as agricultural activities. This is probably a reflection of the high altitudes and short growing seasons in these regions that would make growing crops a riskier business than in the regions farther north. In addition, camelids had been domesticated here for a longer time, which led to a pastoral rather than agricultural economy.

Until recently, the pre-Inka cultural developments of the Cuzco Valley, the heartland of the Inkas, were poorly known. Although a ceramic chronology had

been worked out in the mid-twentieth century by Peruvian and North American researchers (Rowe 1944, 1956; Chávez 1977, 1980), the settlement patterns and political evolution were unclear. There is evidence of Initial Period occupations in the Cuzco region in the appearance of early pottery called Marcavalle (Chávez 1977). This largely undecorated ware has been found at small settlements of adobe houses that have thick middens, suggesting long periods of occupation.

Thanks to the work of a new generation of scholars, both foreign and native-born, this situation has changed. Bauer (2004) notes that the shift to settled village life and agriculture began sometime around 2200 B.C.E., but little is known until the appearance of the Marcavalle ceramics around 1200 B.C.E. By this time, domesticated camelids, guinea pigs, and dogs were being eaten as well as wild animals and some domesticated plants, such as beans and corn. Trade in obsidian and other materials links the Cuzco region more to the Titicaca area to the south than to groups farther north. Nonetheless, no evidence of any social differentiation is evident even though this occupation lasted well into the succeeding Early Horizon (Chávez 1980).

Regarding social developments, the highland regions lagged behind the adjacent coast in the size of the monuments, suggesting smaller groups were responsible for them. Mounds were built at Kuntur Wasi and Pacopampa, and earlier ones continued to be occupied at places such as La Galgada, but these were relatively small compared to those on the coast. This reflects the smaller communities that interacted in the highland regions. The wide variety of ceramic styles that is found throughout the highlands during this period supports the idea of local autonomous groups. Nonetheless, the widespread evidence for trade and exchange among the coast, highlands, and tropical forest clearly indicates that these local groups were in contact with others and were aware of social, economic, and technological developments elsewhere.

Still, the presence of monumental architecture in the highland regions does indicate that common social processes of cultural elaboration were occurring there as well. The basis of these developments was perhaps control of rituals but could also have included trade and exchange with both the coast and jungle regions. Obsidian was already being widely distributed from sources in southern Peru (Burger, Chávez, and Chávez 2000), and at the site of Waynuna in the Cotahuasi Valley of southern Peru, the presence of arrowroot, a tropical forest plant, indicates trade with regions to the east (Perry et al. 2006). Note as well that what could be called luxury items were beginning to appear, and we see marked differences in wealth between individuals appearing during this time. This sets the stage for the greater elaboration of such developments in subsequent periods.

SOUTH-CENTRAL HIGHLANDS

For many years, the Altiplano region was known for a few famous sites, such as Tiwanaku, Chiripa, and Pukara. These were sites that had been known and excavated in the middle of the twentieth century by a variety of Peruvian, Bolivian, and North American archaeologists. Regional patterns of settlement and subsistence information were poorly known. This began to change in the 1980s, and the rate of investigation picked up considerably in the 1990s and into the present millennium. As a result, we now know a considerable amount about the processes of cultural evolution in this region.

It has been known for some time that the central Andean chronological scheme that is so useful in that area is not really relevant in this region. One reason is the lack in this zone of any Chavín or Chavín-related material culture, which defines the Early Horizon. Another is the lateness of the arrival of pottery and possibly agriculture to this area. As a result, the older term Formative is used to identify the period when people settled down into permanent villages based on a herding, fishing, and collecting way of life, with increasing agricultural importance through time. The period is divided into the Early, Middle, and Late phases, based on

ceramics in the Altiplano region (Janusek 2003). The system used here is given in figure 5.12. Due to the nature of cultural developments in this area, I depart from my strictly chronological format and cover events here between 1500 B.C.E. and 250 C.E., or the time that corresponds to the Initial Period, Early Horizon, and beginning of the Early Intermediate Period in the regions to the north. I do this to avoid jumping back and forth geographically just for the sake of demonstrating cultural contemporaneity.

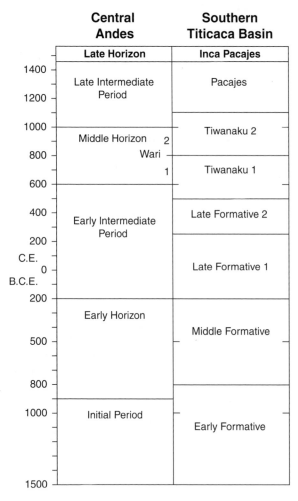

Figure 5.12. Lake Titicaca chronological sequence. Based on Janusek 2008, figure 1.7.

In keeping with one of the themes of this book, I emphasize the environmental effects on cultural developments in this area. These effects have been the subject of both discussion and debate as a result of environmental research in this region. As discussed in chapter 2, on geography and climate, there were shifts in rainfall and temperature throughout the Holocene, and these affected the level of Lake Titicaca, and particularly its southernmost part, called Lake Wiñaymarka (see figure 2.9). Early settlements were all located along the lake, which was dry until around 1500 B.C.E. (Abbott et al. 1997; Wirrmann, Mourguiart, and de Oliviera Almeida 1988). The fluctuating levels affected subsequent cultural developments, including the emergence of the Tiwanaku state, and a dry period and subsequent drop in lake level is seen by some as being a causal factor in the collapse of the state (see chapter 9).

One of the significant results of the research over the past two decades is the clearer identification of the differences between the developments in the northern and southern Titicaca basin. In particular, the role of the site of Chiripa in Middle Formative developments is now seen as much less significant as before, and the Tiwanaku influences in the north are now seen as not as uniform as previously thought (Bandy 2006; Plourde and Stanish 2006; Stanish 2009). These two regions were the heartlands of groups later in prehistory that spoke different languages, Quechua in the north and Aymara in the south, and it is now clear that such differences have deep roots.

Pottery seems to have appeared rather abruptly in several areas of the south highlands, from northern Chile to the Altiplano. Much of it was simple and utilitarian, and appeared in cultures that could be said to be more sedentary, although whether they lived in permanent settlements and used domesticated plants or animals as their principal means of subsistence is unclear.

Early Formative Period (1500–800 B.C.E.)

Surprisingly, one of the earliest of such cultures is found in the drier region south of Lake Titicaca, near Lake Poopó (Janusek 2008; McAndrews 2005). This group, called Wankarani, formed settlements of circular houses beginning around 2000 B.C.E. The way of life was based on camelid herding and the growing of hardy crops such as quinoa and potatoes, supplemented by the hunting and collecting of wild foods. Ritual was important, both at the household and community levels. Subfloor offerings of figurines, stone hoes, and grinding stones were common in the houses, and larger ritual structures were located in each village, where ceremonies to ancestors were conducted (Janusek 2008). Carved stone llama heads (figure 5.13) are common at Wankarani sites, perhaps reflecting the importance of llama caravans and trade to these settlements. Finally, Courtney Rose (2001) finds subtle status differences among households in the different cuts of llama meat, better access to exotic stone tools, and more elaborate pottery. Despite this, McAndrews (2005) finds little evidence of hierarchical political development among the Wankarani settlements. There were, however, some communities with specialized activities, specifically stone carving and metallurgy, but these activities did not impart any discernible economic or political advantages to those communities.

Some of the earliest evidence of copper working in the south highlands appears at Wankarani settlements (McAndrews 2005), where copper smelting evidence was present during the first millennium B.C.E. What exactly was being made from the copper is uncertain. This metal appeared at Chiripa settlements to the north and down into northern Chile, and we can imagine that the spread of metallurgy was in some way associated with the spread of permanent communities in this region.

The earliest sedentary culture in the southern Titicaca basin is Chiripa, named for the site of that name located on the Taraco Peninsula. Thanks to the Taraco Archaeological Project of Christine Hastorf (1999, 2005) and her colleagues, the site can now be placed in its cultural context. Sites belonging to this period are spread across the Taraco Peninsula, averaging about 3.5 ha in area, with populations averaging seventy-seven people per village (Bandy 2006).

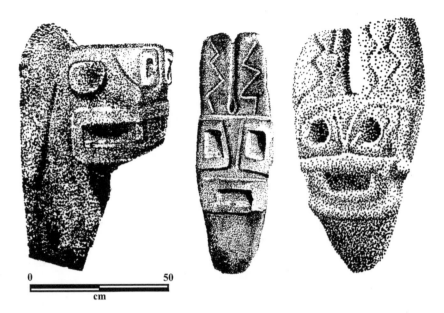

Figure 5.13. Drawing of Wankarani stone figures. From Janusek 2008, figure 3.3, drawn by Jennifer Ohnstad from Ponce Sanginés 1970 and Portugal Ortiz 1998. Image courtesy of John Janusek.

0   50
cm

Subsistence was based on a mix of farming of quinoa and tubers, fishing, and hunting, although domesticated camelids and guinea pigs may have been present (Janusek 2008; Whitehead 2006). Pottery was relatively simple and undecorated at this time, consisting of flat-bottomed vessels with straight sides, although some elaborate serving vessels were also used. Stone sculptures and metal objects suggest the presence of part-time specialists.

In the northern Titicaca basin, the cultural sequence for the Formative is different and much clearer because the subsequent Tiwanaku influence was less pervasive in the region (Plourde and Stanish 2006). Here, the earliest pottery-using culture was Qaluyu, which corresponds to the Chiripa of the southern region. Qaluyu ceramics were somewhat similar to early ones from the Cuzco area to the north and are characterized by bowls and plates with incised or black and red painted designs (Rowe 1956). Stone sculptures of human and animal figures made their appearance at this time, as at Chiripa. The subsistence base of the culture is likewise uncertain; there are abundant Qaluyu sites near regions associated later with raised fields (Janusek 2008), suggesting agriculture was practiced, but few domesticated plants have

been identified. The herding of llamas and alpacas, terrestrial collecting, and fishing were probably the main activities of the occupants.

Middle Formative Period (800–200 B.C.E.)

Starting around 1000 B.C.E., the people at the site at Chiripa built a trapezoidal sunken court that measured 14 by 14 m. Because this is the first evidence of a sunken court, a feature that was maintained among Altiplanic cultures for the next 2,000 years, its appearance is significant. Rare decorated serving vessels (figure 5.14) also appear (Bandy 2006), suggesting that this structure was used for ceremonial purposes that might have involved feasting. This structure was buried at the end of this period, but a similar sunken court was constructed in another part of the site. The presence of a drainage canal beneath this structure marks the appearance of another feature common to later ceremonial structures on the Altiplano. In addition to serving vessels, ceramic trumpets (figure 5.14) and *incensarios* (a type of ceramic vessel used in later cultures for rituals) appear, marking an elaboration of the ceremonialism from the earlier period (Bandy 2006).

Figure 5.14. Chiripa trumpets and decorated serving vessels. From Janusek 2008, figure 3.7, adapted from Bennett 1936. Images courtesy of John Janusek.

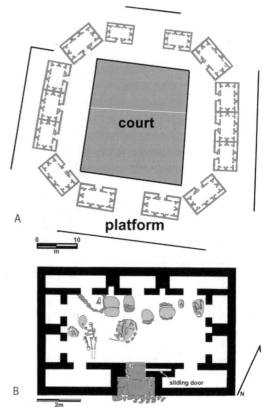

Figure 5.15. Chiripa mound, from From Janusek 2008, figure 3.5. (A) Adapted from Christine Hastorf, Community with the Ancestors: Ceremonies and Social Memory in the Middle Formative at Chiripa, Bolivia," *Journal of Anthropological Archaeology* 22 (2003). (B) One of its ritual structures with sub-floor burials. Adapted from Bennett 1936. Both images courtesy of John Janusek.

At the opening of the Middle Formative, a group of structures was constructed of adobe. The rubble of the lower structure was used as a platform for the one built on top of it, and a fire was made prior to the construction of the new structure (Bandy 2006). This pattern of rebuilding and ceremonially burning has been identified eight times, suggesting repeated ritual use of these structures. Around 400 B.C.E., a thick fill layer was laid down over the uppermost structure, on which a symmetrically laid-out group of fourteen buildings was constructed (figure 5.15A). The arrangement is in the form of a trapezoid, perhaps reflecting the symbolic shape of the earliest structure at the site. In the center of the buildings was a large sunken rectangular court.

Each of the structures was roughly the same in construction features. They all had sliding doors (a recess on one side of the door could have housed a door of perishable material) and bins made up of low walls within the structure (figure 5.15B). They were entered by window-like openings that had elaborate decorations. Each was plastered and painted, and some had burials under the floors. Karen Mohr Chávez (1998) has persuasively argued that these structures were used for the storage of ceremonial objects (Bandy 2006). Burials under the floors suggest they might have been associated with ancestral worship as well, and John Janusek (2008) states that the niches may have housed mummy bundles, although there is no evidence for this. Although each of these structures appears to be similar to the others, the subtle differences in burial numbers argues that each might be associated with a different social group at the site, perhaps a lineage or ayllu.

The sunken court around which these structures were located also had walls with mythical figures carved into them. These structures were probably the places where people came to conduct rituals to the ancestors that included drinking, feasting, and playing music. The playing of music is inferred from one of the common artifacts at Chiripa sites being a ceramic trumpet.

One of the exciting results of the recent investigations conducted on the Taraco Peninsula is evidence that the site of Chiripa, long thought to be the main center of the culture, was just one of several similar contemporary sites (Bandy 2006). In addition, sites such as Lukurmata, located just to the east of the sites studied by Matthew Bandy and Christine Hastorf, had a sizable Chiripa occupation (Bermann 1994), as did the Copacabana Peninsula to the west and regions of the Titicaca Valley to the south. Thus, it appears that the Chiripa culture of the late Middle Formative comprised several autonomous centers with sunken courts surrounded by ceremonial structures. Each was probably surrounded by smaller hamlets that may have been linked to the larger units politically, economically, and/or through religious rituals. Bandy (2006) argues that the emergence of these religious centers enabled the population of the Taraco Peninsula, which was quite dense, to grow without the villages fissioning into smaller units.

It is also significant to note that the appearance of ceremonial structures after 1000 B.C.E. and their elaboration around 800 B.C.E. correspond to changes in the level of Lake Wiñaymarka. Falling lake levels over the period 1000–800 B.C.E. could have been a stressor that led to increased ceremonialism in the groups living on the Taraco Peninsula. The emergence of similar structures reflects shared ritual concepts among the people living there, which in the subsequent period manifested itself in the first widespread religious movement: the Yaya-Mama religious tradition.

In the northern Titicaca basin, the site of Qaluyu was long thought to be the principal center of the culture; however, based on research done by Charles Stanish's Programa Collasuyu and others (Tantalean 2010), we now know that this is incorrect. Qaluyu-type sites are scattered over most of the northern basin, and several are much larger than the Qaluyu site itself. That being said, Qaluyu is still the best known from past excavations, so it merits description.

The site consists of a large mound on which architecture was constructed. Several sunken rectangular courts were built, and there is a large amount of domestic refuse around the sides, suggesting a large resident population. The dates for the structure suggest they were built during the latter part of the Middle Formative, contemporary with the site of Chiripa, although other sites might have been started even earlier (Plourde and Stanish 2006). Evidence of long-distance trade with the Amazonian lowlands to the east is also indicated at this early date.

Late Formative I Period (200 B.C.E.–250 C.E.)

The Yaya-Mama religious tradition is a ceremonial complex that appears throughout the Titicaca basin starting around the beginning of the Late Formative. It is characterized by the use of incensarios, ceramic trumpets, and stone sculpture with stylized male and female figures along with many other symbols, all associated with the use of the sunken rectangular courts (Chávez 1988; Janusek 2008). Bandy (2006) adds decorated serving bowls as a feature that reflects the ritual use of food during the activities conducted at these complexes. That there was a widespread acceptance of this tradition across the Titicaca basin is perhaps an indication of the stresses associated with the decreased rainfall and the subsequent changes in lake level.

Starting around 250 B.C.E., the Titicaca basin saw the development of several of what Bandy (2006) calls multicommunity polities, groups of formerly autonomous villages that were now under the influence of a larger one. Hastorf (2008) notes such polities emerged in several regions of the basin, indicating similar cultural processes, as described for the Taraco Peninsula, were probably operating. Changes during this period included new ceramic styles, the occupation of inland flat plains away from the lake, and an increase in the importance of camelid herding (Janusek 2008). Raised fields began to be built in local regions where the conditions allowed for them (see box 5.2). We can describe the best known of these, the Taraco Peninsula polity, as exemplary of these polities.

BOX 5.2 Raised-field agriculture

As the name implies, raised fields are a means by which low-lying and easily swamped ground is elevated to make an improved surface for planting crops. It is a means of improving land that is marginal for agricultural purposes. Raised fields are found in a wide variety of locations throughout Middle and South America and vary widely in their dates. They also reflect a similar response to different environmental challenges. For example, in Mesoamerica, raised fields are found in the Maya region, where they were used to reclaim swampland for fields. The associated canals between the fields were used for fishing. On the Altiplano, the technique was used for field production in soils with a high water table as well as to elevate fields to reduce frost damage to the crops growing on them.

The basic technology for making raised fields is simple. An individual digs soil up and piles it onto an adjacent area in long parallel rows. Where the water table is high, the excavated regions become canals because they intersect the water table. The adjacent fields are now higher and so can support deeper root growth. The effect is to make a pattern of fields with canals between them. A key element of raised fields is to allow water to circulate through the canals.

Raised fields in the Altiplano region have several advantages over traditional agricultural fields. First, as already mentioned, the field allows a deeper soil layer for plants. Second, experiments have shown that the fields have a tendency to protect plants from frost because colder air flows off the fields into the canals. Third, soil fertility can be maintained over time by either manuring with camelid dung or by dredging up muck from the canal bottoms and adding it to the soil. The advantages are manifested by the much higher yields that are grown on such fields (Erickson 1985).

Raised fields today are built by families and ayllus, which benefit from the increased production. Field systems can be large or small, depending on the need. Extensive regions around Lake Titicaca have the potential for the creation of such fields, and it is obvious from archaeological work that the Tiwanaku elites recognized this potential and used it during Tiwanaku 2.

At the beginning of the Late Formative, there was a significant shift in population on the Taraco Peninsula. Three of the four earlier large villages with sunken courts shrank in size and the site of Kala Uyuni increased dramatically. At this time, a true three-tiered settlement hierarchy emerged (Bandy 2006). Kala Uyuni appears to have dominated the peninsula at this time, but whether its domination was political, religious, or economic is unclear.

In the northern Titicaca basin, the site of Pukara rose to prominence with the beginnings of sunken courts on top of platform mounds, which had begun in the earlier Qaluyu culture. The massive mound at Pukara also consisted of a series of rectangular structures arranged in a horseshoe-shape around the courts. These structures are very reminiscent of the Chiripa structures, indicating contact and communication between the two regions. Carved stone heads are found in niches at the site, possibly suggesting trophy heads (decapitated heads taken from victims to show military prowess or to increase supernatural power) or ancestors. Other mounds in front of the main mound probably also had sunken courts.

A large population lived at the site as well; this is reflected in the quantity of domestic refuse surrounding the main ceremonial platform. Both elite and commoner residences have been identified there, indicating that social differentiation had occurred at the site (Janusek 2008). Charles Stanish (2002) suggests that the site of Pukara was a series of large to small architectural complexes surrounded by and perhaps interspersed with residential zones. Whether there was a strong centralized political power that controlled the site and the region remains to be determined.

Pukara ceramics are beautifully made, with complex motifs that are polychrome and outlined by incisions. Forms included open bowls and *keros,* which are large drinking vessels. Pukara is known for its many stone sculptures, derived from the earlier Qaluyu forms. Human and animal forms are depicted, both in the round and in flat relief. Some scholars have suggested that there is a new emphasis on trophy-head imagery (Hastorf 2008).

During Pukara times, settlements in the northern basin shifted from hillslope farming to floodplain fields, and lake resources also became important. Trade in all directions became much more significant, with obsidian from Cuzco and lowland plants from the yunga zone to the east, probably including hallucinogens for ritual purposes, arriving at Pukara sites (Janusek 2008).

Pukara spread its influence across the northern Titicaca basin, as seen in surveys conducted from Azángaro in the north (Tantalean 2010) to the zone of Chiripa influence. Although some researchers (e.g., Plourde and Stanish 2006; Kolata 1993; Stanish 2002) suggest this shows the political development of an authority at the site of Pukara that brought other regions under its control, others suggest it might have been the result of more indirect influence in regions that were already occupied by the Qaluyu people (Tantalean 2010). Regardless, it does reflect a more uniform cultural manifestation in the northern Titicaca basin during a time when the southern part was less unified. The site of Pukara was clearly the most important center, where religious and/or political authorities ruled over a sizable population of commoners.

Pukara ceased to be a political and cultural power around 250 C.E., as did several of the other centers already discussed. It is at this time that we see the emergence of Tiwanaku as a major player in Altiplano politics (see chapter 8).

Finally, agriculture, pottery, and a Formative way of life appeared in northern Chile around 1000 B.C.E. in the Alto Ramirez phase (Rivera 2008). Agriculture, including quinoa, maize, chili peppers, beans, squash, and gourds have all been found in permanent village sites. The relationship of the ceramics to the domesticated plants suggest that these people were immigrants from the highlands, possibly the Altiplano. Atlatls; metal objects of gold, silver, and copper; the use of hallucinogens; and sophisticated basketry and textiles suggest a well-developed Formative lifestyle. Some objects bearing similarities to the Yaya-Mama religious tradition have also been found (Rivera 2008).

SUMMARY

The period starting around 2100 B.C.E. marks a significant point in the development of the cultures of the north and central coast of Peru. Here, larger groups moved inland, many abandoning what had been their ancestral homes along the coast. They did this because of an increase in the importance of terrestrial plant resources, both domesticated and wild.

Whether this increase in importance was due to a dramatic El Niño or a series of them leading to coastline changes, to population growth, or to migration is uncertain. What is certain is that some individuals in these societies were taking greater control over the labor of their peers than had been the case in the Late Preceramic Period. What is less obvious is the basis on which these individuals were able to gain this control. Many scholars see the control of irrigation as the key, but I am skeptical. It is hard for me to understand how some individuals could make irrigation advantageous when so much area was available. Perhaps families in irrigable regions could grow surpluses that allowed them to build up social or economic debts among their peers (Hayden 1995). It is more likely that they had control over rituals, especially ones that pertained to the new practice of agriculture. Water is never a truly dependable resource along the coast because it is dependent on the amount of rainfall in the adjacent highlands. It is no surprise, as scholars have noted, that the U-shaped pyramid mound complexes are oriented to the east, the source of water for agriculture. Individuals who could claim the ability to control water through supernatural means would naturally be important (assuming they could convince their peers of this power!). As in the previous period, it seems likely that the power of these individuals was based not on coercion but on cooperation.

One possible exception to this was the Casma Valley. If Taukachi-Konkán truly was a palace, then we would have to accept hereditary rule as likely. How rule went from voluntary to hereditary is unclear. The evidence suggests that both rituals and economic controls were important here. Perhaps the volume of food produced was so great that individuals took charge of its redistribution and that through time this system became entrenched, with the same families controlling it. If those families also controlled rituals, the necessary factors for hereditary rule were in place. Still, it appears that these individuals were not benefiting materially, other than by living in a larger home and possibly eating better.

In other regions, the evidence still argues for local groups controlling their own rituals and building their own temples, such as in Lurín Valley and probably other sites in the Norte Chico region. The differences in status were probably not great between members of these societies, and all benefited from their positions in the food-production process.

In the north and central highlands, life was much the same as in the Late Preceramic, although, with the increasing dependence on agriculture, people were more tied to their fields and more dependent on rainfall or irrigation. As such, the emergence of ceremonial centers such as Pacopampa and Kuntur Wasi, as well as the continued use of centers such as La Galgada, Kotosh, and Huaricoto, is understandable. Much like on the coast, rituals for rain and against other disasters, such as drought, hail, and early frosts, would have led to the emergence, or continuance, of ritual specialists. At sites in the north, exchange could have been a mechanism by which individuals began to gain influence over their peers.

It is interesting that the pastoral societies of the central Andes apparently did not develop ceremonial sites, at least ones that have been identified north of the Titicaca basin. Perhaps this is due to their more mobile way of life, moving herds between summer and winter pasture. It is equally interesting that some regions saw a delay in the development of sedentary societies, for example, the Huamachuco basin.

Finally, the processes that led to the emergence of ceremonial centers in the Titicaca basin appear to be distinct from those that led to their appearance along the coast. Sedentism was apparently not as tightly related to plant domestication in this region; rather, the early Formative societies were pastoral societies that also fished and collected plants. That being said, rather quickly after people settled down, they began to construct small ceremonial structures. Why these were important is unclear, although Bandy's (2006) argument that they provided integrative functions that eased social friction could be one explanation. In regions outside the Taraco Peninsula, however, population densities were lower, so this explanation is less compelling.

In both the southern and northern Titicaca areas, as populations increased, the need for integrative practices probably became more urgent, resulting in the widespread use of sunken courts during the Middle Formative and, then, the emergence of the Yaya-Mama religious tradition in the Late Formative I Period. It is also possible that more powerful individuals were emerging at the centers during this time, perhaps either religious specialists or ones involved with trade.

Regardless of the place where an individual lived, there do not appear to be marked differences between the leaders and the led. Although some individuals were buried with greater amounts of goods, the quantity is not enough to think these people could not have accumulated them during their lifetimes. This changed in the next period, both in the north and in the south. Bearing in mind the differences in the time line, marked status differences begin to emerge earlier in the north.

Finally, environmental factors played a role in the cultural developments during this time period. El Niños along the north coast may have led to the abandonment of the major Late Preceramic centers in the Norte Chico. In addition, changes in rainfall and lake level in the Titicaca basin might have influenced cultural developments there. Still, the particular trajectories taken by groups in all these areas were ones based on their previous ways of life. The changes we see were the result of the specific interactions between individuals in the villages where they lived, coupled with the interactions between them and their neighbors. Environmental changes might have played a role, but it is equally likely that groups did not notice the changes from year to year and that the changes we have seen were wholly due to internal, culturally generated factors.

6

OF MASKS AND MONOLITHS
The Early Horizon

One of the most interesting unresolved issues in Peruvian archaeology is what happened to the complex societies that had flourished along the central to north coast during the Initial Period. It is apparent that virtually all the major centers with monumental architecture from the Lurín Valley to Jequetepeque were abandoned or, at least, the construction of major buildings ceased. This appears to have occurred within about two hundred years, starting around 1000 B.C.E.

INITIAL PERIOD COLLAPSE ALONG THE COAST

In some valleys, such as Lurin and Rimac, monumental sites were simply abandoned and there is little evidence for substantial populations in the lower valleys (Burger 1992). Whether the people moved farther inland or stayed in the valleys and their remains have disappeared is uncertain.

Along the north-central coast, the monumental sites were also abandoned, but there is some evidence of what happened to the populations. In the Casma Valley, people resettled in large rectangular compounds just off the floodplain. It is probably significant that the subsistence remains found at these sites show for the first time larger quantities of maize,

which could reflect highland influence at this time. People also placed simple houses on the summit of the Sechín Alto main mound and on the plaza area of Las Haldas (Pozorski and Pozorski 1987). The central staircase to the summit at the latter site was only half finished, suggesting a fairly abrupt cessation of building. There is no evidence of post–Initial Period construction of public architectures at these sites.

Settlements in the north coast valleys between Santa and Lambayeque also reflect the abandonment of the centers that existed, such as at Caballo Muerto, and a general lack of monumental centers to replace them. Early Horizon pottery is found in all these valleys, but few actual sites have been located, suggesting a general diminution of settlements, similar to other regions farther south.

It is unknown what might have caused this widespread collapse of Initial Period societies. It is unlikely that invasion played a role because there is little evidence for it, such as the abrupt replacement of ceramic or architectural styles. Although there is evidence of the movement of highland people into the coastal regions, as previously mentioned, there is little support for an actual invasion and conquest of the extant societies.

Because the collapse seems to have been a general, simultaneous phenomenon, we are tempted to look

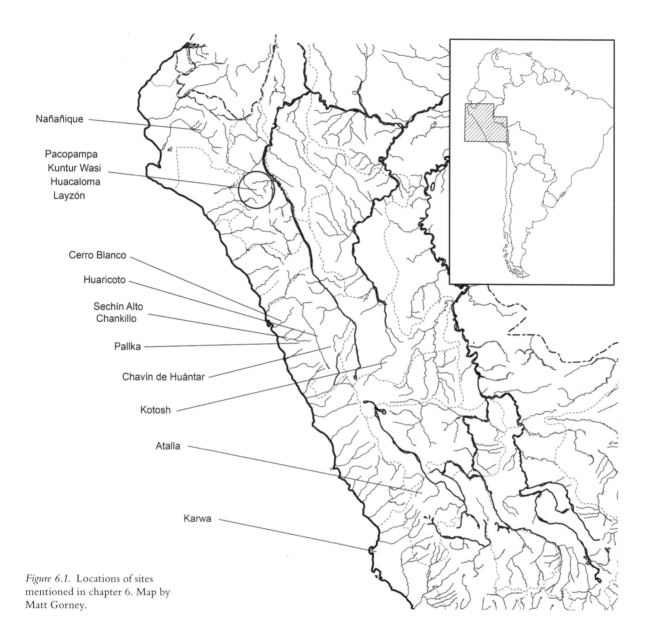

Nañañique

Pacopampa
Kuntur Wasi
Huacaloma
Layzón

Cerro Blanco

Huaricoto

Sechín Alto
Chankillo

Pallka

Chavín de Huántar

Kotosh

Atalla

Karwa

Figure 6.1. Locations of sites mentioned in chapter 6. Map by Matt Gorney.

for environmental causes. But unlike the previously cited evidence for possible earthquakes and El Niño–related disasters at the end of the Late Preceramic Period, there is little support for such a singular event during the Initial Period. There is some support for such an event around 500 B.C.E., but that appears to be too late to account for the collapse by several hundred years. There is some evidence for a marked increase in aridity in the south highlands around 1450 B.C.E. (Chepstow-Lusty et al. 2003) and for low levels in Lake Titicaca around 900 B.C.E. (Moseley 1997; see also the section on the south highlands in chapter 5) that in recent times has been associated with increased El Niño activity along the north coast. Other researchers, however, say this association may not be correct (Fontugne et al. 1999). There is certainly no clear-cut evidence of dramatic damage to these centers that could be attributed to torrential rainfall associated with El Niños.

This leaves the possibility that local and internal factors caused these societies to change so dramatically. Still, such an explanation would need to account for the collapse of all these large centers at virtually the same time. Could the same internal factors have been operating in each valley? To answer this, we must go back and consider the nature of the authority that was in charge at these centers. With the exception of the Casma Valley, most of the corporate authorities in charge of the monumental constructions, and probably other aspects of society such as food production, were probably nonhereditary informal leaders who ruled through persuasion, not coercion. I and other researchers feel the primary source of their authority was the control of rituals and the small surpluses that might have been required for the activities in the temples. As Burger (1992) notes, these authorities might not have been able to convert their sacred knowledge into a more sustained source of power that included coercion and accumulation of wealth. This, however, does not really explain the simultaneous collapse of such authorities.

I wonder if demographic factors, combined with climatic ones, could have been involved in the changes that occurred. As noted in chapter 2, there was a sustained period of reduced rainfall in the highlands starting around 1000 B.C.E. that lasted for two hundred years. Regardless of whether there were increased El Niños, this would have affected the amount of irrigation water available in the coastal valleys. Populations had been rising for over a millennium in these coastal valleys, and agricultural productivity had increased. As long as there was adequate land and irrigation water for the growing populations, the authorities could maintain control through ritual. But as agricultural productivity dropped due to decreased irrigation water,

political crisis might have ensued. Significantly, the crisis might have been brought on even if plenty of land was available.

Although the evidence for such a decrease in irrigation water would be hard to find, the widespread nature of such a phenomenon has the advantage of explaining the collapse of the coastal societies simultaneously. Given that the kinds of gods and rituals conducted were generally the same, at least as reflected in the kinds of temple structures present, we might expect that authorities everywhere could not maintain control over their people. Loss of faith led to loss of authority, and people either abandoned the areas around the centers or reorganized their communities in new social ways. Conditions were perfect for the rise of a new religion that could replace the old ones.

CHAVÍN

Sometime during the late Initial Period, a highly exotic art style began to appear in the north-central highlands, a style that fascinates people even to the present. This art style[1] has been cogently described by Gordon Willey:

> Its themes are anthropomorphic and animal: men, demons, jaguars, eagles, serpents, caimans, and other beasts. These are given fantastic renderings, and there is, especially, a conceit of giving jaguar or feline attributes (fangs and claws) to other animals and men or deities. Serpent heads are also frequently disposed on all parts of the body of the principal animal or human represented in a sculpture. The style is graceful, flowing, essentially curvilinear, and intrinsically and rhythmically balanced. A characteristic mode is an eye with an eccentric pupil, and this, together with the grimacing, fanged mouths of the animals, demons, or gods, gives a somewhat sinister, baleful aspect to the figures. (1971, 116)

The art style was named for the site of Chavín de Huántar, where many sculptures and ceramics that are typical of this style were found in the 1920s by Julio Tello, one of the fathers of Peruvian archaeology. In fact, much like the Olmec, which was thought to have been the Mother Culture for all later Mesoamerican cultures, for a long time Chavín was thought to be earliest manifestation of civilization in the Andes (Tello 1960). This idea has been rejected as a result of the discovery of the earlier monumental sites. Still, this art style did reflect changes that had far-reaching consequences.

A major issue regarding this time period is the relationship of the site of Chavín de Huántar to the art style and their relative placement in time. Excavations by Luis Lumbreras, Richard Burger, and others at the site identified ceramics from a wide area of the Andes, including the north coast and highlands and perhaps the central coast (Burger 1992; Burger and Salazar 2010; Lumbreras 1993). In addition, some of the architectural features of the site, including the basic U-shape of the temples and the presence of a sunken circular plaza, reflect influences from coastal regions. It is important to remember that all these foreign influences, except perhaps the ceramics, occurred earlier in their respective regions than they did at the site of Chavín de Huántar. This has led to the idea that the site was a relatively late center of the art style, although recent work, to be discussed below, suggests otherwise.

It is now generally accepted that the art style represents a set of religious beliefs that was widely but differentially accepted throughout the central and northern parts of Peru, both on the coast and in the highlands. Luis Lumbreras's (1993) and Richard Burger's (1984, 1992) work at the site has indicated that it was a locus of influence for a cult that practiced the religion, but it probably was not the only one and probably was not the earliest. Still, its architectural and artistic attributes make it stand out as a truly unique center of the Chavín religion.

Where this set of beliefs originated is uncertain, assuming it even had a single point of origin. Tello notes that the main animals represented in the art—the crested or harpy eagle; the jaguar; snakes, especially the anaconda; and the cayman—were of tropical forest origin, suggesting that the beliefs developed there. The animals represented, however, if they are as Tello says, range widely, so they do not help in determining the origin. The dates for the pottery and architectural friezes associated with this art style start around 1500 B.C.E. on the north coast (see chapter 5), suggesting an origin in that region. At present, the source of the religious beliefs is uncertain. Indeed, as Rick (2008) and others have suggested, it is likely the religion was supported by many different cults at centers where the art style was manifest. Nonetheless, the religion was associated with dramatic changes in technology, local economies, and sociopolitical complexity (Burger 1988, 2008).

Chavín de Huántar

As an important center of Chavín religion, if not *the* most important center, Chavín de Huántar warrants some additional information. The site is located along the Mosna River, a tributary of the Marañon system, on the east side of the Cordillera Blanca that define the eastern side of the Callejón de Huaylas. The site is dominated by a monumental complex (figures 6.2A and 6.2B), although a large town was also present adjacent to the temples. Based on earlier work by Marino Gonzáles, a Peruvian, John Rowe (1962) defines a chronological sequence for the construction of the monumental complex associated with the major sculptural art. In his sequence, the Old Temple (Building B) was constructed and then expanded twice by the addition of the wings to the south arm to become what is called the New Temple (Building A). During the second expansion, the Black-and-White Portal was constructed as well as a large rectangular plaza defined by two flanking mounds, recreating the U-shape of the Old Temple. Burger (1984) builds on this sequence by associating ceramic styles with the construction features and has also studied the region around the center to understand its sociopolitical context. He identifies three kinds of Chavín pottery, Urubarriu, Chakinani, and Jannabarriu, proposing that they were associated with three phases of temple

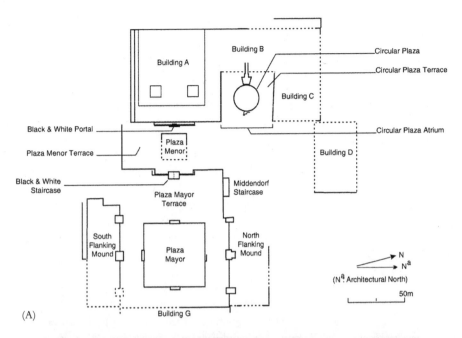

(A)

(B)

Figure 6.2. (A) Map of Chavín de Huántar. From Kembel and Haas 2013. By permission of Springer New York LLC; permission conveyed through Copyright Clearance Center, Inc. (B) Site of Chavín de Huántar. Photo by author.

construction that all date to the Early Horizon proper. This model has been the standard in books on Andean cultures since at least the 1980s.

Beginning in 1995, John Rick and his students conducted extensive research using new and sophisticated equipment and modeling to get a better understanding of the construction sequence of the monumental buildings at the site and the significance of the site to our understanding of the Early Horizon (Kembel 2001, 2008; Rick 2005, 2008; Rick et al. 2009). The map and construction sequence developed by these investigators are included in figures 6.2A and 6.3.

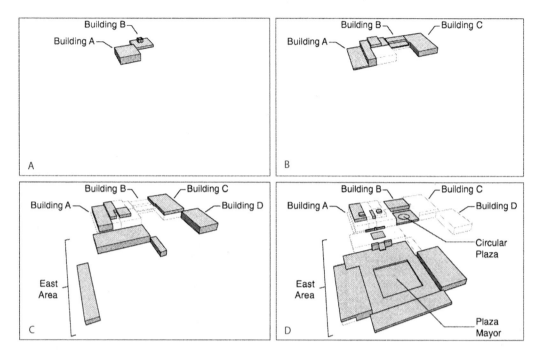

Figure 6.3. Construction sequence for Chavín de Huántar. (A) Stage 1, Separate Mound Stage. (B) Stage 2, Expansion Stage. (C) Stage 3, Consolidation Stage. (D) Stage 4, Black and White Stage. from Kembel and Haas 2013. By permission of Springer New York LLC; permission conveyed through Copyright Clearance Center, Inc.

There are importance differences between Rick's and Kembel's sequence and the traditional one (see figure 6.4). Specifically, the relationship of the ceramic sequence to the architectural one defined by Burger (1984) has been questioned by Rick et al. (2009). The latter note that the original ceramic sequence was based on excavations mainly from outside the architectural complex whereas their data are from both monumental and peripheral contexts. In addition, they have a very large set of radiocarbon dates on which their interpretations are based. They have suggested that Burger's ceramic sequence is problematic, and they can identify only a group of ceramics that could be called *janabarroid,* dating to the period 800–500/400 cal B.C.E., and distinct but as-yet poorly defined ceramics that predate that time. It is obvious that clarifying the relationship between the architecture and ceramics is a critical aspect of future research.

An important point about the recent research by Rick, Kembel, and others is that the majority (27/33) of the radiocarbon dates for the monumental architecture fall into the range of 1200–800 cal B.C.E., with only five falling in 800–500 cal B.C.E. In contrast, in the contexts outside the architectural complex, 27/38 radiocarbon dates fall in 800–500/400 cal B.C.E. This indicates fairly clearly that the main temples at Chavín de Huántar were constructed early on, in the late Initial Period and early Early Horizon, but much of their use fell off during the subsequent time and there was relatively little additional construction.

The second difference between the older and newer interpretations of the chronology of the site is that there are now five major construction stages, with at least fifteen individual phases identified within them (figure 6.3). The first four stages are shown in figure 6.3; during the final stage there

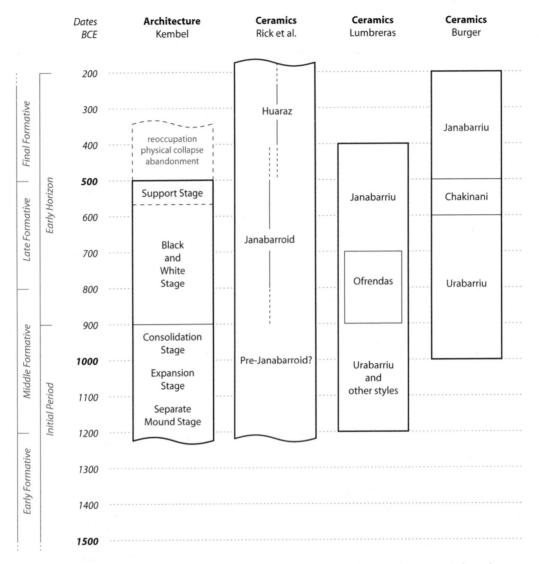

Dates BCE	Architecture Kembel	Ceramics Rick et al.	Ceramics Lumbreras	Ceramics Burger

Figure 6.4. Chronologies for Chavín de Huántar. In Lumbreras's scheme, Ofrendas pottery is an independent group of ceramics within the local tradition. After Conklin 2008, figure 1.2, and Rick et al. 2010, figure 25. Figure by Silvia Rodriguez Kembel.

was little new construction. Within the phases, there were thirty-nine known gallery constructions. What is significant about the new dates from the site is that they show that most of the construction of the monumental architecture occurred during the period from 1200 to 800 cal B.C.E. rather than later. Subsequent to this time, little new

construction was done, but existing structures were more intensively used. In addition, most of the artwork associated with the site was already in place by 800 cal B.C.E. as well, including the Lanzón, the Black and White Portal, the art in the Circular Plaza, and the tenoned heads. The circular plaza and U-shaped pyramid forms, which are seen as coastal in origin, appear prior to this time as well (Kembel and Haas 2013).

Rather than describe the complex set of constructions, I provide here a brief summary; the reader is referred to Kembel (2001, 2008) for a more detailed description. During the Separate Mound Stage of construction, the earliest ceremonial structures were small buildings, which were probably oriented north-south. Even at this earliest stage, galleries for ritual activities were present. During the Expansion Stage, the whole set of constructions of Buildings A and B, and possibly C, were completed, with a series of galleries within each. The orientation of the complex shifted to an east-west line, with a new eastern entrance to Building B centered on the plaza created by the addition on Building C. New platforms and galleries were added during the subsequent Consolidation Stage, with the galleries becoming more standardized in their form. Probably the most significant constructions occurred during the Black-and-White Stage, named for the eponymous portal that was built linking Building A with the Plaza Menor and the Plaza Mayor, the two rectangular courts situated to the east of Building A.

To construct the Plaza Mayor, it was necessary for the builders to shift the course of the Mosna River to the east (Rick 2008), which must have been a prodigious effort. The two rectangular courts were constructed, leading to Building A, although there was no central staircase leading up to the summit. An earlier monumental stairway at the northwest corner of the Plaza Mayor (called the Middendorf Staircase) was incorporated into the new constructions to allow processions to go back to Building B, reflecting its continued importance. More galleries were constructed, and spaces on top of earlier platforms that formerly had been open were enclosed. There is a high order of symmetry to this construction stage, but one that still allowed, and indeed prioritized, access to and the use of many of the earlier galleries and spaces. In particular the Circular Plaza at the entrance to Building B was constructed during this stage, and the three galleries, including the Ofrendas and Caracolas, were built with accesses

from it. It is obvious that Building B and its Lanzón sculpture were still an important part of the rituals conducted at the site, along with the newer ones in Building A: significant efforts were made not only to maintain access to the Lanzón through new gallery constructions but also to enhance its ritual importance, as evidenced by the construction of the Circular Plaza and its staircases that led directly to the Lanzón Gallery. In the final stage of construction, the Support Construction Stage, no major constructions were undertaken, but a major cataclysm, most likely an earthquake, damaged the entire complex, and the walls were shored up at this time. It was shortly after this phase that the center was abandoned.

The final shape of the center was reached during the Black-and-White Stage. Building B (formerly, the "Old Temple"), which was begun during the earliest stage, was entered through the Circular Plaza from the east. This plaza, centered in the U formed by Buildings A, B, and C, was a sunken circular court of a kind that was used on the coast at the same time and earlier. The plaza and its three galleries were built of fill brought in and laid on an earlier platform. The plaza was lined by a lower row of stone carvings of felines and an upper panel of humans carrying conch-shell (*Strombus*) trumpets, spiny oyster (*Spondylus*) shells, and San Pedro cactus. The last could suggest that a significant aspect of the cult was the transformation of shamans or rulers into felines by the use of hallucinogens, especially the San Pedro cactus. The exotic nature of the art style is more understandable in this context.

A wedge-shaped stairway entered the sunken plaza from the east and another exited it from the west, in front of the main entrance to Building B that led to the Lanzón Gallery. The Ofrendas and Caracolas galleries were located to the north and south, respectively, within the fill of the platform. The Galería de las Ofrendas (Gallery of the Offerings) housed the remains of some eight hundred broken pots that were discovered on the floor (Lumbreras 1993). These were from different kinds of pottery and seem to have been offerings; at least some of the pots appear to be from different parts of the Andes, suggesting they were placed there by pilgrims or visitors to the center. Abundant food remains were found among the pots, suggesting the offerings were of food, and it is intriguing to note that 233 burned bones of humans of all ages were also found, suggesting ritual cannibalism might have been practiced (cited in Burger 1992).

The second excavated gallery was the Galería de los Caracolas (Gallery of the Sea Snails; figure 6.5). The significant discovery in this gallery was a large number of *pututus,* carved conch-shell (*Strombus*) trumpets, of the kind seen on the stone sculptures lining the circular plaza. The spires were cut off the shells to make them into the trumpets. It appears that this gallery was used to store the trumpets when they were not in use (Rick 2008). Following on

early suggestions by Lumbreras, archaeoacoustic studies conducted by Miriam Kolar et al. (2012) in the Lanzón gallery and Circular Plaza, indicate that sound, especially of the pututus, was an important factor in the rituals conducted there. It is likely that they were important elsewhere as well, indicated by the prevalence of pututu imagery at the site.

Building B itself contained a group of galleries, which consisted of narrow, dark, internal corridors and rooms connected by ducts for sound and light. One of these galleries housed the imposing figure of the Lanzón (figure 6.6). This sculpture, triangular in cross section and over 4 m high, was one of the principal deities of the temple throughout its use. Galleries were built throughout the site's temple buildings and are a feature largely unique to Chavín de Huántar. Galleries often were multilevel, connected by small

Figure 6.5. Galeria de las Caracolas. Photo courtesy of John Rick, Stanford University.

Figure 6.6. The Lanzón. Photo by author.

Another important deity of Chavín that is less well located in the temporal chronology of the site is the Tello Obelisk. Like the Lanzón, it is a carved granite stone that is meant to be freestanding. The images on the sides are of a cayman with the tail of a bird. Plants such as manioc, achira, peanuts, and chili peppers sprout from various parts of the cayman, suggesting to scholars such as Donald Lathrap (1973) that this deity was associated with bringing domesticated plants to humanity. The original location of this monolith is unknown.

One of the impressive aspects of the construction features of both Buildings A and B is their sophisticated ventilation and drainage systems. Air ducts brought fresh air into and circulated it throughout the temples and also served to bring light into the interior, probably via the polished stone mirrors that are present at the site (Kembel and Rick 2004, Rick 2008). Over 900 m of conduits were also placed in the structures to remove water, and these channels often ran at oblique angles to the halls and galleries. Lumbreras and his colleagues (cited in Burger 1992, 143) noted that the ventilation and drainage systems probably functioned to generate noise as parts of the rituals conducted at the temples. They did an experiment showing that water rushing through the drainage system creates a roaring sound that resonates like applause. According to various researchers, the basic idea of the temple structures was to disorient the individual by making her or him pass through a series of darkened corridors to the place of ritual. The sense of disorientation, if not outright fear, could have been heightened by the sound of rushing water or wind, which could have been channeled through some of the ducts and vents that honeycombed the building.

During the final Black-and-White Stage, Building A was enlarged, and there was an expansion of the plaza system and flanking mounds to the east. Although the basic U-shape was retained, there were now two rectangular sunken plazas, separated by a staircase leading from the larger plaza (Plaza Mayor) to the smaller (Plaza Menor). Between the Plaza Menor and Building A is the Black and White

stairways. Their uses are uncertain, but they could have served as storage facilities for ritual materials or as places for other activities.

Within Buildings A and C the Expansion and Consolidation Stage constructions involved adding more galleries, but ones augmenting, not replacing, the existing galleries. Two rectangular buildings were constructed on the top of Building A, and the east, primary façade of Building A contained doorways suspended many meters above the ground; these were accessed by internal staircases hidden from the view below in the plazas. This would have the effect of making the priests appear out of nowhere.

Figure 6.7. The Black and White Portal. Photo by author.

Portal, an elaborate gateway with two carved columns on either side (figure 6.7). The columns have anthropomorphized birds bearing staffs, and the lintel above has images of harpy eagles or condors advancing toward the center of the lintel.

A series of larger-than-life monstrous stone heads were located along the building's upper courses, just below the roof, though these might actually be from an earlier stage. These heads appear to float in thin air but are attached by tenons to the wall behind them. Burger notes that there seems to be a transition from priests to anthropomorphic creature to felines and other creatures in the artwork of these heads, suggesting shamanic transformations.

This new construction had the effect of greatly expanding the entire temple complex and making it more imposing to the visitor. Surely anyone coming from the river through the large sunken rectangular court and through the portals to the temples could not fail to be impressed. A large number of new stone sculptures were carved, but the basic deities remained the same and were just more elaborately expressed (Burger 1992). While Building B continued to function, Building A was used for additional ritual activities. Those privileged to enter the labyrinthine interiors for special ceremonies were probably a very small, highly elite group.

A new deity, called the Staff God because it carries a ceremonial staff in each of his outstretched arms, appears to have emerged as a central figure of this temple. This figure is represented on the Raimondi Stone, which shows the principal deity with an elaborate headdress. A host of other architectural sculptures were also carved, including the tenoned heads already noted.

During the early phases of construction, the monumental complex sat amid a small community of a few hundred people (Burger 2008). This settlement lived on deer and llamas as well as domesticated plants, although maize was only minor contributor. Shells and fishbones indicate contacts with the coastal region. During the Early Horizon, the population of the town around the monumental complex expanded to perhaps 2,000–3,000 individuals. Several changes were associated with this increase, including new kinds of raw materials, food-consumption patterns, and status differentiation. The presence of obsidian increased at the site, brought from a source located 500 km to the south (Burger and Glascock 2000). Animal remains indicate that meat was now brought to the site already butchered from sites above the center, whereas plant consumption remained the same. Finally, Isabelle Druc (1988) has found through the analysis of the clays used in the pottery that over 30 percent of the ceramics were produced away from the site, indicating a substantial importation of such items, both for temple and domestic uses.

Most significantly, there is now clear evidence that some individuals were more important than others, as reflected in the kinds of high-prestige items they were able to accumulate. In a region adjacent to the temple, gold jewelry, Spondylus shells from Ecuador, cinnabar (a deep red mineral used for coloring pottery and textiles), and exotic pottery were all found, items absent from other areas of the site (Burger 2008). There is some evidence of craft specialization in hide-working and ceramic production as well. All this evidence argues that Chavín de Huántar became a successful and influential center that was benefiting materially from its temple and the religious cult that it served. Burger (2008) notes that systematic surveys in the Mosna drainage have not identified settlements that were similar in size or architectural complexity. This supports the idea that at Chavín de Huántar there

was a political power that controlled the activities of these other sites. Evidence for social segregation during Chavín times has been identified at the settlement of La Banda, across the Mosna River from the site. There are notable differences in the rare raw materials found in certain residences there (Rick 2008).

Kembel and Rick (2004; Rick 2005) have argued that the authorities in charge of the cult and rituals at Chavín de Huántar became less community-serving and more self-serving through time. This is reflected in the marked differences in the prestige items. Such authorities would have come to have more permanent powers and, by extension, greater influence. They see this as a widespread trend throughout this time period.

That Chavín de Huántar was a pilgrimage center cannot easily be denied. It has a cosmopolitan flavor in its iconography, from the use of conch shell (Strombus) and spiny oyster (Spondylus), both from coastal Ecuador, to the ceramics that appear to be from several regions of the Andes. The presence of ceramics from several areas of the coast and highlands, even at the houses of the commoners at the site argues for this too. Aspects of the religious figures as well as the architecture itself are related to other important centers, both coastal and highland. What the recent investigations at the site have indicated is that Chavín de Huántar was not just a final refuge of a religion that perhaps had lost its influence in other regions; rather, it began to develop at the same time as other centers. The emerging elites there took ideas from other regions and built them into their center. In addition, they also used ideas and innovations that were unique to the site and region.

Pilgrims would have seen both new and familiar things on their visit. They probably brought offerings of food, pottery, and perhaps prestige items to be used to curry favor with the powerful deities in the temples. They also would have brought back to their home regions the new ideas and technologies that they were exposed to at the site, or possibly during the trip to and from it.

Distribution of Chavín-Related Sites

As I mention at the beginning of the chapter, many monumental sites along the coast were abandoned at the end of the Initial Period, coincident with the rise of the Chavín religion. As the Chavín religion rose in importance, its influence spread throughout the Early Horizon, although not in a consistent manner. One of the interesting aspects of the Chavín religion is its differential acceptance throughout the north and central highlands and coast. Some societies embraced the religion that formed the basis of the influence; others resisted it (Patterson 1971). I first discuss the evidence for these relationships.

For a long time, the nature of Chavín influence on the north coast was confusing because the Cupisnique (sometimes called Coastal Chavín) ceramics are closely related to some of the Chavín pottery from elsewhere in form, color, and designs. The large friezes on Huaca de los Reyes in the Caballo Muerto complex also were seen as Chavín-related. Now it is evident that they are an early manifestation of the religion and probably one of the sources of the art style. During the Early Horizon, the main monumental sites in the region were abandoned, and the populations apparently dispersed to middle- and upper-valley locations, especially to defensible locations. Although some rich burials have been found in the region, most settlements were small and had little public architecture.

The same is not true of the Casma Valley. The Pozorskis have identified significant changes there that point to the overthrow of the powerful polity located at the Sechín Alto Complex. Originally, the Pozorskis thought the invaders were foreigners, possibly from the adjacent Callejón de Huaylas (Pozorski and Pozorski 1987). As mentioned at the beginning of this chapter, small squatter settlements of rectangular houses appeared at the top of the main mound at Sechin Alto, and other of the main sites appear to be unfinished, with the work abruptly stopped. New settlement forms based on rectangular complexes of rooms then appeared, associated with larger quantities of maize, potatoes, and other crops more typical of the highlands.

Two complexes, Chankillo along the Casma branch and Pallka high up in the valley on the way to the highlands, suggest conflict was now a significant part of life in this valley. Chankillo (figure 6.8) is a walled compound located above the Moxeke branch of the Casma River. This site has been shown to be a fortress and ceremonial center (Cowen 2007; Ghezzi 2006) with an astronomical orientation. It is associated with a rectangular compound and an odd arrangement of thirteen towers located along a low ridge below the fortress/ceremonial center (figure 6.9). The line of towers also has an orientation to the rising sun at both the solstices and the equinoxes (Ghezzi and Ruggles 2007). From a viewing point at a compound door below the structures, an observer would see the sun rising over the northernmost tower on the summer solstice and over the southernmost one on the winter solstice. The nature of the lower valley data now suggests to the Pozorskis that the Early Horizon developments such as Chankillo were probably local and not indicative of a foreign presence (Pozorski and Pozorski 2008). In this scenario, the Sechin polity succumbed to the same local destructive forces as other valley polities did.

Pallka, the other fortified site, is located on a ridge top in the middle valley of the Moxeke branch. It was probably occupied during the Initial Period, but its ceramics and food remains support a more significant Early Horizon occupation, one the Pozorskis argue was associated with an incursion of people from the Callejón de Huaylas. This appears to be a center of a local elite group that affiliated with the Chavín religion and drew their power from their ability to use it for political gains.

In the Nepeña Valley just to the north, there is a remarkable lack of Initial Period sites, suggesting that the population had moved to the Casma Valley to assist with the polity constructions there, although this is uncertain. Both the Pozorskis (Pozorski and Pozorski 2008) and Richard Daggett (1987) argue that the valley might have been repopulated by highlanders bringing Chavín material culture with them because the artifacts found are associated with contemporary settlements in the Callejón de Huaylas

Figure 6.8. Chankillo. Photo by author.

to the east. The site of Cerro Blanco in the lower valley, with its decorated Chavín supernatural figure modeled in clay, is considered by the Pozorskis to have been an actual colony of Chavín individuals (Pozorski and Pozorski 2008). At the beginning of the Early Horizon, settlements are found in the middle- and upper-valley region, although with little public architecture. Toward the end of the Early Horizon, there appears to have been an increase in intravalley conflict, resulting both in more sites being built in defensible locations and in the construction of forts.

The same kind of settlement pattern seen in Nepeña is mirrored in the lower Santa River valley. This valley, which marks the boundary between the north-central and north coasts, has a permanent flow of water with its source high up in the southern reaches of the Callejón de Huaylas. David Wilson (1988) has found a concentration of small settlements dating to this period away from the valley floors and linked to fortresses or refuges on high ridge tops.

The evidence from these three valleys argues for a significant increase in conflict during the Early Horizon, associated with the abandonment of the Initial Period monumental centers. It is uncertain whether the conflict was between the populations of the valleys and their highland neighbors or among intravalley groups. Perhaps a combination of both was involved. Whether the Chavín religion was adopted after the political changes occurred or was part of the justification for them is likewise unclear at this time.

Farther south, along the central coast, Tom Patterson and others found Chavín-influenced pottery

Figure 6.9. The thirteen towers located along a ridge below Chankillo. Photo by author.

appearing during the Early Horizon along with local pottery styles virtually unchanged from their Initial Period antecedents. The former disappeared after a few centuries, suggesting that Chavín religion had less influence there than farther south (MacNeish, Patterson, and Browman 1975; Patterson 1971). Perhaps stronger religious traditions of the local Manchay culture were able to compete with the allure of the exotic religion. It is significant that the first fortresses in this region appear during this period, arguing for an increase in conflict there similar to other regions discussed (Patterson and Lanning 1964).

In the Lurín Valley, there appears to have been a large-scale abandonment of the lower valley, but no fortified sites, at the beginning of the Early Horizon.

Still, the center at Manchay Bajo was in use at the end of the Initial Period and the ceramics from its uppermost constructions show affinities to the Chavín ceramics from the Ofrendas Gallery (Burger and Salazar 2008). This points to the relationships that developed between these centers during this period.

Along the south coast, where there were no major monumental structures, local people seem to have adopted the Chavín religion, indicated by its influence on the Paracas pottery styles there that date to the later part of the Early Horizon (see chapter 7). An important cult center was located near the Paracas Peninsula at a site called Karwa. Here, many painted textiles with pure Chavín motifs and figures were found, unfortunately by looters. The complexity of the designs led Burger (1992) to suggest that the entire Chavín ideology had been imported there intact, with little lost in the intervening 530 km. An interesting distinction is the appearance of a female figure there as a central deity. It is thought that perhaps she represents a wife, sister, or daughter of the Chavín Staff God.

North and Central Highlands

In contrast to the coastal situation at the end of the Initial Period, many of the highland centers not only continued to exist but also flourished during the Early Horizon. Centers and ceramics showing close interaction with Chavín de Huántar are found from Cajamarca south to Huancavelica. In the Cajamarca basin, the sites of Pacopampa, Kuntur Wasi, and Layzón continued to be occupied and expanded, and Chavín-related ceramics appeared during this time (Terada 1985). Monumental walls of cut stone and large staircases cut into bedrock bespeak significant labor expenditures by the local populations.

At Pacopampa, a large rectangular sunken court was constructed on the summit of the mound and stone sculptures with felines and other related motifs were found around it (Rosas and Shady 1970). A similar rectangular plaza was constructed at the summit of Kuntur Wasi along with stone sculptures (Burger 1992), and this construction appears to have been the largest at the site. A series of four tombs were dug into the main plaza, and four individuals were buried with gold crowns, ceramics, *Strombus* shell trumpets carved with Chavín designs, pottery vessels, and stone and shell beads (Burger 1992). Strong Chavín influence is seen in the ceramics at Kotosh as well. All this evidence argues for contacts between the leaders of these sites, or at least participation in the same kinds of religious beliefs. Significantly, most of these sites reached the apogee of their development during the Early Horizon, generally at the same time as the site of Chavín de Huántar itself. However, the new evidence for earlier developments at Chavín de Huántar could argue that it might have been influential in the rise of the other sites.

New sites were founded during this period by devotees of the religion. The site of Nañañique in the upper Piura drainage of far northern Peru has a U-shaped structure that displays Chavín features (Guffroy 1989). Its location suggests that local elites were using the cult to develop a power base that allowed them to control the trade between the Ecuadorian region, where *Spondylus* and *Strombus* are found, and the regions farther south (Bawden 1996). It would be surprising if other such sites in the northern reaches of Peru were not present, lying undiscovered.

The southernmost highland site with Chavín associations is Atalla, located in the province of Huancavelica. At the site, a rectangular structure of stone was built on top of a mound, with burials nearby. The ceramics closely conform to the pottery of Chavín de Huántar itself (Burger and Matos Mendieta 2002).

Between Chavín de Huántar and Atalla, however, there is little evidence of sites showing public architecture or even significant evidence of Chavín influence. Communities continued a basic Formative lifestyle of farming and herding, although some of these aspects were affected by the changes wrought by the Chavín phenomenon, such as an increase in the presence of obsidian.

Change in Chavín-Influenced Societies

All in all, the Chavín religion can be seen as a powerful cultural influence over the entire northern part of present-day Peru. Burger (1988) has indicated that its influence was not restricted to religion alone. Rather, new innovations in metallurgy, textiles, and ceramics appeared that were associated with it. The importance of portable objects made of these new materials, especially gold, and the ideology they represented began a tradition that continued into later societies. These innovations emphasize how a widely accepted religion can open borders to new ideas and stimulate inventions and innovation.

Tello was among the first to determine that the Chavín art style could be recognized across a very wide region, and Burger (1992) notes that there is more similarity among ceramic assemblages over the range of Chavín influence than before, even among societies that shared little previously. The similarities involve the adoption both of forms and decorative elements that were used at the site of Chavín de Huántar. Among the most common motifs are lines of circles and dots, S-shapes, contrasting polished and unpolished zones, and broad incisions. Stirrup-shaped bottles with thickened lips (plate 2B) and flat-bottomed carinated bowls are typical of the shapes used. These influences were often combined with local antecedents to create a new kind of ceramics, reflecting the changing identities of the local potters (Burger 1992). Whether these influences reflect the degree of acceptance of the religion or are simply an expression of interest in the new decorative elements being introduced is unknown; it is likely that some combination of the two was involved and that the combination varied from region to region.

William Conklin (1978), a textile specialist, noted long ago that several new weaving techniques appeared during the Early Horizon. Innovations included the use of paint on the weaving; the use of camelid hair, sometimes dyed, in cotton textiles; new tapestry techniques; and the virtual elimination of twining, the most popular earlier textile-manufacture technique. These new technological innovations are found throughout the area and appear to have spread rapidly, replacing local traditions. A similar revolution occurred in metallurgy. There was a veritable explosion in the use of gold and silver to manufacture cult objects, and advanced techniques were developed to do so (Lechtman 1980). Sophisticated methods for putting together objects by soldering and annealing sheets were also developed (figure 6.10). Full-time craftspeople must have been involved in the creation of both the new textiles and metal objects.

Finally, Burger (1992, 2008) notes that there was a dramatic increase in the volume of interregional trade and the variety of goods being traded. Part of this was due to the expanded use of llamas during this period, beyond their ancestral homeland in central Peru, but much of it must have been due to the

Figure 6.10. Chavín gold plaque. Copyright Dumbarton Oaks, Pre-Columbian Collection, Washington, DC.

increased demand for exotic prestige items such as cinnabar, gold, and *Spondylus*. Along with these items, which usually show up in high-prestige burials and not in the burials of the normal population, are a variety of materials such as obsidian that are much more widely distributed among the entire population at sites. This expanded trade had the effect of stimulating cultural developments in other areas. The site of Atalla emerged at this time as a center of exchange, probably based on its being near both the only source of cinnabar in the central Andes and the northernmost source of obsidian, the Quispisisa flow. Burger and Matos Mendieta (2002) suggest the control of trade in cinnabar and obsidian led to the emergence of leaders who could benefit from the new demand in these materials because there is virtually no evidence for substantial populations in the region prior to the Early Horizon.

There was clearly a link among these new technologies, the expanded trade, and the emergence of

Plate 1. (A) Lomas formations at Mejia, south of Mollendo, Peru, November 1983 during a strong El Niño year. Photo by Michael O. Dillon. (B) Aerial view of the Pirámide Mayor structure of the Sacred City of Caral, with its massive circular court. Photo courtesy of Zona Arqueológica Caral and Christopher Kleigehe.

A

B

Plate 2. (A) Cupisnique bowl with incised designs (ML015246). Museo Larco, Lima–Perú. (B) Chavín stirrup spout vessel with appliqué and punctate design (M.2009.21). Los Angeles County Museum of Art.

Plate 3. Gallinazo negative painted vessel (ML013676). Museo Larco, Lima-Perú.

Plate 4. Moche portrait head vessel (ML000142). Museo Larco, Lima–Perú.

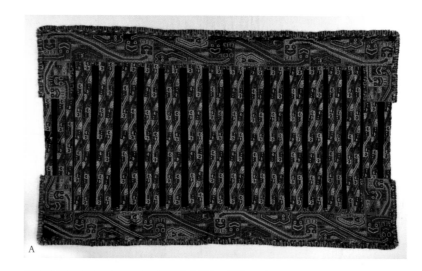

A

Plate 5. (A) Paracas mantle made of camelid fiber in plain weave with stem stitch and loop stitch embroidery (ma-31740025). Los Angeles County Museum of Art. (B) Nasca tunic of camelid fiber with animal figures. Warp-dominant plain weave 1X1; embroidery; plied fringe embroidery (41.2/ 08939). (C) Nasca tunic of camelid fiber with animal figures, close-up of design. B and C courtesy of the Division of Anthropology, American Museum of Natural History.

B

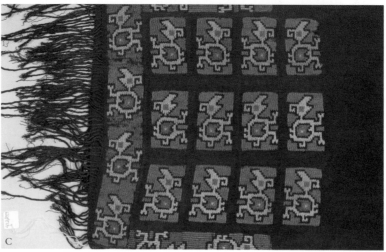

C

A

B

Plate 6. (A) Nasca warrior figure with trophy head (ML040365). Museo Larco, Lima–Perú. (B) Cajamarca Floral Cursive ceramic. Copyright Shinya Watanabe.

Plate 7. (A) Tiwanaku I kero, or drinking goblet. From Janusek 2008, figure 4.20a. Photo courtesy of Wolfgang Schüler. (B) Three classic (post-Algarrobal phase) Chiribaya ceramics from a single burial at El Algodonal. Photo courtesy of Bruce Owen.

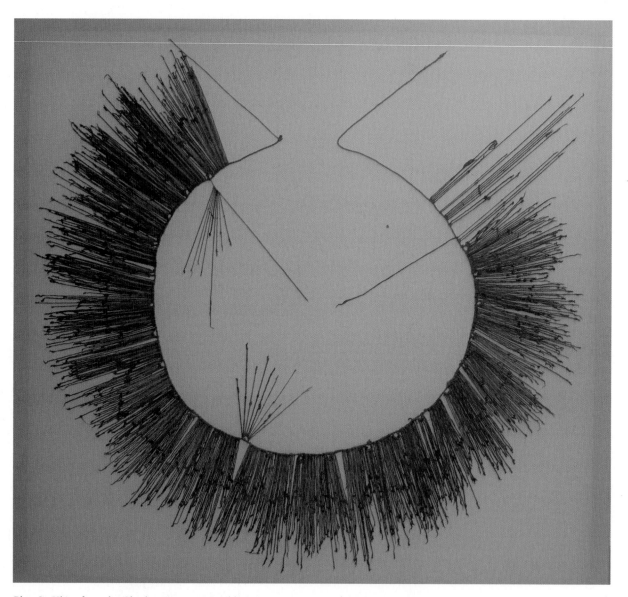

Plate 8. Khipu from the Chachapoyas area, possibly representing a two-year calendar. Located in the Centro Mallqui, Leymebamba, Peru. From Urton 2001. Photo by Gary Urton.

the political authorities at the centers where they developed. It is highly likely that the emerging elites controlled the production of the high-status objects and used it for their own political gain or to justify their positions of authority. The use of new technologies also stimulated craft specialization, which led to changes in the structure of society because more surpluses must have been required to support both the craftspeople and the elites. This occurred at a time when the coastal regions, at least, showed evidence of economic crises. The transformations discussed argue that kurakas (hereditary leaders) had emerged at Chavín de Huántar, as well as at the contemporary coastal and highland centers. Rich burials of individuals at several of these sites support this contention. So, control of both ritual and prestige items allowed individuals to gain authority over their peers, which through time became hereditary power.

CHAVÍN: PEACEFUL RELIGIOUS CULT, AGGRESSIVE POLITICAL FORCE, OR POLITICAL TOOL OF THE ELITE?

That Chavín was a set of religious beliefs that spread widely across the central and northern Andes has been well documented. Burger (1988, 1992) makes the case that it was successful because it was a regional cult, one emphasizing openness, new ideas, and broad themes of integration and synthesis. Its spread was possible in part due to the crisis that befell the coastal communities around the time the cult was developing. The reasons for its success in the highlands are less obvious but probably involved the manipulation of the religion for political purposes by emerging elites (Kembel and Rick 2004).

The site of Chavín de Huántar emerged during the latter part of the Initial Period as a place where different aspects of the religion were brought together in what Burger (2008) calls an "invented tradition." By this he means a tradition in which earlier aspects of other traditions are combined to form a new one that appears to be ancient. The builders of

the site drew on Manchay cultural traditions for the U-shape of their temples, the north-central coastal traditions for the sunken circular courts aligned to the temples, and the north coast traditions for the use of columns. The iconography appears to be of tropical forest origin, judging by the central figures used, but the stylistic conventions were also drawn from the coastal and other highland traditions.

It seems likely that the early priests of the Chavín cult drew together many of these ideas to form a religion that brought adherents from far and wide, as witnessed by the presence of exotic pottery in both ceremonial and domestic contexts. According to Rick (2005, 2008), this was a conscious effort to increase the power and authority of the priests and, by extension, perhaps their access to wealth.

The site of Chavín de Huántar had become the most important site in the central highlands at the beginning of the Early Horizon, and probably earlier. It was the largest center in the region and had by far the most elaborate stone sculpture assemblage, with over two hundred examples having been found. Its drainage and air duct systems, and the internal complexity of the chambers were unparalleled anywhere in the Andes at this time.

The question then becomes, what is the relationship between Chavín de Huántar and the other sites where Chavín influence is manifest? Burger (2008) suggests that the religion spread among local polities that were generally equal in political authority. Chavín de Huántar was one of several centers, including Pacompampa, Layzón, Kuntur Wasi, Pallka, and Cerro Blanco. These were all autonomous but connected through religious rituals and possibly intermarriage and economic activities, such as exchange of exotic materials. In highland regions further south, the priests of the great site formed relationships with less-developed societies to gain access to the materials they desired, both for themselves and their rituals and also as trade items to exchange with groups farther north. This situation also was evident along the south coast, where a particularly strong Chavín influence is seen in the early phases of the Paracas sequence (see chapter 7). The site of Karwa, as noted, was apparently a cult center. Ceramic similarities in the north coast region are present as well. The closeness of the local representations of the Chavín iconography in these areas argues for direct contact between elites at the centers in the two regions.

Other regions avoided or resisted Chavín influence, most notably the north-central coast and the Huamachuco highland region. In these regions, there is little to suggest the presence of the Chavín religion, although the local coastal ceramics do show the typical circle-and-dot motifs and other traits of cult centers elsewhere. Although the Nepeña Valley does have Chavín sites, the influence there can be explained by the movement of isolated groups into the valley at the end of the Initial Period.

In Burger's view, the spread of the Chavín sphere of influence, as he terms it, was linked to the emergence of the site of Chavín de Huántar itself, and the various aspects of this relationship need to be worked out. This view is also argued by Patterson (1971), who suggests that the site was a pilgrimage center. The Lanzón might have been an oracle that drew foreigners to it. The Staff God might have become another powerful image later, although the Lanzón continued to be important. Given the significance of later oracles, such as the one at Pachacamac, this idea is reasonable.

Another view of the spread of Chavín influence has been stated by Shelia and Thomas Pozorski (2008). They agree that Chavín was an amalgamation of ideas from various regions that crystallized into the cult, as recognized by Burger and others. They differ in seeing the elite priests of Chavín de Huántar as consolidating power during the early part of the Early Horizon and then aggressively sending out colonies to other regions as a result of their increasing wealth and power. They argue that Kuntur Wasi, Kotosh, and Huaricoto were all highland outposts and that Pallka and Cerro Blanco were as well. Their evidence that these centers were outposts instead of independent polities is the close similarities in artifacts and iconography. They suggest the lack of such Chavín influence can be seen in the

Casma Valley evidence as well as farther south along the central coast, where either new settlement patterns emerged of a purely local nature (as in Casma) or the Initial Period culture continued with regard to its architectural tenets (as in the Chillón-Rimac region).

Finally, Rick (2008) argues that the evidence from his and his colleagues' investigations at Chavín de Huántar support the view that an elite group actively manipulated Chavín symbolism to gain political authority. Using a model based on Kent Flannery's (1972) ideas, he sees a group of religious specialists, probably based in shamanism, developing a set of religious beliefs during the Initial Period that were accepted by their society due to their system-serving practices. These practices involved interactions with supernatural forces that would help solve societal problems. Through time, this group of specialists became progressively self-serving: "The widespread concept of a shaman's *access* to supernatural power, in part through identity transformation and other-world contact, could be altered into an argument of *intrinsic identity* with such power" (Rick 2008, 34). Later, this power became centralized and used for the political and perhaps personal gain of the elites in charge. His argument differs from Burger's in its focus on the secular political aspects of the individuals involved rather than on the religious aspects. He and others argue that a similar development occurred throughout the region where the Chavín religion was manifest.

At present, it is hard to determine whether one explanation is better than the other. Indeed, the real situation could involve all three explanations. Burger has argued that sites such as Pacopampa and Kuntur Wasi, although they exhibit artifacts and sculptures related to the site of Chavín de Huántar and were contemporary with it, nonetheless show clear evidence of continuities with the artifacts and architecture of the Initial Period settlements that bespeaks local lords incorporating Chavín ideas. The architectural similarities between Pallka and Chavín de Huántar are close but could be the result of local leaders' visiting the latter site and bringing back ideas. Alternatively, the similarities could be due to actual Chavín individuals. Until skeletal populations from these sites are subjected to isotopic analyses or other biological measures, the question of who was in charge of these sites will remain a topic of debate.

Finally, as with most religious cults, the influence of the sites and cults appears to have dwindled with time, in some places quickly, in others more slowly. Nevertheless, Chavín stands as the first example of a truly transformational religious belief in the Andes. It was transformational not only in its religious ideology and how it must have affected its believers but also in its technological aspects. Its emergence also coincides with the appearance of marked social differences among individuals. The portable art that is such an important aspect of the religion played a significant role in its dispersal, and the use of metals and textiles with its symbols reflected a new means of displaying those symbols by an emerging elite. This practice continued through subsequent periods.

This influence of Chavín was developing in the north as the cultures of Chiripa and Pukara were emerging on the Altiplano (see chapter 5). While those cultures continued to evolve in that region, new cultures were emerging from the Chavín-related cultures in the central, north-central, and north coastal and highland regions. This set the stage for the emergence of the first truly large-scale complex societies, the Moche in the north and Tiwanaku in the south.

7

ART AND POWER
The Early Intermediate Period

As the influence of the Chavín religion waned during the period after 200 B.C.E., cultures in the area began to develop more individuality in politics, art, and religion. Continuities to earlier artistic traditions continued, and new designs and production techniques appeared. Powerful leaders emerged based on both religion and politics. Many researchers argue the first true states appeared during this time: the Moche on the north coast and Tiwanaku on the Altiplano. A complex society also appeared on the south coast with the Nasca. Warfare became much more commonplace in many regions, which is reflected in increasing fortifications, skeletal evidence, and warrior motifs on ceramics.

This period is especially unique for the exceptional art that appeared in several of the cultures. The Moche on the north coast created some of the most beautiful ceramics and metalwork ever to have existed in South America, or elsewhere, for that matter (figure 7.2 and plate 4). The contemporary Nasca culture on the south coast also developed exceptional ceramics and continued a sophisticated textile tradition begun by the earlier Paracas culture. The famous Nazca *geoglyphs* date to this period. Specialists today marvel at the skill and sophistication of these works of art. It is no wonder that Wendell Bennett and Junius Bird (1965) choose to call this time frame the Mastercraftsman Period.

THE NORTH COAST

Few settlements or significant public architecture, except Caballo Muerto, have been identified that date to the Early Horizon in this region. Some wealthy individuals' graves have been found, but they are few and far between, suggesting that there was a lack of centralized authorities during this period. The rate of cultural evolution began to pick up starting around 400 B.C.E., resulting in the emergence of the Moche around 100 C.E., the first society that many feel was a state-level polity (but see Quilter and Koons 2012 for a critique).

What happened in those intervening years? The traditional view is that two cultural entities, Salinar and Gallinazo, preceded the Moche and ultimately developed into them. These entities are based on different ceramic styles present during this five-hundred-year period in the region from the Santa River to the Chicama River. Whereas early views had Salinar dated slightly earlier than Gallinazo, more recent work has suggested a contemporaneity between them, and between Gallinazo and Moche (Bawden 1996, 2004). Indeed, Garth Bawden (1996) notes that these two ceramic styles represent material manifestations of groups that shared much in their basic ways of life.

With the disappearance of the Chavín religion in this region, north-coast cultures experienced a serious

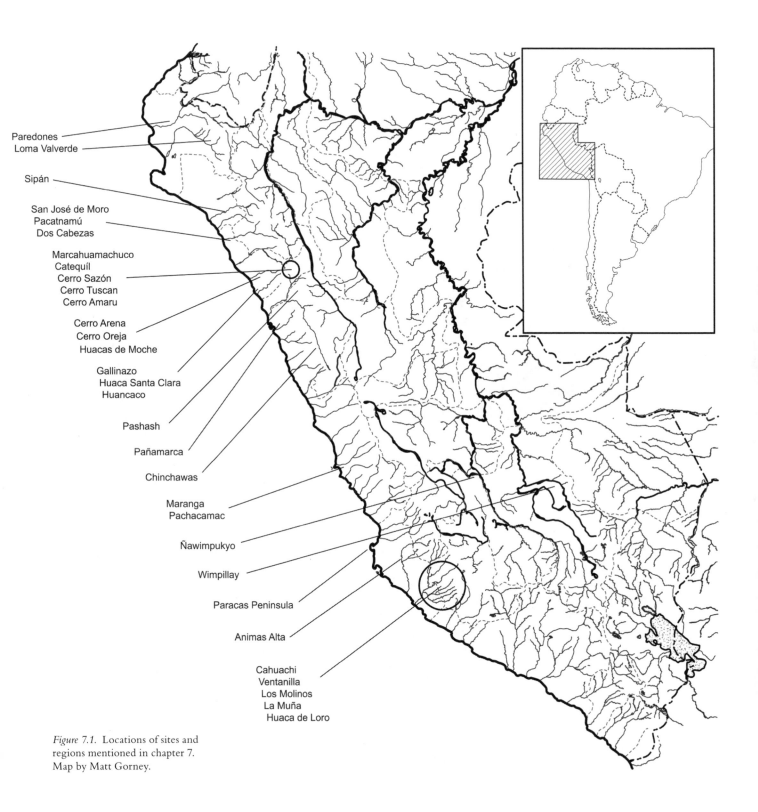

Paredones
Loma Valverde

Sipán

San José de Moro
Pacatnamú
Dos Cabezas

Marcahuamachuco
Catequíl
Cerro Sazón
Cerro Tuscan
Cerro Amaru

Cerro Arena
Cerro Oreja
Huacas de Moche

Gallinazo
Huaca Santa Clara
Huancaco

Pashash

Pañamarca

Chinchawas

Maranga
Pachacamac

Ñawimpukyo

Wimpillay

Paracas Peninsula

Animas Alta

Cahuachi
Ventanilla
Los Molinos
La Muña
Huaca de Loro

Figure 7.1. Locations of sites and regions mentioned in chapter 7. Map by Matt Gorney.

Figure 7.2. Moche fine-line stirrup-spout vessel with warrior figure. Printed by permission, copyright The Metropolitan Museum of Art. Art Resource, New York.

disruption in their way of life. This resulted in new ceramic styles and a dramatic drop in interregional trade, possibly resulting from the reduction of the open communication routes engendered by the Chavín religion. This in turn gave way to more suspicions and conflicts among communities. That the number of conflicts was increasing is indicated by the widespread development of fortified settlements in defensible locations, characteristic of the early part of this period.

In the Moche Valley, the site of Cerro Arena, located on a low ridge overlooking the valley on the south side of the river, became the largest site, with over 2,000 structures (Brennan 1980). Breaking with the earlier tradition seen at Caballo Muerto, there are no pyramid mounds at the site. In fact, there is little evidence of any marked social differentiation, public ritual spaces, or administrative buildings, although

some larger residences near the center of town have been interpreted as being higher status. Significantly, the site does represent a larger settlement grouped together in an urban kind of settlement, a pattern that became more typical of sites on the north coast in later times.

The evidence from the Salinar sites argues that there was no authority strong enough to motivate the population to build large structures. In Gallinazo sites dating to this early time, there is evidence of changes occurring that reflect the emergence of a new elite group. First, an elite pottery style appeared that was decorated using the resist or negative-painting technique, in which a flame-resistant material is placed on a pot and then colored after firing (plate 3). Corporate architecture also reappeared (if it had really disappeared!), and a more dispersed settlement pattern is seen, reflecting a greater security for the population. Canals and fields were greatly expanded as well (Bawden 1996).

In the Virú Valley, the Gallinazo Group of some 30,000 structures is located on the coastal plain and must have housed a very large population. A series of platforms of ritual importance support the idea of a stronger elite, and rich burials near these platforms provide evidence for such a group of high-status individuals. Other Gallinazo platforms throughout the valley mark the emergence of authorities able to control the labor of the farmers, and the appearance of platforms built in sections, a technique that becomes more common with the Moche, argues for some kind of labor tax emerging.

In the Moche Valley, the site of Cerro Arena was abandoned, and the locus of political authority apparently moved upvalley to the site of Cerro Oreja. Cerro Oreja, located near the place where the valley begins to expand after leaving the Andean foothills, is located near the intakes for the major irrigation canals in the valley. It was a large settlement, extending along the river terraces for several kilometers, and was built on a series of terraced platforms rising up the hillside. Like Cerro Arena, the site had no monumental architecture, suggesting perhaps that elites had not emerged here as in the Virú Valley.

A study of the bone chemistry of burials from Cerro Oreja suggests that it was during Gallinazo times that the shift to a more intensive use of maize began (Lambert et al. 2012). Maize is a more storable food that can be used in exchange as well as being a highly nutritious food. It has high water requirements, thus needing significant irrigation. The location of Cerro Oreja near the intakes for major Moche Valley canals is in keeping with the possible increased water needs of this crop at this time.

Gallinazo occupations are also evident in the valleys north of Chicama, even as far as the upper Piura drainage. The sites of Paredones in the La Leche Valley and Loma Valverde in the Piura have Gallinazo or, in the case of the upper Piura, Vicús pottery, which closely resembles the Gallinazo ceramics. Platform mounds at Loma Valverde were built using the same techniques seen at sites farther south.

The evidence from many of these valleys during the 200 B.C.E.–100 C.E. period supports the idea of the emergence of local authorities in each valley directing the irrigation and interaction of the citizenry of that valley, or part of a valley. Exchange between coastal and inland communities continued, and there must have been interactions with highland groups as well. However, at this time there is no evidence for multivalley political unification (but see Fogel 1993).

Moche Culture: Issues of Identification

Moche studies have a long history, from the beginning of the colonial era to the present (Castillo Butters and Quilter 2010; Quilter and Koons 2012). Serious studies began in the early twentieth century, when Max Uhle divided the north coast sequence into Chimú and pre-Chimú phases. In the 1930s, Rafael Larco Hoyle, a Peruvian hacienda owner who lived and worked along the north coast, made widespread and detailed studies of the Moche occupations. He defined the Moche as a relatively uniform culture that originated in the Moche Valley and subsequently spread out north and south by conquest. He saw the Moche as a highly centralized polity

with rulers who controlled the state via coercion and religious activities. According to this traditional view, they supplanted the existing Gallinazo cultures and formed a state-level society that lasted into the middle centuries of the first millennium C.E.

Larco Hoyle (1948) devised the five-phase ceramic chronological scheme that is still used today. This scheme is based on changes in the stirrup-spout libation vessels that form one of the most common Moche ceramic types (figure 7.2). Larco Hoyle notes that the shape and size of spouts and the shape and proportions of the spout and vessel body evolved through time. The scheme is based on a *seriation*, an ordering of vessels in which time is considered the main variable responsible for the similarities and differences among vessels. In other words, the more similar two vessels are, the closer in time they were made. Larco Hoyle defined phases I–V, from earliest to latest. In addition to the form of such vessels, the decorative techniques also changed, from thick-line drawings in Moche I–II to fine-line ones in phases III–IV to complex, crowded imagery in Moche V (Bawden 1996).

As a result of the explosion of research since Larco Hoyle's time, we now know that both the seriation and the concept of the Moche as a uniform state are oversimplified views. Unfortunately, the five ceramic phases are only beginning to be verified using radiocarbon dating, and the chronological placement of each phase holds best only for the Chicama and Moche valleys (table 7.1). There is general agreement that for those two valleys, and for others located to the south, phases I–II represent the emergence of the Moche polity, phases III–IV represent the florescence and expansion of the influence of the polity to other regions, and phase V reflects the transformation of the polity into something else. Even this, however, is being called into question by late dates for Moche IV ceramics from the Huacas de Moche (Lockard 2009; see chapter 8).

Table 7.1 reflects the current view held by most Moche scholars that there was no monolithic Moche polity that included all the north-coast valleys where Moche culture is seen in ceramic, textiles, and archi-

Table 7.1. Phase relationships for the Moche occupations

Dates (cal C.E.)	Southern Moche valleys (Chicama, Moche, Virú, Santa, and Nepeña)	Northern Moche valleys (Lambayeque, Zaña, and Jequetepeque)
800	Pre-Chimú/Casma	Transitional
600–800	Moche IV and V	Late Moche
500–600	Moche IV	Middle Moche
300–500	Moche III	Middle Moche
200–300	Moche II	Early Moche
100–200	Moche I	Early Moche

Source: Based on Chapdelaine 2010.

tecture. Instead, the Southern Moche State, as it is often called, included the valleys from Chicama in the north to Nepeña in the south. The Northern Moche were a set of autonomous polities that existed in each valley, connected by a common set of religious beliefs, material culture, and political developments (Chapdelaine 2010). What relationship existed between the two is only now being worked out.

As a result of the technological achievements of the Moche, plus the detailed scenes on their pottery and building murals, we know much more about them than about other societies. As a preliterate culture, ultimately all we know about them comes from archaeology, but the pottery decorations are so explicit and detailed with regard to the concepts and even individuals portrayed that we can understand a great deal about the Moche, such as their clothing, buildings, subsistence and artisanal practices, religious beliefs and deities, and even what individual people looked like. As such, it is important to discuss Moche ceramics before delving into their general cultural development.

Moche ceramics come in an enormous variety of forms and decorative techniques, but several stand out for their utility to archaeologists. The stirrup-spout libation vessels are one notable kind, as are vessels in the shapes of animals, plants, humans, and landscapes (see figure 7.2). These can be painted in several colors or be plain. A distinctive decorative technique is fine-line painting, in which scenes were painted on the vessels using a thin brush. Many of the ritual scenes to be discussed next were done in this technique, which

largely date to phases III and IV. Finally, there is a whole class of ceramics called portrait vessels (plate 4) because they depict human heads in very realistic detail, including defects such as blindness and scars. Researchers have suggested that such vessels, which are also restricted to phases III and IV and to the southern valleys of Chicama, Moche, and Virú, are actual depictions of important members of Moche society, and some individuals were portrayed during adolescence, during young adulthood, during adulthood, and as prisoners about to be sacrificed (Donnan 2001).

Following the work of Elizabeth Benson, Christopher Donnan, Donna McClelland, Walter Alva, and others, Bawden (1996) notes that the scenes of Moche ceramics are first and foremost an aspect of political ideology, a specific display of the religious beliefs that served the political purposes of the individuals responsible for the pottery. This ideology was based on beliefs that considerably predate the Moche because figures such as the "Decapitator" are known from the Initial Period Cupisnique ceramics of the same region (Cordy-Collins 1992). The religion was based on the ancient belief that shamans could control supernatural forces, moving between the physical and supernatural worlds, often with the aid of animal media. A critical ritual associated with the shamanistic concept was sacrifice, both of animals and humans. Through time, emerging Moche leaders developed political power through their control over such rituals; shamans became priests of the religion.

Donnan (1976, 1978, 2010) notes that much of the ceramic iconography can be interpreted as scenes based on the religious beliefs of the Moche and can be grouped into a small number of themes, probably particular beliefs and the rituals associated with them. Perhaps the most important is the Sacrifice Ritual (figure 7.3). In this scene, sacrificial victims have their throats slit and their blood collected, which is then transferred via other individuals to a powerful and richly dressed individual who drinks the blood. The particular clothes and accessories that the different figures display mark their roles in this ritual. Another theme commonly portrayed is the Warrior Narrative, in which elaborately dressed warriors first parade to war, engage in hand-to-hand combat to capture sacrificial victims, strip the victims of their clothes and weapons, and then parade them naked back to the temples where they will be sacrificed, carrying the victims' weapon bundles on their war clubs. Other themes, such as hunting and burials, denote other aspects of the religious beliefs of the Moche.

For much of the twentieth century, there was a question of whether these scenes on Moche pottery reflected actual events or simply supernatural scenes.

Starting in the late 1980s, archaeological evidence was uncovered that dramatically indicated the former is correct. Tombs discovered by looters but then excavated by archaeologists at Sipán in the Lambayeque Valley recovered individuals who clearly could be linked to figures in the Sacrifice Ritual by their clothing and accessories (Alva and Donnan 1993). Other discoveries at the site of San José de Moro in the Jequetepeque Valley by Jaime Castillo Butters (Donnan and Castillo Butters 1992) recovered others, including the female attendant in the scene.

On the basis of archaeological and iconographic research, Donnan (2010) has defined a Moche state religion that was based on shared symbols that were found on architecture and ceramics, and in burials of important Moche figures, such as those at Sipán. The main symbols of this religion were the weapons bundle, the eared serpent, and the spider decapitator, which together represent over 60 percent of Moche artistic expressions from the Nepeña Valley in the south to the upper Piura Valley in the north. The uniformity of the religion is reflected both in the easy identification of these symbols and in the uniform use of the clothes of the major figures. Clearly,

Figure 7.3. Moche sacrifice ritual theme. From Donnan 2010, figure 1. Drawing by Donna McClelland. Christopher Donnan and Donna McClelland Moche Archive. Courtesy of Dumbarton Oaks Research Library and Collection, Washington, DC.

this religion was shared among the elites in all of the valleys, and the evidence for the Sacrifice Ritual indicates it was commonly practiced by the warrior-priests who ruled in these valleys.

Unlike in the Nazca region (discussed later in the chapter), textiles are not well preserved on the north coast; hence, fewer examples are known. Still, like the ceramics, the textiles are very consistent with regard to their structure (Donnan and Donnan 1997), and they are largely of cotton, with only the tapestries using wool. This suggests to Christopher and Sharon Donnan that camelid wool, probably from the highlands, was a more valued material due to its scarcity. A collection of 181 textile fragments from Pacatnamú contained examples of several kinds of clothing that were represented on the ceramics, including shirts, loincloths, headcloths, and bags. This information, like the burials from Sipán, indicates that the Moche pottery tradition was based in reality rather than myth.

Moche Culture: Origins and Evolution

We can now return to the discussion of Moche origins. Around 100 C.E., the site of Huacas de Moche,[1] on the south side of the Moche River, emerged as the main settlement of the Moche polity (figure 7.4; Uceda 2010). The site was founded during the Moche I–II phases, but it expanded greatly at the beginning of phase III. The site of Huacas de Moche is the only major Moche site in the Moche Valley at this time, indicating a centralization of power by the rulers who lived there. Bawden (1996) argues that what appeared at this time was the political ideology that is manifest in the Moche III–IV highly decorated ceramics, an ideology that was espoused by a new elite that gained authority through its use. This ideology spread through the Moche and Chicama valleys early in the fourth century C.E., probably by peaceful means because there is little evidence of fortifications at this time.

The site is dominated by two main pyramids, the Huaca del Sol and the Huaca de la Luna (Temple of the Sun and Temple of the Moon, respectively, names given by the Spaniards). Huaca del Sol was originally cross-shaped, 380 by 160 m, and at least 40 m tall (figure 7.5). It is estimated that 143 million adobe bricks were used in its construction. Like the earlier Gallinazo platforms in the Virú Valley, the Huaca del Sol was made in sections that were unbonded, that is, had no interdigitating of the rows to strengthen them. The bricks in different sections have over one hundred distinctive maker's marks, suggesting that they were made and put in place by certain social groups as part of a mit'a-like tax system (Hastings and Moseley 1975). Only a part of the structure remains, due to the Spaniards diverting the Moche River to erode it and expose the treasures that may have lain inside. Excavations on the mound have revealed that it had funerary and administrative functions because both tombs and evidence of feasting have been found on its summit structures (Chapdelaine 2006).

The Huaca de la Luna, in contrast, is a large structure that probably had multiple functions (figure 7.6; Chapdelaine 2006; Uceda 2001). Certainly it was a temple where Moche priests conducted important rituals of sacrifice, but it also might have served administrative functions and possibly as a residence (Uceda 2010). The structure is a series of rooms and corridors adorned by elaborate polychrome murals of the spider decapitator and other supernatural representations. It was built in five major phases, each simply larger versions of the previous one. Santiago Uceda (2001) suggests the rebuilding may have been part of ancestor worship, with important priests buried and a new temple built above them.

Evidence of sacrifices at the Huaca de la Luna was identified by Steven Bourget (2001), who discovered corpses of males splayed in a courtyard of the temple in mud that must have originated in an El Niño downpour. Most showed evidence of battle injuries, both previous and recent, and many had their throats slit in ways that are reflected in the Sacrifice Ritual (Verano 2001). Their sacrifice during El Niño events suggests the reasons for the ceremony.

Research at the Huacas de Moche since 1995 has indicated that the core of the center was at least 60 ha in size, with nearby associated areas of food and resource

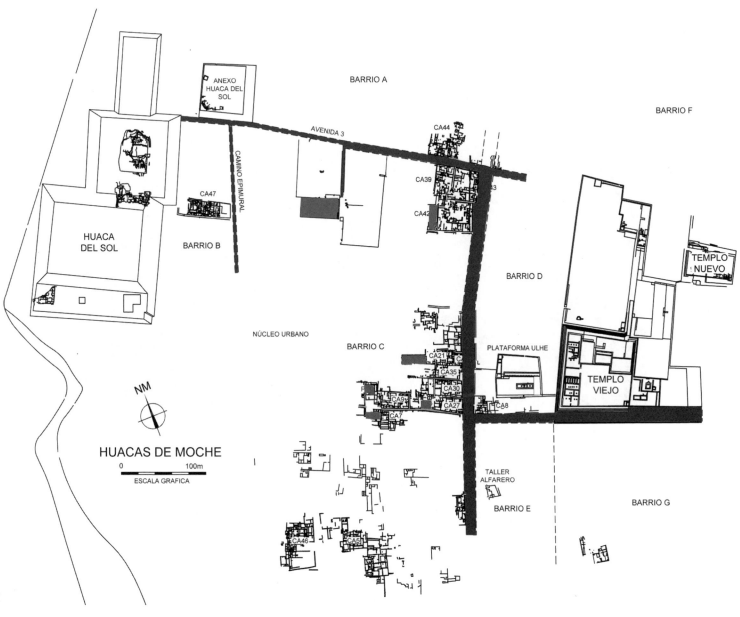

Figure 7.4. Map of Huacas de Moche site. Image provided by Proyecto Huaca de la Luna.

producers extending out to a radius of about 10 km. Between the two huacas was a large settlement of elite residences and workplaces of the artisans who toiled to produce rich goods for them and others outside the set-tlement. Workshops for metal, ceramic production, weaving, and lapidary activities were all present; however, farming equipment was lacking (Chapdelaine 2009). Claude Chapdelaine (2006) identifies an upper

Figure 7.5. Huaca del Sol. Photo by author.

class and middle class there, based on the size of the compounds, the quality of their construction, and other aspects. Burials support a three-tier social hierarchy as well (Donnan and Mackey 1978).

Santiago Uceda (2010) suggests that the roles that the two main structures at Huacas de Moche played changed through time, as did the relationship between the urban core inhabitants and the ruling elite at the site. In 100–600 C.E., he believes, the Old Temple at Huaca de la Luna (the part previously described) was the primary temple at the site because the Huaca del Sol was much smaller at that time. Workshops were controlled by the rulers, who might have lived at the Old Temple and directed the rituals of sacrifice there. Craft production was mainly for these rituals, and not part of a wider distribution

network. After a mega-El Niño around 600 C.E., however, this system fell apart, and a new secular urban elite developed to challenge the power of the priests. At that time, the workshops became controlled by the urban elite for their own uses. The Old Temple was abandoned, and a New Temple, much reduced in size, was constructed to the northeast of the Old Temple. The Huaca del Sol became the major temple at this time and was greatly expanded to reflect that new authority.

Because the two structures at Huacas de Moche represent the largest labor investment of any Moche site, plus the evidence for high-status residents there, the site is thought to have been the capital of the Moche polity starting in phase III. Under the direction of its rulers, agricultural fields and canals were expanded and many

Figure 7.6. Huaca de la Luna. Photo by author.

rural villages were founded to produce the surpluses needed for the projects of the polity (Billman 2010).

Many of the same traits seen in the Moche Valley are mirrored in developments in the Chicama Valley, its larger neighbor to the north. The sites of Huaca El Brujo and Huaca Cao Viejo along the coast are seen as major settlements where the Moche rulers lived. Cao Viejo has a series of spectacular friezes (figure 7.7), some depicting the early stages of the Sacrifice Ritual. Research at the Huaca de la Luna has identified a similar pair of friezes there (Uceda 2010). There are smaller sites with platforms upvalley from the coast, suggesting to Régulo Franco Jordan, Cesar Gálvez Mora, and Segundo Vásquez Sánchez (2010) that a tiered hierarchy of sites and social positions was present in the valley at this time. Lesser elites lived in the upvalley centers and mediated trade between their regions and more distant locations such as the Cajamarca basin in the highlands to the east.

According to many scholars, the polity that developed based at Huacas de Moche began an active conquest of the valleys to the south (Chapdelaine 2010). This conquest occurred in 300–600 C.E. and marked the high point of Moche influence. In the Virú Valley, that this was a conquest and not just cultural influence is indicated by three changes (Bawden 1996): (1) a shift in agricultural production from the north side of the river to the south, (2) the introduction of Moche lords into the valley to oversee its activities, and (3) the abrupt appearance of Moche ceramics and platforms that symbolized their power over the local inhabitants. A tomb of a warrior priest, much like the ones found at Sipán, indicates these Moche lords had all the trappings of Moche authority.

Recent research in the valley, however, now questions whether it was subjugated or incorporated (Bourget 2010; Millaire 2010). At both the platform sites of Huaca Santa Clara and Huancaco, there are

Figure 7.7. Huaca Cao wall motifs. Photo by author.

Gallinazo occupations dating later than the Moche occupations in the valley. Christopher Millaire (2010) argues these sites were like city-states, controlling their own hinterlands but independent. They were conquered by the Moche, but they were administered through indirect rule, so that the local elites continued to direct the actions of the locals but for the benefit of their Moche overlords.

In valleys farther south, such as Santa, the Moche conquest was clearly direct and led to the major reorganization of the conquered settlements to accommodate the tribute requirements of the conquerors (Chapdelaine 2010; Wilson 1988). These doubtless included food and materials for the construction of the temples at Huacas de Moche. More than that, Chapdelaine argues that there was probably a massive immigration of Moche colonists during Moche IV, with the relocation of the local inhabitants to the middle and upper reaches of the valley. A major ceremonial site was constructed in the lower Nepeña Valley at the site of Pañamarca. This site had several large murals with typical Moche warrior figures on them, the largest of which was a depiction of the Sacrifice Ritual. It is significant that there are no major Moche sites in the middle- or upper-valley re-

gion, where the ceramics suggest the presence of groups from the Recuay culture of the adjacent Callejón de Huaylas (Daggett 1984). Scenes on Moche ceramics showing Moche and Recuay warriors in combat indicate that there was conflict between these two powerful groups, conflicts that may have played out in the frontier zones such as the middle Nepeña Valley. South of Nepeña, there was only a minor Moche presence, suggesting these were places founded to maintain a frontier against groups from farther east and south but also to act as places where trade goods could enter the Moche realm (Makowski 2010).

In sum, the evidence from the valleys south of Moche suggest that the rulers of Huacas de Moche sent military groups to subjugate the local inhabitants, but how they ruled these provinces after their conquest varied from indirect rule in Virú to direct rule in the Santa and lower Nepeña valleys.

In the valleys north of Chicama, the situation was quite different, and there is debate as to the nature of the Moche presence in this region. As seen in table 7.1, the five-phase sequence of ceramics does not work in the valleys here. The early view saw Moche culture in this region as being the result of its conquest by Moche rulers centered at Huacas de Moche. Now it is generally accepted that this was not the case (Bawden 1996). There is evidence from the upper Piura Valley of a Moche I–II presence there during the time when the Moche polity in the core area was just forming. Goldwork from burials and ceramics from this region closely resemble those in the region farther south. In contrast, the area between the Jequetepeque and La Leche valleys shows little evidence of such occupations. Moreover, in contrast to the southern Moche region (south of Moche Valley proper), there is no abrupt replacement of Gallinazo ceramics by Moche ceramics in this region; indeed, the Gallinazo style pottery persists in the northern valleys throughout the rest of the Early Intermediate Period at some sites, indicating that the groups using them did not accept the Moche ideology, either passively or through coercion. Other aspects of culture also remained the same, such as the kinds of houses and burials seen in both.

It is only in the elite art that differences exist between Gallinazo and Moche ceramics. The exquisite ceramics of the Moche, with their detailed scenes of religious beliefs, are associated with elite burials and power centers, not the rural villages. They represent the ideology of power and a set of beliefs associated with the manifestation of that power. In contrast, Gallinazo elite wares have much less decoration, yet they continued to be made at centers where the Gallinazo leaders lived and ruled. Thus, the emergence of the Moche political ideology that was seen in the Moche and Chicama valleys during Moche I–II continued to expand northward during subsequent centuries of this period. Some local elites apparently adopted the Moche political ideology while others did not. The tombs at Sipán reflect a local group that did accept it; it is an interesting fact that these tombs far surpass in richness any tombs found farther south. Although this could be a function of the fact no other unlooted tombs have been found elsewhere, it could also reflect a situation in which local leaders in the northern valleys were at least as powerful (as measured in wealth) as the rulers who lived at Huacas de Moche.

Evidence from the upper Piura Valley also suggests that local elites adopted Moche ideology for their own uses. A large quantity of metal objects in the Moche style looted from cemeteries in the Loma Negra region were made using local technological processes but display Moche concepts. The iconography is subtly different from that of the southern region as well, indicating a local adoption of certain beliefs but not others. The use of different colors of paint on local ceramics also supports this idea (Bawden 1996, 2004).

Evidence from the Jequetepeque Valley shows a much different kind of political development (Castillo Butters 2010). During Gallinazo times there, a political authority developed that was based at Dos Cabezas and that unified the lower-valley region. As Moche culture arrived in the valley, control spread to the southern part of the valley. The expanding populations were accommodated through the construction of a major irrigation canal that opened new fields for exploitation. Finally, during the later part of the sequence, corresponding to Moche IV farther south, the entire Chamán River to the north was opened up to exploitation by the construction of four canals that had their intakes in the Jequetepeque Valley, all close together. The groups living along each canal developed their own elite centers but were integrated by common Moche rituals and elite burials conducted at sites such as San José de Moro (Dillehay 2001) and Pacatnamú (Donnan and Cock 1997). That there was conflict among these elites is suggested by the presence of fortresses near the major centers on each canal. Castillo Butters argues that these groups occasionally came together for common purposes, such as defense against outside aggression, but then fractured. The Moche elites in this valley developed what he calls an opportunistic state system. Similar arguments might be made for what happened in the Zaña, Lambayeque, and La Leche valleys farther north. Clearly, there was no conquest of these northern regions by a military force operating out of the Moche-Chicama region (Shimada 2010).

The emergence of the Moche rulers in the fourth century reflects the appearance of a new and more powerful ruling class based on hereditary rule. According to Bawden (2004, 122) and others (e.g., Donnan 2010), they were able to accomplish this by grounding their justification to rule in ancient myths and cultural practices of the region, as well as manifesting the roles of the major mythological characters in reality. The rulers took the roles of powerful figures that dated back to Initial Period iconography and played out the rituals for the public good. By virtue of conducting the rituals, they gained the power of the supernatural forces they were supplicating. Apparently, the Moche lower classes were accepting of this new power arrangement because it was maintained for three centuries.

In like fashion, Quilter and Koons (2012) have challenged the concept that the Moche were a state-level society, based on the kinds of evidence just provided. In their view, the Moche do not fit the criteria that researchers have used for defining statehood. They suggest that "Moche was a religious system that realigned the political economies and social relations of the North Coast" (ibid., 138). They argue that even in the southern Moche region, the valleys were never truly incorporated into a hierarchical state. As more evidence is uncovered, the true nature of Moche sociopolitical organization, it is hoped, will emerge.

In the seventh century, things began to unravel for the ruling elite of Moche society. A series of devastating El Niños have been documented for this period, and influence from the Wari polity, which had spread both to the adjacent highlands and along the coast from the south, spelled doom for the status quo. The southern valleys became independent, although how is uncertain, and the political power that was centered at the site of Huacas de Moche disappeared. Perhaps the rulers who had tied their power to the supernatural forces that had been so benign were unable to maintain their control when environmental and social crises appeared. The multiple sacrifices of warriors at the Huaca de la Luna might reflect the priests' efforts at supplicating the gods. When the powerful lords at Huacas de Moche fell, the alliances on which the lords in the northern valleys based at least some of their authority were shaken as well. The Moche civilization was nearly at an end. (These dramatic changes are discussed further in chapter 8.)

THE CENTRAL COAST

The Early Intermediate Period occupations of the region between Nepeña and Ica are relatively poorly known, even though it was the early focus of research in Peru. Although much is known about the earlier societies of this region, much less has been discussed about the cultures of this period. The general pottery style of this time and region of the central coast is called Lima, and it developed out of the post-Chavinoid styles of the area. In terms of sociopolitical architecture, pyramid mounds were still present, and one site, Maranga in the Lurín Valley, is considered to have been a ceremonial center for the region (Shimada 1991). It has around a dozen mounds, of which the largest was the Huaca San Marcos, which measured 300 by 120 by 30 m. Sites in other valleys indicate similar population centers (Patterson and Lanning 1964; Willey 1971), but there is little evidence that a multiregional polity existed at this time.

Note that the site of Pachacamac in the Lurín Valley, which would rise to major religious and political significance in the Middle Horizon, was founded at this time; a small temple and other structures date to this period (Shimada 1991). Whether the oracle that existed during Inka times, and that is presumed to have been the source of the power of the site in the Middle Horizon, was functioning at this time is uncertain.

THE SOUTH COAST

The Nasca culture occupied the arid coastal valleys from Cañete to Acarí, and possibly further south. It developed out of the preceding Paracas culture of the Early Horizon, but it never achieved a level of complexity comparable to its contemporaries, the Moche. It did rival the Moche in the excellence of its

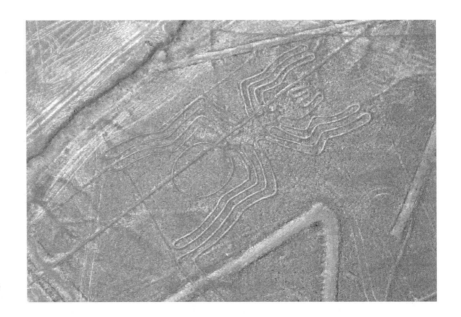

Figure 7.8. Nazca biomorph. Photo courtesy of John Henderson.

ceramics, and the geoglyphs the Nasca left on the pampa floors still intrigue both scholars and the public (figure 7.8).

Regarding chronology, this region is where the Rowe stylistic seriation that forms the basis for the period system used in this book was developed. Because of this detailed ceramic chronology, based on fine differences in pottery styles, scholars usually refer more to the particular phases than to actual calendrical dates. Part of this practice comes from the difficulty in comparing the phases across valleys where dates may be different (for a discussion of these issues, see Silverman and Proulx 2002, 37). Nonetheless, to facilitate some sense of temporal development, phase numbers can be equated to dates, although it is best to lump phases into general periods of time until finer radiocarbon chronologies for the individual phases are determined. The ceramics in question began in the Early Horizon and extended to the end of the Early Intermediate Period. I follow here Donald Proulx's (2008) dates for Nasca and Anne Paul's (1991) dates for Paracas/Ocucaje, all uncalibrated (table 7.2), and list them with general period terms and the ceramic descriptors associated with them.[2] The equivalent dates for Ocucaje 10 and Nasca 1 in table 7.2 reflect the uncertainties regarding the exact dates for these periods.

Paracas

To understand the development of the Nasca, we must return briefly to the Early Horizon Paracas culture. The term *Paracas* refers to two distinct cultures, called Paracas Cavernas and Paracas Necropolis (sometimes known as Topará); to a textile style; to a ceramic style; and to a geographical region centered on the Paracas Peninsula. As mentioned in chapter 6, the Chavín cult was influential in the early phases of the Paracas ceramic-style sequence, although it disappeared entirely by the end (Menzel and Dawson 1964). Paracas Cavernas pottery is decorated with post-fired resin paint, meaning that the decoration was applied after the pot was fired, and was made with pigments in some kind of vegetable matrix so they adhered to the surface of the pot. The most common forms are bowls, double-spout bottles, spout and head bottles, ollas, and collared jars decorated in up to five colors. In contrast, Topará ceramics are thin-walled and undecorated, but very well made.

Table 7.2. Phase relationships and dates for south coast occupations

Phase	Date	Period	Descriptor[a]
Nasca 9	Post–700 C.E.	Middle Horizon	Chakipampa
Nasca 8	650–700 C.E.		Disjunctive, Huaca de Loro
Nasca 6–7	500–650 C.E.	Late Nasca	Proliferous
Nasca 5	400–500 C.E.	Middle Nasca	Transitional
Nasca 2–4	1–400 C.E.	Early Nasca	Monumental
Nasca 1	100 B.C.E.–1 C.E.		Proto-Nasca
Ocucaje 10	100 B.C.E.–1 C.E.		
Ocucaje 9	200–100 B.C.E.		
Ocucaje 8	300–200 B.C.E.		
Ocucaje 7	400–300 B.C.E.		Chavín influence ends
Ocucaje 6	475–400 B.C.E.		
Ocucaje 5	525–475 B.C.E.		
Ocucaje 4	600–525 B.C.E.		
Ocucaje 3	700–600 B.C.E.	Early Horizon	Chavín influence begins

[a] *Descriptor* is a term used in the literature that reflects changes in both the figures that are painted on the vessels and their complexity (Proulx 2008).

In 1925, Julio Tello and his colleague Toribio Mejía Xesspe (Tello 1959; Tello and Mejía Xesspe 1979) began work on the desolate Paracas Peninsula, where they discovered a series of cemeteries and occupation zones containing Paracas Cavernas and Topará ceramics. At the Wari Kayan Necropolis, they discovered a large subterranean tomb with 429 mummy bundles. These were high-status individuals who were wrapped in elaborate embroidered textiles and placed in large open baskets. The textiles, some of which measure a square meter or more, were made of cotton and alpaca wool, and the designs are often so complex and detailed that they amaze modern weavers by their sophistication (plate 5A; see Paul 1990 for other colored examples). Topará ceramics are associated with the Necropolis burials, which are found more commonly in the two valleys to the north of the peninsula. The burials at Paracas are distinct from those of the earlier Paracas Cavernas people, who buried their dead in a different fashion and with undecorated textiles. Scholars consider the two to have been distinct cultures that both buried their dead on the peninsula, probably for religious reasons.

The Topará people also lived in the upper Ica Valley to the south, whereas the Paracas people lived in the middle and lower valleys. Cavernas-related pottery in Ica is known as Ocucaje, and it is also found in the northern valleys of the Río Grande de Nazca drainage. People in these valleys lived in small farming communities along the rivers, although some ceremonial sites are known. The site of Animas Alta in the Ica valley is said to have been a regional center, with thirteen mounds, storage facilities, and a plaza. One of the mounds had an elaborate frieze with anthropomorphic figures, including the Oculate Being on an interior wall (Massey 1991).

On this basis, Proulx (2008) argues that Paracas society was organized at a chiefdom level, with powerful shamans as leaders or sharing power with political leaders. The evidence, however, does not strongly support such a level of complexity, except for the elaborate burials of the Paracas Necropolis and the presence of some gold objects in the Ocucaje 10 burials (Silverman 2002). I agree with Silverman (2002) that there is no good evidence of ranking at the end of the Paracas period and that these societies were still organized along tribal lines. The individuals buried with elaborate textiles or gold objects were perhaps important lineage or ayllu heads but lacking broader political and social authority.

Several traits that became more pronounced in later Nasca society also appear in Paracas. Trophy heads and trepanation (sometimes spelled trephination), the practice of cutting out a section of the skull wall, possibly to relieve pain or let evil spirits out, were both evident. Trophy-head taking, probably connected with agricultural fertility, was a common practice, and burials with ritual costume paraphernalia such as gold mouth masks indicate that individuals dressed up as supernatural figures during rituals. Several of the figures that are prominent in Nasca iconography also appear on the Paracas textiles. The use of ceramic musical instruments, panpipes, drums, and trumpets, is another trait recognized at Paracas sites (Silverman 2002).

Nasca

It is an unusual archaeological circumstance that the shift from Paracas/Ocucaje to Nasca ceramics is based on a single change: the switch from post-fired resin painting to slip painting. Slip painting is a process in which pigments in a clay solution (the slip) are placed on the pot, which is then fired; this bakes the color onto the pot. It is clear from the design elements on early Nasca pottery that it evolved from the late Paracas ceramics. The shift in decorative technique marks the official beginning of the Early Intermediate Period Nasca culture, but little else actually was modified. Nasca evolved from the Paracas culture with the basic way of life continuing unchanged. Early Nasca society was based on farming villages along the drainages in this region. Most settlements were small, although there was often a larger-than-usual village in each drainage or part of a drainage that might have been the residence of a more important person or family. Farming of typical Andean crops—maize, beans, manioc, and squash—provided the mainstay of the diet, and camelids and guinea pigs seem to have been the main protein sources. In contrast to their contemporaries farther north, ma-

rine resources were not as important to the Nasca, although they do turn up in domestic sites. Patrick Carmichael (1991; cited in Silverman and Proulx 2002) finds no Nasca sites along the ocean, so what marine resources were used must have been caught by fisherfolk who visited the ocean periodically.

After Nasca ceramics developed from the Paracas ones, they became increasingly complex in their decorations. There was quite a bit of innovation, and new mythical figures appeared. This probably is due to the emergence during this period of a cult at the site of Cahuachi.

In contrast to the ceramics, Nasca textiles actually became less impressive in their decorative elements through time. Few textiles are known from the first two phases; however, by Phase 3, textiles were less elaborate than the late Paracas textiles, even though this phase arguably represented a cultural high point of the society (plate 5, B and C). The focus was on needlework along the edges of the textiles, rather than covering the entire textile with design elements. Silverman (1993) and others suggest that this was due to a preference for ceramics as the cultural medium for iconographic representations. Ceramics could be more easily and quickly produced than the elaborate textiles, and the demand for such representations had reached the point where weaving could not keep up with it.

During Early Nasca times, the site of Cahuachi, located in the Nazca Valley, stands out in its uniqueness. This site consists of forty mounds of varying sizes and shapes, but very little evidence of permanent residents (figure 7.9). The mounds are scattered along the valley side in a place where water emerges in the Nazca River from underground sources. Helaine Silverman (1993), who has worked extensively at the site, argues that it was a true ceremonial center, probably a pilgrimage center where Nascans came for cyclical rituals associated with agriculture. The different kin groups from different areas constructed their own mound for their own rituals. They came and stayed long enough for the rituals and then returned home. Katharina Schreiber and Josué Lancho Rojas (2003) suggest that a small elite group might have lived there that were in charge of rituals at the largest temple. Several of the famous Nazca lines lead directly to Cahuachi, and some even line up with particular mounds there, suggesting specific relationships between the groups who built those mounds and the associated figures (Silverman 1993). The site was used for only a few centuries and was abandoned at the end of Phase 3. It became a massive cemetery for later cultures, which continued to believe it was a place of sacred power.

Nasca religion was very uniform across the Ica–Rio Grande de Nazca region during Phase 3, reflecting the widespread participation of the populations there in the cult at Cahuachi. Proulx (2008) notes that the Nascans believed in nature spirits rather than deities. The spirits were represented by animals and sea creatures, many of which were represented as geoglyphs. Ceremonies to appease these spirits were conducted by shamans or priests dressed to look like them. Consumption of hallucinogenics, particularly the San Pe-

dro cactus, was a part of these rituals, as was the playing of music on the panpipes, drums, and trumpets, found at the sites and seen on the ceramics.

As in Paracas times, the taking of trophy heads during conflicts was a common feature of Nasca society. These were prepared by removing the brains and cutting a hole through the forehead to attach a carrying string or band. The lips were pinned shut with thorns, perhaps to keep a malevolent spirit in. Proulx (2001) thinks trophy heads were part of agricultural fertility rites, to assure the successful growth of plants. Rituals associated with these beliefs probably occurred in individual villages because the discovery of such heads in burials is widespread, although not common.

Perhaps the most famous aspect of Nasca culture is the famous geoglyphs, found scattered on the dry pampas between the river valleys. The geoglyphs were made by scraping the dark stones off the surface of the desert, exposing the lighter soil beneath.

Figure 7.9. Cahuachi. Photo courtesy of Helaine Silverman.

They consist of two kinds: geometric shapes and biomorphs. The former are actually much more common and consist of lines, trapezoids, squares, and other rhomboids (figure 7.10). They can be large or small. The biomorphs, which number about forty, are larger than life, and include monkeys, killer whales, birds, a few plants, fish, and simple human figures (figure 7.8). These are the main figures in Nasca art and religion.

The meaning of the geoglyphs has been much discussed by both scientists and amateurs; the latter includes Erich von Däniken, who attributed them to extraterrestrials who used the lines as landing fields for their airships (for an excellent summary and exhaustive bibliography of the more reasonable explanations, see Silverman and Proulx 2002, 163–192). Maria Reiche, a pioneer in the study of the geoglyphs, thought they were astronomical; however, Anthony Aveni (2000), an astronomer with interest in ancient cultures, did a detailed study of the lines and figures and failed to find any significant alignments. He did find many mounds of stones with lines radiating out from them. He and Silverman (1990) suggest that these were ritual pathways between the villages and irrigation zones. Johan Reinhard (1988) argues that the lines were related to the worship of mountain deities that were the source of rainfall and irrigation water. Solid figures are often found pointing upvalley, suggesting a link to the mountains, the source of the precious irrigation water. David Johnson, an amateur geologist, and his colleagues (2006) have found some intriguing, although limited, evidence that some of the solid figures may point to underground aquifers as sources of water. If such were proven to be the case, it would indicate an impressive knowledge of geology by the ancient Nascans.

The geoglyphs were constructed and used over many centuries, even after the demise of Nasca culture (Clarkson 1990), and it is likely that they served

Figure 7.10. Nazca lines. Photo courtesy of John Henderson.

different purposes at different times. Although the amount of space they cover is impressive, 3.6 million m² (Moseley 2001, 202), it is probable that each individual glyph was constructed by a small group, maybe no more than a few related families, so the amount of work involved was actually quite small.

Following that line of discussion, we can ask, what kind of society was Nasca during the early period? There are two views. The first, championed by Silverman and Proulx (2002), states that the society that lived in the Ica and Rio Grande de Nazca drainages was organized as independent groups, ayllus or groups of ayllus, that had their own irrigation systems and fields and that were largely autonomous from other similar groups living around them. These groups built the ceremonial mounds at Cahuachi and conducted their own rituals there following a cycle that was probably similar to others around them. Some civic-ceremonial sites exist in each of these drainages that might have been secondary ritual centers. Silverman (1993) suggests that there might have been some form of paramount chieftaincy and that the position rotated among the different independent groups, much like a cargo system.

In her 1993 book on Cahuachi, Silverman notes that there might have been a political capital at the site of Ventilla that contrasted to the religious center of Cahuachi. Ventilla is located across the pampas to the north of Cahuachi and is linked to it by a major transpampa geoglyph. What role Ventilla played in intervalley politics is unclear, however, and Schreiber and Lancho Rojas (2003) note that the site is not as large as was originally estimated. Clearly, excavations are needed at this important site to determine what role it played in early Nasca society.

The other view is one stated by Markus Reindel and Johny Isla (1999; Isla and Reindel 2006), who claim Nasca was a state-level society based on their research in the Palpa tributary of the Rio Grande drainage. They see a first-order political capital at the site of Los Molinos, with secondary centers at other sites in the valley and tertiary settlements below them. They argue that there is sufficient differ-

entiation in the burials and material culture to say that different classes existed and that production was controlled by the elites at the centers.

Some of the disagreement between these two views is about what criteria define a state as opposed to a less complex sociopolitical level. Based on the information present, I agree with Silverman and Proulx (2002) and support the idea that Nasca society was simpler than a state. Although it is true that there was social differentiation in the architecture, burial patterns, and artifact production, none is marked enough to convince me that a true state-level society was operating. The lack of specialized production centers for ceramics, metallurgy, and textiles, as well as the lack of elite representations on the pottery supports this. If such data are discovered in the future, then this interpretation may change.

In the southern branches of the Rio Grande system, much less political complexity is evident, and so the issue of statehood is not pertinent. Only a few sites with what might be called civic-ceremonial architecture are evident, and the population densities were much lower. It is likely that the populations in these valleys also participated in the Nasca cult at Cahuachi because fine Nasca ceramics are found at sites throughout the region.

Around 300–400 C.E., significant changes occurred in the Nasca region. Perhaps most significant, the site of Cahuachi was abandoned as a ceremonial center, and the cult that used it must have declined in importance. Still, the Middle Nasca saw the greatest extent of geoglyph construction, and Silverman (1993) argues that ritual practices shifted from the ceremonies at Cahuachi to the use of the figures. The reasons for the collapse of Cahuachi are uncertain, but ritual overload of the system combined with stresses produced by emerging elites, drought, and flooding all have been put forward (Silverman and Proulx 2002).

Around 400 C.E., dramatic changes began to occur in the ceramics that continued until the end of the period. Heterogeneity among valleys in the ceramics suggests that the integrating influence of Cahuachi had declined and local potters were experimenting with new ideas. Human representations increase, including both naked female figures with elaborate tattoos on their bodies and male warrior figures. Richard Roark (1965) notes an increase in militaristic themes in general, which suggests warfare was becoming a more significant part of life. New forms and decorative elements increase, and during Late Nasca times, marked Moche influence appears in several ceramic features (Proulx 1994).

A significant new design element beginning in Nasca 5 is the male warrior figure holding a trophy head (plate 6A). These individuals are no longer dressed as spirits but are claiming power for themselves. This suggests elites are vying for individual power in their own regions at this time. Although there is variation in the burial practices and quantity of goods during Nasca 5, the appearance of very elaborate tombs at the site of La Muña in the Palpa valley argues for the authority of these new elites (Isla and Reindel 2006). Sites also become fewer but

larger, perhaps in response to greater conflict between polities in the different parts of the valleys and among valleys.

In the valleys south of the Ingenio River, a unique system of underground canals that tapped subterranean aquifers flowing down from the Andes was developed during Middle to Late Nasca times (Schreiber and Lancho Rojas 1995, 2003). Water flowing downslope under the ground could be reached by digging canals into the earth that intersected these aquifers. By digging circular holes down to the canals, they could be used as wells in addition to irrigation (figure 7.11). These systems, called *pukios,* or filtration galleries, are located in the middle reaches of the southern valleys, in sections where the water coming down from the Andes goes underground. Schreiber and Lancho Rojas (2003) note these parts of the valleys were sparsely occupied until the development of these systems during Middle Nasca times. Whether they were controlled by the emerging elites

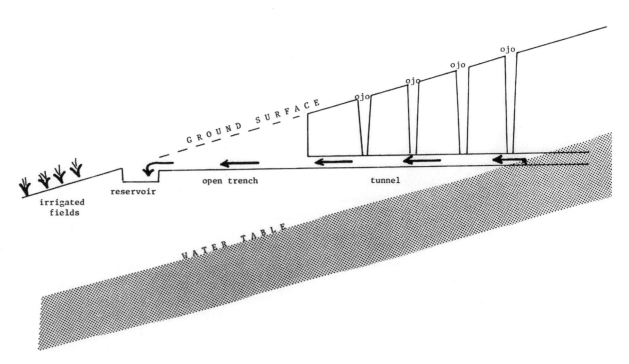

Figure 7.11. This diagram is of a historically modified Nazca puquio. Most original puquios are open trenches that intersect the water table. Drawing by K. Schreiber.

is uncertain, but Schreiber and Lancho Rojas believe they were.

Although the decades-long droughts of the sixth century, documented in the ice core data from the eastern Andes (Thompson et al. 1985), cannot account directly for the fall of Cahuachi, the significant stresses they brought to bear on Late Nasca societies must have been responsible for some of the changes seen in the settlement patterns and some of the sociopolitical developments. As the amount of water flowing down from the highlands decreased both in the rivers and subterranean aquifers, problems with the irrigation systems must have increased. The use of the filtration galleries clearly would have been a response to these problems. Silverman and Proulx (2002) suggest the appearance of female figurines may represent a new emphasis on fertility that might also be reflected in the increased trophy-head themes. Finally, the increase in geoglyphs during this time might indicate an increased ritual effort to increase the water sources.

By the seventh century C.E., Nasca culture was changing dramatically, to the point that it is no longer called "Nasca" (Silverman and Proulx 2002). The Huaca de Loro, or Nasca 8, occupations were very different from those of the previous phase, in ceramics, in burial practices, and in the evidence for their interactions with the emerging Wari culture to the east. This is also a time when Nasca ceramics show the strongest influences from other regions, such as the Moche. Nasca 7 and 8 reflect a time of increased interregional exchange of ideas that were markedly different from previous times (Schreiber 1992).

From Acarí south to the Chilean border, little is known of the occupations from the Initial Period to the Middle Horizon. A few sites and scattered cemeteries have provided tantalizing clues as to developments in this region, but few broad-scale surveys have been conducted. It is clear that there were interactions between the local people of the far south and the Nasca people because isolated Nasca pots have been discovered as far south perhaps as Arica (Silver-man and Proulx 2002). The technique of cross-knit looping appears much earlier in the collections from the latter region, so it probably represents a technique developed there that diffused northward. Joerg Haeberli (2006) conducted an analysis of textiles said to come from the Sihuas Valley and suggests on that basis that Nasca 2 and 3 people moved into the far southern region, introducing Nasca iconography to the local inhabitants. The locals then took this iconography and developed their own version of it, which was reintroduced back into the Nasca region as the Proliferous style. If this proves to be correct, then it suggests that the far south coast, at least to the Camaná-Sihuas-Vitor drainage, was more influential in the development of the Nasca style than previously realized.

Summary of Coastal Developments

In the north and south coastal regions, more complex societies developed during this period as populations continued to increase due to the success of the agricultural lifestyle, supplemented in the north by mixed maritime resources. Powerful leaders emerged who learned how to control other sectors of society to increase both their power and wealth. Moche leaders used conflict and ritual to build their power base, and they expanded trade to obtain exotic materials that were used by artisans under their control to create exceptional works of art for corporate and personal uses.

Along the south coast, and perhaps the central coast as well, emerging elites did not construct large monuments with the labor under their control. I interpret this to mean that they did not have the population base to do so. Still, the distinctions in status developed through this period show that society was differentiating. It is likely that the smaller valleys in this region were responsible for the more limited social developments because the emerging leaders controlled only smaller populations. Why no single group rose to control more of this region, as occurred in the Moche society, is uncertain.

THE NORTH AND CENTRAL HIGHLANDS

The Early Intermediate Period in the north and central highlands is a relatively poorly known era. The research in different river basins suggests that a Formative way of life largely continued from previous times in some regions, with people living in small villages, farming and herding in the different altitudinal zones. Typically, however, there are more sites present, implying that populations had increased through time. In fact, by 500 C.E., we see the emergence of complex societies in several regions, yet little research has been done to tell us what these developments were.

In the northern basins of Peru, at the end of the Early Horizon, the major sites of Pacopampa, Layzón, and Huacaloma were abandoned, perhaps due to the collapse of the Chavín religion. In Cajamarca, a new pottery type developed, made out of a distinctive white clay called kaolinite. Curvilinear designs were painted on these ceramics, which were much coveted by people in other regions (plate 6B). They show up in the Moche region and as far south as Ayacucho. To date, no sites with monumental architecture have been discovered for this culture, and even its production and distribution systems are unknown.

John and Theresa Lange Topic have been working in the Huamachuco basin south of Cajamarca since the early 1980s, and as a result, we know a considerable amount about the developments there. This is a region that appears to have remained culturally isolated from the major influences around it until the end of this period. No Chavín sites or ceramics have been identified there, despite Chavín influence to the west, north, and south; Moche influence is also entirely absent, despite this region being located up the valley of the Moche River (J. Topic 2009). During the early part of the Early Intermediate Period (200 B.C.E.– 300 C.E.), sites began to cluster around larger communities where circular, linear, and curvilinear gallery structures are located. These are buildings with groups of rooms around an open patio space. Such structures are a hallmark of later occupations in the region, and it is significant that they make their appearance during this time. They were probably the residences of local leaders and their families. Trade increased, and ceramics from the Recuay area to the south appeared during this time (J. Topic 2009). The basic economy was one of farming and herding.

During the subsequent time (300–600 C.E.), monumental architecture appeared at several sites, heralding the emergence of a group or groups that were organizing labor for such constructions. Marcahuamachuco, the largest site, occupied a zone at the top of a prominent plateau and is divided into two main sections (T. Topic 2009). The northern part of the plateau is residential and composed of circular galleries of two to three stories. Domestic debris suggests the galleries were residences, although they had centrally located patio rooms where objects used communally might have been stored. The variability in size and elaboration of these galleries argue for differences among the groups that occupied them, which were probably lineages.

The southern part of the plateau was a ceremonial and residential zone, demarcated by a major wall with a single entrance on the side opening to the circular galleries, which were 300 m away. A group of curvilinear galleries, probably also residences for some other segments of society, was present, but the main focus of this area was the Cerro de Castillo, which occupied the highest point on the plateau. A Great Plaza was located at one end, around which were several niched halls. These were massive buildings, sometimes 8 by 48 m under a roof, that consisted of thick walls with niches high up in the interior. Human bones were found in the walls of these halls, and they have high percentages of spoons, cups, and decorated ceramics inside. John and Theresa Lange Topic interpret them to be places of ancestral worship, where feasts in honor of the ancestors buried in the walls were conducted (J. Topic 1986; T. Topic 2009). The Castillo, a five-story spiral building of unknown function, formed the center of the site, which also included numerous rectangular and round smaller structures.

The amount of labor involved in the construction of Marcahuamachuco, which continued into subsequent periods, was enormous and reflects a large and well-coordinated construction force. Based on several lines of evidence, Theresa Lange Topic argues that there was no central authority organizing the labor; rather, it was simply built by groups of ayllus that worked together. Three kinds of burials are found at the site, but none bespeak marked inequalities in their burial goods or size. The Topics believe that Marcahuamachuco was a focus of lineage-based ceremonies and that the site was occupied only during ritual times. After such rituals were conducted, the people returned to their villages in other parts of the basin (T. Topic 2009).

Two other sites located within an hour's walk of Marcahuamachuco, Cerro Sazón and Cerro Tuscan, also had monumental architecture in the form of rectangular and curvilinear galleries. These two sites might have been the political center of the polity at this time. A fourth site, Cerro Amaru, also located near the other three, was a shrine related to water, where elaborate wells were excavated that included offerings (Topic and Topic 1992). Catequíl, a shrine that was famous during Inka times, was first occupied during this period to the south of the Huamachuco basin. Population size and aggregation increased during this period, with many sites located near the later Inka road, implying an early version of the latter was first constructed during this time.

An interesting, but poorly known culture defined as Recuay, was centered in the Callejón de Huaylas during the period about 1–700 C.E. This culture is largely known from its beautiful white pottery, virtually all of which comes from looted burials. Some is made of kaolinite, like the Cajamarca ceramics, but more is made of red clay over which a white slip was applied. Few domestic sites are known from this culture. The ceramics display a high level of skill, although it is unlikely that specialized potters were responsible. No major Recuay centers are known; however, the site of Pashash, located at the northern end of the Callejón de Huaylas, might qualify (Grieder 1978).

Work at the site of Chinchawas by George Lau (2002a, 2002b) has added much to our understanding of this culture. Regarding subsistence, the Recuay was a farming and herding society that also participated in long-distance exchange. The people were apparently organized in egalitarian communities that lived in large fortified settlements, although some large sites might have been centers of political authority.

Lau (2002b) found that the practice of ancestor worship emerged as an important aspect of Recuay culture following the disappearance of the Chavín religion in the region. With warfare becoming a more serious problem, both with groups such as the Moche and between Recuay communities, local leaders in the kin-based system developed different practices to retain authority. No institutional leadership roles emerged, except possibly at major centers such as Pashash, but local leaders used feasts and ceremonies to gain power over their communities (ibid.). Burial practices during the Early Intermediate Period and into the Middle Horizon consisted of individual tombs of leaders, often associated with stone sculptures. The figures on the sculptures are interpreted as ancestor figures.

This brings up the stone sculpture tradition that appears at this time in the Recuay culture. The tradition consisted of carvings in the round and in *bas relief*, which was probably part of the architecture. The figures, all about 1 m tall, represent males and females, although animal figures are also known (figure 7.12). Lau (2002b, 2008) states that these were part of ancestor cults and represented lithified members of the community. A figure of a male flanked by two felines, called the Central Figure Scene (Lau 2002b), shows considerable variability in design elements, so it is not considered a deity but was probably an ancestor of the group who used the figure in mortuary contexts.

Little is known of the cultures that occupied the Puna of Junín and the Upper Mantaro valley region farther south at this time. What has been found sug-

Figure 7.12. Recuay stone sculpture. Photo by George Lau.

landscape (Lumbreras 1974). In addition, irrigation canals were placed to bring water to the terraces from streams coming down from higher altitudes. The irrigation increased the reliability of water over the irregular rainfall of the region. This irregularity in rainfall, both seasonally and over longer periods, might be the main reason for the development of irrigation in this region. The irrigated terraces allowed the population to increase during the period and led to the appearance of a new settlement pattern of large villages, each surrounded by a series of smaller hamlets, mostly at higher elevations.

Although there is little to argue for increasing social complexity, at the site of Ñawimpukyo, some public architecture and what are interpreted as elite residences nearby appeared (Leoni 2006). At the top of the hill on which the site sits, a walled ceremonial area, the East Plaza, which is 82 by 45 m, was built. Inside it, a circular structure made up of three concentric walls was built with a narrow entrance into it. The entrance is oriented toward Rasuwillca, the highest mountain in the Ayacucho Valley. Grinding stones and camelid-bone clusters argue for some ritual activities, perhaps associated with feasting in the circular temple. In the rest of the East Plaza, a cache of ritually broken ceramics (a practice that might anticipate the ones seen in later Wari society), evidence of a food preparation area, and walls suggesting other rooms with ceremonial functions were identified. Leoni (2006) argues that the temple was a sacred location where rituals associated with mountain-deity worship were conducted for the people of the site, as well as for those from the area around Ñawimpukyo.

To the west of the East Plaza, a complex of rooms was excavated that bears a resemblance to the later Wari orthogonal patio groups (see chapter 8). On the basis of this similarity, Leoni suggests the complex might have housed an elite group that was in charge of the rituals at the East Plaza, although there is little artifactual evidence to support this view. Still, the site does argue for emerging status differences on the basis of differential access to the sacred spaces in the ceremonial part of the site.

gests small farming and herding communities existed in these regions that remained largely autonomous and independent of the developments around them.

In the Ayacucho region, one of the two great Middle Horizon societies, Wari, would emerge at the beginning of the Middle Horizon. The culture from which it developed is called Warpa. Other than its ceramic styles, little is known about this society. During the Early Intermediate Period, this region did, however, experience an increase in agricultural technology that has not been identified in other regions. The appearance of agricultural *terraces,* artificially flat surfaces created by building a retaining wall and then filling in with soil behind it, marks an important innovation in farming of the steep Andean

Whereas it was originally thought that Ñawimpu-kyo was perhaps the capital or political center of Warpa society, the site is now seen as just one of several important towns that were probably competing for terraced land, irrigation water, and other resources. Emerging elites at these centers conducted rituals for the good of their communities. One of these towns, Huari, would rise to dominate the rest in the succeeding Middle Horizon.

Like other highland regions discussed in this chapter, the Early Intermediate Period occupations in the basins around Andahuaylas and Cuzco are defined by distinctive ceramic styles; however, there is little evidence of marked social development. In both regions, there is little evidence of an emerging hierarchy or social differentiation (Bauer 2004; Bauer and Aráoz 2010). In Andahuaylas, the Qasawirka ceramics date to 300–1000 C.E. and are found at small to large sites with agropastoral economies.

In the Cuzco region, Chanapata ceramics followed the Marcavalle ceramics around 500 B.C.E., and there was the development of a diversified settlement pattern of a few large and many smaller sites. Bauer (2004) suggests the emergence of a chiefly society based at Wimpillay, the largest site in the Cuzco region. He notes the existence of other sites of comparable size in adjacent regions and likens the sociopolitical development there to that of Pukara farther south. He cautions, however, that more research is needed to support this conjecture.

Starting around 1 C.E., Qotakalli ceramics replaced the Chanapata ceramics, and this marks a dramatic shift in decoration. Chanapata ceramics were primarily black decorations on red slip; Qotakalli ceramics were black or black and red on a creamy white slip. Qotakalli pottery was present from 1 to 1200 C.E., and it is found at sites that started with a mixed agricultural and pastoral economy, but then shifted to intensive maize cultivation (Bauer and Aráoz 2010). In terms of sociopolitics, Brian Bauer (2004) suggests that a cluster of large villages located under modern Cuzco might have been the locations of elite households or ayllus that emerged at this time. Another cluster to the south and east might have been another, and others could have existed in adjacent regions. Although no single center dominated the region, population growth during the period led to political differentiation. The basis for the political power is not known at present.

Both the Andahuaylas and Cuzco regions fell under Wari hegemony in the Middle Horizon, but the nature of the local responses to this foreign influence are yet to be worked out.

Summary of North and Central Highland Developments

Developments in the north and central highlands followed a similar trajectory to those in the adjacent coastal regions, with the exception of the Moche region, which stands out in its high level of sociopolitical complexity during this period. Although social inequalities began to emerge in the Huamachuco and possibly Ayacucho and Cuzco regions, they did not represent the level of developments we see in Moche society. It is uncertain why these regions lagged behind the Moche, but the lower population densities and generally smaller communities probably are responsible, much as in the south coast region. Ranking and hereditary inequalities are often associated with increasing population densities (see chapter 2). It is particularly curious that the regions in the north highlands did not develop like their coastal neighbors, even though the people of the two zones were in contact and shared material culture. This suggests to me that the highland societies maintained their own distinctive ways of life despite their knowledge of status differences that existed along the north coast. This situation changed in the subsequent period when a new cultural influence, Wari, spread across this area from the south. Cultural developments in the south coast and central highlands appear to be more on parity, and the increased evidence for contacts between these two regions at the end of the Early Intermediate Period shows contacts between them were probably increasing.

THE SOUTH-CENTRAL HIGHLANDS

The early part of the Early Intermediate Period (the Late Formative 1 Period in the local sequence), 200 B.C.E.–250 C.E., for this region is covered in chapter 5. The subsequent developments during the Late Formative 2 Period, 250–500 C.E., relate to the rise of Tiwanaku, the great center and cultural influence that spread across this region after around 500 C.E. Therefore, they fall more appropriately into the next chapter, and I describe them there.

8

CLASH OF THE TITANS?

Tiwanaku, Wari, and the Middle Horizon

The Middle Horizon, or specifically the time between 600 and 1000 C.E., marks the emergence of two powerful political and religious entities: Tiwanaku and Wari. Their influence was such that there is little to discuss from elsewhere in this book's geographical focus (except the north coast) other than their development and spread. Until the past decade, one of the most intriguing features of these two polities was the use of very similar iconographies as their corporate styles. Indeed, the similarities are so close that some early investigators mistook one for the other. For many years, Wari ceramics from coastal contexts in Peru were defined as "Coastal Tiahuanaco," reflecting the lack of information about Wari as a discrete center (Goldstein 2005).

Even after the discovery of Wari, Tiwanaku was considered the main source of influence on Wari development because Tiwanaku had been discovered and described earlier and because a scatter of early radiocarbon dates suggested Tiwanaku had developed earlier. Now, it is much less clear how each culture influenced the other and whether the development of one of them had primacy over the other. That being said, the reasons for their common religion remain elusive. We begin by returning to the south-central heartland of Tiwanaku, beginning in the Late Formative II Period, around 250 C.E.

THE SOUTH-CENTRAL HIGHLANDS

Late Formative 2 (250–500 C.E.)

The Late Formative and Tiwanaku Period (500–1100 C.E.) history of the south-central highlands is dominated by the development of the Tiwanaku polity, which had its capital at the site given the same name. The site has been known since the sixteenth century, when Cieza de León, a soldier with Francisco Pizarro, visited and described it. Excavations and architectural studies began in the nineteenth century, with several projects in the twentieth century by both Bolivians and foreigners. The site and region was the focus of the Wila Jawira research project in the 1990s, a major multidisciplinary project directed by Alan Kolata (1996, 2003a).

Some confusion exists in the traditional ceramic sequence for the culture (Janusek 2003). Building on the work of several earlier archaeologists, Carlos Ponce Sangines, the great Bolivian archaeologist, described a five-phase sequence of ceramics in 1981, labeled I–V. But the earliest three phases have not been confirmed by more recent work, with the result that confusion exists regarding the dating of the early phases of development. As such, more recent work has tended to call the period of the early emergence of the culture, which corresponds to Ponce

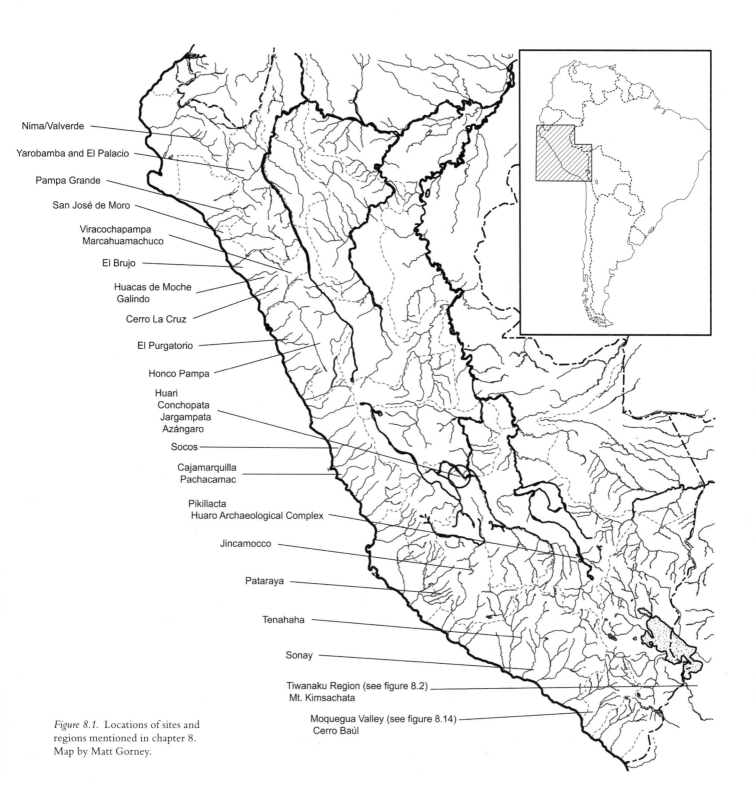

Nima/Valverde

Yarobamba and El Palacio

Pampa Grande

San José de Moro

Viracochapampa
Marcahuamachuco

El Brujo

Huacas de Moche
Galindo

Cerro La Cruz

El Purgatorio

Honco Pampa

Huari
Conchopata
Jargampata
Azángaro

Socos

Cajamarquilla
Pachacamac

Pikillacta
Huaro Archaeological Complex

Jincamocco

Pataraya

Tenahaha

Sonay

Tiwanaku Region (see figure 8.2)
Mt. Kimsachata

Moquegua Valley (see figure 8.14)
Cerro Baúl

Figure 8.1. Locations of sites and regions mentioned in chapter 8. Map by Matt Gorney.

Sangines's phases I–III, the Late Formative. The time period when the Tiwanaku emerge as the major power on the Altiplano, the Middle Horizon of the central Andean sequence, is now called the Tiwanaku Period and is divided into Tiwanaku 1 (500–800 C.E., formerly the earlier part of phase IV) and Tiwanaku 2 (800–1100 C.E., formerly the later part of phase IV). The time period after the fall of Tiwanaku, comparable to the Late Intermediate Period elsewhere, is here called the Pacajes Period (1100–1470 C.E., formerly phase V). Following Janusek (2008), I use this chronological system here (see figure 5.12).

During Late Formative 2 times, the influence of Chiripa seems to wane for reasons that are unclear. At this time, there is a fairly dramatic increase in the level of Lake Wiñaymarka, suggesting increased rainfall in the region. Whether this affected cultural developments is not certain. It is likely that the emergence of Tiwanaku as a major center had something to do with the loss of Chiripa influence.

One significant change that occurred during the Late Formative was a shift of settlements away from the lakeshore and river edges toward more inland locations. Many were now away from the lake and rivers, suggesting changes in subsistence. Herding became more important than it had been, and farming provided more of the diet than previously. This shift led to other changes that were associated with the rise of Tiwanaku and related centers (Janusek 2008).

At this time, the Bolivian Altiplano had several multicommunity polities, including ones centered at Tiwanaku, Lukurmata in the Katari Valley to the north, Kallamarka, Kala Uyuni along the shore of Lake Wiñaymarka, and Khonkho Wankane in the Machaca area to the south (figure 8.2). Each of these was a large residential site, and all had ritual structures as well. The structures were typically sunken trapezoidal courts on platforms. Stone sculptures continued to be in use as well, although the figures on them changed.

Janusek (2004a) notes that Tiwanaku was occupied and was one of the major centers in the Titicaca

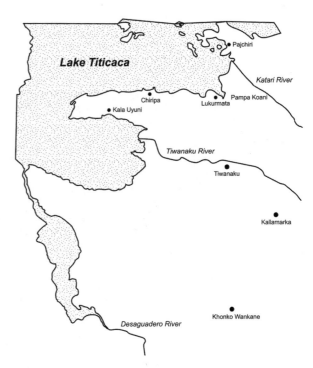

Figure 8.2. Map of region around Tiwanaku, showing site locations. Map by Matt Gorney. Adapted from Janusek 2008, figure 3.4.

region. Two of the principal monumental structures at Tiwanaku, the Semi-Subterranean Temple and the Kalasasaya platform, were constructed at this time (figure 8.3). Recent work by Alexei Vranich (2009) has shown that an early version of the Semi-Subterranean Temple was constructed with a north-south orientation, perhaps during the early part of the period. Its entrance was aligned to the Southern Cross constellation and the peak of Mt. Kimsachata, an important mountain located to the south (Benitez, cited in Vranich 2009, 20). Typical of later Tiwanaku architecture, the court was constructed of large sandstone pillars separated by smaller ashlars and fieldstones. Effigy heads showing great variety were placed in the walls (figure 8.4). The fact that many show distinct facial expressions and cranial features suggests to Janusek (2008) that they represented the ancestors of the groups who made up the center at this time. Alternatively, they may represent deities or the *wak'as* (sacred objects or places) of conquered groups incorporated into the expanding political sphere of the city (Kolata 2003b). In the center of the court was at least one monolith, and perhaps more, which might have been the representation of a collective ancestor of the entire community (Janusek 2008).

Sometime in 300–500 C.E., the Kalasasaya monumental platform was built on an earlier elite residential compound. It measures 128 by 119 m. It is significant to note that there is evidence of a 2-m-high platform underlying the entire monumental core, which, in turn, is underlain by drainage conduits that drew water off the platform during periods of high rainfall (Vranich 2009). The Kalasasaya compound faces east, in contrast to the Semi-Subterranean Temple, and marks a new ritual orientation. A wide staircase led to a shallow sunken court. Beyond that was a small platform that was used in association with the western wall of the compound, called the Balcony. Hallways and rooms were also located in other areas of the platform and may have housed the remains of rulers or lineage figures (Kolata 2003b). The main wall of the first level was made of huge sandstone blocks with ashlars and other stone in between, similar to the Semi-Subterranean Temple. Vranich (2009) argues that the Kalasasaya replaced the Semi-Subterranean Temple as the main ritual structure of the city during the Late Formative Period.

During Late Formative times, the Kalasasaya served as a ritual center, a possible repository for elite ancestor mummies or their representations (Kolata 2003b), and an astronomical calendar. The last warrants further discussion.

Figure 8.3. The Semi-Subterranean Temple and Kalasasaya platform at Tiwanaku. From Janusek 2008, figure 43A. Photo courtesy of John Janusek.

Figure 8.4. Effigy heads along wall of Semi-Subterranean Temple. Photo courtesy of Alan Kolata, Proyecto Wila Jawira.

The Balcony of the Kalasasaya is constructed of beautifully fitted andesite ashlars, representing some of the finest stone carving at Tiwanaku. The source of the andesite is 90 km to the northwest, across Lake Wiñaymarka. The other three sides were constructed of sandstone that was quarried locally. This marks the west side as the most important part of the platform. The top of the Balcony originally consisted of eleven (one is now missing) 4-m- tall monoliths of andesite, regularly spaced at 4.6-m intervals. From the central platform between the sunken court and the Balcony, a viewer could see the sun setting over the southernmost pillar at the summer solstice and over the northernmost pillar at the winter solstice. The sun set over the sixth pillar on the equinoxes. The other pillars also marked important times in the solar year (Benitez 2009). During the equinoxes, the setting sun could be seen from the Semi-Subterranean Temple, up the central staircase, and through the Kalasasaya. This calendar must have been significant in the timing of rituals conducted by the priests of the temple.

Tiwanaku apparently expanded rapidly at the end of the period, to perhaps 1 km² and became the largest site in the region. It is hard to determine how early it expanded or how large the settlement of Tiwanaku was during the Late Formative period because many of these deposits are buried deeply under the subsequent ones. Still, research by Carlos Ponce Sangines (1981, 1995), Kolata's project, and others who followed have identified both residential and ritual areas in Tiwanaku, although the latter were probably local shrines. Still, the size of the Kalasasaya platform and its layout argue that the religious leaders at Tiwanaku were controlling a sizable labor force over a long period of time. Whether this marks the emergence of hereditary leadership is uncertain but likely. Regardless, the group in charge may have been relatively small.

A site that rivaled Tiwanaku during the Late Formative 1 period was Lukurmata, located along the shore of Lake Titicaca, at the mouth of the Katari Valley (Bermann 1994). Here, a population concentration led to the site growing beyond the size of other settlements, probably due to its location between agricultural areas and the lake. During Late Formative 2 times, a large rectangular plaza was constructed that probably served for ritual meetings and ceremonies (Janusek 2004b). By the end of the period, the site had expanded to 30 ha and was clearly the largest community in the region.

Another site that probably rivaled Tiwanaku at this time was Khonkho Wankane, located across the Kimsachata-Chilla mountains to the south (Janusek 2008). This site rose to importance around 1 C.E., when a sunken rectangular court and massive platform were constructed. To the east of the court, an elite compound of residences was built with its own staircase to the court. To the north, a large plaza was probably used for gatherings of the communities under the ritual authority of the elites there. Another large rectangular platform with residences was built to the east of the plaza. After 250 C.E., a large Dual-Court Complex was built to the east of the plaza for additional rituals (Janusek 2008).

It was not just settlement patterns that changed during the Late Formative 2 period. A new religious belief developed out of Pukara iconography based on two main themes: the Camelid Woman and the Feline Man. Similar to the themes identified in Moche art, many of the designs on the ceremonial ceramics deal with these two figures, which must have been important elements of the religion. They seem to reflect the Andean concept of duality, with the woman holding a llama and associated with plants (figure 8.5A) and the man holding a trophy head and a knife (figure 8.5B). Janusek (2008) suggests the ap-

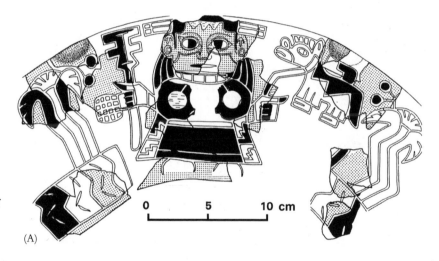

Figure 8.5. (A) Camelid woman motif on Pukara pottery. (B) Feline Man motif on Pukara pottery. Drawings courtesy of Sergio Chávez.

(A)

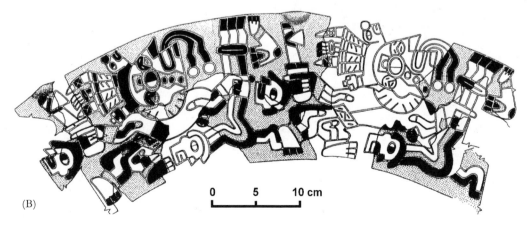

(B)

pearance of trophy heads during this period might reflect increased militarism and conflicts among settlements.

Stone sculptures became more elaborate and detailed. The sculptures appear to represent ancestors, as did their predecessors in the Yaya Mama tradition. Other stone carvings are of abstract symbols. How these may relate to an integrated religion that also included the Camelid Woman and Feline Man is uncertain. It is also clear that a new aspect of religious ritual was the consumption of hallucinogens, available from the yunga zone to the east. A set of paraphernalia used in snuffing such substances (figure 8.6) is common at sites of the period (Bermann 1994; Janusek 2004b). Tablets, spatulas, spoons, and tubes with iconographic symbols on them are found from the Altiplano down into the Atacama Desert.

Figure 8.6. Tiwanaku snuffing tablet. Photo courtesy of Mario A. Rivera.

Due to its high quality, ceramic production is seen as being controlled by specialists. In addition, distinct Qeya ceremonial wares appear to be restricted to particular ritual contexts. This suggests control over their production and producers by the religious authority (Janusek 2008). Altogether, Late Formative II societies appear to have been more complex, which is reflected in the presence of powerful individuals or groups that controlled ritual from different, politically autonomous sites. The degree to which they controlled other aspects of society, such as trade and food production, is less clear. The widespread similarities in the iconography, material culture, and architecture of this time indicate that cultural concepts were broadly shared. We can imagine that leaders at these major centers were in contact with each other, perhaps even intermarrying. It is unfortunate that there are so few burials that date to this period that could tell us more about the social structure of this pre-Tiwanaku culture.

Tiwanaku I (500–800 C.E.)

This period begins with the appearance of a series of new red-slipped ceramics. In contrast to the Late Formative, now most households have access to these ceramics, which were used in ceremonial activities. The emergence of the site of Tiwanaku as the major religious and political center of the Altiplano occurred early in this period, although it may have occurred before. Janusek (2008) suggests it became the primary center as a result of the merging of two Late Formative centers that had been based at what became the two major ceremonial complexes of the unified city: the Kalasasaya and Pumapunku.[1] In contrast to Wari (discussed later in the chapter), there is no compelling evidence that Tiwanaku's influence, which spread from the northern edge of the Altiplano to central Bolivia and northern Chile in the south, spread through militarism. Rather, the site became a pilgrimage and trade center, "a noncentralized federation of ayllus, ethnicities, and polities" (ibid., 108). The economic base of the center was raised-field agriculture and camelid herding. To understand the influence of the center, we must begin with a description of the city itself and its historical development. Also note, as Vranich (2009) cautions, that Tiwanaku was modified often by its designers, pillaged by later cultures for its stones, poorly excavated by early investigators, and had its major monuments reconstructed more than once in modern times, making an accurate reconstruction of its features for any given time period difficult, if not impossible.

THE CITY OF TIWANAKU Alan Kolata (2003b), the director of the Wila Jawira Research Project that provided the data on which our recent understanding of the city and society is based, discusses two important principles on which the city was planned. The first is a concentric cline of the sacred, whereby the residences of the inhabitants of the city were located in relation to the important religious buildings. The closer to the main religious structures an individual lived, the higher that person was in the sacred hierarchy, which translated to higher social status. Excavations in the city residential areas support this basic principle.

The second principle is cardinality related to the path of the sun. The major structures at Tiwanaku and the residential barrios were all oriented largely to the cardinal directions, with the most important religious structures facing east. This east-west orientation was based on the importance of the Cordillera Real range to the east, especially Mt. Illimani, and Lake Titicaca to the west. Kolata (2003b) notes that only from the summit of the Akapana pyramid, the largest of the ceremonial structures at the site, can both be seen simultaneously. It is no wonder the highest elite chose to live there.

Regarding the architecture of power at Tiwanaku and other Tiwanaku sites such as Lukurmata, Pajchiri, and Khonko Wankane, the most important buildings were all made following the same design: a platform with a sunken interior court (Kolata 2003b). This form originated in the earlier Pukara and Chiripa cultures, but it was greatly elaborated by the leaders of the main settlements. In addition to these features, the principal structures included carved monuments and nonresidential sectors. Thus, there was a deliberate pattern and design that was followed at the major sites, one that doubtless reflected the cosmology of the culture.

The ceremonial core of Tiwanaku consisted of two groups of structures, the Akapana, Semi-Subterranean Temple, and Kalasasaya complex to the northeast and the Pumapunku to the southwest. Both Kolata and Janusek feel these might have been centers of two distinct moieties or communities that merged into a single political entity at this time.

The northeast complex was originally surrounded by a moat that both physically and symbolically separated the activities and the individuals who dwelled there and conducted the activities. Traces of other moats to the east suggest that another symbolic barrier was built as the city grew, to separate the earlier and presumably higher-status groups from newer ones.

The current configuration of these monuments masks a temporal factor in their construction. As mentioned in the previous section, both the Semi-Subterranean Temple and the Kalasasaya were constructed during the Late Formative Period but were probably reconstructed and added to in later periods, which included the addition of the Bennett monument to the Semi-Subterranean Temple. During the Tiwanaku I Period, the Akapana was constructed as a major ceremonial focus that prohibited the earlier rituals from being conducted—the view of Mt. Kimsachata from the Semi-Subterranean Temple was now obscured. This suggests that a shift in the religion may have occurred. During this same time, the Pumapunku was constructed as a new focus and possible entry into the ceremonial city.

The Akapana was designed to be one-half of an Andean cross, a common motif in the architecture and art of Tiwanaku (figure 8.7). The main access to the summit was from the west, and individuals entered (if they were allowed!) the main staircase from a large plaza. It was built of seven terraces of decreasing size, and the construction features of the first terrace, which is actually the foundation of the structure, were similar to those of the Kalasasaya. The walls were constructed of cut stones that were carefully fitted, with large uprights between which were placed smaller ashlars. The upper six terraces had flat stone panels instead of the ashlars, and Kolata (2003b) thinks these may have had metal plaques or textiles that covered them, providing sacred and possibly political information to the masses who saw them. A sunken court was placed on the summit of the structure. Unfortunately, this court was completely destroyed by looters centuries ago.

Kolata (2003b) feels that the Akapana was meant to represent a sacred mountain, and several architectural features support that idea. A complex drainage system of stone-lined canals draws water off the summit and out of the sunken court. Rainfall flows out over the edge of the terrace below and then is channeled into another underground canal, only to flow out over the next terrace. This system of outside-inside movement of the water continues until the water flows out from the lowest foundation wall and into a large underground canal that brings the water to the Tiwanaku River. This sophisticated system mimics the Kimsachata Range to the south, where rainfall flows onto the summits and then goes into subterranean streams, only to reappear as springs lower down, which then deliver water to other subterranean aquifers and ultimately to the valley floor, where the water becomes the main source for irrigation and drinking (Kolata 2003b). Thus, the Akapana symboli-cally represents the source of water on which the culture depended.

Further evidence of this association is found in the layers of small green stones that are found interspersed with the clay fill of the upper terraces and covering the summit. These green stones come from the streams flowing down from the Kimsachata range and must have been laboriously collected and transported to the Akapana. Kolata (1993) suggests they represent the source of the water for the city and perhaps elements of the powerful wak'as that dwelled there.

In addition, Kolata notes that the Akapana sits amid the main moat of the city, in a location that could represent the sacred mountain on the Island of the Sun in Lake Titicaca. Thus, it represented a symbol of the world order of the culture. On the first and second levels of the structure, human burials and a large ceremonial offering of ceramics indicate activities associated with the Akapana. Twenty-one incomplete but correctly articulated bodies were found along the first terrace, and Kolata (2003b) suggests many more probably exist in unexcavated zones. The bodies of men and children might have been either mummy bundles or human trophies (Blom et al. 2003). Studies of the bones indicate that many were foreigners, and those in particular showed evidence of trauma, arguing for violent deaths (Knudson et al. 2004). The ceremonial ceramic offering consisted of hundreds of fine polychrome vessels (figure 8.8), many with the motif of trophy

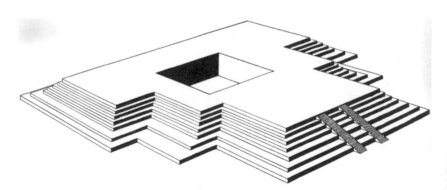

Figure 8.7. Idealized partial reconstruction of the Akapana, showing tiers and stairways. Drawing courtesy of Alan L. Kolata.

heads or *chachapumas*, warriors in puma masks who hold severed heads in one hand and axes in the other. The association between these vessels and the human remains suggests the latter were probably sacrificial. Kolata (2003b) believes that the remains might be trophies of conquered peoples, brought there to become part of the earth shrine of the city.

Although most scholars suggest the Akapana was begun around 500 C.E., recent reanalysis of the fill for the lower revetment of the foundation suggests it may be the latest structure at the city, dating to perhaps the seventh century (Vranich 2009).

The second monumental complex of Tiwanaku was the Pumapunku platform, which was begun around 500 C.E. The structure consisted of a main staircase on the west side that entered a large court. Beyond the court was a massive portico through which people passed to a large plaza located below the portico. William Isbell and Vranich (2004) suggest that the Pumapunku was the main entryway for pilgrims to the city. Coming from the southwest, they would first view the ceremonial core from the portico as they passed through it. If this hypothesis is correct, it suggests that the rulers of Tiwanaku were developing a sense of the power of the city as a pilgrimage center and using that power to their advantage. If this structure and community were the center of an earlier moiety, it would also suggest that the leaders were now in some way subservient to the elites of the other moiety that controlled the Akapana and Kalasasaya complexes.

There were other structures that existed in the city center. The Kantatayita was a small ceremonial structure located to the east of the Semi-Subterranean Temple and to the northeast of the Akapana. The main feature of this structure was a large *maquette,* or model of a sunken court on a platform. Its function is unknown, although Janusek (2008) makes the reasonable suggestion that it might have served to organize ritual dances in other areas. The presence of an ornately carved architrave indicates an important portal was probably a part of the original structure as well but has since been removed.

This brings up one of the significant aspects of Tiwanaku architecture that make it distinct among ancient Andean cities: the prominence of large portals. The most famous of these is the Gateway of the Sun (figure 8.9), but many others existed, although few

Figure 8.8. Ceramic offering from the Akapana with human remains. Photo courtesy of Alan Kolata, Proyecto Wila Jawira.

are still standing or in their original positions (Isbell, Protzen, and Nair 2002; Vranich 2009). The elites of the city made use of large portals through which people were channeled by decorating them with religious icons. The portals were also a means to inspire awe because of their size and architectural sophistication. They marked the transition between the secular world outside the portal and the sacred world within the court or room that would have been entered. Whereas some of these portals, such as the ones in the Puma-punku, must have been experienced by thousands of individuals, others in more restricted areas would have been accessible to only the honored few. This access must have been a means by which privileged individuals identified their higher status and were made aware of their responsibilities to the elites who allowed the access. We can imagine that such access was not free; offerings and wealth must have been part of the honor of entering such restricted spaces.

Evidence of social inequalities at Tiwanaku appear during this period and become more apparent in the succeeding one. In addition to the probable elite residence at the top of the Akapana, there were

two compounds behind the Kalasasaya where the Putuni complex was later constructed. One consisted of a kitchen and food-preparation area along with additional rooms, and the other was a mortuary complex. The tombs of the latter had no remains, and the excavators of the complex suggest that the original bodies were removed and relocated in the Putuni complex when it was built later (Couture and Sampeck 2003). The location of the complex argues for a very high status for the individuals living there.

As Tiwanaku grew during this period, new residential compounds were constructed farther out from the ceremonial core. These were probably the homes of groups of families, perhaps ayllus or other kin-based groups (Janusek 2008). That they were lower status is reflected in their construction of sod blocks on cobblestone foundations, rather than finely cut stone, and by the lack of fine wares in their domestic trash. They contained food-preparation regions, sometimes craft production, and ritual spaces. Evidence of feasting in some areas with little evidence for other domestic activities suggests com-

Figure 8.9. The Gateway of the Sun. Photo courtesy of John Janusek.

mon areas where perhaps relatives or guests were fed, either for social or ritual reasons. If we assume that the city by now had become a major pilgrimage center, this could have been one way that temporary visitors were accommodated or fed while visiting.

Evidence that not all Tiwanaku residents were the descendants of its original inhabitants comes from biological markers, ceramics, and food preferences. Deborah Blom (2005) finds that there were two kinds of head deformation practiced by the people who lived at Tiwanaku, in addition to keeping the natural form (figure 8.10). Deformation is a means of identifying ethnicity in the Andes, and here too it must have been a means to visually indicate to which group an individual belonged. Moreover, Blom has found that individuals with different head shapes were in the same burial, suggesting intermarriage. These biological data are some of the stronger pieces of evidence arguing for ethnic and social diversity at Tiwanaku.

Janusek (2003) notes that there were marked differences in the ceramics in different parts of the site in addition to those based on status distinctions. He finds pottery types that are more common in other regions of the Altiplano in some compounds, suggesting the origins of the inhabitants lay outside the city itself (although the presence of Tiwanaku-style ceramics as well reflects the importance of such objects in status displays). Finally, Melanie Wright, Christine Hastorf, and Heidi Lennstrom (2003) find that quinoa and cañihua, both local crops, formed the largest part of the agricultural diet of the citizens of the city, followed by tubers. But they find that maize, a high-status crop due to its importance in making *chicha* for ritual and social events, was *not* most common in the high-status areas such as Putuni or Akapana. Instead, they find it was more prevalent in lower-status contexts where the ceramics found are associated with warmer regions where maize grows.

Thus, it is clear from multiple lines of evidence that people from outside Tiwanaku moved to the city and both lived alongside and married individuals from the city. It is likely, however, that the highest-status lineages that resided within the ceremonial core were some of the original occupants of this zone, who laid claim to direct links to the deities or ancestors and powers that were worshipped in the sacred enclosures of the city.

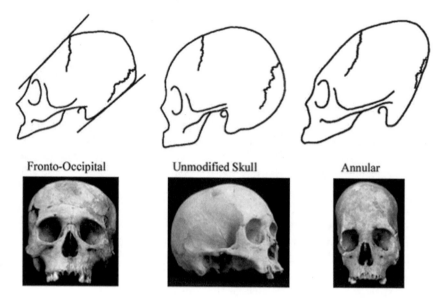

Fronto-Occipital **Unmodified Skull** **Annular**

Figure 8.10. Different types of Tiwanaku head forms. Drawing and photos courtesy of Deborah E. Blom.

Similar to the megalithic portals, large carved monoliths were prominent aspects of Tiwanaku. Most scholars today support the idea that these monoliths represent ancestors of the ruling lineages of the city (Kolata 2003b). The two main figures are represented on the Bennett Stela and the Ponce Stela (figures 8.11A and 8.11B); the former is carved from sandstone and the latter is carved from andesite. The Bennett Stela was placed in the Semi-Subterranean Temple around the beginning of the Tiwanaku Period, and although it faces south today, Kolata (2003b) argues it probably faced west when originally erected. This would be so it faced the Ponce Stela, which is located in the central sunken court of the Kalasasaya and faces east. As Kolata aptly describes the rationale for this arrangement, "This sculptural ensemble brilliantly expressed Tiwanaku elites' political legitimacy, their esoteric knowledge, and their moral authority. They were powerful visual statements that overtly linked Tiwanaku's ruling dynasty with the mythic past, with the time of ethnic origins, and with the proper and necessary functioning of the natural world" (2003b, 198).

Both the Ponce and Bennett stelae display a richly costumed individual holding a kero (ceremonial goblet) in one hand and a snuff tablet in the other. The Ponce Stela has images of fish and appears to be associated with lake or river resources (Janusek 2008). In contrast, the Bennett Stela figure has elaborate images of plants such as maize and columnar cactus prominently displayed on its clothing and body. These two plants are used for preparing chicha and a mescaline compound for inducing hallucinations, respectively. The abundance of both chicha brewing and serving vessels in ceremonial contexts at Tiwanaku and other sites and the common discovery of paraphernalia for snuffing hallucinogens at other sites indicate that these two activities were prominent aspects of Tiwanaku religion.

Thomas Zuidema (2009) has made a compelling case that the Bennett Stela is actually an elaborate calendar, used by the elite for reckoning time and setting a ritual calendar. This use would support the importance of having such a calendar that is also re-

Figure 8.11. (A) Bennett stela. Photo courtesy of Clare A. Sammels. (B) Ponce stela. Photo courtesy of John Janusek.

flected in the solar observations made from the Balcony of the Kalasasaya.

Other monoliths share the same basic features of these two stelae but differ in the particular motifs that they display. Janusek (2008) argues they might represent the ancestors of distinct groups of elites at Tiwanaku and that having the particular ancestor of a group enshrined in a temple such as the Kalasasaya or other high-status structure reflected its status and the critical importance of its lineage in the religion and politics of the city.

One final monument that merits description is the Gateway of the Sun, or Sun Portal (figure 8.9). This portal today sits in the northwest corner of the Kalasasaya, but its current location makes no sense with regard to the layout of the platform or the powerful images on it. The main figure on this portal is an individual holding a spearthrower in one hand and darts in the other. The figure appears to be standing on a dais of some kind and has thirty attendant figures in three rows facing it, fifteen on either side. The middle row of each side is a condor with upraised face, and the other two rows are human figures holding staffs. A band of heads in a zigzag row forms the base of the depiction. The figures and the designs also have decorations of birds, fish, felines, and plants that are common to other Tiwanaku architecture. The figure's rayed headdress could be a representation of the solar corona, making this figure a solar deity or a representation of solar power. Zuidema (2009) has identified a solar calendar in the layout of the main figure and the band of heads at the bottom. On the basis of this iconography, Janusek (2008) suggests that the Sun Portal might have orig-inally been located on the central platform and that through it elites could watch the solar events over the Balcony uprights.

THE TIWANAKU ECONOMY Where were crafts produced in the city, and by whom? One of the hallmarks of a state-level society is craft specialization, but there is little evidence for this in the investigations that have been conducted. Given that only a tiny percentage of the 4–6 km^2 site has been excavated, this is not surprising, and it is possible that craft workshops might have been located away from elite areas, especially those that produced noxious by-products, such as ceramic production and metallurgy. A workshop for producing ceramics was found over 1 km to the east of the main core of the site, at a place called Ch'iji Jawira. A group of households produced large storage jars, cooking and serving vessels, figurines, and special forms called *sahumadores* and incensarios (figure 8.12; Rivera Casanovas 2003). These forms were used in many areas of the site, so it is difficult to say that the occupants worked for any particular group. The relative lack of fine wares at Ch'iji Jawira suggests that such wares were produced elsewhere. Ponce Sangines (1981) and David Browman (1981) argue that fine wares must have been manufactured by specialists, either for elite uses at the site or for trade (plate 7A).

Evidence for other crafts, especially metallurgy and textiles, is even scarcer. Few examples of textiles have been found in the humid soils of the Altiplano, although examples are known from the dry environments of northern Chile. The examples found show that the figures on the main monuments probably

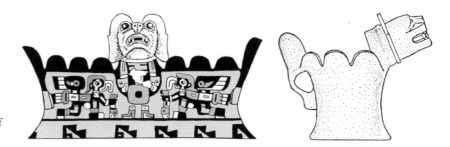

Figure 8.12. Incensario. Courtesy of John Janusek.

depict actual clothing that was worn. But who made the clothing and whether there was any elite investment or control are uncertain. In contrast, Heather Lechtman (2003) has made a preliminary study of the bronze artifacts from Tiwanaku, and she notes that the technical aspects needed to produce the objects argue for state control. One of the uses of bronze at Tiwanaku was to bond the ashlar masonry together by pouring the molten metal into depressions in adjacent sides. These cramps (as they are called) are unique in prehistoric Andean monumental buildings, and they were made of a special bronze alloy (Lechtman, pers. comm. 2015). Although metal objects were uncommon at Tiwanaku, they reflect a new technology that was probably developed by elites for their own uses.

Stone tools for domestic uses were made from locally available materials in most households (Geisso 2003). Basalt and obsidian, however, were materials imported from southern Bolivia and Peru, respectively, and were largely restricted to the urban core; their importation was controlled by the religious authorities. Obsidian and chert projectile points were highly standardized, and Martin Geisso argues that they represent a kind of taxation required by the state of urban inhabitants. Therefore, it seems unlikely that there were workshops for the production of any stone tools.

In addition to the production of crafts, there are the obvious questions about the food required by the urban residents of Tiwanaku: how it was produced, and even more important, how and by whom it was distributed. Because of the altitude and environment of the Altiplano, many staples of the Andean diet cannot be grown there, foods such as maize, beans, chili peppers, fruits, and nonfood crops such as coca and psychotropic drugs. These had to be grown at lower altitudes and imported into the city. Nevertheless, the majority of the food used in the city, hardy crops like quinoa and cañihua, was grown or collected on the Altiplano.

The three major subsistence activities were farming, herding, and fishing. Kolata (1993) makes the argument that these roles were probably played by different ethnic groups known through historical records. The Pukina, now extinct, lived along the shores of the lake and down to the eastern warmer climates, and they might have originated the intensive raised-field agriculture. The Uru were fisherfolk who lived along the lake and rivers but who now are nearly extinct as well. The Aymara, a vibrant culture still today, were pastoralists and tuber farmers of the high puna. A key to the success of Tiwanaku might have been how the three ethnicities, plus others perhaps, were coordinated into a functioning unified polity.

During the Tiwanaku Period, the most important agricultural activity was the farming of raised fields. The adaptive value of raised fields has been well documented by modern studies of both rebuilt ancient fields and experimental plots (Erickson 1985; Kolata et al. 1996). Yields increase greatly over non-raised-field agriculture in the low-lying zones near Lake Titicaca, where the water table is very high.

Raised fields began to be used in the Middle Formative in the region of Huatta, Peru, but they became a focus of local community productivity during Tiwanaku I. On the Koani Pampa at the mouth of the Katari River, individual communities that existed on the piedmont zone above the pampa developed their own field systems and canals, and grew food for their own uses, although few were in operation during this period (Janusek 2004b). In the Tiwanaku Valley, most raised fields were concentrated on the north side of the valley near settlements for ecological reasons (Janusek 2008). At this time, Janusek (2008) feels, there was no political control over the fields; rather, elites at Tiwanaku worked through local community leaders to obtain food surpluses, probably in return for crafts or trade goods.

In addition to raised-field farming, the terracing of hill slopes and *qocha* farming were also practiced, albeit to a lesser degree. Terracing was conducted along the lower slopes of hills to lessen erosion and increase flat planting beds. Because of later expansion of such terracing by the Inkas, it is difficult to know how much existed during Tiwanaku times. Qochas were ponds or depressions that were dug out in areas with low water tables. They had a formal organization of furrows that ringed the depression and canals that directed water both around the margins and through the middle. They could be filled and used for aquatic resources, drained and used for fields, and during fallow periods, used to pasture herds of camelids. Thus they were multifunctional. A series of qochas were found in the Mollu Kontu sector of the city, where they might have served for either food production or for camelid pasturage. Other qochas have been found scattered around the drier sections of the Katari, Tiwanaku, and Desaguadero valleys. Probably both qochas and terraces formed another aspect of the diversified economy (Janusek 2008).

Herding was another important economic aspect of Tiwanaku because of the importance of llamas and alpacas to trade, subsistence, and ritual. As mentioned, the city and Altiplano population were dependent on lower-altitude communities for certain crops and for other goods as well, such as salt, wood, and metallurgical supplies. Such resources were brought to the region by llama caravans; similar caravans still ply the ancient routes, for example, from the highlands of Cuzco to the Pacific coast through the Colca Valley. Alpaca herds were important for providing the wool from which cloth and textiles were made. Maintaining large herds of camelids was critical to the economic well-being of Tiwanaku, and it is likely that specialized herders were involved with this activity. Where the vast herds were quartered is not clear, but it was probably in the upland regions where forage would have been plentiful and where the herds did not compete for agricultural land.

In addition to being used for caravans and cloth production, camelids played an important role in the diet. Webster and Janusek (2003) note that 70 percent of the faunal remains from Tiwanaku I sites were from young camelids, probably llamas that were specifically bred for their meat. Camelids also provided dung that could be used as fuel for fires in a region where wood was scarce. Finally, as mentioned earlier, camelids served ritual functions as sacrifices and were prominently displayed as part of the iconography of both monuments and ceramics. This importance stemmed from their value to the Tiwanaku economic system.

Finally, fishing played a role in the Tiwanaku economy, but a much reduced one. Although the resources of Lake Titicaca were very important to the Early and Middle Formative settlements of the region, by the Late Formative they began to be supplanted by camelids as the importance of inland locations increased (Janusek 2008). Yet they were clearly significant enough to also form a part of Tiwanaku iconography, perhaps more as a link to a time when the ancestors of the later people lived closer to the shore and used such resources. Although the Uru today are largely a marginalized culture, Janusek (2008) suggests that they might have been a much more influential group during Tiwanaku times because they controlled the lake and its resources, including the means to access andesite for the important monuments of the city.

So how was this vast hinterland of special-interest groups, local communities, ayllus, and ethnicities integrated into a cultural entity? It is clear from settlement studies that there were four levels of site size, ranging from hamlets under 3 ha to the cities of Tiwanaku and Lukurmata. To many scholars (e.g., Ponce Sanguines 1981; Stanish 2002), this argues for a state level of bureaucracy, whereby goods and labor moved up the hierarchy, and orders and ritual information moved down. Other scholars, such as Kolata (1993), Janusek (2008), and Paul Goldstein (2009), suggest that no centralized governing authority was in charge of the economic relations just described. Rather, powerful elites centered in Tiwanaku, and probably more than a single dynasty, negotiated power with elites in other centers, especially in Lukurmata, and perhaps also in Khonkho Wankane. These elites, in turn, worked with leaders in smaller communities near their centers to gain what they needed. Although this system does seem to have been hierarchical, it differed from a true state system in the inability of the higher levels to coerce the lower levels to do what they wanted.

But what did the people at the lower echelons of the power hierarchy get for their labor and surpluses? Certainly they were involved in rituals that were conducted by the leaders and elites, and it was this sacred knowledge that was the basis for the inequalities that developed through the Formative and into the Tiwanaku Period. Lineages that had could trace their ancestry to founding individuals also could argue that they were the "keepers of the faith" and controlled the ritual information critical to the functioning of the society. The astronomical information designed into the Kalasasaya was just one such form of information used by the emerging rulers of Tiwanaku. But it is also evident that there was a considerable amount of *commensalism* (the sharing of food and drink) that cemented bonds of kinship and politics. The presence of large vessels for making chicha, and the quantities of serving vessels in certain areas at the major sites reflects this, as do the presence of large kitchens and food debris. Surpluses provided by the local communities were, in a sense, given back at large feasts sponsored by elites and during special festivals throughout the year. Such festivals were probably associated with religious rituals so the local people could see how the products of their efforts were being used to assure the continuance of society.

THE HINTERLANDS Thus far, we have only discussed the development of the city of Tiwanaku and its relationship to nearby settlements in the valleys to the north and south. But we defined Tiwanaku as a powerful political and religious entity that spread its influence over a large geographical area. What was that area, and how did Tiwanaku influence the regional cultures that existed in those regions? To explain this, it is useful to use Janusek's (2008, 202) concepts of concentric rings of influence: a core area consisting of an inner and outer heartland, near peripheries outside the core, far enclaves or peripheries outside of them, and the frontier region at the margins of the influence of the city. The core region was just discussed. We now turn to the more distant regions (figure 8.13).

The near peripheries include the greater Lake Titicaca basin and the regions to the east, descending into the yunga zone. The most important site of the outer heartland was Lukurmata. The site expanded into a major center during this period, focused on a ceremonial complex on a ridge that was surrounded by a moat, as at Tiwanaku. A sunken temple constructed of ashlars formed the major part of this complex, although it varied in specific details from the Semi-Subterranean Temple at Tiwanaku (Bermann 1994; Janusek 2004b). The ceramics were similar to those at Tiwanaku, but the elites at Lukurmata also used a variety of shapes not common at Tiwanaku. Some burial practices were different as well. These differences support the idea that the Lukurmata elite were distinct from those at Tiwanaku.

During the period, the population of the city expanded beyond the moat, as at Tiwanaku, and a variety of craft-producing residential complexes were founded. One of these specialized in making flutes out of llama bones. Residential compounds were planned in advance, and subterranean canals took away waste. Significantly, all new constructions were oriented, more or less, to the cardinal directions, in marked contrast to the Formative buildings. Although not as rigidly uniform in their orientation as the compounds in Tiwanaku, their conformity suggests an acceptance of the cosmological canons on which it was based (Janusek 2004b). The abrupt adoption of Tiwanaku-style ceramics with the characteristic iconographic motifs, particularly those associated with ceremonial drinking, supports this view as well.

In contrast to Tiwanaku, where living in proximity to the city core was a measure of how important an individual was, status was based on other measures in Lukurmata. The residences closest to the temple on the ridge were not the best houses nor did they have the best tools (Janusek 2004b). Rather, the residential compounds where the panpipes were made appear to have been higher in status as determined by their material remains and the construc-

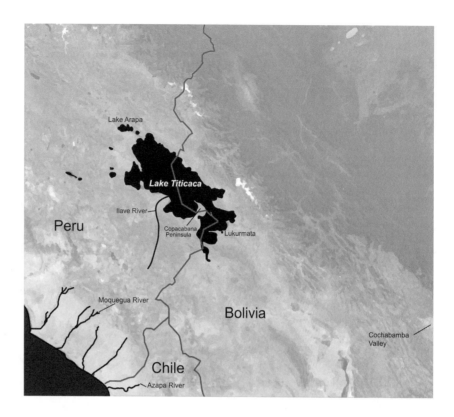

Figure 8.13. Map of Altiplano and vicinity, showing regions and site locations. Map by Matt Gorney.

tion techniques used. Janusek suggests this might be because they were on a major route from Lukurmata to Tiwanaku, although other factors might have been in play as well.

Lukurmata was at the west end of the Katari Valley, yet there is no good evidence that it controlled any of the towns or communities elsewhere in the valley. Raised-field agriculture was beginning to play a role in the local economy but not a significant one. Most farming was done along the piedmont zones around the valley proper, and fishing activities were conducted along the lakeshore. Janusek (2004b) argues that what control Lukurmata had over such communities was mediated through the local leaders of the small communities and through control of rituals at the sunken temple and perhaps elsewhere at the site. The elite status of the individuals at Lukurmata was also no doubt related to their interactions with the Tiwanaku elite.

Tiwanaku influence was extensive, but uneven, along the western edge of Lake Titicaca during Tiwanaku I (Stanish et al. 2005). To start, there is little evidence of a Tiwanaku presence in this region prior to Tiwanaku IV (of the old system, which corresponds to late Tiwanaku 1 in the system here); political developments were restricted to local zones around small centers. Sites with Tiwanaku IV ceramics, however, were found in regions associated with raised fields and terraced lands from the Copacabana Peninsula to the Ilave River (see figure 8.13). Ceremonial centers with sunken court complexes were found, often as expansions of earlier pre-Tiwanaku settlements. At this time, Tiwanaku established a major presence on the Island of the Sun, including large sites and the giving of offerings (Seddon 2005). The incorporation of this island, which would become one of the most sacred locations of the Inkas a millennium later, argues that it might have been claimed by the Tiwanaku elite as a place of origin as well.

Between the Ilave River and the vicinity of the modern city of Puno, Tiwanaku influence is much less evident and entirely concentrated along the lake. In contrast, from Puno north to Huatta there are many sites all associated with raised-field farming. It is clear that the region around Puno was an actual enclave of Tiwanaku, probably including individuals from the heartland. Why this region was considered more important than the intervening areas is unclear at present.

Continuing to the northwest, there is little evidence of Tiwanaku presence in the zone of Lake Arapa and north until around 700 C.E. (Stanish 2009). At that time, Tiwanaku established many settlements along the edges of lakes Titicaca and Arapa, focusing, as in the regions to the southeast, on zones of raised-field agriculture. An autonomous culture, termed Huaña by Stanish, existed adjacent to this region and occupied the rich farmland of the northern Altiplano. The two cultures apparently did interact but remained independent. The presence of Tiwanaku colonies within the Huaña territory does suggest that these interactions might have been more complex than previously thought.

According to Janusek (2008), the far peripheries included regions adjacent to the Altiplano that provided resources to the core and that, in turn, participated in the culture of Tiwanaku to some degree. In some places, such as the Moquegua Valley of southern Peru, there was a strong interaction, including the presence of Tiwanaku individuals and colonists in these distant lands. In other places, local individuals participated in the culture, absorbing Tiwanaku material culture for their own purposes.

Thanks to Michael Moseley's Programa Kuntisuyu and the subsequent research that expanded it, we know a considerable amount about the Moquegua Valley of far southern Peru (figure 8.14). This valley is of considerable interest during the Middle Horizon because of the evidence of Tiwanaku presence there and also the presence of a Wari enclave adjacent to

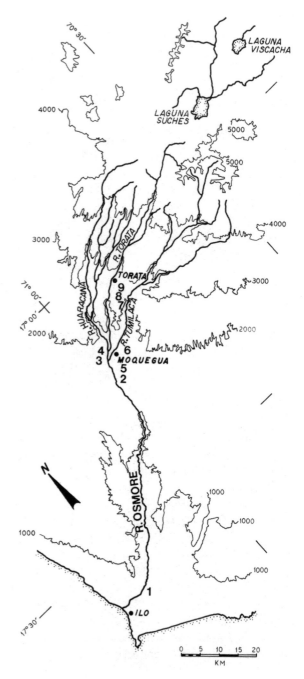

Figure 8.14. Map of Moquegua Valley, showing locations of Tiwanaku-contemporary sites. From Moseley 1991, figure 2. Map courtesy of Michael Moseley. Key to site numbers: (1) Chiribaya, (2) Omo, (3) Cerro Trapiche, (4) Cerro Echenique, (5) Chen Chen, (6) Los Cerrillos, (7) Tumilaca, (8) Cerro Baúl, (9) Cerro Mejia.

Tiwanaku settlements (discussed in the Wari section of this chapter).

The Huaracane occupation dates to the Early Intermediate Period of the valley. At this time, settlements were located just above the valley floodplain in locations where simple canal irrigation could be practiced. The middle valley was fairly densely occupied by people using simple ceramics and living on low semicircular terraces (Goldstein 2005). There is little to suggest social differentiation, although a few sites have boot-shaped tombs associated with Pukara ceramics. The size and construction techniques of these tombs, plus the evidence for prestige goods associated with them, argues they were for an emerging elite group. This group was probably responsible for the interaction with the Pukara culture to the east.

Between 500 and 700 C.E., groups using a distinctive style of ceramics that are closely similar to those from Tiwanaku started arriving in the Moquegua Valley. These ceramics are divided into two distinctive style groups, called Omo and Chen Chen for the sites where they are best represented. The Omo-style inhabitants arrived first and settled away from the valley floodplain in regions that would not have threatened the Huaracane settlements. Goldstein (2005, 2009) argues they were probably pastoralists

from the Altiplano, perhaps from near Lake Titicaca, based on the ceramic affinities (see box 8.1 for other evidence). There is no evidence of interaction between these earliest settlers and the Huaracane locals.

Around 700 C.E., there was a major El Niño event in the valley that eroded hillsides, destroyed irrigation canals and fields, and remodeled the landscape. This event must have been catastrophic for the Huaracane farmers along the floodplain. After this event, agriculturalists using Omo-style ceramics occupied the regions adjacent to the floodplain, regions that had been abandoned by the Huaracane. After this initial colonization, another group moved into the mid-valley using the Chen Chen–style ceramics. These people settled to the southwest of the initial inhabitants and used their own style of ceramics, yet buried their dead and oriented their settlements in the same way as the Omo inhabitants. On the basis of a variety of indicators, Goldstein (2009) argues these two distinct groups probably were social groups such as ayllus that migrated to the Moquegua Valley from different regions in the Tiwanaku heartland, although these cannot at this point be identified. Biological distance studies by Deborah Blom et al. (1998) have shown no differences between the Omo and Chen Chen populations and those from the Tiwanaku heartland.

BOX 8.1 Isotopic studies and the Middle Horizon

Traditional ways of identifying what people ate and where they were born or emigrated to were based on the macrobotanical remains of plants and animals and the study of burials and their associated artifacts. Yet these procedures yield only indirect results; plant and animal remains show the presence of such materials but do not indicate how much was consumed, and burials may reflect the movement of people or just trade in objects. New analytical techniques that identify the isotopes of different elements and their ratios are now beginning to yield more specific information that was previously unavailable.

One of the most exciting new techniques used in Andean studies is strontium *isotope* analysis. Strontium is an element that occurs in rock, groundwater, plants, animals, and humans. It has four isotopes. The ratio of two of them, strontium-87 (^{87}Sr) and strontium-86 (^{86}Sr), varies according to local geological conditions, so it can be used to identify the movements of people between regions. The ratio of these two isotopes in human bone and tooth enamel can be used in subtly different ways. Tooth enamel is set in the first several years of an individual's life and varies little after that, so the ratio $^{87}Sr/^{86}Sr$ in an individual's enamel indicates the region in which the individual lived her or his early life (assuming the ratio has been determined for the region). The ratio of the two isotopes in bone, however, changes because bone is replaced through time, so the isotopic ratio in an individual's bone indicates the place where the individual was living at the end of her or his life. Both kinds of analysis allow the archaeologist to determine whether an individual was born in the particular region where her or his bones were found or immigrated from elsewhere (Slovak, Paytan, and Wiegand 2009).

An example of how this technique has shed new light on the Middle Horizon is Kelly Knudson et al.'s 2004 study of skeletons from the sites of Chen Chen and Tiwanaku. Chen Chen has often been regarded as a Tiwanaku colony, based on the architecture and ceramics. A small sample of individuals tested for strontium isotope ratios supported that at least two of the people at Chen Chen were from Tiwanaku. Nonlocal individuals were also identified from the Putuni Palace at Tiwanaku and were interpreted as dedicatory offerings. This indicates that the sacrifices were probably nonlocal people. Another study (Slovak, Paytan, and Wiegand 2009) shows that at least one individual in the Middle Horizon Ancón Necropolis site near Lima was probably born in Ayacucho. This supports the contentious hypothesis that the site of Ancón might have had political links to Wari, although weak ones.

Another way that isotopes are increasing our knowledge of ancient societies is through the study of carbon isotopes, in addition to their utility in dating. Different plants take up different isotopes of carbon, specifically ^{13}C. Plants using what is called a C_3 metabolic pathway have lower percentages of ^{13}C than those using a C_4 pathway. The only plant of major importance that uses a C_4 pathway in the Andes is maize; all other crops are of the C_3 type. To use this technique, however, the researcher also has to be aware of other inputs to the diet because marine resources also have higher percentages of ^{13}C. Brian Finucane (2009) has used this technique to indicate that maize agriculture was the foundation of the Wari Empire, in contrast to earlier cultures that were based on traditional Andean crops. Analyzing skeletal materials from pre-Wari and Wari proveniences, he found clear evidence of a principal reliance on maize, which stands in contrast to other regions of the Andes where maize was more of a supplement or even a condiment, as he notes. This also contradicts previous ideas that a dependence on maize was largely a late development of the Inkas.

In addition to the evidence for the importance of maize to the Wari, Finucane, Patricio Maita Agurto, and William Isbell (2006) have found that the Conchopata inhabitants were foddering their camelids on maize, probably on the cobs and leaves, rather than simply taking them to pasture on the puna, as modern herders do. The identification of higher levels of C_4 plants in these animals, the most likely of which was maize, led to this conclusion. This discovery reflects a different herd-management practice than previously known and again shows the importance of applying new analytical practices to archaeological data.

These studies show some of the exciting new and more nuanced details about ancient societies that can be identified using new analytical techniques.

It is evident from mortuary differences that through time social differences continued to develop. In several local cemeteries, a few adult males were buried with ear spools and four-cornered hats, emblems of authority in this society. These were probably local leaders. In contrast, a group of elite tombs at two sites that had above-ground structures over chambered tombs housed individuals with exquisite jewelry and Tiwanaku tunics with the principal deities on them (Goldstein 2005). These individuals probably represented the highest echelon in the status system, perhaps individuals who ruled groups larger than a local ayllu. Still, Goldstein argues such individuals were local people, not governors sent from the heartland.

The evidence for a Tiwanaku I occupation of the Moquegua Valley represents the clearest proof that people from the Altiplano colonized this region, as opposed to simply influencing it indirectly. The reason for this probably lies in the dramatic El Niño event that allowed the movement of Tiwanaku people into the region. Where did the Huaracane inhabitants go? It is uncertain, but it is possible they migrated down the valley to the coastal zone or perhaps laterally to other valleys north and south. Regarding the former possibility, around 700 C.E., the local Late Formative Chiribaya ceramic style appears (Lozada et al. 2009), and its emergence perhaps heralds a merging of the local coastal groups with the immigrant Huaracane population. Biological evidence supports the local origins of the Chiribaya people (see chapter 9).

In the valleys farther south, there is evidence for Tiwanaku influence but through more indirect intervention. Tiwanaku vessels and other objects from the heartland appear in valleys such as Azapa in northern Chile, but their relative paucity and association with local material indicates to Janusek (2008) that there were no enclaves in these regions. Rather, as in other regions discussed, the local elites were increasing their own status by interacting with Tiwanaku. The ceramics of the local Cabuza group are heavily influenced by Tiwanaku, and other aspects of their culture also incorporated foreign elements of the dominant culture. In contrast, Goldstein (2005) suggests that there were Tiwanaku enclaves in the region that occupied mid-valley areas not occupied by the local Cabuza groups. He thinks that the Tiwanaku elites were "a trade diaspora community whose impressive cultural associations permitted it to attract clients, inspire emulation, and exert a dominant political influence over its hosts" (Goldstein 2005, 111).

As in Moquegua, the Cochabamba Valley of southeastern Bolivia began to show Tiwanaku influence around 500 C.E. Ceramics from the core are used along with the local pottery styles. It is interesting to note that the kero form (plate 7A) that was such an emblem of Tiwanaku culture probably originated in this region (Janusek 2008). Cochabamba is an excellent maize-growing region, and it is likely that it was this crop that drew Tiwanaku people to the region. On the basis of ceramic styles and the abundance of maize found there, the Ch'iji Jawira zone of the city was perhaps occupied by people from this zone. Trade through Cochabamba brought social developments to the local elites in charge, and Tiwanaku ceramics and other elements of culture such as the drug cult spread throughout the region (Janusek 2008).

Finally, at the frontiers of the Tiwanaku sphere of influence are places such as San Pedro de Atacama in Chile. Located 800 km south, and thus perhaps a month's journey from the city, this oasis has ample evidence of Tiwanaku presence, although the nature of the presence is debated. A large number of Tiwanaku objects, especially textiles, ceramics, snuffing tablets, and gold artifacts have been found in graves from the several sites in the vicinity. Still, Janusek (2008) argues that the overall percentage of such objects is quite small relative to the locally produced materials. On that basis, he argues that San Pedro, like Azapa, was probably a trade hub managed by local elites who benefited from their exchange with Tiwanaku.

In summary, during the Tiwanaku I Period, the city expanded, both in terms of its size and complexity as well as in terms of its influence in other regions. The center had become a major ritual focus through careful observations of celestial movements, and its religion was accepted by both the commoners and elites in the heartland. People from more distant lands were attracted to the center both for trade and religion, and local elites who controlled such trade increased their prestige (perhaps) through gifts or exchange of Tiwanaku objects for foreign products. But even as the agricultural productivity of the heartland was intensified through raised-field and hill-slope technology, more food was needed by the population centers, engendering both an expansion along the shores of Lake Titicaca and a diaspora of herders and agriculturalists to places such as Moquegua. Yet, as Janusek notes, there might not have been a strongly centralized bureaucracy that developed this expansion. The heartland was multiethnic and pluralistic, and the powerful ancient lineages in charge of rituals at the Akapana, Kalasasaya, and Pumapunku needed to negotiate their power through the local and regional leaders. The use of feasts and celebrations was the principal means to do this, but these came at a cost: the spiraling need for both food and drink to put on such celebrations. These needs led to changes in Tiwanaku society and its influence after 800 C.E.

Tiwanaku 2 (800–1100 C.E.)

This period can be characterized as one when there was a centralization of the political economy of Tiwanaku. The city began a major reconstruction process that resulted in the concentration of elite power in the core of the city and a much more prominent display of authority. Outside the core, there were changes that were the result of these internal shifts, such as an increase in the production of maize in the Moquegua Valley. Most of the Katari Valley was now given over to state-controlled raised-field production that was directly under Tiwanaku authority rather than mediated through Lukurmata (Janusek 2008). In essence, the negotiation of power among the elite lineages of Tiwanaku and their regional and local leaders was subverted to favor the city leaders.

THE CITY OF TIWANAKU In Tiwanaku, the process of urban renewal is evidenced by the substantial remodeling of the Akapana. Recycled ashlars are found in the modified retaining walls, indicating that they were part of a previous construction phase. Who proclaimed the need and oversaw the work is uncertain. Rituals involving llama and human sacrifices are evident in the piles of bones found along the foundation terrace. The Pumapunku platform was modified by reducing access to the sunken court.

Some of the most significant information concerning the centralization of power comes from the changes in elite residential architecture during this period. On top of the Akapana, around the central sunken court at the summit, there were a series of rooms that contained large quantities of serving vessels and food remains, suggesting ritual feasting and drinking. Six burials beneath the carefully constructed floors, five individuals facing a sixth one, suggest the final resting places of the ritual specialists who conducted the activities in the court (Kolata 2003b). This might suggest that the highest elite in society were associated with such ceremonies, although it does not preclude their being involved in other activities or that other individuals might have been comparable in status as well.

In addition to the burials on the Akapana, the two elite compounds behind the Kalasasaya were covered over and the Putuni residential-ceremonial complex was constructed on top. Part of this complex was a platform surrounded on three sides by niches that Couture and Sampeck (2003) think may have housed the mummy bundles of the ancestors that had been located in one of the razed structures. Alternatively, they could have been the locations for ritual objects used in the ceremonies on the platform. Vranich (2009) notes that this building was made entirely of recycled ashlars, possibly from the Kalasasaya itself, indicating that the elites of Tiwanaku were willing to sacrifice older structures for newer ones. The other part of the Putuni complex was an elite residence with a plaza that was covered by chicha-brewing jars that had been smashed. An adjacent residence had the remains of gold, copper pins, silver, and jewelry. Thus, another of highest elite Tiwanaku groups lived behind the Kalasasaya and conducted private ceremonies near their residence. This contrasts with the more public ceremonies conducted in the earlier structures that had been modified.

It is important to note that to reach the Putuni platform, individuals had to travel across the entire Kalasasaya platform and then pass through a narrow door and passageway to reach the temple complex. All the walls of this passage were of andesite, and the view from the passageway to the temple framed the sacred Mt. Kimsachata (Vranich 2009). This all suggests that only the most important individuals were able to participate in whatever rituals and feasting were done there.

During this period, much of the region within the inner moat was renovated into elite ceremonial zones (Janusek 2008). Two compounds were constructed over earlier ones. The first was a poorly made kitchen and chicha-preparation area, where animal remains and chicha-brewing jars were found. The other was a well-made zone with high quantities of luxury items but also evidence of feasting and drinking. This evidence suggests that much of the urban core was now dedicated to commensalism, and given that there probably were many of these kinds of compounds located in the urban core, it indicates a city that had become focused on ritual feasting and drinking, probably among elites and nonelites to cement bonds of friendship and mutual assistance. Janusek (2008) argues that the different compounds housed competing lineages who traced their ancestry to different rulers, much like the later Chimú and Inka.

THE HINTERLANDS The pressures of such ceremonial activities spurred changes in the productive parts of the Tiwanaku economy. First, Tiwanaku vessels were now mass-produced to accommodate the increased demand for them. More important, the raised-field system came to be dominated by the elites in Tiwanaku, who reorganized the Katari Valley system to increase production of food for the ceremonial life of the city. The city of Lukurmata, long a sister city to Tiwanaku, was largely abandoned (Bermann 1994). Its location in the food-production system was appropriated by elites in Tiwanaku, leading to its demise. How this happened is unexplained.

Perhaps the Tiwanaku elites were able to convince the local farmers that they could provide some advantages that the Lukurmata elites could not; perhaps the latter moved to the city and were incorporated into the Tiwanaku elite.

By Tiwanaku 2, the site of Khonkho Wankane was also largely abandoned, although this decline may have started earlier, during Tiwanaku 1 (Janusek 2008). Like Lukurmata, the evidence suggests that the Tiwanaku elite focused their interests and special favors on the groups living nearer the Desaguadero River, where raised-field farming could be conducted. As in their expansion out of the heartland northwestward, it was the desire for food that drove geopolitical considerations in the region south of the core.

By 1000 C.E., the city of Tiwanaku was a large multiethnic community of elites, commoners, craftspeople, and pilgrims. Great festivals may have continued to be celebrated in the major structures, but now other rituals took place in smaller, more private venues such as the Putuni platform. Elites conducted competitive feasting of important clients from outside the city and of nonelites who provided the resources for the feasts. These events became increasingly common and probably expensive to maintain. Pressures mounted on the elites and their followers to provide such festivals. A long period of higher rainfall had led to the expansion of raised-field agriculture throughout the Titicaca basin, and trade brought in maize, metals, and other materials for the chicha and the rituals necessary to the elites' statuses. But this increase in commensalism had sown the seeds of problems that would arise at the beginning of the Pacajes Period (see chapter 9).

Associated with the reorganization of the Katari raised-field systems, maize production in the Moquegua Valley was also transformed into a Tiwanaku elite-controlled activity. During the Chen Chen phase, new field systems were opened in the flat pampas along the river floodplain, drawing water through long irrigation canals and from spring-fed aquifers (Goldstein 2005). Possibly representing a different social group, these agriculturalists became focused on food production and storage. The site of

Chen Chen itself had massive storage facilities far beyond the needs of the local community.

As the Chen Chen colonists became more tied into the Tiwanaku cultural sphere, they incorporated a new element of its power: a ceremonial center modeled on the platform and sunken-court architecture of Tiwanaku. At the site of Omo M10, a temple complex of three courts was constructed on a hill above the settlement. The lowest terrace was a simple open courtyard, although with a large circular area defined in it, possibly for dances. Above that was a rectangular court entered through a narrow staircase. Above that was the Upper Court, clearly the most sacred place in the complex and, indeed, in the valley. Its foundations were constructed of carefully cut and polished ashlars, on top of which were laid adobe bricks to finish the walls. Stone slabs and adobe-covered lintels mimicked the elaborate architectural features of the Tiwanaku city temples (Goldstein 2005). Ichu grass roofs covered some of the rooms. In the center of a series of rooms was a sunken rectangular court that had some kind of monolith located centrally. The monolith is gone, but the hole in which it was placed still exists. Thus, the temple mimics closely Tiwanaku structures such as the Akapana and Kalasasaya.

In contrast to the rituals conducted at Tiwanaku, there is an absence of ceremonial drinking and serving vessels in the temple. Offerings throughout were composed of incensario vessels for the burning of offerings, animal sacrifices, and simple plainware vessels (Goldstein 2005). Exotic stones, such as lapis lazuli (from Chile) and malachite, and *Spondylus* from Ecuador were also found. A rare tapestry fragment with the Tiwanaku "Sacrificer" figure on it also indicates the presence of high-status individuals in the temple.

The construction of a Tiwanaku-style temple complex where rituals could be conducted for a privileged few, probably by the most important members of society, reflects the strong influence that Tiwanaku had on its colonists in the valley. Whether the elite priests were from the Altiplano or were locals is unknown. But the presence of the temple is a symbol of the authority demonstrated by the city elites in the province of Moquegua. As Goldstein notes, "Tiwanaku colonists constructed corporate architecture that replicated the grandeur of homeland monuments and provided a stage for public ceremonies that reified and legitimized central power. Increasingly, the actors in these rites saw themselves as citizens of a province rather than colonists affiliated with kin groups" (2005, 320).

Was Tiwanaku a state? Many trees have been killed to feed publications in the search for an answer to this question. Unlike Wari, for which the evidence is perhaps more compelling for statehood (Isbell and Schreiber 1978), Tiwanaku does not clearly exhibit the criteria that archaeologists have come to expect for a culture to be called a state. Although the evidence is better for the southern Altiplano region, the nature of the political reach of Tiwanaku beyond that region has been debated, except for the Moquegua Valley. Even the evidence from Moquegua now seems to point to colonies sent by local groups from the Altiplano rather than state-organized colonies (Goldstein 2009). State-level criteria include ascribed status; a bureaucracy to carry out state functions; intensive agriculture providing surpluses; well-developed and full-time occupational specialization, especially regarding crafts; formal religion with full-time specialists; and coercive power. Funerary evidence supports the existence of ascribed status for Tiwanaku and the multitiered settlement pattern is inferential evidence for a hierarchy of political positions, possibly reflecting a bureaucracy. Craft specialization is present, and other occupations, such as herding, agricultural, and fishing, have been identified. Intensive agriculture is evident in the raised-field systems. The monumental architecture, carved monoliths, and iconography on the ceramics is the best evidence for a formalized religion. Coercive power is not necessarily obvious because there is little evidence for any militarism by Tiwanaku. The abundant evidence of Tiwanaku interaction in external regions all points to trade or local elite emulation.

In contrast, Paul Goldstein (2009) has noted that Tiwanaku does not fit easily into traditional models of ancient states. He notes that "Tiwanaku central authority was a ritual suzerainty that coexisted with the persistent autonomy of corporate groups" (ibid., 295). The state, and its ruler if one existed, operated only through negotiations with these powerful corporate groups. The city of Tiwanaku displayed its influence through its image as a pilgrimage center. But its political authority seems to have been limited to the region around Lake Titicaca, and even there, the lineages at the capital were not omnipotent, as in other states.

WARI IN THE MIDDLE HORIZON

The other cultural power of the Middle Horizon was Wari.[2] As mentioned at the beginning of the chapter, due to the similarity in iconographic features of the ceramics from both Tiwanaku and Huari (and Wari-related sites), for a long time Wari ceramics were included as a derivative form of Tiwanaku pottery. Later, with the better description of Huari and its ceramics in the 1950s (Bennett 1953; Rowe 1956), the independence of the two centers was firmly established.

Huari emerged as the primary center of this culture at the beginning of the Middle Horizon, around 600 cal C.E. At this time, it eclipsed other Huarpa centers that had existed, such as Ñawimpukyo. The reasons for its emergence are not clear. We know little about the site because of the terrorist activity of the Sendero Luminoso, which originated in Ayacucho and prevented any serious work at the sites during the 1980s and into the 1990s. Still, building on previous work by Bennett (1953), Lumbreras (1960), and others, William Isbell's Huari Urban Prehistory Project identified several sectors of distinct activity and an architectural style that was different from Tiwanaku and from any other Andean society (Isbell 1991). New research since the mid-1990s has advanced our understanding of this complex site and its relationship to other settlements in the Ayacucho Valley.

The building style that defines Wari occupations, both in the capital and in its provincial centers, is called orthogonal cellular architecture (Isbell 1991). Isbell discusses thirty different characteristics of this style, divided into the domains of form, technology,

and concept. Some of the important characteristics of form include orthogonal layout, *patio groups* consisting of central open patios surrounded by narrow rooms and a low bench, rectangular compounds of patio groups enclosed by high walls (figure 8.15), and sealed chambers for mortuary or ritual uses. Technology traits include a rigid hierarchical order in the construction sequence of buildings across a site, walls with double faces and a rubble core, drainage canals under the floors, clay and plaster coatings on the finished walls, and corbels or wall setbacks to support the upper stories. Conceptual characteristics include buildings confronting the natural landscape rather than blending in with it, a sense of closure and privacy in the compounds and patio groups, modular architectural units, no foci of public activities, and periodic interment and renewal of public structures.

The uniformity of this style is one of the hallmarks of Wari influence from its farthest southern boundary to its northern one. That being said, one of the curious features of Wari influence is its irregular distribution. There are many regions with no centers, although the presence of Wari ceramics in the intervening areas does argue for some kind of interaction between Wari people and locals.

THE CITY OF HUARI Let us begin by discussing Huari (figure 8.16). The site appears to have grown by the coalescence of smaller villages at the beginning of the Middle Horizon (Isbell 2008). A ceremonial area, Vegachayoq Moqo, is located in the western part of the site (Bragayrac 1991). This area began as an elite residence that was interred and had a D-shaped temple built on top of it (figure 8.17). This temple, of a shape that is also typical of Wari centers, was a place where ritual feasting and drinking occurred, with the smashing of serving vessels as a part of the activities. Later, the site served as a funerary monument (Isbell 2008).

Across a wide avenue to the south of Vegachayoq Moqo is a complex called Monjachayoq, where a complex tomb was located deep underground. Its form and organization argue for its being a royal burial location (Isbell 2004), probably one of many

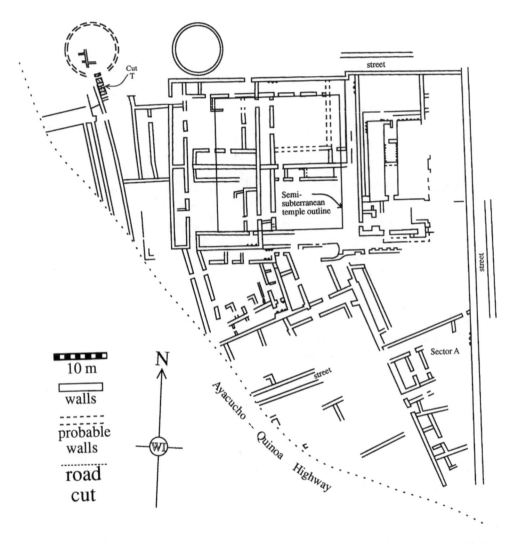

Figure 8.15. Moraduchayoq compound, Huari, an example of Wari orthogonal organization. From Isbell, Brewster-Wray, and Spickard 1991, figure 21. Courtesy of William Isbell.

at the site. To the southeast of this complex is the Moraduchayoq compound, the location of extensive excavations by the Huari Urban Prehistory Project (Isbell, Brewster-Wray, and Spickard 1991). Here, a square, semi-subterranean temple constructed of finely cut stones was found, dating to the early Middle Horizon. The form and technology suggest strong similarities to the semi-subterranean temples of the Tiwanaku region. The significance of this temple is uncertain; it could reflect a copying of the form by early individuals from Huari who visited the Altiplano or the use of Tiwanaku stonemasons for the work, a possibility suggested by Isbell (2008).

This temple was interred and a large orthogonal cellular compound was constructed on it. Although domestic debris was found in the excavations, a large quantity of fancy serving vessels suggest that entertaining in the main patio must have been an import-

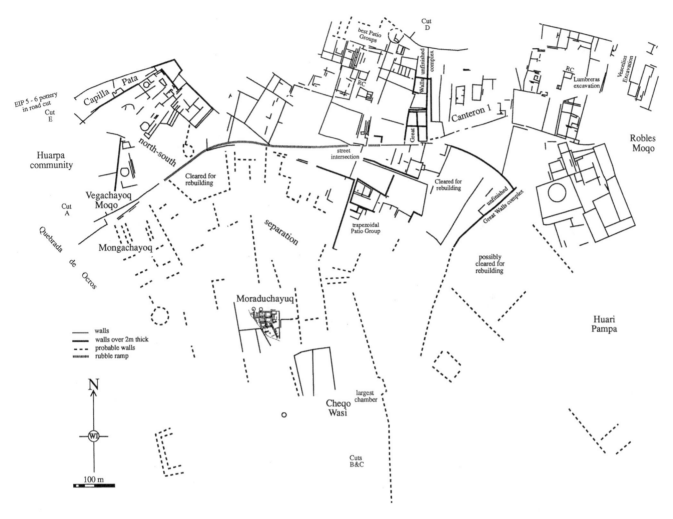

Figure 8.16. Map of site of Huari. From Isbell, Brewster-Wray, and Spickard 1991, figure 4. Courtesy of William Isbell.

ant function of this compound. We do not know who was being fêted, but Isbell (2008) suggests they were low-level managers or workers who brought goods into the city from elsewhere. The residents, then, were middle-level managers.

A final area of excavation at Huari was Cheqo Wasi (Benavides 1991). This badly looted area was a funerary sector, as indicated by the many tombs and the remains of over one hundred individuals found there. Tombs of different kinds existed, but the cut

stone chambers with more than one individual are the type identified by Isbell (2004) as the elite graves. A D-shaped structure at Cheqo Wasi included both tombs and a carved monolith that might have been a guardian deity. Thus, this sector was not just funerary but ritual in nature as well.

Other areas of the site probably reflect similar uses; certainly there are the remains of other compounds like Moraduchayoq present. Isbell (2008) argues that most of the core just described was proba-

Figure 8.17. Vegachayoq Moqo, showing the D-shaped temple. Photo courtesy of José Ochatoma Paravicino.

bly ceremonial at the beginning of the occupation of the city and, indeed, may well have been the magnet that drew people to the site. In Middle Horizon 1A (see figure 5.12), the iconography shared with Tiwanaku appeared on pottery and some textiles, indicating the incorporation of a new pantheon of gods. During this phase, Wari influence also spread, as most of the centers have ceramic and architectural features that link them to the city during this time. When the city reached its largest size, it probably covered roughly 2.5 km² and had a population of 20,000–40,000 people.

Like Tiwanaku, sometime in the ninth century, a dramatic change occurred that led to new architectural forms appearing at the city (Isbell 1991). The orthogonal cellular architecture was replaced by monumental compounds that were elongated and trapezoidal. A major clearing of old buildings took place to make way for news ones that were never built. The city apparently was abandoned at the end of Middle Horizon 2, although Finucane et al. (2007) suggest this abandonment did not occur until the mid-eleventh century. The fact that some provincial centers continued to function until the tenth or perhaps eleventh century (Malpass 2001; Williams 2001) could support this later date for the administrative collapse.

Although the layout of Huari was fundamentally different from Tiwanaku (Isbell and Vranich 2004), emphasizing closed compounds with high walls separated by narrow streets, and no particular organization is seen, there are some aspects of overall design that could suggest the city might have been a pilgrimage center as well (Isbell 2008). There are large zones above the city with evidence of occupation that might have been places for pilgrims to enter the city. Still, their movements through the city were probably very different from those coming to Tiwanaku, which might have been their very reason for coming. No great plazas or courts were present, so smaller groups must have entered the compounds and the D-shaped structures.

In fact, we could make the argument that there was no centralized authority at Huari, much like the argument that there may not have been one overarching ruler of Tiwanaku. Although there is clearly a hierarchy of statuses present in both architecture and mortuary structures (Isbell 2004), there is no evidence identified yet to argue for one house or individual being preeminent over the others. Of course, it is possible that such a residence might still be found after additional investigations. But before we decide on this issue, let us turn to the evidence for Wari influence outside the city.

THE HINTERLANDS Conchopata is located a mere 10 km from Huari. The site is estimated to have covered approximately 20–40 ha at its greatest extent, although much of the site was destroyed by the construction of the Ayacucho airport and the encroachment of urban dwellings, including a large military base. The site rose to fame when Julio Tello discovered a group of oversized urns with Tiwanaku-like iconography on them in 1942. The urns most closely matched another group discovered at Pacheco in the Nazca Valley earlier, and that led to the style being named "Coastal Tiahuanaco." Later, in 1977, another offering of these large urns was discovered at the site (Knobloch 1991). Conchopata was originally thought to be a community of potters (Pozzi-Escot 1991) on the basis of the evidence of quantities of ceramic-manufacturing activities found at the site. There are several workshops present at the site that support this activity (Peréz Calderón and Ochatoma Paravicino 1998).

Salvage work in the early part of the new millennium has provided additional information about the site (Isbell and Cook 2002). First, a variety of mortuary practices has been identified, which suggests that the community was hierarchically organized. Second, the discovery of patio groups and D-shaped structures indicate that more than ceramic production was practiced at the site. Isbell and Cook argue that the patio groups identified were probably elite palaces, but their funerary structures are less elaborate than those found at Huari, suggesting the elite at Conchopata might have been subservient to the higher individuals at the capital. This remains to be supported with further research. But the site continued to be occupied throughout the Middle Horizon, supporting the argument that Huari might not have been abandoned at the end of Middle Horizon 2.

In discussing Wari expansion, I use the chronology of site construction defined by William Isbell in 1991, with modifications based on more current work. In 1991, Isbell argued that the mountaintop site of Cerro Baúl was probably the first provincial center, based on the Wari conquest of the Moquegua Valley early in the Middle Horizon. This is hypothesized largely based on similarities of the stonework of the subterranean temple at Huari to the Putuni temple at Tiwanaku (Isbell 1991, 304–305). However, we now know that Cerro Baúl was not built until the early seventh century C.E. (Williams and Nash 2002), and the Putuni temple was constructed even later, perhaps around 800 C.E. Thus, it seems more likely that the fine stonework was an independent invention at Huari, as Isbell (2008) has more recently suggested.

Isbell (1989) argues that the small site of Honco Pampa in the Callejón de Huaylas was probably the second provincial center constructed as Wari military forces marched north to confront the polity of Marcahuamachuco in the Huamachuco Valley. The site has a few patio groups and D-shaped temple structures (which it shares only with Cerro Baúl and Huari) but no cellular organization or perimeter wall. This suggests to Isbell that it must date to an earlier time than the emergence of the cellular orthogonal style in Middle Horizon 1B.

The next center to be built was Viracochapampa, in the Huamachuco basin (figure 8.18). This somewhat enigmatic site was located about 3 km from the Late Intermediate Period center of Marcahuamachuco and across the valley from it. The two main architectural forms at the site are what John Topic

(1991) calls niched halls and galleries. Niche halls are long rectangular buildings with rounded corners and niches located along the walls. Galleries are very long, narrow rooms that often abut each other at right angles and that share open patios. They are similar to the patio groups of Huari; the niched halls are more similar to structures found at Marcahuamachuco.

John Topic (1991) agrees that Viracochapampa is an early Wari site because it lacks the formal organization of later sites and because the niched halls and galleries have local antecedents. On the basis of the last point, and the lack of such structures in the regions farther south, he argues that the patio group and niched halls are probably local building styles adopted by Wari.

Significantly, Topic also discusses evidence that it was probably local workers under Marcahuamachuco elites that constructed the site, rather than Wari elites. Few Wari ceramics are found at the site, and there is abundant evidence that the site was never finished. Wari presence is also noted at a local shrine called Cerro Amaru and a few other sites, but Topic suggests it was trade and religion that brought Wari individuals to Huamachuco. He also believes their presence was short-lived and that the local elites probably ended the relationship after a brief period. An interesting fact to note concerning the chronology of Wari sites is that Viracochapampa is argued to have been an early site, yet it was abandoned relatively shortly after it was begun and was probably never really used to any great extent.

During Middle Horizon 1B, significant changes took place throughout the central Andes because Wari sites appear in several regions. This corresponds to the emergence of the cellular orthogonal architecture. Whether it was the new changes in the city that stimulated developments elsewhere or vice versa is not known because radiocarbon dates are not accurate enough to make the determination.

To the north of Huari, the small administrative center of Jargampata was built, which is associated with a group of domestic residences (Isbell 1977). It is a small site, only 0.1 ha in size, but it does have a section that Isbell (1991) argues was used for feasting local workers. The site no doubt reflects the emergence of the city and its need for food from surrounding areas.

Jincamocco in the Carhuarazo Valley to the south of the Ayacucho region was also built at this time. There is a formal Wari compound at the site that covers 3.5 ha, but the total site area is around 17.5 ha (figure 8.19; Schreiber 1991). The compound was divided into two halves, with the northeastern half being left largely open, perhaps as a corral for llamas. The southwest half was divided into four blocks of rooms. The one section that could be trenched indicated the presence of several patio groups connected by corridors. The entire enclosure was built on an earlier local village that was moved to make room for the enclosure.

The construction of the Wari compound was not the only change wrought by the intruders from Ayacucho. A substantial number of agricultural terraces were built, and two other Wari enclosures were located near them. Local communities were focused along the tuber- and grain-growing ecotone to maximize productivity. It is likely that Jincamocco was constructed to serve as the center for maize production, at least some of which may have been sent to Huari. The location of the site along a major north-south road of the time supports this contention (Schreiber 1991).

Another center built during Middle Horizon 1B is the site of Pikillacta, located in the southern Lucre basin, about 30 km from Cuzco (figure 8.20). This is the largest provincial center known, approximately 2 km². Within this large area, the main compound is 745 by 630 m (McEwan 1991) and consists of three sectors of patio groups; a sector of smaller conjoined rooms often thought to be storehouses; and two outer, walled areas called *canchones,* which might have served as corrals for llamas and alpacas, although excavations in one of them discovered deep and extensive middens, suggesting they functioned as trash deposits. The site is impressive for the size of its walls, some of which still stand 12 m high, and for its marked orthogonal plan despite its being located

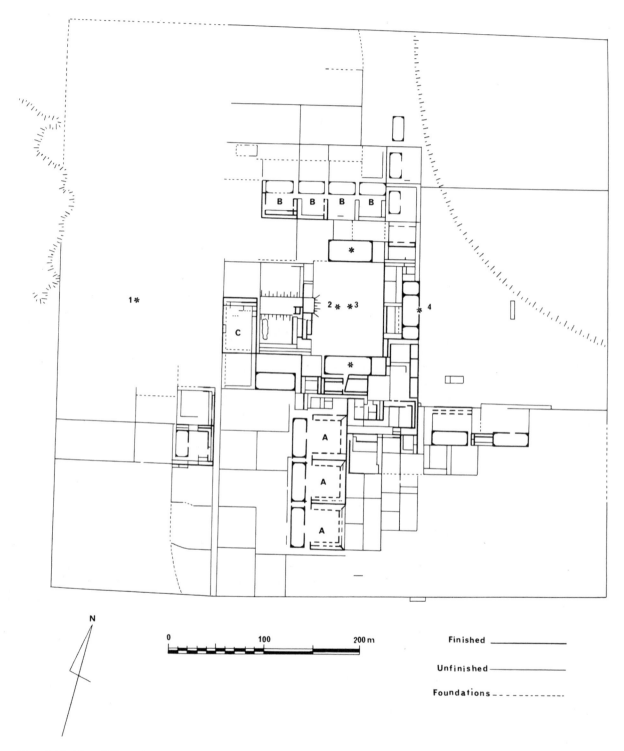

N

| 0 | 100 | 200 m |

Finished ————————

Unfinished ————————

Foundations — — — — — —

Figure 8.18. Map of Viracochapampa. From J. Topic 1991, figure 2. Huamachuco Archaeological Project, directed by John and Theresa Topic.

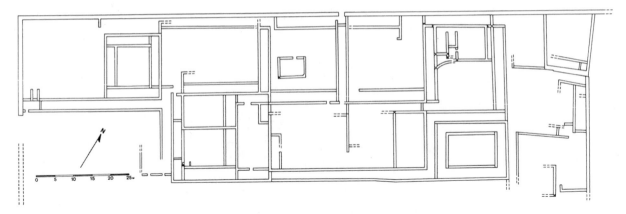

Figure 8.19. Map of the portion of Jincamocco exposed by wall trenching. The total size is uncertain. From Schreiber 1991, figure 5. Drawing by K. Schreiber.

on undulating terrain, with the lower portion of the site 80 m below the upper portion (figure 8.21).

Gordon McEwan (1991) notes several peculiarities of this site. There are very few corridors or accesses to many of the seven hundred structures and hardly any doorways to the outside. One of the notable points about some of the patio groups is the large number of rectangular galleries around the central patios; they are sometimes three deep. Another element of interest is the presence of large trapezoidal niches in at least two structures that are very similar to the ones in the niched halls at Viracochapampa. As previously mentioned, this feature might have originated in the Huamachuco area and been adopted here for the same uses, whatever they were. Finally, for a site the size of Pikillacta, there is no source of water for the city, although the discovery of a deeply buried canal suggests that such a source might yet be discovered. The nearest source today is Lake Huacarpay, located about 1 km away. This might be an indication that the inhabitants of the site were not particularly concerned about security, in contrast to researchers who feel the site was fortified.

McEwan (1991) finds evidence for a significant occupation of the site, in contrast to earlier reports of the scarcity of surface artifacts. He found thick and extensive middens in two areas of the site, and the diagnostic artifacts suggest a Middle Horizon 1B–2A occupation, dates supported by radiocarbon samples from the site. In the northern sector of the site, the region thought to be the storehouse area, excavations revealed cooking wares, food remains, and hearths, arguing for the small rooms being residential. McEwan suggests the laborers at the site might have been housed there or that it could have been for a garrison of troops.

One of the interesting points about Pikillacta is the evidence that all the architecture is based on three basic forms: large square rooms, narrow rectangular galleries, and small rectangular rooms with rounded walls. These three forms were combined to make five structural types that formed the repetitive nature of the site architecture, most of which was residential though some was ceremonial.

The site served three purposes. It was the residence of a small group of elites who lived in the center of the site and performed administrative duties associated with Wari political functions. The two largest structures at the site are located in the center of the city; one appears to have been dedicated to rituals and the other to administration. Mary Glowacki (1996) identifies imperial Wari ceramics that, along with the architecture, argue for some

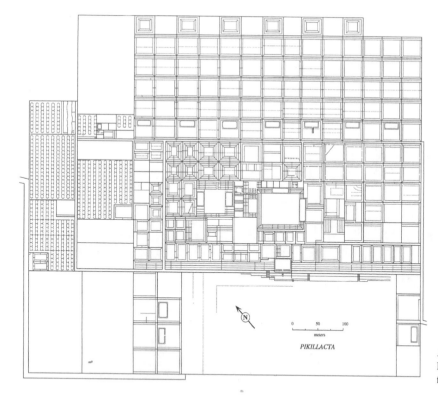

Figure 8.20. Map of Pikillacta. Drawing by Gordon McEwan, from McEwan 2005.

ceremonial feasting and drinking, although not much. Thus, residential, ceremonial, and administrative tasks were carried out by the occupants, some of whom were probably Wari administrators while others may have been local laborers who came to construct the site.

Studies of the architecture of the site suggest that only the central sector was fully built and occupied. Other sectors were laid out but never finished, as was the case at Viracochapampa. The midden analysis also suggests that the site was never fully operational, suggesting a less intensive occupation than the size of the site indicates (Glowacki 2002).

The site of Pikillacta is part of a larger occupation of the Lucre basin by Wari people. Sites are located at all the main entrances to the basin, suggesting control functions, and other sites were located near a local shrine or around the basin. The fact Pikillacta

is located not far from the northern boundary of the Tiwanaku area of influence suggests that this control might have been based on concerns about their powerful southern neighbor. According to McEwan (1991), the site was probably occupied for two hundred years and then abandoned.

Until the late 1990s, Pikillacta was considered the main Wari site that controlled the Cuzco region. However, with the discovery of the Huaro Archaeological Site Complex, located 17 km southeast of Pikillacta, the nature of the Wari influence in this region must be reconsidered. The complex, consisting of over twenty sites clustered in an area approximately 9 km², was occupied earlier than Pikillacta and apparently continued to be used later (Glowacki 2002). Although the research there is preliminary, excavations at several sites have identified a zone of agricultural production, an elite resi-

Figure 8.21. Photo of a portion of Pikillacta. The largest central plaza in figure 8.20 is seen at the left center of this photo. Photo by author.

dential and administrative site (Qoripata), and a temple zone.

Excavations at Qoripata provided data on several aspects of a Wari frontier settlement. A large, face-neck jar was discovered with a unique iconography showing Nasca and Tiwanaku influences (a color illustration of this jar is provided in Glowacki and McEwan 2001, fig. 14). Other ceramics show earlier Pukara relationships. Two female burials represent dedicatory offerings, and one had copper *tupus* (pins for closing a shawl) and a smaller burnt offering nearby of a bone snuff tube and two copper snuff spoons (Glowacki 2002). In contrast to Pikillacta, there was an abundance of ceremonial keros found at Qoripata, suggesting ritual drinking. The fine architecture and ceramics, evidence for *Spondylus,* and patio and site layouts argue that Wari elites used the site for hosting social and ritual events for important

people, some of which may have come from external areas.

Glowacki and McEwan (Glowacki 2002; Glowacki and McEwan 2001) have presented the following as a working hypothesis explaining the evidence for Wari occupations in the southern Cuzco region. The lack of an orthogonal layout in the Huaro Complex, plus the ceramics, argue that this region was the earliest occupied by Wari personnel in the region. Later, Pikillacta was built in the Lucre basin because it had a large open area and perhaps to open up that region to exploitation. With the evidence of Tiwanaku influence showing up in the region, perhaps security considerations were also a factor in the location of the site. Regardless, many of the Huaro sites were abandoned about the same time as Pikillacta, although at least one site, Cotacotuyoq, continued to be occupied into Middle Horizon 2. Evidence for the sudden abandonment of Qoripata suggests the retreat from this region may have been abrupt and based on hostilities.

The final site that dates to the Middle Horizon 1B is Cerro Baúl, located in the upper Moquegua Valley, well beyond the traditional southern frontier of Wari influence in the Sihuas Valley. As noted in the section on Tiwanaku, the middle part of this valley was the focus of intense occupation and exploitation by Tiwanaku peoples during the Middle Horizon. The nature of the interaction between the Wari occupants of Cerro Baúl and the people of the Tiwanaku polity in the rest of the valley is an interesting question that is still being worked out.

Certainly one of the main points not under dispute is that the site of Cerro Baúl represents an intrusion by people from Wari areas of influence (Moseley et al. 1991). The site has all the features of a Wari provincial center: D-shaped ceremonial structures, patio groups, kitchens for cooking feasts for large numbers of people, and even a brewery for making large quantities of chicha (Williams 2001; Williams and Nash 2002; Moseley et al. 2005). In addition to the site itself, which sits atop an impressive mesa towering 600 m above the valley floor, there are two other Wari-related settlements nearby. The longest canal in the entire valley was dug to bring water to terraced fields constructed to feed the population brought in from elsewhere. A hierarchy of architectural features at these sites indicate that the inhabitants of Cerro Baúl were the highest elites, who had access to goods that others did not have. The other two sites had progressively less access to elite goods, and there were architectural distinctions indicating further hierarchical subdivisions. The site went through a major reconstruction around 900 C.E., when most of the existing buildings were constructed over the earlier structures (Williams and Nash 2002). This late reorganization corresponds to the late shift in architecture at the site of Huari, although the reasons for both remain obscure.

The Wari people arrived either before the Tiwanaku settlers or at about the same time. The reasons for the appearance of this colony at this time are un-known. Perhaps it was simply to create a further location for imperial interests, especially food production, although the existence of turquoise-like minerals could have been another reason. Probably it was also to extend the frontier of Wari influence at a time when Tiwanaku was also expanding, although the presence of Tiwanaku settlements farther north contradicts this explanation.

Cerro Baúl continued to function into the tenth century, when the site was ceremonially closed and abandoned (Moseley et al. 2005). It is unclear why the descendants of the first Wari colonists left. Causes might have been the collapse of the capital around this time or increasing tensions with the local Tiwanaku-influenced groups in the valley.

The final provincial center I discuss was also the latest. Azángaro is located in the Ayacucho Valley, approximately 15 km north of Huari. It dates to Epoch 2 and probably later. The fact the site is in the chaupiyunga zone suggests that its location might have been selected to provide crops of that zone to the city (Anders 1986). The site is unusual in that it has both the formal orthogonal architecture in the typical form and also irregular structures that appear to be local in nature (figure 8.22). Excavations by Martha Anders (1991) indicate that the two are contemporary, so explanations for the latter must involve social aspects rather than temporal ones.

The formal compound is 175 by 447 m, or 7.5 ha in area. It is composed of three sectors, designated south, central, and north. The south sector has irregular architecture, both outside the main compound and between the south and central sectors. Nonetheless, these controlled the main access routes to the other parts of the compound. The central sector is a series of rows of small conjoined rectangular rooms that were accessed through a central corridor. Anders interprets them as housing for workers at the site, much like the similar rooms at Pikillacta. The north sector is an area of patio groups, although only the west side of the sector appears complete.

Anders (1991) suggests that local elites were placed in charge of the compound, and Wari officials allowed them to use their own architectural styles,

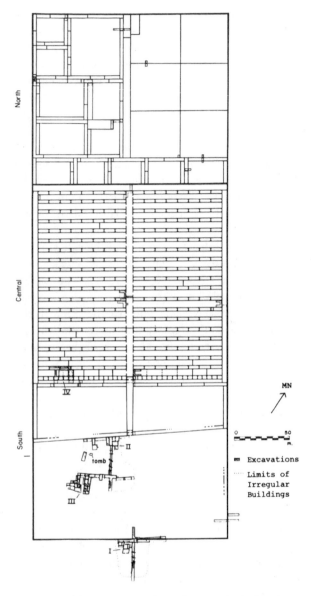

North

Central

South

MN ↗

0   50
        m.

IV

Tomb

II

III

I

■ Excavations

⋯ Limits of
Irregular
Buildings

Figure 8.22. Map of compound at Azángaro. Map by Martha
Anders, used courtesy of her estate.

the moiety principle, and that the site functioned as
a calendrical and ceremonial center. On comparisons to the Inka *zeq'e* system, she sees the arrangement of the rooms in the central sector as "the material expression of two calendar counts and the stage
for the performance of rituals connected with the
calendrical and agricultural rounds" (ibid., 192).

A more recent reanalysis of Anders's dates and two
new ones from Azángaro has called this interpretation into question (Finucane et al. 2007). It now appears that the local architecture, originally interpreted as the local leader's residence during the Wari
occupation, actually post-dates the main compound,
suggesting that after the fall of the center at Huari,
the site continued to be occupied. With this information, it appears that the actual Wari compound
was used into the Late Intermediate Period by
non-Wari local elites.

The site was occupied by Wari personnel for a
brief period, perhaps only one hundred years. Its
construction corresponds to the time when the second major reorganization was occurring at Huari,
and so it might reflect sociopolitical changes at the
capital.

The sites discussed so far represent the major
known settlements that pertain to the Wari polity.
Until the 1990s, there was no evidence for Wari architecture in the coastal zone (Cerro Baúl and Pacheco were in the mid-elevation zone), although
Wari and Wari-related ceramics are abundant, from
the Sihuas Valley in the south to at least the Chicama
Valley in the north. With more survey work being
conducted away from the population centers of the
coast, however, new sites are appearing that fill this
lacunae in our knowledge.

Pablo de la Vera Cruz and I located the site of
Sonay in the upper Camaná River (Malpass 2001).
This site is a small compound, approximately 50 by
35 m, divided into two sectors, although a third sector was destroyed by the construction of the modern
irrigation canal for this part of the valley (figure 8.23). The northern sector has three patio groups
plus a fourth area that was probably a residence for
the occupants of the compound. The site has very

perhaps as a means to gain their participation in the
provincial system. The irregular structures are in the
same architectural style as the local ones, and the
majority of the ceramics are local as well. Anders
argues there was dual leadership, possibly based on

late dates, 940 and 1000 C.E., and remarkably few artifacts of any kind. It appears to have been a very brief occupation. Due to the lack of information about earlier sites, it is difficult to say who was in charge of the center. Although our earlier interpretations suggested direct Wari control, it now seems more likely that a local individual directed its construction, someone very familiar with Wari formal architectural canons. It is interesting to note that the dates for this compound correspond to the time of major changes at Cerro Baúl and Huari, and so may be related in some fashion.

The next valley to the north of Camaná is the Ocoña River; the upper reaches of this river are known as the Cotahuasi River. This region is not really coastal in that it is much higher than 2,500 m above sea level. A Wari center was found in this valley, called Tenahaha[3] (Jennings and Yépez 2001). Tenahaha is irregularly shaped and shows variability from the Wari canons, and the ceramics are considered local imitations. Justin Jennings and Willy Yépez argue that the site was a communal meeting place for the valley, where individuals came to discuss issues, share information, and bury their dead.

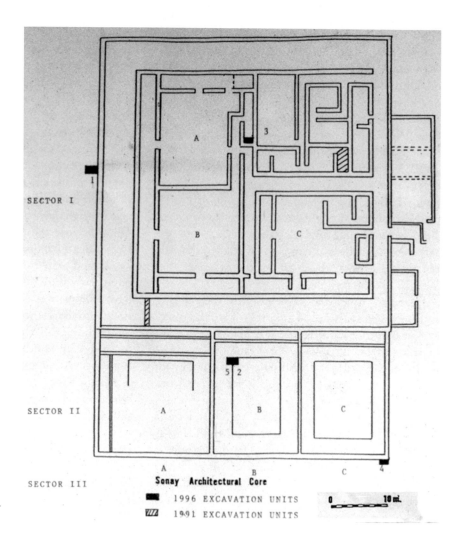

Figure 8.23. Sonay Compound. Drawing in the author's collection.

Changes during the Middle Horizon in the valley argue that Wari influence was pervasive, yet there is little evidence of direct contact. A model of globalization is suggested in which influence from the site of Huari spread out through intervening regions, each region ultimately taking the aspects that were appropriate to its particular situation (Jennings 2010). This model could also account for the evidence from Sonay.

The site of Pataraya is a small, orthogonal Wari center located in the upper reaches of the Aja River in the Nazca area (Edwards 2010). Evidence of textile manufacturing at the site and its location along a major route to the central highlands suggest that Pataraya was important in the movement of cotton from the coastal zone to the capital at Huari.

In addition to the discovery of these Wari centers of administration, other changes along the coast document the impact of Wari during the Middle Horizon. In the Nazca region, evidence for significant Wari influence has been found in the change in funerary practices beginning in this period (Isla 2001). Isla argues that the change to mummy bundles in tombs in the form of a *barbacoa* reflects a conscious change imposed on the local population by the Wari polity. How this was imposed is not stated. The general change from Nasca pottery styles to one called Atarco, which incorporates Wari themes while remaining distinct, also indicates the influence that Wari had in the region.

In regard to ceramics, a mention of the offering deposit found at Pacheco is in order. Like the offerings at Conchopata, this find was a huge collection of sherds from very large urns and other vessel forms, many with the distinctive iconography of Wari. It was uncovered by Julio Tello in 1927, but his report was never published. Dorothy Menzel (1964) uses this material to define the early Robles Moqo style, which she associates with Middle Horizon 1A. The find is termed an offering because it appears that the vessels were deliberately broken and discarded as part of some kind of ritual. Thus, a kind of offering associated with Wari activities is found at this site, but little else has been published concerning its context. This and the previous information do suggest that there was close contact between the Nazca region and Ayacucho at the beginning of the Middle Horizon, a fact supported by the Wari influence seen on late Warpa ceramics with Nasca influences as well.

Farther north, in the central-coast region of the Lurín, Rimac, and Chillón valleys, only the site of Socos in the Chillón Valley has been identified as a Wari occupation, although its description is brief (Isla and Guerrero 1987). The site map shows a rectangular compound but no patio groups, and it has been suggested that the Wari ceramics there were emulations of pottery from the heartland (Jennings 2006).

Nevertheless, significant changes occurred in this region at the beginning of the Middle Horizon that could reflect Wari influence (Shimada 1991). The site of Maranga was abandoned, but another major center was built in the Rimac Valley at Cajamarquilla. Shimada (1991) and others (e.g., Paulsen 1976) argue that these major changes were associated with the droughts of the sixth century that reduced the flow of water to the coastal valleys. It is possible, although difficult to prove, that the oracle at Pachacamac might have risen to importance at this time as well. Because the Middle Horizon significance of Pachacamac is bound up with its adoption of Wari icons, and hence religion, this would explain its popularity; in response to an environmental crisis, a new religion was adopted by local religious practitioners to maintain or increase their authority. Certainly the significance of Pachacamac seems to have increased in Middle Horizon 2A, which fits well with this interpretation.

Middle Horizon ceramics from the central coast also show affinities to those from Ayacucho but have distinctive motifs that set them apart. Most notable of these is the Pachacamac griffin, a bird-feline figure found on ceramics from this region. This figure is found widely along the coast but never in the highlands, suggesting to Menzel (1964, 1968) that Pachacamac was a rival of the Wari religion along the coast, and that the coastal sites were independent of Huari. Pachacamac appears to have exerted its independence from Wari as a political center during Middle Horizon 2B because its pottery is then more widely distributed from the Chicama Valley in the north to Nazca in the south (Menzel 1964). The appearance of Pachacamac iconography at both Pacatnamú and Batán Grande on the north coast attests to a strong relationship between these two regions, one that Shimada (1991) argues might have been related to the control of the *Spondylus* trade with coastal Ecuador.

THE FRONTIERS OF WARI For a long time, the north-central coast from Chancay to Nepeña was poorly known during this period. Ceramic styles were defined, but little evidence for political developments was apparent. As a result of more recent research, particularly by Melissa Vogel (2003, 2011), we now know that a powerful polity known as Casma emerged during the Middle Horizon in this region. This polity, which had its capital at El Purgatorio in the Casma Valley, grew out of the local cultures after the Moche state lost control over its southern valleys at the end of the Early Intermediate Period. The culture is recognized by its ceramics and architecture, although the nature of its political structure is still being worked out. El Purgatorio was a large site, 5 km², located along the Casma branch of the river. It is composed of four sectors, with what Vogel (2011) calls platform/plaza complexes, a small platform with a rectangular plaza in front of it. In additional, there were large free-standing compounds of rooms, and terracing with densely packed residences. Cemeteries have been found as well, although the majority has been heavily looted. A second major site, Cerro La Cruz in the Chao Valley, may have been a secondary political center or a relatively autonomous center. Vogel (2011) has identified ceramic attributes that indicate the Casma elites were in contact with the Sicán, Wari, and central-coast polities. Ceramic workshops at the two main sites reflect craft specialization, possibly under elite control, and makers' marks on other pottery from outside these settlements suggest tribute or taxation. It is un-

known at this time on what basis the elites justified their authority, but the presence of multiple elite residences and compounds argue for no clear hierarchy. The Casma polity continued into the Late Intermediate Period.

I describe the evidence for Wari influence along the north coast separately at the end of this chapter because the evidence there reflects more of a continuation of local cultural developments with an overlay of Wari influence than any significant change.

To round out my discussion of Wari influence, the nature of Wari influence in the Cajamarca region north of Huamachuco is still unclear. Wari ceramics are found sporadically throughout the region and in private collections, although whether these were Wari trade items or imitations is unclear (T. Topic 1991). Daniel Julien's survey of this region identified three sites that he affiliates with Wari by their architecture (cited in Jennings and Craig 2001). In addition, the widespread appearance of Cajamarca ceramics at many sites in the Wari sphere of influence, even as far south as Cerro Baúl, argues for trading interactions between the groups of Cajamarca and those under Wari control (Lau 2008; Toohey 2011). The site of Coyor has been suggested to have been a political center during the early part of the Middle Horizon (D. Julien 1993), which in the local chronological sequence is called Middle Cajamarca. This site may have been responsible for this trade.

There are two sites with Wari architecture located in the Cajamarca region (Watanabe 2001). Both the site of Yarobamba and the complex called El Palacio include rectangular compounds that are generally thought to be affiliated with Wari because they are different from the local architecture. The presence of Wari sherds supports this view. The two sites are relatively close together, within 15 km of each other, and were occupied until the end of Middle Horizon 2. Given these two areas are the only places where Wari influence is manifest, it appears they coexisted with the local Cajamarca culture, much as the Wari occupants of Viracochapampa coexisted with the Marcahuamachuco elites in the Huamachuco region to the south. It is perhaps through sites such as

Yarobamba and El Palacio that Wari material culture spread down to the Late Moche groups on the north coast.

The Nature of Wari Influence

What, then, was the nature of Wari influence? What kind of a political organization was Wari? In 1978, William Isbell and Katharina Schreiber discussed the evidence that supported the idea that Wari was a state-level polity. These include the presence of a multitiered settlement system, intrusive Wari sites, and intercommunication between centers by a road system. Schreiber (1992, 267) elaborates on this information and develops the idea that Wari was an imperialist state, based on its rapid (perhaps in 50–100 years) spread to and control over a large environmentally and ethnically diverse area. She argues for the concept of a Wari *mosaic of control* over the region from Cajamarca to Cuzco, including the regions of the coast. This means that in some regions Wari exerted direct control by building its own administrative centers, such as in the Carhuarazo Valley, whereas in others it exerted indirect control via the use of local leaders and political centers. Implicit in this view is the idea that Wari was an expansionist state, manifesting its power and control over other regions, sometimes through military might and other times through alliance or other means.

In contrast, other scholars have argued for different kinds of influence rather than military might. Shady Solís and Arturo Ruiz (1979) suggest that Wari was one of several powerful political groups that were contemporaries and had intense interaction, including the sharing of ceramic and other styles throughout this period, but that Wari was not dominant over the others. The lack of evidence for contemporary polities as powerful as Wari at this time tends to discredit this idea (Schreiber 1992). Likewise, Menzel's (1964) original idea that Wari influence was the result of proselytizing missionaries has fallen out of favor due to evidence for the prominence of administrative centers in the regions discussed.

On the basis of a detailed study of the evidence from the Huamachuco region, John and Theresa Lange Topic (J. Topic 1991, 2009; T. Topic 1991) argue that Wari did not exercise direct control over that region but that there was a peaceful interaction with local people that was mutually beneficial. Wari was mainly interested in trade with Cajamarca farther north to obtain *Spondylus* and Cajamarca ceramics, a trade that was also helpful to the local elites at Marcahuamachuco. Wari may also have had ritual expertise that was of interest to the locals, represented by the Wari presence at the shrine at Cerro Amaru. This led the local elites to participate in the construction of the Wari center at Viracochapampa, which shows local architectural traits. They likely also provided labor (J. Topic 2009). The evidence of burning at Viracochapampa and Cerro Amaru suggests that the peaceful coexistence might have come to an end and that the Marchahuamachuco elites drove the Wari personnel out. What this interpretation suggests is that the northernmost boundaries of Wari influence were not based on militarism but cooperation. Nevertheless, the situation in Huamachuco was different from the areas farther south. How different remains to be worked out in those areas.

It seems clear to me that Schreiber (1992) is correct in her assessment that Wari exercised different means of influence in different regions. I disagree that Wari control was always based on militarism because the evidence from Huamachuco contradicts this. In contrast, Schreiber's own work in the Carhuarazo Valley is clear evidence for direct control, and the dramatic settlement changes that occurred in that valley can best be explained via militarism. The evidence from Pikillacta and Huaro suggest that the initial Wari interests were probably based more on trade and religion, as in Huamachuco, but that, later, militarism may have played an increasingly important role, perhaps as Tiwanaku expanded northward.

The evidence from Cerro Baúl also supports the early colonization of the upper Moquegua Valley, but one that could have been a source of conflict.

The construction of the main canal feeding the Wari sites would have reduced the water available to Tiwanaku-influenced groups in the middle valley (Williams and Nash 2002). Still, there is no clear support for warfare between the two at this time, and over the succeeding two centuries, there is evidence of Tiwanaku ceramics at the ceremonial heart of the city. Patrick Williams and Donna Nash suggest that this reflects interaction between the elites of the two societies. In contrast, Goldstein (2009) notes that there is very little evidence of interaction between the Moquegua villages and the Wari sites nearby, suggesting little interaction between the lower levels of the two societies. Williams and Nash (2002) also point out that the destruction of Chen Chen villages, that is noted as occurring at the end of the Middle Horizon, took place when Cerro Baúl was still functioning and that, at that same time or

shortly thereafter, the site itself was ritually closed and burned. So militarism might be an aspect of the Wari control over the upper Moquegua Valley.

Finally, the discovery of oversized urns at Conchopata that have warrior figures on rafts suggests the importance of warfare in the affairs of Wari (figure 8.24; Isbell and Cook 2002). (This is discussed further in the section on Wari-Tiwanaku interactions.)

Was Wari a state? I agree with the majority of others in saying, by traditional archaeological indicators, the answer is yes. There is a multitiered settlement pattern in the Ayacucho region, and the argument can be made that the provincial centers outside Ayacucho were second-order settlements that were developed through direct control from the capital of Huari. Note that every large provincial center except Azángaro was associated with smaller

Figure 8.24. Conchopata oversized urn and conch boat warriors. Photo and drawings by William H. Isbell, Conchopata Archaeological Project.

support or religious centers nearby. In addition, Nash and Williams (2009) have noted that obsidian appears to be a material that can be used to track imperial control at the provincial centers in that the source of the Cerro Baúl obsidian was not the closest source but the one nearest to the capital. Smaller centers such as Tenahaha, Sonay, Socos, and Pataraya might have served state needs through local leaders, although what those needs were are hard to identify. Craft specialization appears to be well developed in the heartland, although less well in the provinces. There is evidence from funerary patterns for a multi-tiered and hierarchical social system with ascribed status. There is a corporate art style and a formal religion, as witnessed by the use of D-shaped structures and offering deposits.

It is less evident, however, how extensive Wari control of its hinterland was. Justin Jennings (2006) has suggested a modified model to explain the peripheral-site data. He notes that the smaller sites along the coast and inland do not conform well to direct control by Huari elites because they show considerable architectural and ceramic variability. He argues that these regions were connected to the capital by trading activities with the local elites, who emulated Wari canons for their own purposes. This also explains other regions where Wari ceramics and architecture are either absent or local imitations. In his model, Wari as a state had direct control over only three regions, the Carhuarazo Valley, the Lucre basin of Cuzco, and the Moquegua region, in addition to, of course, the Ayacucho basin.

Related to this suggestion is the nagging question, was the Wari political apparatus truly hierarchical or was it more heterarchical? So far, there is no clear evidence for a single ruler of Huari, although such evidence might still be found with more work at the site. Isbell's (2004) hierarchy of mortuary structures at Wari centers in Ayacucho is suggestive but inconclusive. If militarism was a feature of Wari expansionism, we could conclude that someone had to be in charge of the armed forces and, more important, had to be making decisions about where to direct the armed forces. Could a heterarchical political body

conduct such campaigns? Although there might not be a good ethnographic example of such a body, I agree with others, such as Silverman (1993), Goldstein (2009), and Quilter and Michele Koons (2012), in thinking that perhaps traditional views of what a state is and how it functions might not be as appropriate for the Andes as has been previously thought. We should continue to think about alternative possibilities.

Another question that has not been answered in any satisfactory way is *why* Wari expanded and why so rapidly. It is difficult to determine this archaeologically anywhere, and with a lack of written documents speaking to motivations, it is particularly difficult in the Andes. Still, there are several factors that can be considered. The first is a population expansion in the heartland that might have required increased food from other regions. Population figures are hard to extrapolate, but this is a possibility because agricultural intensification began in the Ayacucho Valley in the Early Intermediate Period with the construction of terrace systems and irrigation. But if population pressure were the dominant cause of expansionism, then we might expect an ever-expanding circle of conquests outward from Ayacucho; this is contradicted by the evidence presented here, especially the late construction of Azángaro.

Most scholars suggest that the severe drought documented for the end of the sixth century (Thompson et al. 1985) could have caused a drop in food production that led to the rapid Wari expansion during Middle Horizon 1B. This would have the same effect as an increased population with stable food resources. Mary Glowacki and I (2003) have suggested a related idea about how this drought motivated Wari expansionism. Noting the relationship between major centers such as Pikillacta and Viracochapampa and major religious locations such as high mountain peaks or shrines, we feel that Wari elites may have been attempting to control powerful supernatural forces that, in turn, controlled water for agriculture. It is reasonable to believe that Wari would have been as interested in supernatural controls over water as in human ones. Given that Wari is the one of the first major cultures to rely extensively on maize (see box 8.1), which requires significant water inputs, the need to manipulate supernatural forces is understandable.

WARI AND TIWANAKU: CLASH OF THE TITANS?

This chapter has a question mark after this phrase for a specific reason: What was the nature of the interaction between these two great polities? It should be clear from the preceding information that the two societies were fundamentally different in their political natures and the ways their influence spread. Yet the two shared a common set of religious beliefs that were manifested in similar iconographies displayed in different media. How can this situation be accounted for?

Since the differentiation of Wari from Tiwanaku, there has been a tradition of thinking that the use of Tiwanaku iconography at Wari locations was the result of the diffusion of the concepts from the Altiplano to Ayacucho. But with better dating of the appearance of this iconography, William Isbell (2008) has demonstrated that the figures appeared at the same time at both centers in a way, he argues, that must indicate representatives from each society met to work out the details of the adoption of the religion by both. Isbell has suggested the somewhat cumbersome term Southern Andean Iconographic Series (SAIS) to be used when discussing this system of symbols.

The SAIS comprises three major elements: a Staff God, a Rayed Head, and Profile Attendants. These three elements have their classic configuration on the Gateway of the Sun at Tiahuanaco (see figure 8.9). The Staff God is the most important figure, followed by the Rayed Head, which is probably an abbreviated version of the Staff God. Finally, the Profile Attendants make up subordinate figures that appear to be kneeling or running toward the Staff God. At Tiahuanaco, these images are best displayed in stone sculpture: the Gateway of the Sun, and the Ponce and Bennett monoliths. At Huari, they are represented on ceramics, most notably at Conchopata on the oversized urns from offering deposits. Once adopted, the specific motifs and figures were modified by each society to the point that scholars have little difficulty identifying them.

Where did the SAIS pantheon originate? At present this is unknown. Isbell (2008) notes that aspects of the pantheon can be identified in Pukara art, the Yaya-Mama religious tradition (the Rayed Head only), and on snuffing paraphernalia from northern Chile, but none of these has a complete set of icons. Thus, we are left with the idea of a synthesis of existing ideas that emerged during the later part of the Early Intermediate Period, probably somewhere in the southern Andes. In 1983, Isbell made an intriguing suggestion that leaders at both emerging centers might have been converted to a common religion by itinerant healers from the eastern Andes, who synthesized the religion from earlier religions in the region. Although he has moved away from that idea in more recent publications, it seems that something like that scenario might be the ultimate source of the religion. We can hope that future research will answer this fascinating question.

Finally, we reach the central question of the chapter, what was the nature of the interactions between these two great polities? They shared a common set of religious beliefs but manifested them differently. Their capital cities were dramatically different in their layouts, basic organizing concepts, and construction techniques. The methods of expanding their influence were different, and they probably spoke different languages. What happened along the frontiers of these two great identities, as Isbell (2008) calls them? At Cerro Baúl, where the evidence for direct contact is clearest, it appears they coexisted for centuries, although perhaps not without some tension. Yet elites from the Tiwanaku settlements were feasted at the center of Cerro Baúl. In the region around the modern city of Arequipa, most settlements were Tiwanaku-related, but there were small centers of Wari affiliation nearby (Cardona Rosas 2002; de la Vera Cruz pers. comm. 2010).

The discovery of oversized urn fragments at Conchopata with warrior figures supports the idea that Wari might have used military might in their expansion. That the warrior figures are on rafts (figure 8.24) suggests the intriguing possibility that there was conflict between Wari and other groups on a body of water—either Lake Titicaca or the Pacific Ocean?

Isbell (2008) has made the observation that Wari much more significantly changed the societies with which it came into contact than Tiwanaku did. There seems to have been a greater motivation on the part of Wari personnel to transform the non-Wari groups, or perhaps the Wari culture was more attractive in some sense to non-Wari societies. In contrast, Tiwanaku did not act like a classic empire, attempting to mold its subjects into a form modeled on the capital, an idea shared by Goldstein (2009). The two societies seemed to be able to coexist well, and perhaps the mutual religion they shared was a factor in that coexistence.

THE NORTH COAST: MOCHE DECLINE OR TRANSFORMATION?

Probably no part of the Moche sequence is more poorly understood than the Moche IV–V transition that took place beginning in the sixth or seventh century. Still, we now have a much better understanding of this critical period than previously. Dramatic changes took place in the Moche world during this time (Bawden 1996; Castillo Butters 2001; Chapdelaine 2010). Moche influence disappeared in the southern valleys that had been conquered during the earlier phases, and large regions of cultivable land in the northern valleys were abandoned. The site of Huacas de Moche was abandoned as well, although the Huaca de la Luna may have continued to function. Large population centers appeared inland where the narrow middle valleys open up into the coastal plain, and there were major changes

in the corporate art of the Moche elite.

Traditionally, the Moche decline was thought to have occurred at the beginning of Middle Horizon, and many thought it must have been related in some fashion to the arrival of the Wari Empire from the adjacent highlands. The lack of radiocarbon dates from the major centers and the shift from Moche IV to Moche V ceramic forms suggested this relationship. But we now know that Moche society at the Huacas de Moche continued into the seventh century, even as new centers such as Galindo were emerging. It is also evident that Moche IV and V ceramics were used at the same time, although the latter continued for a longer time after the former disappeared. Finally, it is now clear that there is virtually no evidence for a Wari presence in the Moche region and that the changes that occurred were due to internal factors, not external influences (Chapdelaine 2010). Let us turn to those changes.

One of the most significant developments that occurred during this period was the disappearance of Moche occupations from the valleys south of the Moche Valley. This region, which had been brought under Moche control during Moche III and IV (see chapter 7), apparently was able to free itself at this time (Wilson 1988). Local groups exhibited pre-Moche forms of settlement and a new multivalley polity emerged based in the Casma Valley. This rejection of Moche rule may have been the result of other dramatic changes occurring in the heartland.

These changes were due to environmental factors and internal stresses. At the outset, it is clear that both of these factors were responsible to a greater or lesser degree, and the relative effect they had depended also on the region of the Moche polity. For example, environmental factors might have played a more significant role in the developments in the Moche Valley than in the Jequetepeque Valley.

Regarding the environment, it is evident from both archaeology and climatic studies that the sixth century was a time of great perturbation. As noted in chapter 2, there were two extended droughts in the Andean highlands in the sixth century, one lasting sixteen years and the other thirty-one years. Precipitation dropped in each period by 30 percent. On the coast, this would have had the effect of significantly reducing water in the rivers for irrigation. This was one cause of the abandonment of fields. Another cause was a series of large El Niños that led to severe erosion, as witnessed at the Huacas de Moche site (Moseley and Deeds 1982), where a low platform in the middle of the area between the two huacas was covered by a layer of water-borne silt. The same has been suggested for the abandonment of the El Brujo complex in the Chicama Valley (Franco Jordan, Gálvez Mora, and Vásquez Sanchéz 1994, cited in Bawden 1996) and of the Nima/Valverde site in the Upper Piura River to the north (Kaulicke 1993, cited by Bawden 1996). Moseley (1987) finds evidence for the stripping of several meters of soil from the landscape as a result of such El Niños, which would have devastated the fields of the Moche.

It was not just the El Niños that caused destruction; the resulting silts and sands that were eroded from hillsides were blown into the irrigation canals, especially on the south sides of the river valleys (the winds are ever from the southwest). The platform at Huacas de Moche was covered by such sands, as were other areas up to the Jequetepeque Valley. This problem would have been a persistent one that far outlived the immediate destruction caused by El Niño rainfall.

These factors led to a dramatic decline in the amount of food produced by the Moche agricultural systems in most of the valleys in the north. One result of this was a movement to sites located upstream at the valley necks. In the Moche Valley, the evidence presented shows that large-scale destruction at the site of Huacas de Moche was followed by the absence of Moche V pottery.[4] There is some evidence of the continued use of the Huaca de la Luna and a much reduced residential community, but the diverse city that had existed was gone (Castillo Butters and Uceda 2008). Still, Chapdelaine (2010) suggests the elites were able to maintain their control over part of the Moche Valley population from the Huaca de la Luna until the end of the eighth century, when the site was finally abandoned.

During the seventh century, a new site, Galindo, rose to importance; it was located at the valley neck on the north side of the Moche River, near to where the intakes for the main irrigation canals of the valley are found (Lockard 2008, 2009). This suggests the location was chosen to control this source of power and to avoid the wind-blown sands that were destroying the fields on the south side of the river.

Galindo was a fundamentally different site, one that broke many of the traditions of earlier Moche settlements. First, it was a true urban center, with many thousands of inhabitants of both high and low status, and the architectural evidence indicates that there was a strict segregation of classes (Bawden 2001; Lockard 2008, 2009). The lower class lived on a steep slope isolated by a large wall. The elites lived in larger houses in another part of the site and had higher-protein diet in the form of llama meat (Bawden 1996, 288). Perhaps the most significant difference was the appearance of a different kind of architecture for ceremonial activity. The *cercadura* was an enclosed area with high walls, within which smaller rooms were used for the important activities of the elites. Gone was the tradition of building a large platform mound.

Another departure from earlier Moche traditions was the burial practices found, both for high- and low-status individuals. The appearance of a royal compound, a large area enclosed by a tall wall within which was a residential complex and burial platform, marks the beginning of a new tradition that continued in later times. The people of the lower class began to bury their dead in an extended position within the house rather than in cemeteries, both new traits. Higher-status individuals were buried between houses in stone-lined tombs near the cercaduras that contained much better funerary objects. A final new characteristic of the site was the appearance of large-scale storage with controlled access. This warehouse section was located on a slope above the cercaduras and separated from the lower-class housing by a quebrada and high walls.

Bawden (2001) also notes how the ceramics changed in significant ways. The tradition of using portrait vessels disappears, indicating that the depiction of local rulers was no longer considered appropriate. More important, the narrative scenes such as the Sacrifice Ritual disappeared as well, indicating a rejection of the earlier religious ideology that had been the basis for such scenes. In elite contexts, the ceramics that replaced the traditional Moche pottery were different in both form and decoration, and showed heavy central-coast influence. Bawden (2001) argues that the elites adopted the more pan-Andean Wari-related ceramics as a new form of power, replacing the earlier, and now discredited, source of supernatural power. Perhaps this reflects similar motivations that led to the adoption of Chavín after the collapse of the Initial Period polities.

Bawden (1996, 2001) notes that all these new features indicate a fundamental shift in the social order at Galindo. The elite were maintaining their status through segregation and exclusion. Status differences were now marked, probably due to the fact that so many low- and high-status people were living together in close quarters. Whereas the ceremonies conducted at the Huacas of Moche were public and open, conducted in large plazas on the tops of highly visible platforms, the ones at Galindo were carried out in secret, behind high walls, shielded from the prying eyes of the lower class. In addition, the lower class was dependent on the elites for food and water. Finally, there is clear evidence in the royal compound for a paramount ruler who separated him- or herself from the rest of society and was buried separately. Society in Moche V times had become a much more hierarchical and segregated one. This is not to say the lower class had become more powerless; to the contrary, Bawden (2001) suggests the burial practices of this group were a means of maintaining a social identity in the face of the new conditions of segregation from power.

More recent research at Galindo by Greg Lockard (2008, 2009) suggests a new interpretation of this site relative to other sites in the Moche Valley. He finds there is a significant overlap in dates for Moche IV ceramics from the Huacas de Moche and Moche V pottery from Galindo. He suggests that perhaps the different forms reflect different social groups and that the changes seen at Galindo reflect a new social order there, whereas other groups using Moche IV pottery continued the older traditions. This is in accord with Chapdelaine's (2010) interpretations of the data from the Huacas de Moche.

That being said, Lockard (2008) also notes there was some continuity between the authorities at Galindo and the earlier Moche rulers at Huacas de Moche. He notes that one of the major monuments, the Huaca de las Abejas, shows architectural similarities to earlier Moche structures, and an analysis of the fine-line drawings also show that some earlier scenes were still used. This suggests that the earlier religious beliefs continued at Galindo, although in a modified form.

Galindo was abruptly abandoned around 800 C.E., although squatters' houses appeared in the former elite zones at this time. What happened to the center is unclear; indeed, what happened to its inhabitants is also unknown. The lower classes probably returned to ancestral locations elsewhere in the Moche Valley. If the elite still existed, they had become insignificant to the point of questioning applicability of the term or, perhaps, they too moved elsewhere.

In the Chicama Valley, Lockard (2009) notes the same issue with the dating of Moche IV and V ceramics is present. He argues that Moche IV ceramics continued to be used into the eighth century there as well. The sites of Moche IV were apparently all abandoned at the end of the eighth century, although the reasons for this are unclear (Gálvez and Briceño 2001). There was severe El Niño damage to the site of Huaca Cao Viejo, but the researchers note that it had been partially dismantled prior to the rainfall damage.

A different situation is seen at the site of San José de Moro in the Jequetepeque Valley, north of the Chicama Valley. Here, a Late Moche cemetery provided a series of burials that allowed different conclusions about Moche V life to be drawn. Luis

Jaime Castillo Butters and Christopher Donnan (Castillo Butters 2001; Donnan and Castillo Butters 1992) have identified burials that can be linked to figures in the Sacrifice Ritual, specifically, the female attendant who brings the cups of blood to the two main figures. The site itself was a ceremonial center and probably also had political influence in the valley. It is located at the juncture of the main north-south path and the route to the highlands from the coast. Located on the north side of the valley, it was largely spared the problem of the sand invasion that plagued the Huacas de Moche site.

A notable development of the Late Moche Period in Jequetepeque was the sudden appearance of fine-line drawings (see figure 7.2) that had been absent in the periods previous to this one. Castillo Butters (2001) attributes this to the migration of potters skilled in this technique from the southern valleys, where it was present earlier. The scenes that were depicted are much more restricted than in the southern region. Significantly, humans as the central figures almost disappeared entirely, a fact Castillo Butters interprets to mean they had become the deities that were still represented.

The elites at San José de Moro also differed from those known from elsewhere at this time (and few other sites dating to this period have been as well excavated) by the inclusion of a large number and wide variety of foreign ceramics in their burials. Pots from Cajamarca and Wari in the highlands, and central-coast locations farther south were present (Castillo Butters 2001). Individuals of lower status had local replications of such pots, showing an effort to emulate the upper status. At the end of the Late Moche Period, the fine-line drawings disappeared along with the boot-shaped tombs that had been the characteristic elite tomb shape since Middle Moche times (ibid., 2001). To Castillo Butters, this marks the end of Moche society, although he notes that this really reflects the disappearance of the elite segment of society that was responsible for the production of such ceramics and burials in such tombs.

Castillo Butters (2001) notes that the evidence suggests two things about Late Moche elites at the site. First, they had the means and motivation to gain access to a wide range of exotic ceramics from non-Moche regions. This represents an opening of the north-coast society to external influences, to which it had been resistant previously. Second, the Moche were incorporating foreign elements into their ideology in a fashion that was distinct from their ancestors. Wari influence (by way of Cajamarca rather than directly up the coast) is seen first in elite tombs and then more widely as a local hybrid of Wari and Moche ceramics that was adopted by the middle and lower classes. Bawden (1996) and Castillo Butters (2001) see this syncretism as a reflection of the elites' needs to adopt new religious concepts to maintain their hold on authority. Although their way of life was not as different in other respects from earlier times, their source of religious power was waning and needed an infusion of new ideas to be effective.

But evidence from elsewhere in the Jequetepeque Valley and the regions adjacent to it is hard to construe as supporting the interpretations just presented. In the Zaña Valley, there is a moderate Late Moche occupation, but Dillehay (2001) sees this valley as being a buffer zone between the polities located in the Jequetepeque and Lambayeque valleys to the south and north, respectively. A significant Cajamarca presence above the middle reaches of the valley served to restrict occupations in that region. In the lower Jequetepeque Valley, 322 Moche sites from all periods were recorded, with small, intermediate, and large centers noted (Dillehay 2001). Significantly, sizable fortresses were located on hilltops, reflecting defensive considerations that most probably date to Late Moche times.

Dillehay (2001) describes a situation similar to the one Castillo Butters discussed for the region in the Late Moche Period (see chapter 7). The settlement pattern for the Zaña and Lambayeque valleys is one of enclaves of small villages close to one or two large settlements, all located near tracts of irrigable land. Fortresses near such settlements reflect the need for security, and it is likely that the conflict was between local factions rather than external forces. Dillehay argues that there might not have been any clear hierarchical arrangements of sites but, rather, shifting alliances among enclave centers. Like Bawden, he argues that smaller centers may have experienced greater autonomy than many specialists believe, making the political situation much more complex than previous descriptions imply.

The final region where there is good evidence of Moche V changes is in the Chancay tributary of the

Lambayeque Valley. Here, the site of Pampa Grande was founded during the Moche IV–V transition (Shimada 1994). Radiocarbon dates suggest an overlap with the occupation at Galindo (Lockard 2009). Like Galindo, it was located at the valley neck near where the two main irrigation canals for the valley have their intakes. It was built in a short period of time and was the home to thousands of people of distinct statuses. The site is very different from Galindo, being centered on a large elite precinct (figure 8.25) consisting of an enormous platform mound, the

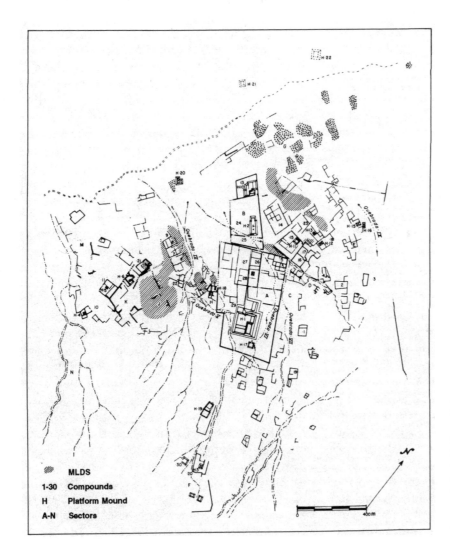

Figure 8.25. Simplified architectural map of the site of Pampa Grande, showing the locations of formal storage complexes, sectors, huacas, majored walled compounds, and concentrations of multilateral depressions (MLDs). Drawing by Gerrman Ocas and Izumi Shimada. From Shimada 1994, figure 7.3. Courtesy of University of Texas Press, copyright 1994.

Huaca Fortaleza (figure 8.26), which was 270 by 180 by 38 m in size, and a series of smaller platforms and compounds. The construction technique is different from Huacas de Moche, consisting of rooms filled with rubble rather than adobe bricks.

Significantly, Shimada (1994) has shown that the ceramics at the site reflect that two distinct social groups occupied it, the Gallinazo and Moche. The former lived in the region of the city called the Southern Pediment, and the latter lived on the Northern Pediment. The Gallinazo appear to have been of lower status, based on their ceramics and architecture and the fact they were largely segregated from the elite parts of the site, which were all on the Northern Pediment. This situation suggests that the Moche rulers of the city compelled the Gallinazo inhabitants of the valley to move to the site and work for them.

Shimada (2000) finds that craft production was well organized and tightly controlled by elites at the site. Specific workshops for copper working, pottery making, cotton weaving and sewing, cooking, chicha making, lapidary, and shell working were found. Often, the workshops did only part of the production process for an industry, such as ginning the cotton before it was spun and woven. The craft production was overseen by supervisors, who provided the workers with food and drink, probably in the context of reciprocity. *Spondylus* production was restricted to the elite compound, and Gallinazo and Moche craftspeople worked in separate, isolated complexes.

Pampa Grande was occupied for only about 150 years and was abandoned around 700 C.E. The site saw a violent end—most of the major elite structures, particularly the ceremonial ones, were burned in an intense fire. No reoccupation of the central part of the site is noted, and it is likely that the entire site was abandoned, with the lower classes possibly returning to their ancestral homes elsewhere in the

Figure 8.26. The rear of the Huaca Fortaleza at Pampa Grande. Photo by author.

valley. Shimada (1994) favors the view that the destruction was due to an internal revolt, and it is possible that the Gallinazo segment of the population was responsible.

It is only after the fall of Pampa Grande that Wari influence appears in the Lambayeque Valley, suggesting that the elites at the center had been strong enough, both militarily and ritually, to hold back the influence from the highlands. With its fall, the resistance disappeared, and the remaining people were more amenable to the concepts of a different cultural influence coming to them from elsewhere. It is likely that the Wari influence was via Cajamarca intermediaries rather than direct contact with Wari individuals. The lack of Wari influence in the Cajamarca region also supports this interpretation.

Moche culture did not disappear; it transformed into something different through foreign influences and the inability of its elites to maintain conformance to its religion. This inability was probably strained to the breaking point by climatic factors, especially El Niños and periods of drought in the adjacent highlands. Still, as the last vestiges of Moche culture disappeared, new cultural identities emerged to replace them. These are the subject of the next chapter.

9

AUCA RUNA, THE EPOCH OF WARFARE
The Late Intermediate Period

The time after the Middle Horizon was marked by the emergence of local political groups throughout the Andean region. It is also a time period for which we can begin to use the power of written documents to understand what was happening. Several of the Spanish chroniclers asked groups in different areas what life was like before their conquest by the Inkas. Although this information is even more questionable than that pertaining to the Inkas themselves, it still affords us a means other than archaeology to learn about the past.

Guaman Poma described the time before the Inkas as *Auca Runa,* a time of war, when people abandoned their villages for hilltop strongholds. Although this was certainly true in many regions, note that warfare was not widespread over the entire Andean area. Many of the more combative groups were led by *cinchekona* (singular, *cinche*), powerful leaders who could command the allegiance of followers through charisma or coercion. One of these groups was the Inkas, which started out as just another political power localized near Cuzco. As discussed in chapter 10, the Inkas were unique in being able to forge an enormous empire through conquest.

With the waning of Tiwanaku and Wari influence, local cultures began to develop their own distinctive cultures, although many had never entirely lost them during the Middle Horizon. Something

that is often misunderstood is that populations continued to expand during this period. The cultures of the north coast became more complex rather than less, and many other regions experienced the development of political structures that had not been present previously. The populations became large enough that conflicts became more common, and the Late Intermediate Period settlement patterns in many regions are marked by fortifications and defensive locations in many regions. It was indeed a time of strife for many, as the chroniclers reported.

THE NORTH COAST

By the end of the eighth century, Moche culture as defined by its iconography and ceramics had disappeared. The major sites of Pampa Grande and Galindo had been abandoned, and their populations had dispersed throughout their respective valleys. Before examining what happened next, I present a brief digression into ethnohistory, for it is at this time that we begin to have information from colonial Spanish documents that mention the oral traditions of the local people of the north coast. Two traditions described in these documents in particular have been the subject of much debate concerning whether they are based in historical fact or pure

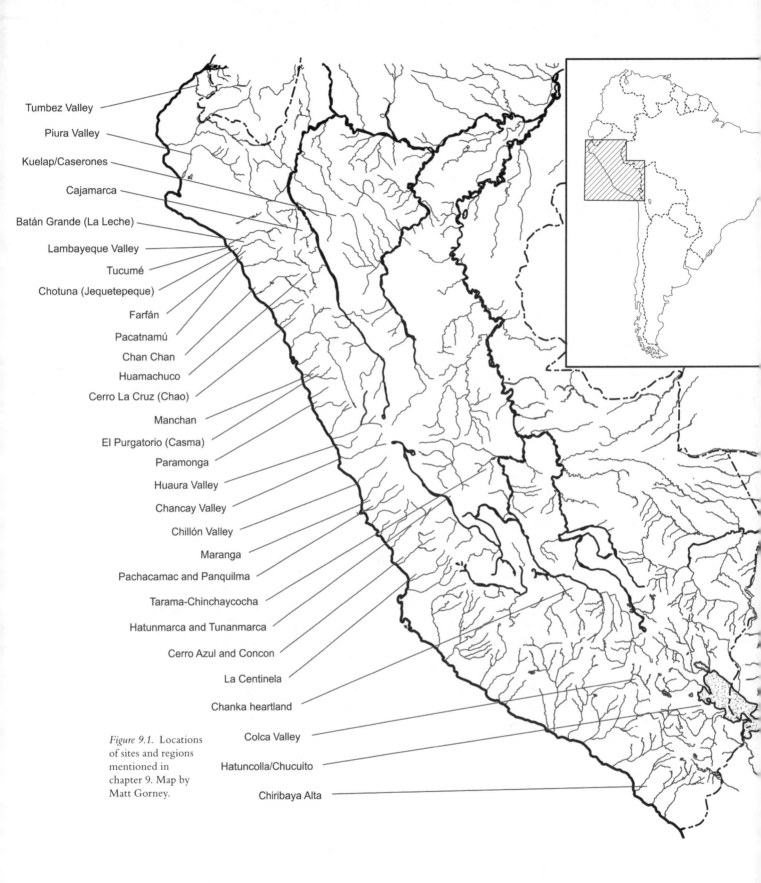

Tumbez Valley

Piura Valley

Kuelap/Caserones

Cajamarca

Batán Grande (La Leche)

Lambayeque Valley

Tucumé

Chotuna (Jequetepeque)

Farfán

Pacatnamú

Chan Chan

Huamachuco

Cerro La Cruz (Chao)

Manchan

El Purgatorio (Casma)

Paramonga

Huaura Valley

Chancay Valley

Chillón Valley

Maranga

Pachacamac and Panquilma

Tarama-Chinchaycocha

Hatunmarca and Tunanmarca

Cerro Azul and Concon

La Centinela

Chanka heartland

Colca Valley

Hatuncolla/Chucuito

Chiribaya Alta

Figure 9.1. Locations of sites and regions mentioned in chapter 9. Map by Matt Gorney.

myth. These are the legends of Naymlap and Taycanamo.

According to Cabello Balboa, writing in 1586 (cited in Donnan 1990), a powerful leader named Naymlap arrived on the coast of Lambayeque with a fleet of balsa rafts. He had a wife, Ceterni, and a host of people who came with him, including forty different officials who attended to his needs. He also brought a green idol called Yampellec, which was a representation of him. He built a palace at a place called Chot and a palace nearby for his wife. He lived in the valley for the rest of his life, learning the culture of his adopted home. When he died, his son, Cium, took over as ruler, and he and his wife, Zolzdoñi, had twelve sons who in turn had large families.

After Cium, there was a succession of nine other rulers followed by Fempellec, the last of the line. He decided to move Yampellec from Chot, but this was resisted. For some reason not specified, presumably to achieve the move, the Devil appeared to Fempellec in the guise of a woman, and Fempellec slept with her. Upon the consummation, torrential rains began to fall and did not stop for thirty days. When the rains stopped, famine and other hardships for the people of the valley lasted for a year. Knowing that it was Fempellec's actions that caused this, the priests tied him up and threw him in the sea, drowning him.

Following Fempellec's death, the Lambayeque Valley went "for many days" without a ruler before a leader named Chimú Capac came and conquered the valley with an army. He placed another Chimú named Pongmassa in charge of the region. It was apparently during the time of Pongmassa's grandson, Oxa, that the region fell to the Inkas, although this is not stated specifically; rather, there were five more rulers before the Spaniards arrived.

A second legend relates to the founding of the Chimú dynasty in the Moche Valley. According to the *Anonymous History of Trujillo* written in 1604 but published in 1936 by Rubén Vargas Ugarte and translated into English by Rowe in 1948, a man named Taycanamo arrived in the lower Moche Val-

ley on balsa rafts (like Naymlap) and settled there. His son Guacricaur conquered the settlements in the lower valley, and his son, Ñançenpinco, conquered the rest of the valley up to the mountains. The latter then expanded the Chimú conquests from the Santa River in the south to the Jequetepeque Valley in the north. After this, there is a period of consolidation for several generations before Minchançaman conquered the coast from the Santa Valley southward to the Chillón River and northward to the Tumbez Valley. Apparently, soon after these conquests, Minchançaman was conquered by the Inka Topa Yapanqui (probably Thupa Inka Yupanki; see chapter 10) and was taken to Cuzco in chains.

In a related legend, Antonio de la Calancha (1638, translated by Philip Means and published in 1931) provided an account of the conquest of the Jequetepeque Valley by the Chimú. This account states that the valley was conquered by a general named Pacatnamú, who was given the privilege of ruling the province by the (unnamed) Chimú leader. He built an administrative center for the valley. Although this might suggest that the site of Pacatnamú was the center, in fact, it is now known from excavations that the general's administrative center was the site of Farfán.

If there is any validity to these stories, and there are those who deny this (Rowe 1948; Zuidema 1990), then it appears that Naymlap existed prior to the Chimú conquest of the Lambayeque region, but how much earlier is unclear. If the number of rulers who succeeded Naymlap is accurate, and the conquest of the Lambayeque Valley took place in the mid-fourteenth century (see later in the chapter), then the date would be sometime in the eleventh century, assuming twenty-five years per generation. The legend of Pacatnamú takes place within the time frame of the legend of Taycanamo and seems to reflect the specific general that Ñançenpinco sent to conquer the Jequetepeque Valley. It is difficult to place the founding of the Chimú line in historical time using the legend of Taycanamo because of the vagaries of how many successors existed between Ñançenpinco and Minchançaman. Let us turn to the archaeological record of this region to see what evidence supports or contradicts these oral histories.

After the fall of the Moche V centers at Galindo and Pampa Grande in the eighth century, a new ceramic style developed in the Lambayeque region, called Sicán, or Lambayeque.[1] The hallmark of this new style was a monochrome blackware, which replaced the polychrome pottery so typical of the Moche tradition. For utilitarian ceramics, new stylistic elements based on stamping the outside of the pot with decorated paddles (*paleteada*) also appeared. The principal figure in the Sicán iconography is called the Sicán Deity, a figure with huge ear spools, comma-shaped eyes, and the clothing of a ruler (figure 9.2). His head is often seen on the necks of libation vessels, frequently with serpent heads or attendant figures on either side. Images of the Sicán Deity are also commonly found on textiles and metal objects (Shimada 2000). He had an alter ego called the Sicán Lord, who is considered to have been a human either mimicking the deity or transformed into him. Shimada (2000), following Menzel (1977), argues that the Sicán Deity was a synthesis of earlier concepts drawn from both the Moche and Wari. This supports the idea presented in the previous chapter that a new syncretistic religion emphasizing both the old and new was needed by an emerging elite to justify their rule as a result of the crisis that occurred at the end of Moche V.

Politically, the fall of Pampa Grande left a power vacuum that was not filled by any powerful rulers for a century or so. The poorly known Early Sicán Period (750/800–900 C.E.) marked a transitional time when prototypes of the Sicán Deity emerged on blackwares and local copies of fine Cajamarca ceramics became common (Shimada 2000). No monumental architecture is known from this period, suggesting that political power was diffused across small communities where the new religion was developing. However, this changed at the beginning of the Middle Sicán Period (900–1100 C.E.), when there was a cultural florescence marked by several traits: a distinctive art and religion based on the Sicán Deity; a veritable explosion of crafts, especially ceramics and metallurgy; the return to constructing massive platform mounds; elite shaft tombs; and widespread trade with regions to the north and east (Shimada 2000). These traits reflect both continuity and innovation in this culture.

Figure 9.2. Sample of the Middle Sicán logographic paleteada designs. Upper left corner: Sicán Deity face, Huaca Las Ventanas, South Sector, site of Sicán. Lower left corner: Undetermined design, surface collection, looted platform, Sector III, Cerro Huaringa. Upper right corner: Double-spout bottle design, Huaca Las Ventanas, South Sector, site of Sicán. Lower right corner: Seated mythical feline (or fox) design, Huaca del Pueblo Batán Grande, Trench 4 (1983). Remaining (small) pieces: Two are Sicán Deity face design and the last is undetermined, surface of Huaca Botija, site of Sicán. Photo courtesy of Izumi Shimada.

The center of Batán Grande emerged in the La Leche Valley as the capital of a powerful polity. The center of this great site, called the Sicán Religious Funerary Precinct (shortened to just the Sicán Precinct) included more than twelve major pyramids; the largest, Wak'a Corte, was more than 250 m square at the base. Izumi Shimada (1995), who excavated this site, discovered the burials of two rulers near the major pyramid, one with five individuals (one adult male, two adult females, and two juveniles) and over a ton of copper, gold, and gold-alloy artifacts buried with him. Intriguingly, this individual was buried upside down in a seated position. The clothing and objects buried with him match those of the Sicán Lord; the objects interred to accompany him to the next world are also similar to those of the Sicán Deity, indicating the two were one and the same (Shimada 2000). Another burial, located on the opposite side of the pyramid, had less metal wealth, but twenty-three bodies, all but one young females, plus parts of over twenty-five camelids.

Dental studies of the individuals in both graves indicate that they were closely related (Shimada et al. 1998). Ground-penetrating radar studies of nearby areas of the site suggest there are many more deep-shaft tombs awaiting excavation, including one directly under the center of the Wak'a Loro (Shimada 2000). In contrast, commoner burials have been found in residences or workshops, and are simple shallow pits below the floors.

One of the main activities that intensified during the Middle Sicán Period was trade with other regions. It has been suggested that *naipes,* I-shaped arsenical copper ingots (figure 9.3), were a kind of currency; their distribution overlaps with T-shaped copper objects called axe-monies that were used in southern Ecuador at the same time. The overlap in the distributions of the two in northern Peru suggests both could have been used for trade. The large quantities of *Spondylus* and *Strombus* shells in Sicán burials, both from Ecuador, would have been a main trade item, but emeralds from Colombia were also

Figure 9.3. Naipes. Upper row, from the looted Middle Sicán tomb at Huaca Menor. Lower row, from other huacas at the site of Sicán. Photo courtesy of Izumi Shimada.

greatly desired by the elites. Gold from the Marañon basin to the east was clearly a reason for exchange with that region, and Sicán wares have been found in that region near a gold mine (Shimada 2000).

Many other Sicán centers arose during the end of the Middle Horizon and beginning of the Late Intermediate Period, especially in the La Leche and Lambayeque drainages. One of the most intriguing was the site of Chotuna, in the Jequetepeque Valley. Its name, of course, suggests it could be the location of the palace of Naymlap, and the site of Chornancap, 1 km to the west, seems a likely candidate for the palace of his wife, Ceterni. Work at the site by Christopher Donnan (1990) could neither discredit nor affirm the possibility that Chotuna was Naymlap's residence, although he found grounds for believing that the individuals, if they were real, could have lived either during the Early or Middle Sicán phases. On other grounds, Shimada (1990) believes neither is the location of the main characters of the legend, a view shared by others.

Shimada (2000) makes the case that the Middle Sicán polity was a Vatican-like state that controlled the region between the upper Piura River and the Chicama Valley, with cultural influence that spread a good deal farther, as previously noted. He notes the presence of marked status distinctions in architecture and burials, control of trade and craft production by a distinctive elite, and a four-tiered settlement hierarchy with the Sicán Precinct as the capital. What is missing at this time is an understanding of *how* this state emerged over a relatively short period (about one hundred years; Shimada 2000). Like so many other centers of power I have discussed in this book, the Sicán Precinct is a group of twelve major mounds that seem to be duplicates of each other, although varying in size. Was there a single ruler, or were there multiple leaders who competed with one another? It is possible we are seeing a dynastic situation, as described in the Naymlap legend, in which sons succeeded fathers and each perhaps built his own mound and burial complex. Such was the case with the subsequent Chimú. Whether the dynasty was one founded by an individual named Naymlap will probably never be known.

The major pyramids at the Sicán Precinct were burned in a huge fire around 1050–1100 C.E., although the commoner residences only a kilometer away were not. Likewise, no other center was torched, suggesting that it was the ruling elites who were the focus of the destruction. Why this occurred at this time is uncertain, although there is the evidence for the onset of a major drought in the adjacent highlands (Shimada et al. 1991; Thompson et al. 1985) that could have reduced water levels and caused field abandonment, as was discussed for the earlier Moche. A large El Niño, or a series of them, contributed to the political unrest around 1100 C.E. As Shimada (2000) suggests, perhaps the economic costs of the trade and worship of the elite class also contributed to the downfall of the rulers.

Subsequent to these catastrophes, the irrigation systems were rebuilt and fields renewed. Nevertheless, the evidence suggests dramatic changes in the culture that herald the beginning of the Late Sicán phase. The Sicán Deity and Sicán Lord conspicuously disappeared from the ceramics, suggesting the belief in the omnipotence of the deity and its alter ego were no longer accepted. The focus of political power at this point shifted to the site of Túcume (also called El Purgatorio), downstream from Batán Grande in the La Leche Valley. There, a huge ramped pyramid, the Huaca Larga (figure 9.4), continued the tradition of powerful rulers building such edifices for their uses. It is intriguing to wonder how a local second-order lord at the site was able to claim religious and political power at this time, but Shimada (2000) suggests that someone there was able to reunify the elite lineages (or coordinate new ones, if those at Sicán had been killed). Much of life for commoners continued unchanged in this period, and metalworking and trade continued as well. The site flourished until sometime in the late fourteenth century, when it fell to warriors from the powerful Chimú center of Chan Chan.

To understand the emergence of the last great power to rule the north coast prior to the coming of

Figure 9.4. Huaca Larga at Tucumé. Photo by author.

the Inkas, we turn again to the ethnohistorical legend of Taycanamo. The legend suggests an initial appearance of a conquering ruler, his and his children's consolidation of the lower Moche Valley, and then two periods of expansion north and south.

Archaeologically, the two phases of expansion are hard to identify, but research projects in this area, starting with the Chan Chan–Moche Valley Project (Moseley and Day 1982) and work by Carol Mackey and colleagues (Mackey 1987; Mackey and Klymyshyn 1990; Moore and Mackey 2008) have greatly clarified the timing of the Chimú expansion. According to Mackey (2009), the consolidation of power in the Moche Valley by the Chimú, whether Taycanamo and his son and grandson or not, took place between 900/1000 and 1200 C.E. The conquest of the Jequetepeque Valley occurred around 1300/1400 C.E., and shortly afterward, around 1350–1380 C.E., the valleys to the Casma Valley

were brought under Chimú rule. A final expansion to the La Leche Valley in the north, possibly concurrent with the expansion south, took place between 1350 and 1400 C.E. At present, it appears that the area under active Chimú control extended only from the Casma Valley in the south to the La Leche Valley in the north, although their influence spread as far as Piura in the north and the Chillón Valley in the south through alliances and trade. The ubiquity of Chimú blackware ceramics outside their zones of control attest to this additional influence.

What we know from archaeology is that sometime after Galindo was abandoned, the city of Chan Chan was founded. It was located along the coast in the northern part of the Moche Valley (figure 9.1). This city became the largest mud-brick city in the world under the rule of the great Chimú kings, extending over a total area of 20 km^2 (figure 9.5). There are four kinds of architecture at the site: *ciu-*

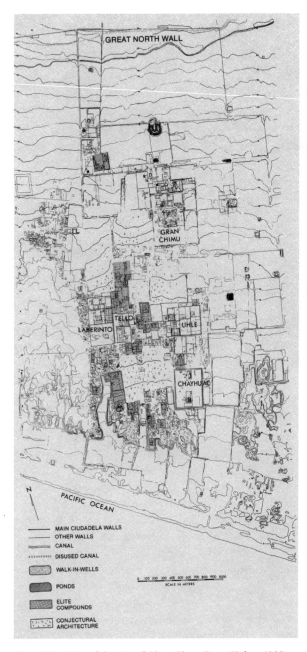

Figure 9.5. Map of the site of Chan Chan. From Kolata 1982, figure 4.6. Courtesy of Alan Kolata.

dadelas, or Great Compounds; elite compounds;, small, irregularly agglutinated rooms (*SIARs*); and five small mounds, probably religious structures. Of

note is the relative insignificance of the last structures, a break from the earlier Moche tradition. The main architectural components of Chan Chan are the nine named ciudadelas (Figure 9.6). Each ciudadela had three major sections, divided by massive walls with only a few entryways through them. The outer walls were as tall as 9 m. Each had walk-in wells, large ramped excavations that reached down to the water table and were the source of water for the occupants. A central section had a series of small U-shaped structures called *audiencias* (figure 9.7). These heavily decorated structures are thought to have been the living quarters and workplaces of bureaucrats because they are often associated with storage facilities. Whether for bureaucrats or other purposes, Moore and Mackey (2008) note that these structures were state symbols of authority because they are found at many Chimú centers both great and small throughout their realm. The ciudadelas at Chan Chan average over two hundred storerooms, by far more than any other kind of structure (Mackey 1987). Finally, most ciudadelas contain a funerary mound within the compound, where the king and his retainers were buried. The burial function marks these compounds as the residences of the highest nobility in the kingdom.

Each of these ciudadelas was the residence of a king and his family, as well as a place where royal administrative activities were conducted. The fact that there are nine of them, approximately the number of rulers in the oral history of Taycanamo and his descendants, suggests each son built his own compound upon becoming king. The rest of the former king's family continued to reside in his compound and use its support resources, a situation called *split inheritance.* An alternative view is that of Rafael Cavallaro (1991), who suggests that the ciudadelas were built in pairs at the same time. This and other ethnohistorical information has led Patricia Netherly (1990) to suggest that Chan Chan was ruled by dual kings, one primary and one secondary, who both lived in such compounds. If this is true, then pairs of the ciudadelas were in use contemporaneously rather than all nine being used sequentially.

Figure 9.6. Ciudadela at Chan Chan, showing central sector where audiencias are concentrated. Photo by author.

Better dating of the compounds in recent times, however, does argue for their sequential construction rather than dual construction, although Cavallero's interpretation cannot be ruled out.

Not in question is the hierarchical nature of the society at Chan Chan. In addition to the ciudadelas, thirty-five elite compounds (figure 9.8) are found interspersed among the ciudadelas, sometimes sharing outer walls. These compounds, which greatly vary in size, share some high-status features with the ciudadelas, such as walk-in wells and audiencias. But they lack funerary features and are smaller than the Great Compounds (Klymyshyn 1982). Ethnohistory again tells us that there was a middle level of bureaucrats, lesser elite who dwelled in Chan Chan and whose function was to maintain the flow of goods through the center. There is little doubt that these were the functions of the residents of the elite compounds.

Finally, occupying large areas on the west and south edges of Chan Chan are masses of SIARs (figure 9.9; J. Topic 1982, 1990). The *quincha* (cane-and-mud) structures housed the workers of the city, mostly craftspeople responsible for creating the high-status goods of copper, textile, wood, and other materials for the residents of the elite compounds and Great Compounds. SIARs were both residences and workshops. John Topic (1990) suggests there were subtle status differences among the occupants of the SIARs, with some who were located in closer proximity to ciudadelas being royal retainers who worked directly for the royal families. In contrast, the bulk of the workers lived in *barrios* and manufactured a variety of items whose basic elements were manufactured elsewhere. The audiencias in houses interspersed among these barrios probably were used to provide the raw materials needed. The residents probably depended on the

Figure 9.7. Audiencia at Chan Chan. Photo by author.

elite compounds for food, water, and raw materials, which they then converted to goods that returned to the upper classes, although many of the items were utilitarian goods whose ultimate destination was the working class of the empire. Topic suggests the barrios might have been kin-based guilds.

A question that is not often addressed concerning the hierarchical nature of the Chimú society is, how did it function as a state? What power did the existing king have relative to the ciudadelas of the previous ones? For the Inkas, we know that the wealth of a king stayed with his family and that the new king was required to amass his own, using the power of the state (i.e., the army) as the mechanism. This was accomplished using a cadre of professional Inka soldiers along with masses of warriors from conquered groups. Whether the Chimú had a comparable system is uncertain. Likewise, was the wealth of the previous rulers kept by their families, or did the new ruler gain control over it in some fashion, distributing it as he saw fit?

A related question is, what were the relations between the ciudadela occupants and the elites at secondary centers? Were the latter members of the royal family from Chan Chan? Alternatively, if local rulers were incorporated into the political hierarchy, were they related to the current and former rulers? If the flow of tribute was not controlled by a single person but, rather, the different ciudadelas, it suggests a rather complicated and potentially competitive situation.

At its height in the fourteenth century, Chan Chan may have had a population of 30,000–40,000, all of whom were thought to be nonfood producers. Part of the enormous volume of food for the city was produced in the Moche Valley, where the Moche canal system was expanded to maximize productivity (figure 9.10). When the Moche canals failed to provide sufficient food, the 80-km-long Moche-Chicama Intervalley Canal was built (IV on figure 9.10). This canal was constructed to bring water from the Chicama Valley to field systems located to the north of Chan Chan. Whether it ever actually carried water is uncertain; if it did, the total area under cultivation in the valley reached over 200 km², much more than the modern system in the valley (Moseley and Deeds 1982).

As previously mentioned, the Chimú also conducted a series of conquests to the north, conquering the former Sicán centers and establishing a center of authority at Túcume, the earlier Sicán center. Whereas

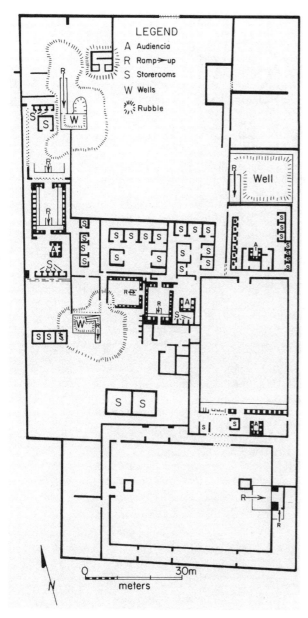

LEGEND
A Audiencia
R Ramp→up
S Storerooms
W Wells
☼ Rubble

Well

Figure 9.8. Type I elite compound at Chan Chan. From Klymyshyn 1982, figure 6.1. Courtesy of A. Ulana Klymyshyn.

most authors note that the Chimú also extended their rule all the way to the central coast near Lima, Carol Mackey and Ulana Klymyshyn (1990) suggest that their actual political control reached not much further

south than Casma. Evidence for these conquests is seen in a series of Chimú centers built for administrative purposes in the conquered valleys. Mackey (1987) notes that the Chimú demonstrate the classic settlement hierarchy of a state, with four levels above the basic village. Chan Chan was the largest site and the unquestioned capital of the empire. Below it were three regional centers, Túcume in the La Leche Valley, Farfán in the Jequetepeque Valley, and Manchan in the Casma Valley. These centers are recognized by their size, the presence of Chimú administrative or royal architecture (burial platforms at Farfán and Túcume, audiencias, and compounds built to existing canons), and ceramics. Third- and fourth-order settlements are recognized by Chimú construction techniques and decoration and ceramics. Even though these four levels can be identified archeologically, note that no valley has examples of all four.

The Chimú exercised different methods of control in the different regions they conquered (Mackey 2009). In the Jequetepeque Valley, they built new compounds at an earlier center (Farfán) instead of occupying the old capital (Pacatnamú), thus diverting political power away from the latter. They also leveled the Sipán compounds and built their own on top of them. After the takeover of Túcume, they built new compounds on the two largest Sicán compounds, but built them in local architectural style rather than using Chimú architecture. Local lords also continued to live there in other compounds, probably reflecting joint rule. At Manchán, a new center was constructed, but both Chimú compounds and local elite compounds were built, again, suggesting joint rule. In the Jequetepeque and Lambayeque valleys, the Chimú installed members of the royalty, as shown by the presence of burial platforms. In contrast, at Manchán, nonroyal elites were installed, although still Chimú by ethnicity. Local rulers continued to be used in the political hierarchy at all these centers, as shown by the local architecture and ceramics. Thus, the Chimú used a variety of political means to rule the valleys they conquered.

Mackey (2009) notes that the somewhat limited data on hand argue that the aim of the Chimú pro-

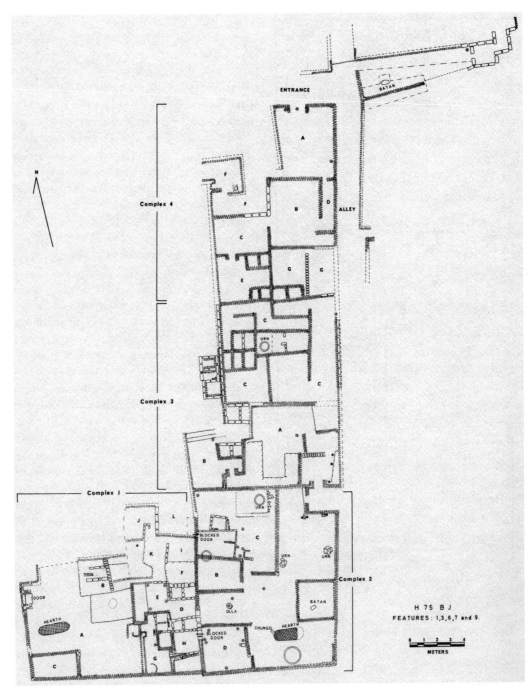

Figure 9.9. Drawing of a compound of SIARs at Chan Chan. From J. Topic 1982, figure 7.2. Courtesy of John Topic.

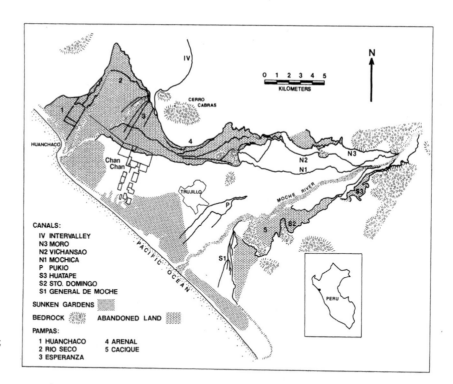

Figure 9.10. Moche Valley canal system. By permission of Maney Publishing, from Ortloff et al. 1985; permission conveyed through Copyright Clearance Center, Inc.

vincial policy was to maintain the local lords at the lower levels of the administrative hierarchy. In all the valleys where there are regional centers, there are third- and fourth-ranked centers that continued to function with little evidence of direct Chimú control. Such centers were in charge of specific tasks, mostly agriculture but also some craft production. Such lower-level lords were probably the individuals invited to the larger centers on special occasions to be fêted with food and drink to maintain their loyalty and productivity. The other side of that coin was probably punishment for failure to serve the Chimú in the ways deemed appropriate.

The Chimú were a seafaring group, much like the previous Sicán and Moche. An early Spanish exploration off the Ecuadorian coast captured a large raft with sails. While the cultural affiliation of the raft occupants is uncertain, this raft may reflect the kind of vessels used by the Chimú. Because Ecuador was the nearest source of the coveted *Spondylus* shell, the appearance of

Chimú traders off the Ecuadorian coast would not be surprising.

The reasons for Chimú expansionism involve ideological and economic factors (Mackey 2009). The north coast was an important area in Chimú mythology, including the probable location from whence came Taycanamo. Thus, controlling this region may have had ideological importance. Control over the trade in *Spondylus* from Ecuador is considered a strong reason for conquering Túcume, which until that time had been a major player in such trade (Heyerdahl, Sandweiss, and Narváez 1995). The Jequetepeque and Casma valleys were gateways to highland communities that provided resources not present on the coast but valued by Chimú elites, such as camelid hair for textiles and metallic ores.

Environmental factors have also been suggested as being important in the Chimú expansion. The large El Niño(s) of the period 1050–1100 C.E. is suggested to have been the reason for Ñançenpinco's conquests to the Jequetepeque and Santa valleys (Kolata 1990). The destruction of the Moche Valley irrigation system required the Chimú to find food from other valleys rather than rely only on the products of their own. Minchançaman's later conquests of the Lambayeque to Casma region might have been a response to a fourteenth century El Niño flood as well.

The incorporation of the Lambayeque region was associated with a late spurt of growth at Chan Chan and a reorganization of the city (Cavallaro 1991, cited in Shimada 2000; Klymyshyn 1987). The ciudadelas became more standardized at this time, twenty-seven of the thirty-five elite compounds were constructed, and the supervisory structures within the barrios were built as well. These changes were the result of the greatly increased amount of tribute entering the city, and the concomitant need for more supervision. Whether artisans from conquered areas were brought to Chan Chan (as the Inkas did later) is unknown; certainly metal production continued at the site of Batán Grande in the La Leche Valley under Chimú control (Topic 1990).

Chimú religion has been partially identified through figures on friezes, ceremonial drinking cups (keros), ceramics, and textiles (Moore and Mackey 2008). Four principal deities have been recognized: the Staff God, Plumed Headdress Deity, Chimú Goddess, and Moon Animal. The first and last are deities that were ancient in the Andes and along the north coast and that probably represent continuities from earlier religious beliefs, modified to provide new power to the elites who wielded them. The Staff God was certainly an emblem of royal power because it is the only figure to be preserved in architectural friezes inside the ciudadelas. It and the other figures were standardized in a way that reflected their use as a corporate art style, a visual representation of the power of the state over its conquered subjects.

In summary, by the beginning of the 1400s, the Chimú were the largest sociopolitical group in the Andes and were unrivaled in their wealth and political power. Beginning as a group who developed in the Moche Valley, the leaders expanded their political control both north and south over a period of four centuries. The Chimú capital of Chan Chan developed through time by the construction of administrative architecture reflecting the emerging political system based on hereditary rule of powerful kings. A middle level of bureaucrats also developed to mediate the flow of goods in the city from the lower class craftspeople to the rulers. An economic system based on conquest and trade also developed to import raw materials to the capital. Whether the finished luxury products remained there or were used in the political system, as they were with the Inkas, is unclear. Regardless, by the middle of the fifteenth century, the Chimú were the unparalleled power of ancient western South America.

That wealth of the Chimú drew the Inkas to the region and led them to conquer it (see chapter 10). They took the best of the craftspeople to Cuzco and divided the empire into a series of smaller groups that were incorporated into the Inka decimal administrative system. No doubt some local rulers continued in power, but under Inka hegemony, others were killed and replaced. The day of the Chimú was at an end.

THE NORTH-CENTRAL AND CENTRAL COAST

Until recently, very little was known of the Late Intermediate Period cultures in the region from the Huarmey to the Supe valleys. As just discussed, this region interacted with the Chimú state to the north, but how many valleys, if any, were incorporated is uncertain. Sites such as Paramonga in the Fortaleza Valley are often identified as Chimú, but this is due to the presence of Chimú ceramics at the sites, which were probably trade wares.

As mentioned in chapter 8, the Casma polity emerged in the region between the Casma and Chao valleys. This polity continued into the Late Intermediate Period. Its two main sites, Cerro La Cruz in the Chao Valley and El Purgatorio in the Casma

Valley, continued to be occupied; the latter was the probable capital, whereas the former could be considered a northern border center (Vogel 2003, 2011). The two sites were conquered by the Chimú in the fourteenth century, although the nature of their incorporation into the empire is still uncertain.

For the central coast, there is a larger body of information from ethnohistorical records about the groups of this region. Following early Spanish writers, the term *señorío* is often used to describe the polities that existed in different valleys and even in different parts of the same valley. The term refers to a local ethnic group under the rule of a hereditary chief. There is particular confusion between the archaeologically defined ceramic styles noted in this region and the identification of the señoríos of the historical record. For example, the Chancay ceramic style is known from the Huaura Valley in the north to the Chillón Valley, but the señorío responsible for it is uncertain. Craig Morris and Adriana von Hagen (1993) suggest it was the Collique, a group identified by Maria Rostworowski (1977a), one of the foremost Peruvian ethnohistorians. Jalh Dulanto (2008) and Ramiro Matos Mendieta (2000) argue that the Collique señorío was restricted to the lower Chillón Valley. Whether the ceramics were due entirely, partially or not at all to this group is not known. Due to their location in the same geographical setting, it is reasonable to believe that they were at least partially responsible. Francisco Vallejo (2010) and others have discovered ceramic complexity in the Huaura Valley in the Norte Chico that will make connecting ethnohistorical groups to archaeological styles challenging.

Chancay ceramics and textiles are well-known due to their superb craftsmanship. Unfortunately, due to this quality and the proximity of Chancay to modern Lima, virtually all Chancay archaeological sites have been badly looted (Matos Mendieta 2000). Nonetheless, Andrzej Krzanowski (1991a, 1991b; cited in Dulanto 2008) notes the presence of a distinctive monumental architecture called *montículos piramidales tronco-cónicos* (truncated cone-shaped pyramidal mounds) at sites that correspond to the Chancay ceramic style in the Huaura and Chancay valleys. These were (probably) administrative structures consisting of a small pyramid with a ramp on one side surrounded by rectangular rooms and open spaces, all enclosed by a wall. Several of them can be found at the same site, indicating that there were duplicate individuals in charge of the activities in these buildings. This might suggest there was no central authority in charge of society. Eri Azami and Oliver Velásquez (2010) find craft production associated with the open patios of some of these mounds, similar to what is found at Chimú sites farther north. If particular crafts were associated with particular mound groups, then it could suggest a more complex economic system that might warrant a more centralized authority to run it. More research is needed to clarify this important point.

Nonetheless, we do know that there was an elite class, as recognized by the elaborate burials of individuals with hundreds of ceramic vessels and ornate textiles using different techniques of decoration (Matos Mendieta 2000). Tapestry, brocade, laces, and painted textiles are found, often embroidered with figures of gold, silver, or feathers. The ceramics are a distinctive off-white slip with black line designs, mostly of geometric forms. A common form is an urn with a human head as the neck.

Thanks to the work of Maria Rostworowski (1977d), we know the Ichsma, or Ychsma, señorío existed in the lower reaches of the Rimac and Lurín valleys. Most scholars, such as Rostworowski and Matos Mendieta, argue that Pachacamac was the main religious and political center of this señorío. Following the ethnohistorical research of Rostworowski, Alberto Bueno Mendoza (1982) has argued that the Ychsma was a kind of religious confederation, with local leaders from the surrounding regions coming to Pachacamac to conduct rituals for their particular groups (López Hurtado 2010). A contrasting view has been presented by Peter Eeckhout (2003, 2004), who suggests that there was a principal authority who lived at Pachacamac and ruled the surrounding regions.

The difference in the viewpoint of these scholars relates to the presence of a distinctive architecture of power in this region and site, the *pirámides con rampas* (pyramids with ramps). These are compounds consisting of a rectangular enclosure with a mound of several tiers within that are linked by ramps (Shimada 1991). They are found in groups at sites in these two valleys, and they are similar both to the Chancay compounds and the Chimú ciudadelas. The interpretation of Bueno Mendoza (1982) and others is based on the fifteen pyramids with ramps at the site of Pachacamac being occupied at the same time by the regional rulers who came there to conduct their particular rites and homages to the image of Pachacamac located there. Eeckhout's interpretation is based on these structures being occupied by the successive rulers of the site, who built a new one upon replacing the previous ruler. Until better dates are provided for these compounds, which model is correct remains to be proven.

Work by Enrique López Hurtado (2010) at the site of Panquilma, located a day's walk upvalley from Pachacamac, has recovered significant data suggesting what kinds of elites interacted with the individuals at Pachacamac, either as direct participants or under the aegis of the ruler at the site. Sector 1 was a zone of three pyramids with ramps and associated residential structures. Each was briefly occupied, but all had large funerary chambers with evidence of feasting associated with them. The excavator's description does not make it clear whether this zone was post-Inka; he does note an abundance of Inka ceramics in the sector. Sector 2 was separated from sector 1 by a walkway and was a zone of elite residences, again with associated funerary structures but smaller in size. Finally, Sector 3 was located at a distance from the other two sectors and was a residential zone for the commoners. Here, burials were located in groups away from the houses. López Hurtado interprets the information as indicating that the elites were maintaining their status by ancestor worship and that there was probably competition between elite lineages for status and possibly access to prestige items. If Panquilma is representative of other sites in the region, it indicates a social landscape of competing elite groups that occupied different sections of the river valleys. If such groups can be linked to the pyramids with ramps at Pachacamac, it will lend strong support to Bueno Mendoza's model of political organization for this region.

Pedro Espinoza (2010) has hypothesized that there was a distinct polity in the Rimac Valley, centered at Maranga, that was independent of Pachacamac until the Inkas conquered the region. He notes the differences in architectural features between the two centers and suggests a different cult may have been located at Maranga. As part of their political transformations, the Inkas replaced the local cult with priests from Pachacamac after their conquest of the zone, perhaps to expand its religious authority and, by extension, their own political power. The burning of Sector 1 at Panquilma (López Hurtado 2010) might reflect a similar pattern of Inka conquest in the Lurín Valley.

In addition to the other *etnías* (ethnic groups) identified on the central coast, Rostworowski (1977, 1978–1980) mentions the Guarco and Lunahuaná as inhabiting the Cañete Valley south of Lurín. The former inhabited the lower valley with their main center at Cerro Azul, and the latter were located upvalley with their principal temple at Concon (Matos Mendieta 2000). Rostworowski's research indicates they were distinct political entities, but their material culture was very similar, indicating close ties between them (and emphasizing the difficulty of differentiating such polities archeologically!). Cerro Azul (Marcus 1987) consists of a group of eight elite residences surrounded by smaller structures devoted to fish storage. Both elite and commoner graves have been identified, as have different occupations. Marcus interprets the site as the center of a local polity that controlled fishing and farming activities for the valley.

The research along the central coast indicates the diversity of late pre-Hispanic political and ethnic entities, and the challenges in differentiating them. It is hoped that, as archaeological research continues, the true nature and extent of these entities and their links to ethnohistorical groups will be identified.

The archaeological and ethnohistorical information for the region farther south is somewhat clearer, perhaps due to the size of the valleys and the distance between them in this region but also due to the lack of modern urbanization that has occurred. The Chincha Valley was the location of a powerful etnía that controlled maritime trade along the coast as far as the north coast and perhaps even Ecuador. The lord of Chincha was allowed the privilege of being carried in a litter next to the Inka ruler, reflecting the importance of this maritime trade to the Inkas. Maria Rostworowski (1977b) describes the Chincha society as specialized into villages of farmers and fisherfolk, which is supported by the archaeological research of Daniel Sandweiss (1992). In addition, there was another group of specialists, the *mercaderes* (merchants), whose job it was to conduct trade along the coast, particularly in *Spondylus*.

The capital of the polity was the site of La Centinela, located at the mouth of the valley. This site had a series of nine large compounds, resembling the mounds with ramps from the Lurín Valley, that surrounded a main truncated pyramid mound that stood over 40 m high (Morris and Santillana 2007). The compounds were most likely the residences of elite lineages at the site. Morris and Julián Santillana (2007) suggest that the pyramid was the location of the oracle of Chinchaycamac, the main deity of the Chincha people.

THE SOUTH AND FAR-SOUTH COAST

That the Chincha polity was more developed than others along the south coast is reflected in both the number of settlements with monumental architecture (over thirty) and a series of roads that linked La Centinela with nearby and more distant locations (Wallace 1991). The roads extended to the Pisco Valley, indicating the integration of the population of at least the lower part of that valley into the Chincha polity. Canziani (1992, cited in Morris and Santillana 2007) has found major Chincha sites not only in the lower valley but in the central valley and upper-neck region, suggesting a possible hierarchical arrangement of settlements. That, in turn, could

argue for a complex political entity in the valley that reinforces the ethnohistorical descriptions of the culture (Rostworowski 1977b).

The remaining valleys of the south coast (Pisco, Ica, and the Nazca drainage) have been suggested to have been the seats of local political groups, none particularly centralized (Dulanto 2008). Although centers such as Ica Vieja in the Ica Valley may have been political or religious centers (Menzel 1959) based on the presence of mounds there, little other evidence supports the idea that political power was focused in a small number of individuals. In fact, the evidence from Nazca (Conlee 2005) argues that there was an increase in the number of local elites vying for power in the different drainages and that centralized authority did not exist.

Less still is known of the political developments in the far-south coastal region, from Acarí to the Chilean border, with the notable exception of the Ilo/Moquegua drainage. As in the areas farther north, distinctive ceramic styles of adjacent highland regions, such as Chuquibamba in the Majes region and Churajón in the Arequipa region, have been defined, but the nature of the polities and ethnicities responsible is less well understood.

Thanks to the Programa Condesuyo and subsequent research conducted by its members and others, we know a great deal more about the Ilo/Moquegua region than other valleys of this area. During the Middle Horizon, the middle and upper parts of this valley had been under the sphere of influence of Tiwanaku, although the Wari Empire was present, as marked by the colony located at Cerro Baúl and Cerro Mejía (see chapter 8). Around 1000 C.E., this situation changed; the Wari colony was abandoned and Tiwanaku influence waned.

Even before the beginning of the second millennium, a new cultural manifestation developed in the coastal zone of Ilo and the lower Moquegua Valley. This culture is known as Chiribaya, and it was largely restricted to the zone below the narrow region where the river water reappears after flowing through subterranean aquifers for around 15 km. This natural phenomenon seems to have been a cultural border throughout the pre-Hispanic sequence in the region. Tiwanaku influence did not penetrate this zone, although some researchers have argued the opposite (Stanish 1992). Research by Jane Buikstra and colleagues (Lozada et al. 2009) indicates that Chiribaya emerged as a discrete cultural entity around 700 C.E., contemporary with the earliest Tiwanaku colonies in the mid-valley region. Skeletal comparisons of the Tiwanaku and local pre-Chiribaya populations showed a clear clustering of Chiribaya with the latter, not the Tiwanaku.

Chiribaya is recognizable as a vibrant ceramic (plate 7B) and textile tradition, both media using many different colors and designs of abstract symbols and exotic creatures. It emerged out of the simple fishing and agricultural cultures that existed in this region from early Formative times. It is evident that the south-coastal pattern of distinct farming and fishing communities was also present here (Lozada et al. 2009). Fisherfolk were found to have had distinct ceramic styles as well as annular head deformations, whereas the farmers had other styles and fronto-occipital deformation (see figure 8.10).

Politically, the Chiribaya are described as having differentiated elites and commoners, with the former living at the site of Chiribaya Alta, located about 7 km upvalley from the coast. This site, the largest in the region at this time, had nine cemeteries, most of which contained farmers but one contained fisherfolk. Cemetery 7 was apparently an elite cemetery because the individuals there had larger quantities of burial goods and camelid offerings. The analysis of the camelids from this site and others supports the idea that camelid breeding was an important occupation in this region and may have been one supervised and controlled by the elites (Lozada et al. 2009).

Chiribaya society came to a dramatic end sometime in the fourteenth century as a result of a major El Niño that struck the entire coast at this time. Subsequent to the destruction, many Chiribaya sites were abandoned and the inhabitants apparently moved upvalley.

The post–Middle Horizon history of the middle and upper valleys indicates a gradual loss of Tiwanaku influence followed by population movements into previously unoccupied regions (Rice, Stanish, and Scarr 1989). The final occupation of the Omo site was only a fraction of the 4-km^2 zone of the previous occupation where the Tiwanaku temple had been located. The site was also fortified. Tiwanaku-style ceramics from the Altiplano disappeared, replaced by locally made forms, although much of the iconography continued to be used. One important exception to this is the hallmark of Tiwanaku state style—the Front Faced or Gateway God motif—which disappeared completely and was replaced by a stylized flamingo. This suggests a rejection of the Tiwanaku state religion but the retention of some of the beliefs during this critical transitional time. According to Bermann et al., this succeeding Tumilaca Period

> is characterized by the disappearance of monumental architecture and hierarchical site arrangement. Settlements become more widely distributed and uniformly-sized, and were usually either fortified or strategically located. Tumilaca Period ceramics display increasingly little identity with the altiplano prototypes of Tiwanaku V. Moreover, the Tumilaca Period does not demonstrate a unified "Moqueguan" approach to ceramic technology, choice of form or decorative style. It is, instead, defined by a diversity that suggests extremely local, rather than regional, patterns of production and distribution. (1989, 273)

Sites were now found over a wider range of locations, including in the upper valley for the first time. The Otora tributary of the Moquegua was opened to agricultural use, and terrace and irrigation systems were constructed to feed the local population. There were, however, no monumental structures or other evidence of any hierarchical control, and these settlements appear to indicate the movement of people into new regions after the authority of Tiwanaku disappeared. In the lower and middle valley, the locus of occupation in the previous period, sites were still present but were located on steeper slopes or in defensible positions.

During the succeeding Otora Period, we see a complicated pattern of settlement that reflected migrations from two different regions, the Altiplano and the coast. The former is identified by a colony of Qolla individuals, the latter by Chiribaya people, both in the Otora Valley. Stanish (1989) argues that this brief period represents a multiethnic, heterogeneous colonization of the region. This evolved into a more homogeneous culturally unified region during the following Estuquiña Period, which was much more broadly distributed across the upper reaches of the Moquegua tributaries and even into the adjacent Tambo Valley. Nonetheless, there was little political organization, even into the later stages of the Late Intermediate Period. What is present is the emergence of local elites who could control limited areas of resources, but by what means is uncertain.

THE NORTH HIGHLANDS

In the Cajamarca Basin, there was a marked decrease in the number of sites from the previous period, from forty-six to twenty-five, during the Late Cajamarca Period (850–1200 C.E.). The quantity of fine ceramics that were characteristic of this Cajamarca tradition also fell. Both Daniel Julien (1993) and Jason Toohey (2011) see this information as reflecting a collapse of the earlier political order and the subsequent emergence of local political units that were autonomous and competing. Sites were now located in defensible locations or displayed defensive structures, suggesting concerns over security. The decrease in interaction with the adjacent coastal zone during this period supports Toohey's (2011) conclusion that politics, including conflict, were more internal to the Cajamarca region than external at this time.

During the Final Cajamarca Period (1200–1532 C.E.), there was an increase in the number of sites to forty-eight. A settlement hierarchy begins to emerge, with three large sites located in different parts of the Cajamarca region. Using Spanish documents about the Inka political organization of the region, Julien

(1993) argues that these were the centers of small chiefdoms that became *warangas* (units of 1,000 taxpayers) under the Inkas. The three centers were probably autonomous units, as each had elite housing and fine ceramics, indicating the emergence of a ruling group. Variability in the ceramic substyles of the region also supports the autonomous nature of these local polities during this period (Toohey 2011). The presence of different substyles at each center suggests that there was exchange among the elites in this region that has been mistaken for political homogeneity and centralization by earlier scholars.

For Huamachuco, the next area south, a similar pattern seems to have developed. John Topic (2009) suggests the major Middle Horizon center of Marcahuamachuco might have lost its political preeminence because no new major constructions have been identified, only reconstructions of earlier buildings. With the development of this political vacuum, three site clusters are seen, each with a large site with more elaborate architecture. Topic (2009) argues this indicates the emergence of three independent political entities that probably interacted economically because each has access to only certain resource zones, not all of them. The lack of fortifications or defensible locations also suggests cooperation among these entities during this period. The developments here thus seem to parallel those of the Cajamarca region to the north.

Before proceeding south, I now discuss the Chachapoya culture that existed to the east of both Cajamarca and Huamachuco. This region is noted for its cloud forest environment, in contrast to the more traditional puna-quechua-yunga zones of the regions farther south. This region was famous, infamous even, during the Late Horizon for its resistance to and rebellions against the Inka. Although the region was continuously occupied from the Preceramic Period onward (Church and von Hagen 2008), monumental architecture appears only at the end of the Middle Horizon or perhaps the beginning of the Late Intermediate Period. A Chachapoya identity is apparent in ceramics, architecture, and settlement patterns at the beginning of the latter period. Warren Church and Adriana von Hagen (2008) attribute this to the growth and fissioning of ayllus, some of which may have been ranked while others were more egalitarian. During this period, hundreds of sites were occupied, mostly above 2,900 masl, with several sites such as Kuelap and Caserones having more than four hundred structures. A distinctive architectural style using slabs of cut limestone laid in decorative patterns emerged during this time (figure 9.11). Many of the larger sites sit atop ridges, although whether this was for defense or economic reasons is unclear.

Subsistence was based on wild game, guinea pigs, and camelids for protein, and tubers and high-altitude grains for carbohydrates (Church and von Hagen 2008). Extensive field systems surrounded many sites. Although the size and specialized architecture in some of the larger sites and mortuary differences suggest sociopolitical hierarchy, Church and von Hagen argue that the evidence for marked complexity is scarce. The settlement patterns do not support such an interpretation, either.

All in all, the evidence suggests that there were political inequalities present, warfare and sorcery as well as trade and accumulation of wealth having been the means to greater power for certain individuals or perhaps ayllus (Church and von Hagen 2008). Yet there is little to suggest political centralization, and the evidence from the Late Horizon and historical documents suggest a system of autonomous centers that were able to form a confederacy in the face of external threats, especially the Inkas.

CENTRAL HIGHLANDS

There is little known about the Late Intermediate Period cultures of the regions between Huamachuco and the Puna of Junín. In contrast, the region that includes the main part of the Puna of Junín and the valleys that descend from it to the east is referred to as Tarama-Chinchaycocha, following the names of the Inka provinces defined in the area. Research here by several investigators, notably Ramiro Matos Mendieta and Charles Hastings, indicates a significant cultural transformation during the Late Intermediate Period (Parsons, Hastings, and Matos Mendieta 1997). A large-scale survey of the region

Figure 9.11. Chachapoyas slab architecture at Gran Pajatén. Photo by Gregory O. Jones. From the Jones Pajaten Archive, courtesy of Columbus State University, with assistance from Warren Church.

covered 800 km² of puna and 500 km² of the valley area. The survey indicated that the region was occupied by two distinct specialized groups, puna herders and valley cultivators. These two used similar ceramics and lived in similar kinds of structures. Yet there were distinctions in burial practices between the two regions, indicating other distinctions also existed between the two occupationally specialized groups. Using a model based on ethnographic and ethnohistorical work, the researchers suggested that the two groups developed social and ritual interactions at special activity sites along the boundary between the two zones that allowed each group access to the products of the other while maintaining their distinctiveness. They also identified evidence of probable moiety differences within each group and possibly between them as well. Although no marked political differences were present in the region, the nature of the economic, social, and political interactions of these two groups reflects the complexity of the cultural activities during this period.

One of the best-known regions in this period is the Upper Mantaro River valley where the modern towns of Jauja and Huancayo are located. This region was the focus of study by the Upper Mantaro Archaeological Research Project (UMARP), headed by Timothy Earle, Terence D'Altroy, Catherine Scott, and Christine Hastorf (Earle et al. 1983; D'Altroy 1992). Building on the work of Matos Mendieta (1959, 1975), David Browman (1970), and others, the goal of this project was to understand the changes effected by the Inkas on the local Wanka group that inhabited this region. Combining archival and archeological research, the project identified dramatic changes in the Late Intermediate Period political and domestic economies prior even to the arrival of the Inkas.

Ethnohistorically, the Upper Mantaro region was occupied by two or three ethnic groups. The three often mentioned were the Hatunxauxa, the Lurinwanka, and the Ananwanka. The latter two possibly reflect a moiety division of a single group, but the Hatunxauxa were identified as having been separate.

All three are collectively called the Wanka, reflecting the Inka name of the province after it was conquered. The province may have had as many as 60,000 inhabitants at the time of the Inka conquest (D'Altroy 1992).

Archaeologically, the Late Intermediate Period is divided into two phases, Wanka I (1000–1350 C.E.) and Wanka II (1350–1460 C.E.). During Wanka I, sites were located in all ecological zones and the population densities were low. Houses consisted of one or two circular structures opening onto a small patio. There was no evidence of conflict; the sites were neither fortified nor located in defensible positions. And there is no evidence of any political centralization or corporate architecture. The population during this period is estimated at between 4,000–6,500 people (D'Altroy 1992).

Significant changes occurred during the subsequent Wanka II phase. The population increased significantly to almost 60,000, a tenfold increase. Most settlements now were found on hilltops or other defensive locales, and many had multiple walls around them. Two settlements, Hatunmarca and Tunanmarca, dominated the northern Yanamarca Valley region at the northern end of the Mantaro region. Both have evidence of elite residences, identified by access to better foods, more exotic materials, and high-status items. Yet most activities were still conducted in the households, both elite and commoner. D'Altroy (1992) interprets this to indicate that the elite households were controlling the materials but not labor. The evidence also suggests the development of hostilities was mainly a means for local leaders of ayllus to gain power and prestige and possibly more wives for larger households. The positions of power were likely passed down to capable sons, indicating the emergence of hereditary inequalities, although perhaps at an incipient level. Conflict for the Wanka was an intravalley activity among members of the same or closely related ethnicities. The somewhat surprising lack of evidence for any public or ceremonial structures (the presence of a large plaza in the center of Tunanmarka might possibly reflect some civic space) is interpreted as being the result of these ethnicities' using their political capital for warfare rather than construction activities.

Following Henry Wright (1984), D'Altroy (1992) interprets the Wanka as a complex chiefdom during the phase preceding their incorporation into Tawantinsuyu. He notes that such societies "are not well differentiated politically but exhibit hierarchical ranking of distinct social groups. . . . [They] typically exhibit periodic warfare, shifting alliances, and appropriation of land" (D'Altroy 1992, 69). Alternatively, given the incomplete nature of the emergence of the elites at this time, the Wanka could be described as a transegalitarian society, following Brian Hayden (1995).

For the region of modern Ayacucho, the heartland of the Wari culture, the transition to the societies that followed has not been well documented. In fact, the reasons for the Wari collapse are not understood, and even the date when the political authority that ruled from the site of Huari disappeared is uncertain. There is evidence that the city was undergoing a great transformation in the ninth century, with a significant change in its overall organization (Isbell 1997a). The traditional orthogonal architectural units and D-shaped ritual structures were abandoned or greatly reduced in occupation. Smaller irregular compounds were constructed that were bounded by massive walls. Janusek (2008), following Isbell (1997a), suggests this represents a fragmentation of the old centralized bureaucracy and the emergence of competing kin groups.

It is notable that the major Wari provincial centers were abandoned at different times and under different kinds of circumstances. Jincamocco and the other Wari sites in the Carhuarazo Valley were abandoned around 800 C.E., at the end of Middle Horizon 2, as was Azángaro in the Wari heartland. More violent ends are suggested for the settlements in the Cuzco area, Qoripata, and possibly Pikillacta (McEwan 1996; Glowacki and Malpass 2003). Viracochapampa in Huamachuco was carefully closed and abandoned, and there is some question concerning how intensively it was ever occupied. Finally, in the Moquegua Valley, the site of Cerro Baúl was perhaps one of the latest major Wari sites to be abandoned, sometime around 1000 C.E. The abandonment was done after the ritual burning of several of the buildings (Moseley et al. 2005).

What seems to have occurred is some kind of major upheaval at the site of Huari, perhaps around 800–850 C.E. This must have affected the interactions between the elite groups at Huari and those in the provincial centers. If centralized control disappeared, then the local Wari rulers at the centers could decide what pathways they wanted to pursue. Some perhaps closed up the centers and returned to the homeland, whereas others stayed and faced violent repercussions, either by local people or perhaps foreigners. The evidence from Moquegua is particularly complex, but it does suggest that there was a pattern of conflict and killing that involved both Tiwanaku descendants and Wari personnel (Williams and Nash 2002).

Little is known about the groups who inherited the political landscape of the Wari near Ayacucho or Apurimac. Ethnohistorically, this region was occupied by the Chanka, the group most famous for its role in the accounts of the rise of Pachakuti, the ninth Inka king. In these accounts, the Chanka laid siege to Cuzco, causing the reigning king Wiraqocha Inka to abandon the city. Pachakuti rallied the people of the city to its defense and, with the supernatural turning of field stones into soldiers, defeated the Chanka, driving them back to their homeland, where they were conquered. Thus began the Inka expansion (I discuss this story in chapter 10). Until recently, we could say little about the kind of society that the Chanka had. Lumbreras (1974) suggests that after the fall of Wari the populations of the large centers dispersed into smaller communities, many on the summits of hills. The people lived in round houses attached to one another and buried their dead in circular mausoleums or simple graves. Whether these two burial types reflect status differences is unknown, but community buildings and other markers of status are noticeably absent.

Thankfully, this picture is now clearer due to a research project by Brian Bauer, Lucas Kellett, and Miriam Aráoz Silva (2010). The first thing that this project found was that the term *Chanka* properly refers only to the ethnic group that lived in the region of Andahuaylas, a province in the Department of Apurimac, which lies between the Department of Ayacucho to the west and the Department of Cuzco to the east. Other groups sharing some general traits, such as those enumerated by Lumbreras, lived in nearby regions. Collectively, these groups are often called the Chanka Confederation in the literature.

In contrast to the view given by the Inkas that the Chankas were a powerful chiefdom-level society capable of invading and conquering the Inkas themselves, Bauer, Kellett, and Aráoz Silva (2010) find little evidence for such political unification or centralization. The Late Intermediate Period sites were generally located on ridgetops and situated far from each other and consisted of irregular groups of circular houses with no apparent distinctions. Only two larger settlements were found, but they showed no clear evidence of political power. Bauer, Kellett, and Aráoz Silva argue they were probably complementary moiety centers rather than political foci: "Currently we find no archaeological evidence to suggest that the Chanka were a highly stratified or uniquely powerful ethnic group at the time of the Inca expansion. . . . Powerful Chanka leaders, or a loose confederation of central Andean ethnic groups, may have briefly arisen near the end of the period with the legendary Chanka-Inca war, but they have left few material correlates to be identified" (2001, 93).

On archaeological grounds, it would seem, then, that the Chanka war may have been an overexaggeration on the Inkas' part for political ends. For the moment, I defer discussion of the rise of the Inkas, the next group to the south, until the following chapter. Note, however, that the Inkas began as another of these generally undifferentiated cultures, much like the others just discussed here. How and why they emerged as the dominant power is that much more interesting because of their unremarkable beginnings.

SOUTH-CENTRAL HIGHLANDS

Some preliminary research has been conducted on the Middle Horizon to Late Horizon sequence for the Colca Valley, which is the name for the upper reaches of the same river that is called the Majes and Camaná River lower down (Brooks 1998; Denevan 1987; Malpass 1987; de la Vera Cruz 1987; Wernke 2003). A survey of and testing at sites in the central Colca identified some evidence of Wari presence, mainly in the development of terracing in the vicinity of the town of Coporaque. Subsequent to the collapse of Wari, local towns emerged that controlled the terrace systems adjacent to their towns and were probably independent. The groups expanded the rain-fed terrace systems as their populations increased. The Late Intermediate Period ceramic style, called Chuquibamba, is probably associated with these occupations. When the Inka arrived in the region, they redistributed the population and increased agricultural productivity by constructing a new system of irrigated terraces, including reservoirs, below the earlier system (Malpass 1987).

The final region to be discussed is the Altiplano, the former home of the Tiwanaku culture. The period I discuss here is the Pacajes (1150–1430 C.E.), although the story begins where it left off in chapter 8, in the late Tiwanaku 2 Period (or Tiwanaku V of earlier chronologies, 1000–1150 C.E.; Janusek 2005). This brief period saw the collapse of the Tiwanaku civilization and its evolution into a series of localized groups that later developed into powerful chiefdom-like societies that confronted the Inkas.

Alan Kolata and his colleagues (see Kolata 1996 for a list of these scholars and their work) see the reason for the Tiwanaku collapse as the extended drought that began in the eleventh century. This reduction in rainfall is identified both from the ice cores in the Quelccaya glacier and a steep drop in the level of Lake Titicaca (Kolata and Ortloff 1996; see chapter 2). They note that this reduction in rainfall would have affected the outlying colonies such as those in Moquegua first because their systems of agriculture were more directly dependent on rainfall.

The raised-field systems would have been buffered against such reductions because they were dependent on groundwater sources that would have dropped more slowly. Hence, the colonies and external regions under Tiwanaku influence would have fallen victim to hard times prior to the heartland, which is supported by the archaeological evidence of the loss of Tiwanaku influence earlier in those regions. As the drought intensified, however, the level of Lake Titicaca dropped as the water table dropped, causing the raised fields to become stranded. The pattern of field use and subsequent abandonment does support such a model. As the raised fields were abandoned, food surpluses dropped and the system of commensalism on which Tiwanaku had been developed was no longer tenable; the system collapsed.

This environmental model has been challenged by Clark Erickson (1999), who notes that Kolata and colleagues smoothed over the many smaller increases and decreases in the Quelccaya record and focused on longer-scale changes. He notes that the collapse actually started 100–200 years earlier than the major drought of 1245–1310 C.E. He discusses how major droughts were historically always followed by periods of increased rainfall that would have mitigated some of the major effects discussed by Kolata and others. He also notes the many ways that present farmers and those of the recent past coped with severe droughts. Kolata et al. (2000) have responded to these criticisms, citing various differences in both interpretation and data analysis. Nevertheless, a critique of both the ice-core and Titicaca sedimentation data on which Kolata et al.'s model is based (Calaway 2005) suggest that the data are not sufficiently detailed to support the view of an extended drought and drop in lake levels at a time that would have caused the collapse.

Janusek (2008) uses this argument to come up with a human agency-based description of the collapse. He notes that a process of decentralization of the population of the Tiwanaku Valley was already underway before 1000 C.E. Local groups may have been taking control of local food production, perhaps forcing the rulers in the city to increase their control of the Pampa Koani raised fields. This led to a decline in the population and influence of Lukurmata.

Throughout Late Tiwanaku V, Tiwanaku was progressively abandoned, one residential sector at a time. The center was all but abandoned by 1150 C.E., with many of its main structures more like shrines than active sacred spaces. There is ample evidence that the abandonment might not have been totally peaceful. The elite residence at Putuni was completely razed around 1000 C.E. (Couture and Sampeck 2003). Most of the megalithic monuments, including many of the large doorways and monoliths, were systematically defaced or destroyed, and it is not unreasonable to suggest much of this destruction occurred during this time (Janusek 2008). As Janusek states, "More profoundly than the razing of the Putuni Palace, the ritualized destruction and defacement of icons representing elite ancestors targeted ideological foundations of power and legitimacy among Tiwanaku's elite. I argue that much of it was wrought just as Tiwanaku's population—elite and commoner—fragmented into conflictive factions, and as powerful gestures of symbolic violence" (2008, 296).

It is not surprising that the period before 1000 C.E. also marked the time when Tiwanaku influence declined in the Moquegua Valley, and there is evidence of systematic destruction of the sites associated with the Altiplano city. This would have further damaged the system of food distribution for the inhabitants of the city and might have compromised the ability of elites to provide the quantities of maize chicha that were part of the important commensalism on which the society was based.

As the crisis deepened, people began to abandon the Tiwanaku Valley in favor of other regions. Some of the new Late Intermediate Period settlements in the upper Moquegua Valley appear to be groups from the Altiplano (Owen 2005), and the region to the south of Tiwanaku also experienced an increase in population. In addition, the ancient boundary between the Katari and Tiwanaku valleys reemerged with a series of fortified sites appearing in the Taraco hills separating the two drainages. It is at this point that the possibility of a reduction in rainfall simply exacerbated an already difficult situation, leading to the final abandonment of the city and the collapse of its state-sponsored material culture.

Post-Tiwanaku Developments on the Altiplano

Janusek (2005, 2008) has provided an excellent description of the developments on the southern Altiplano that occurred as a result of the collapse of the Tiwanaku polity. First, there was a dramatic reduction in the population of the region of Tiwanaku and the adjacent Katari Valley, although the number of sites dating to this period increases by a factor of three. This evidence suggests that sites were not occupied for long periods, an interpretation supported by excavations showing ephemeral occupations. Second, the Pampa Koani raised-field systems were now the locations of residences for people, indicating that they were no longer in use for agriculture. The drier conditions of the twelfth century would have made agriculture more difficult in general, but the lower water table resulting from the drop in Lake Titicaca affected the raised-field systems directly. These two factors support the idea that people shifted to a greater use of camelids at this time. At the time of the Spanish conquest, this region was known for its extensive herds of camelids, which were owned by powerful lords of particular regions. This situation apparently began to emerge during the twelfth century.

The sites of Tiwanaku and Lukurmata were reduced in size as well, although this process began in Tiwanaku V, as previously mentioned. These settlements were now the same size as others located along the lower piedmont zones. Although less work has been done on sites of this period, it seems likely that these towns were the precursors of the systems of *cabaceras* or *markas* that existed when the Spaniards arrived. These political units were often based on the concept of duality and were composed of aggregates of ayllus. Indeed, this entire region was divided in the sixteenth century into two major divisions, *Urkosuyu* and *Umasuyu*, and Janusek makes a strong

case for the boundary being along the Taraco hills that divide the Tiwanaku and Katari valleys.

Supporting his argument are the changes in ceramic assemblages and burial practices that appeared during the Pacajes Period. With the collapse of the sociopolitical centers, the distinctive ceremonial and commensal wares of the polity disappeared. The large storage vessels called *tinajas* that were used for brewing chicha for feasts became almost nonexistent, and the ones still in use were much smaller, reflecting the more limited feasting that was going on. Open bowls with different designs largely replaced the fancy decorated wares of Tiwanaku 2. The different designs on such bowls in Urkosuyu and Umasuyu reinforces the idea of a social boundary between the two regions. In contrast to the decorated wares, the undecorated forms from the Tiwanaku period largely continue in use with little evidence of change.

A change in burial practices is also a feature of the Pacajes Period. Tiwanaku burials were typically in subterranean cist tombs, but in this period new above-ground tombs appeared. These are of two types. In the Umasuyu region, slab cist tombs made an appearance, which were above-ground structures of adobe on a cobble foundation. They were used for multiple burials, probably of family or other kin, and could be reopened as new members were interred. This marks a significant shift from the previous period when burials could not be reopened. In the Urkosuyu region, *chullpas* (burial towers) appeared that fulfilled a similar function but were much more visible on the landscape (figure 9.12). Following Isbell (1997b), Janusek (2004b) argues that these represent visible boundary markers and justifications of social territories during a time when such boundaries were more fluid due to increasing mobility.

In the northern part of the Altiplano, the two best-known ethnohistorical cultures of the Late Intermediate Period were the Qolla and the Lupaqa. The former had their capital at Hatuncolla, north of the modern city of Puno; the latter had their capital at Chucuito, south of Puno. These could be considered the ethnic equivalents of the Pacajes, the group

Figure 9.12. Late Intermediate Period chullpa. Photo by Elizabeth Arkush.

just described, who were the next ethnic group to the southeast of the Lupaqa. The documents pertaining to these ethnicities describe a situation in which powerful lords maintained control over groups of ayllus whose leaders were subservient to the *caciques* (principal lords). The two caciques of the Lupaqa were Martín Cari and Martín Cusi, who were the leaders of the Upper and Lower moieties of the Lupaqa. The economy was based on herding and tuber cultivation, although colonies were created in the lower valleys to the east and west where they cultivated crops such as maize (Murra 1972). The control of other ecological zones for economic purposes is called the zonal complementarity model. An important historical document, the 1567 *Visita* [census] *Hecha a la Provincia de Chucuito de Garci Diez de San Miguel en el Año 1567* (Espinoza Soriano 1964), notes that there were Lupaqa colonies in the Sama, Moquegua, and Tambo valleys. Stanish (1989), however, has found that the Altiplano influences in the upper Moquegua drainage were of Qolla affiliation, as indicated by similarities in tomb type, architecture, and ceramics. Lupaqa influence is noted only during the Late Horizon, indicating that the

system of Lupaqa colonies was probably a result of Inka policies. Nonetheless, the model of zonal complementarity fits with the evidence for Altiplano colonies in the western valleys.

It is interesting to note that the Inka oral histories given to the Spaniards after their conquest described the Qolla and Lupaqa as powerful señoríos that were a threat to the Inkas. Their early conquest was described as necessary to prevent the powerful adversaries to the Inkas' south from threatening their existence. Kirk Frye and Edmundo de la Vega (2005), researching the Lupaqa, and Elizabeth Arkush (2006, 2008, 2011) researching the Qolla heartland, find little archaeological evidence of centralization or hierarchy. More typical were small habitation sites located near fortified ones, indicating an increased concern over security. Arkush (2008) suggests it was the drought and concomitant collapse of Tiwanaku that led to the shift to hilltop living for the Qolla and that warfare developed only some centuries after the settlement shift. The warfare is explained more as a result of environmental conditions leading to resource competition early on that became a cultural pattern continued by emerging warlords. That being said, like the Chanka case discussed earlier, the amount of political unification and centralization for the Altiplano region may have been exaggerated by the Inkas to glorify the exploits of their kings.

Farther south in the Altiplano and in northern Chile, similar local ethnicities and political polities developed through the Late Intermediate Period. Some of these are discussed in chapter 10, which deals with the development of the Inka Empire.

SUMMARY

The Late Intermediate Period represents a time of cultural heterogeneity and increasing conflict. From Cajamarca in the north to the Altiplano, we see the development of regional cultures defined by changes in ceramics, burial practices, and settlement patterns. In some regions, such as the north coast, cultures continued to develop greater levels of complexity, which reached an apex with the Chimú, clearly the largest and most hierarchical polity in South America at the time. In other regions, societies actually became less complex, such as the heartlands of Wari and Tiwanaku. With the decline of both Wari and Tiwanaku, local polities emerged both in their heartlands and elsewhere when local leaders found means to increase their own power base and that of their social groups. With the ethnohistorical records that begin to be available for this time period, sometimes these cultures can be linked to distinct etnías.

Although certainly not universal, it is evident from many regions that conflict and warfare, both interregional and intravalley, became a common feature of life. The causes of these conflicts appear to have been competition among groups for power or perhaps territory, although the former seems more likely in most cases. Settlements often shifted to defensible locations, although not everywhere. The stage was set for the emergence of the Inkas.

10

EXPANSION AND EMPIRE
The Inkas and the Late Horizon

Our literate knowledge of the Inka Empire begins in the 1530s, when the Spanish *conquistadores,* led by Francisco Pizarro, invaded it. There are some eye-witness accounts of the conquest that provide invaluable information about the empire and its main features by the individuals who were intent on dismantling it (for excellent descriptions and assessments of such sources, see D'Altroy 2003, chap. 1; Rowe 1946).[1] Later, other Spanish writers (e.g., Betanzos 1996; Cobo [1653] 1979, 1990]; Sarmiento de Gamboa [1572] 1960) provided descriptions of the empire or aspects of it. In the sixteenth and seventeenth centuries, native writers began to provide their own information on the empire, drawn both from their ancestors and from other sources, such as the *khipu kamayuqs* (khipu record-keepers; *khipus* were knotted-string accounting devices). Two of the native writers who are most notable are Garcilaso de la Vega and Felipe Guaman Poma de Ayala. Both of them were men of mixed ancestry, although Garcilaso de la Vega left Peru when he was only fifteen and Guaman Poma de Ayala was involved in Spanish administration for much of his life before writing his magnum opus. Much of Garcilaso de la Vega's *Royal Commentaries of the Incas* ([1609] 1966) has been discredited, particularly his historical sections, although his descriptions of Inka customs continue to be useful. Guaman Poma de Ayala's ([1584–1615] 1980)

protest letter to the king of Spain is also suspect historically, but it provides over four hundred illustrations of the Inka way of life that are invaluable (figure 10.2). Finally, two more general kinds of information about the Inkas and even the epoch preceding them come from official census visits, called *visitas*, by Spanish Crown authorities, and from colonial litigation by natives who attempted to gain back land or other resources through the Spanish court system. The former provide useful summaries of the populations, land uses, and natural resources of various areas while the latter gives insights into specific land disputes and native systems of labor.

> The meteoric rise of Inka power was filled with charismatic leadership, arduous campaigns, spirited opposition, divine aid, heroism, treachery, and wise rule—in short, all the elements of history's grand sweep as told by the victors. (D'Altroy 2003, 62)

This quotation emphasizes one of the main issues in understanding how the Inkas created their empire: we have mainly the word of the Inkas about how they did it. The perspective of the vanquished is seldom heard, and when it is, the narrative was recorded often decades after the events that were discussed. But even the Inka informants themselves

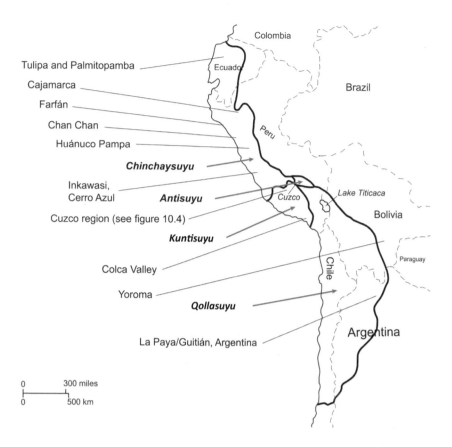

Figure 10.1. Locations of sites and regions mentioned in chapter 10. Map by Matt Gorney.

were problematic because their empire had been riven by a five-year-long civil war that pitted different factions against each other. Most sources we have for the Inkas were written by the victorious faction, who had largely exterminated their rivals—men, women, and children—prior to the arrival of the Spaniards.

There are many reasons to be cautious of the written documents about the Inkas in addition to the ones just noted (Julien 2000). The Spaniards, whether Crown officials, travelers, or conquistadores, were coming from a very different culture than the one they were describing, and so they attempted to explain the Inka customs in language their readers could comprehend. Nowhere is this more significant than in the details of Inka royal succession and religion. In addition, early authors were free to copy

each other's works, so an error early on could be repeated in later documents. It is also true that the Inka informants had their own agendas and so had reasons to misinform their interviewers. Still, as most Inka scholars note, the Inkas had something to say about their empire (C. Julien 1993), and we should listen to them, keeping in mind the cautions noted.

Archaeology provides another means of understanding how the Inka Empire worked, and it is complementary to ethnohistory (Malpass 1993; see also chapter 1). Until the 1990s, the bulk of what we knew about the Inkas was from the documentary sources. Now, however, the quantity of archaeological research focused on the Inkas has increased enormously, with the result that we have a much broader understanding of their empire, both how it devel-

Figure 10.2. Illustration from letter by Guaman Poma de Ayala to the King of Spain. From Guaman Poma de Ayala (1584–1615) 1980.

oped and how it incorporated conquered people (Bauer 1992, 2004; Bauer and Covey 2002; Covey 2006; D'Altroy 1992; Malpass 1993; Malpass and Alconini 2010). The research around Cuzco by Bauer, Alan Covey and others (e.g., McEwan, Chatfield, and Gibaja 2002) in particular has greatly clarified the nature of early Inka state formation in the Cuzco region.

In this book, I take a middle ground between emphasizing historical records and archaeological data in trying to understand who the Inka were, how they rose to fame, and how they managed to form such an immense empire in a relatively brief period of time. I consult the chronicles to see what the Inka said about these matters, and I discuss the archaeology to verify, question, and elaborate on the chronicles.

INKA ORIGINS: MYTH AND REALITY

The Inkas, like every people, had myths concerning where they came from and how the world came to be. Like other preliterate societies, there were different versions of the origin myth, or at least different chroniclers recorded myths that varied in content. In general, however, the Inkas attributed the origins of the world to their creator god Wiraqocha, who formed the world, the sun, moon, and stars, starting at Lake Titicaca (Betanzos 1996). The Inkas were formed in the vicinity of Cuzco before Wiraqocha moved on, finally leaving the coast and sailing west across the Pacific Ocean.

Most versions of the origin myth of the Inkas state that there were four brothers and four sisters that came out of a cave called Tambo T'oqo (often spelled as Tambotoco) at the site of Pacariqtambo, south of Cuzco.[2] Non-Inkas came out of other caves nearby. The eight Inkas paired off as couples, with one couple, Manqo Qhapaq and Mama Oqllu, being the principal pair. The eight began a search for fertile land where they would settle. According to Sarmiento de Gamboa ([1572] 1960), at this early time the ayllus of one of the non-Inka groups, the Tambo, were divided into two moieties, Hanan (Upper) and Hurin (Lower), by Manqo Qhapaq and Mama Oqllu. The entourage then moved northward, until they reached the Cuzco Valley, although two brothers were lost along the way; one was sealed back up in the cave of origin for his aggressive ways and the other turned to stone. The third brother tossed a golden rod into the air that sank deep into the ground. This was the sign that meant the Inkas had found their home, but they had to displace the local inhabitants before they could settle. After terrible fighting, the indigenous occupants were displaced and Cuzco was founded and was divided into four quarters. The first Temple of the Sun was built as well.

As D'Altroy (2003, 51–52) notes, this myth weaves many aspects of Inka thought and belief together, and justifies the social order as the last Inka kings saw it. The myth identifies a separate creation for the royal lineage and a divine origin for it. It also defines several sacred places in the landscape that pertain to the story and so gives credence to Inka ownership of them. It sets out the moiety division of the social organization and the reason for the subservience of other non-Inka to the royal line. The myth also identifies the quadripartite division of the capital and the Sun Temple as original aspects of the Inkas. Finally, the myth legitimizes the marriage of royal brothers and sisters. The practice was adopted late in the history of the empire to maintain the purity of the bloodlines of the ruling families.

According to the Inka oral traditions, eleven or twelve kings followed Manqo Qhapaq's rule (see box 10.1). Different chroniclers give different accomplishments to these kings, especially the kings prior to Wiraqocha Inka. It is not certain who did what, due to both the contradictions among the different accounts and the Inkas' lack of a precise means of counting time. Once a person reached adulthood, her or his age was not important. As a result of this, we do not know exactly how long it took for the Inka Empire to expand. The chronology that is cited most often is that of Rowe (1946), who uses a careful accounting of the accomplishments of the last three kings of the unified empire (Pachakuti, Thupa Inka Yupanki, and Wayna Qhapaq) plus the timing of the civil war prior to the Spanish arrival to define dates for the latest rulers. Although this chronology suggests that the empire developed in less than a century, radiocarbon dates from the southern part of the empire suggest that the expansion out of Cuzco occurred earlier than 1438 C.E. (D'Altroy, Williams, and Lorandi 2007). Still, the radiocarbon dates do not put the southern expansion at much more than perhaps a century earlier.

BOX 10.1 Chronology of Inka kings

The following is a list of Inka kings who followed Manqo Qhapaq:*

1. Manqo Qhapaq
2. Zinchi Roq'a
3. Lloq'e Yupanki
4. Mayta Qhapaq
5. Qhapaq Yupanki
6. Inka Roq'a
7. Yawar Waqaq
8. Wiraqocha Inka
9. Pachakuti Inka Yupanki (1438 C.E.)
10. Thupa Inka Yupanki (1471 C.E.)
11. Wayna Qhapaq (1493 C.E.)
12. Atawallpa (1531–1532 C.E.)

★ From D'Altroy 2003, with possible dates of rule for the last four kings taken from Rowe 1946.

As noted in chapter 9, the Inkas were one of many local ethnic groups during the Late Intermediate Period. They can be identified archaeologically by the appearance of a ceramic style called Killke (figure 10.3; Dwyer 1971; Rowe 1944), which can be linked to the later imperial Inka ceramics. This style began to appear in the vicinity of Cuzco after 1000 C.E., not surprisingly as Wari influenced waned, and it spread across the region as the influence of the Inka ethnic group spread.

Of critical importance to the Inka imperial expansion was the political, economic, and religious consolidation of the area around Cuzco. Without a strong foundation, the Inka could never have developed the state apparatus to rule the empire they conquered. As a result of research over recent decades (Bauer 1992, 1996, 2004; Bauer and Covey 2002; Bauer, Kellett, and Aráoz Silva 2010; Covey 2006; McEwan 2006; McEwan, Chatfield, and Gibaja

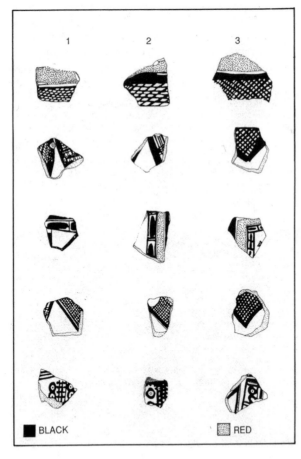

Figure 10.3. *Killke* pottery from Cuzco and Paruro: column 1, *Killke* Pottery from the Cuzco Valley (after Rowe 1944: 16, figure 1; 19, figures 11, 12, 16, and 21); columns 2 and 3, *Killke* Pottery from the Province of Paruro. From Bauer 1992, figure 6. Courtesy of University of Texas Press, copyright 1992.

2002), we now have extensive archaeological data from the region around Cuzco on which to base ideas about how and why this consolidation happened. Over 1,200 km² of land encompassing an 80-km-long north-south transect was surveyed by Bauer and Covey (2002). These lands included the region around Cuzco and areas occupied by several other ethnic groups. In addition, work by McEwan, Melissa Chatfield, and Arminda Gibaja (2002) at the site of Choquepukio southeast of Cuzco has provided additional information about Inka state origins (figure 10.4).

For the vicinity of Cuzco, there was a significant increase in the population during the Late Intermediate Period that corresponds to both local growth and immigration, either voluntary or forced. The south side of the Huatanay River had been occupied during the Middle Horizon, and now several large villages were founded on the north side and provisioned by the construction of several large terrace systems (Bauer and Covey 2002). These were probably controlled by elite lineages in Cuzco that used the surpluses to both support workers there and promote their self-interests. Cuzco itself grew to be a major town or even small city, the seat of the emerging polity.

Using both the chronicles of the early interactions with ethnic groups around the Inkas and the archaeological surveys, we can determine that the Inkas employed a diverse set of strategies to integrate the region around their capital, including marriage alliances, coercion, treaties, and outright militarism (Bauer and Covey 2002; Covey 2011). This suggests there was no overall strategy to expand their territory but, rather, ad hoc activities that resulted in this consolidation. Given the fact that the Inka were competing with several nearby powerful groups, such as the Ayarmaca to the north and the Pinahua and Mohina to the southeast, political activities could be seen as reflecting a strategy of self-preservation as much as anything.

The Paruro region to the south of Cuzco was sparsely settled by groups that lived near areas of agricultural land, and this pattern continued after

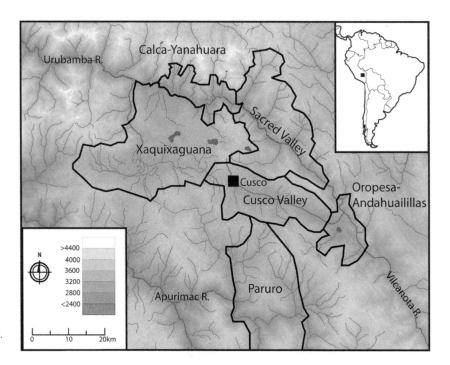

Figure 10.4. Map of region studied around Cuzco by various researchers. Map courtesy of R. Alan Covey.

the appearance of groups using Killke ceramics. It is apparent that this region was incorporated relatively easily and with no evidence of major conflict. As a sidebar, this is the region where Pacariqtambo is located, and there is no good evidence that this region was in any way special prior to the Inkas' incorporation of it. Bauer (1992), however, has found evidence that the site of Maukallacta, which displays several significant features including high-quality architecture, might well have been built there to preserve the myth of Manqo Qhapaq. Maukallacta means "old town" in Quechua, and it was probably the original Pacariqtambo. The present town of that name was created as part of Viceroy Francisco de Toledo's *reducción* policy in the 1570s. Bauer also interprets the adjacent site of Puma Orco as the possible location where the Inkas believed their ancestors had emerged from Tambo T'oqo. By creating an actual location that corresponded to their origin myth, the Inka kings gave credence to the myth and their divine right to rule as the sons of deities.

The Limatambo group located west of the Inka heartland was incorporated in a fashion similar to that of the Paruro region (Heffernan 1989, cited in Bauer and Covey 2002), as were the groups of the Vilcanota/Urubamba region to the east (Covey 2006). To the north and northwest of Cuzco, the chronicles suggest that the Ayarmaca were absorbed through intermarriage between the Inka and local elites in the two regions. Other groups such as the Quilliscachis, Huayllacan, and Cuyo were more difficult, resisting the Inkas and so requiring military conquest to subjugate them. The Cuyo were particularly independent, and when they were finally subdued, many of the inhabitants were resettled in the coca-growing lands to the east or on Pachakuti's royal estate at Pisaq (Bauer and Covey 2002).

Finally, we have research that indicates that the region to the southeast of Cuzco followed a very different trajectory to its incorporation. During the early part of the Late Intermediate Period, a sparsely settled buffer zone between the Inkas and the Pinahuas developed that reflected the hostilities between the two groups. The earlier settlement pattern showed a series of villages along the valley bottom, but all of these were abandoned at the start of the Late Intermediate Period. Only the site of Tipón, a large, heavily fortified settlement and group of agricultural terraces, was occupied at this time. To the southeast, the Pinahua probably had their capital at Choquepukio, a site that came to prominence after the collapse of the Wari center at Pikillacta, located across the Huatanay River from the site.

Excavations at Choquepukio have revealed a new dimension to the idea of Inka origins, according to McEwan, Chatfield, and Gibaja (2002). One of the major architectural features at the site is the niched hall (a large building with niches in the walls). Similar niched halls were used at Pikillacta for ancestor worship, as indicated by the presence of human bones and feasting vessels. These halls all dated to the Late Intermediate Period. Their size and function could be related to the later Inka *kallankas,* long single-room structures that also had niches (figure 10.5). While kallankas were not used for ances-

tor worship, the form might have been adopted from the Choquepukio niched hall.

In addition to the architecture, the excavations at Choquepukio revealed a different kind of ceramic style called Lucre (figure 10.6). These ceramics are found in this region and farther to the southeast and appear to be similar to ceramics of the Mollo culture of Bolivia (McEwan 2006). Chatfield (1998; cited in McEwan, Chatfield, and Gibaja 2002) notes the style is more similar to imperial Inka ceramics in technological attributes than the Killke style is, although the imperial Inka pottery shares more motifs with the Killke. The keros and bowls are of forms and colors that reflect Wari influence, thus connecting the makers of the Lucre ceramics with the earlier Wari occupants. In contrast, the local Middle Horizon ceramic style of Cuzco, called Qotakalli, shares few features with the Wari ceramics but is more closely linked to Killke.

This evidence, taken together, suggests that the origins of the Inka material culture came from two sources: the local inhabitants of the Cuzco area, who

Figure 10.5. Great Hall (kallanka) at Huánuco Pampa. Photo by Mahlon Barash, 1965. Reprinted by permission.

Figure 10.6. Lucre ceramics. Photo courtesy of Gordon McEwan.

were using Qotakalli ceramics, and the people around Choquepukio, who made Lucre pottery. When the Inka finally incorporated the Pinahua and Pukina of this region, they merged the Killke motifs with the technological attributes of the Lucre style to create the imperial form.

McEwan (2006) takes this evidence further with the intriguing suggestion that a group of Titicaca basin people may have moved to Choquepukio, bringing their ancestral mummies and ceramic styles with them and placing them in the niched halls. This idea finds tenuous support in the chronicle of Fernando de Montesinos (1882), who wrote a controversial history of the Inkas that mentions a migration to Cuzco from Tiwanaku. Garcilaso de la Vega, who was the son of an Inka princess, also stated that Manqo came from the shores of Lake Titicaca in his rather romanticized 1609 history of the empire. In addition, the Inka Creator, Wiragocha, was said to have originated at Lake Titicaca. All these sources, as questionable as they might be, could be seen as supporting the idea that the original Inka couple Manqo and Mama Ocllo, and thus by extension all the Inkas, came from Titicaca, not Pacariqtambo. Although this is an intriguing hypothesis, much more evidence is required before it gains greater acceptance.

It is certainly evident that through a variety of strategies the Inka built up a secure region of loyal allies in the regions around them. Bauer (1992) notes that the evidence from Paruro, which has been supported by his and Covey's later studies in other regions, indicates the Inkas had already become an integrated heartland by the Killke Period. Covey (2011) notes that the Late Intermediate Period groups most easily integrated were those who existed in upland communities, whereas the Inkas and other more intransigent groups occupied the fertile valley bottoms. The allowed larger communities to develop that were more accustomed to communal work and thus could expand at the expense of their more isolated, less organized neighbors. As this incorporation advanced, the better lands not already occupied were claimed by Inka royalty as estates.

As the political integration of the area around Cuzco developed, social distinctions between the Inkas and non-Inkas emerged that became important for the later development of the Inka state. As the chroniclers note, there was a hierarchy in the social organization of the heartland that is generally agreed on, at least by Garcilaso de la Vega, Guaman Poma de Ayala, and Pachacuti Yamqui Salcamayhua, the three who were probably best able to speak to this issue (Bauer 1992). At the top was the Sapa Inka, the Inka king, and the royal *panaqas,* groups made up of the descendants of the earlier kings. Like the Chimú, the Inkas practiced split inheritance, a system in which the chosen heir of the Sapa Inka followed his father but the rest of the wealth and land accumulated by the dead king went to his other relatives: the queen and his other sons and daughters. These panaqas used the wealth and land to support the cult of the dead king. There was the typical Andean use of moieties as well: the panaqas of the first five kings belonged to Hurinsaya, and the later kings belonged to Hanansaya.[3]

Below the king and royal panaqas were ten other ayllus, divided into the two moieties, Hanansaya and Hurinsaya. The origins of these ayllus differ with the chronicler referenced. Guaman Poma de Ayala's ([1584–1615] 1980) notes they came with Manqo to Cuzco from Pacariqtambo and lived in Cuzco. Garcilaso de la Vega ([1609] 1966) states they were the original inhabitants of the town of Cuzco when Manqo arrived.

The final social group in the Inka social hierarchy was the *Inka de Privilegio* (Inka-by-Privilege). These were groups that lived in the vicinity of Cuzco but that were clearly lower in status than the Inkas, although higher than conquered groups. Guaman Poma de Ayala again notes that they originated in Pacariqtambo with Manqo but lived in regions farther outside the city than the noble groups already described. Garcilaso de la Vega states these were the indigenous inhabitants of the region around Cuzco who were not Inka but who were given the privilege of calling themselves by that prestigious term by Manqo after he arrived in the valley.

Therefore, what is agreed on by these two chroniclers, and by Pachacuti Yamqui Salcamayhua ([1613] 1950), another respected indigenous chronicler, is that status was reflected both in genealogical closeness to the Sapa Inka and proximity of the group to Cuzco. The kings and their lineal relatives were the highest nobility, followed by a group of nonroyal nobility. At the bottom were the local ethnic groups who existed in the regions around Cuzco.

Given the archaeological evidence discussed here, it is apparent that local groups existed in the Cuzco region long before the Inkas emerged as an identifiable group in the eleventh century C.E. As such, the Inka de Privilegio were probably the groups incorporated early into the state sphere of influence. The distinction between the panaqas and the nobles of Hanansaya and Hurinsaya was one of ancient ancestry: the original leaders of the Late Intermediate Period Killke group that lived around Cuzco became the panaqas, and the nonrelated ayllus that lived there as well became the nobility. By virtue of their being part of the original ethnic Inka group, they were higher in status than the groups incorporated into the Inka political organization later. The Inka de Privilegio were critical to the crystallization of the Inka state as early taxpayers, food producers, and soldiers, but they also played important roles in the administration of the empire as it expanded.

Before moving on, we should note the roles the *Qoya,* or principal wife of the Sapa Inka, played in the affairs of state. First, starting with Thupa Inka, the Qoya had to be a full sister of the king to keep the bloodline pure. This also had the effect of reducing competition for this position among rival kin groups. D'Altroy (2003) makes the point that the queen had considerable influence, as did the mother of the king. Because of split inheritance, the wife played the role of liaison with the rest of the king's family and often benefited from this position. The king's mother was influential in assisting in the selection of her son's marriage partners, and so also played a significant role in politics. The fact that the wives and mothers of kings were singled out for execution by rivals points to the importance of their positions.

THE EMPIRE EXPANDS

One of the most famous mythohistorical aspects of the rise of the Inkas is their glorious defeat of the rival Chankas in a great battle around Cuzco (introduced in chapter 9). In the most often repeated version of this battle, the Sapa Inka, Wiraqocha Inka, the eighth king, fled the city along with his heir, Inka Urqon, in the face of an advancing Chanka army. Another son, Inka Yupanki, remained and mounted a defense of the city along with other nobles. The Creator god Wiraqocha appeared to Inka Yupanki before the conflict, assuring him of victory. The battle was won with the help of stones that were transformed into warriors. These stones were collected and housed as sacred relicts called *pururaucas*. With this victory, Inka Yupanki was given the additional honorific of Pachakuti. At this point in the narrative, he either asked for his father's blessing or took the throne outright. He then set out to rebuild Cuzco before commencing the wars of expansion.

D'Altroy (2003), whose description of the expansion of the empire I follow here, notes that different chroniclers stated that the Chankas were subjugated during the reigns of either the fifth, sixth, eighth, and ninth rulers, or are not even mentioned. In light of Bauer, Kellett, and Aráoz Silva's (2010) archaeological research in the homeland of the Chankas (see chapter 9) and the other information provided by archaeological research in the vicinity of Cuzco, it seems most likely that Pierre Duviols's (1980) skeptical suggestion that the Chanka war was largely a fabrication to glorify and justify the power of the Inkas is closest to the truth.

Most of the chroniclers attribute the expansion of the Inka Empire to the last three undisputed rulers:[4] Pachakuti, his son Thupa Inka, and his grandson, Wayna Qhapaq. What the chroniclers do not agree on is who conquered which regions. In this book, I follow Marti Pärssinen's (1992) reconstruction of the empire and its expansion. The main difference between this reconstruction and others (e.g., Rowe 1946) is the uncertainty surrounding the conquests attributed to Pachakuti and his son. The Inka kings often sent their heirs on military excursions while they were young, entrusting them to capable generals who could teach them the fine points of warfare before they assumed their position as Sapa Inka. This is what probably happened with Thupa Inka, who was sent by Pachakuti with his generals early on. Therefore, it is hard to discern whether it was Pachakuti or his son who expanded the empire northward. Hence, the conquests of the two are simply com-

bined. An important observation about the empire is that it was actually those two who created it; Wayna Qhapaq only extended its borders slightly in Ecuador and Bolivia.

It is uncertain what brought about the first expansions out of the Cuzco region after it had been integrated into an early state. D'Altroy (2003) indicates that several factors were probably important, including the significant drought of the late thirteenth and early fourteenth centuries, the importance of effective leadership in the succession of a king to power, personal ambition, and the desire for wealth and other resources. Ideology was also a factor because the Inkas believed they were meant to civilize the world around them. Conrad and Demarest (1984) suggest that split inheritance was a cause of the expansion because new kings had to find new land for their uses because all the land near Cuzco had been claimed by the panaqas. This, however, has been questioned by D'Altroy (2003, 85); he notes that even Washkar was still developing estates near Cuzco.

Although the causes of Inka expansionism were multiple, we do know that the first advances were to the south. In fact, the first excursion may have been by Wiraqocha Inka (Rowe 1946, 203–204). The groups of the Altiplano region, particularly the Lupaqa and Qolla, are described by the Spanish sources as having been a clear threat to Inka power.[5] According to Cieza de León ([1551] 1967), the Lupaqa had defeated the Qolla before the Inkas arrived and agreed to an alliance with the Inkas. Pachakuti is said to have conquered the Lupaqa with the aid of Chanka warriors after the Lupaqa rebelled against him. Having secured the southern flank of the empire, he then turned his interests to the north.

Several campaigns were launched against groups in the central highlands, with early ones extending the empire to around Cajamarca. This was done with the help of the Chanka, who apparently did not get along with the other members of the army and fled north. The Inka generals in charge pursued them and actually conquered lands farther north than Pachakuti had declared. It is possible that at this time the Inkas came into conflict with the Chimú, who may have had alliances with the Cajamarca lords. Whether they actually defeated them at this time is unclear; other chroniclers state their defeat was at the hands of Thupa Inka in a later campaign.

When the victorious Inka army returned to Cuzco, Pachakuti had the generals in charge executed for insubordination, although D'Altroy (2003) suggests that the real reason was that he feared their increasing influence. It is at this time that Pachakuti turned the reins of the army over to his sons. More campaigns were launched northward, and in some of these, Thupa Inka, Pachakuti's son, was sent to learn the art of war under his older brother, Yamque Yupanki, a skilled general. Thupa Inka was largely given charge of the armies, perhaps as a result of being chosen as the heir by his father and began the conquest of Ecuador, a process that continued for decades, into the reign of his son Wayna Qhapaq. Thupa Inka may also have been the one who finally crushed the Chimú because it was under his command that Minchançaman, the Chimú ruler, was brought in chains to Cuzco. The Ecuadorian campaigns were bloody and costly because the local groups fought savagely to maintain their sovereignty.

Upon the conquest of much of Ecuador, Thupa Inka returned to Cuzco to visit his ailing father. It might be at this point that he conducted campaigns against the central and southern coastal regions, although there is confusion among the chronicles as to the timing of that event. When it did occur, it was a difficult campaign, taking several years, especially to subjugate the Cañete Valley. The site of Inkawasi was constructed specifically for this campaign, and after their defeat, the inhabitants of the valley were relocated to other regions. At this time, the Late Intermediate Period site of Cerro Azul became the administrative complex for the valley (D'Altroy 2003).

Turning his focus in the opposite direction, Thupa Inka led two campaigns into the jungle to the east of Cuzco. Neither of these was particularly successful, but in the second one, according to a common story reported in several chronicles, an Altiplano warrior reported to his homeland that the king had been killed. This set off a rebellion among the Qolla and Lupaqa that took the Inkas several years to quell. When they did, they exacted a terrible revenge by flaying the rebellious leaders and impaling their heads on stakes as warnings to others.

Having returned the Altiplano to the empire, Thupa Inka continued his march of conquest southward through Bolivia and northwest Argentina. He set up a series of fortifications along this border with the lowlands to maintain security for the conquered regions from attacks by tribes in the regions beyond. He then crossed over into modern-day Chile, defining the southernmost point of the empire at the site of Cerro del Inga, located 95 km south of modern-day Santiago (Rossen, Planella, and Rubén Stehberg 2010). His reasons for stopping there vary, from the resistance of the local Mapuche and Araucanian groups to Thupa Inka's feeling that he had been away from Cuzco too long, to the need to put down rebellions in the northern provinces. It is likely that a combination of these factors was responsible.

Thupa Inka turned back north and split his armies into factions that marched north on both sides of the Andean chain. The nature of the Inka conquests in Chile is particularly difficult to interpret because of the lack of Spanish documents that pertain to this region. Local groups here were successful at challenging the Spaniards for over a century, so the memory of their brief period of subjugation by the Inkas had already faded. It is also difficult to determine whether the far southern region of modern Peru was conquered at this time or another time. It is likely that it was conquered as the armies returned to Cuzco, although the archaeological remains in most regions are very limited and ethnohistorical sources are scarce.

The exact date of Pachakuti's death is uncertain, with some Spanish sources stating it occurred prior to Thupa Inka's southern campaign and others stating it occurred while he was in the south. Regardless, it is apparent that Thupa Inka conducted no more major campaigns after his return to Cuzco. Rowe (1946) gives the date of Thupa Inka's death as

1493 C.E., when his son Wayna Qhapaq became Sapa Inka. According to tradition, the first thing that Wayna Qhapaq did was make a royal inspection of the empire, both to make his presence known and to reinforce Inka rule symbolically. He first attempted a conquest, or perhaps reconquest, of the Chachapoyas of the northern Peruvian montaña, which finally succeeded after much effort. He also visited Bolivia and northwest Argentina, setting up a massive system of farms for growing maize near Cochabama (Wachtel 1982) using conquered people from the northern provinces as workers, and he reinforced the forts along the southeastern border. He then set out to expand the empire farther into Ecuador.

Most of Wayna Qhapaq's life and military career were spent in these campaigns, which were difficult and costly in human lives. The northern boundary of the empire was established approximately at the modern border between Colombia and Ecuador. Efforts to expand eastward and westward were largely unsuccessful, and the Inkas appear to have relied more on trade with groups at these margins than on actual conquests (Lippi and Gudiño 2010; Salomon 1986). A footnote to the history at this point is that, when the Chiriguano of the eastern Bolivian lowlands had invaded the empire, they were accompanied by a Portuguese explorer, Alejo García. This brief encounter marks the first visit by a European to the empire, although the date is unknown.

Sometime in the mid-1520s, European-introduced epidemics arrived in Ecuador, having traveled down from Mexico or perhaps the Caribbean. Wayna Qhapaq became one of the many victims, dying in 1528. Unfortunately for the empire, his heir also died, leaving no chosen son to be the next Sapa Inka. I discuss what happened next at the end of this chapter.

THE POLITICS OF EMPIRE

It is one thing to subjugate a large number of ethnic groups. In the Andean world, where hand-to-hand combat was the main battle strategy, all one needed was a larger number of warriors and effective leaders. The Inkas had both, assuring they would win most battles and therefore be able to expand their political control. If we follow the Spanish documents concerning the means by which the Inka expanded, those just outlined, then we would believe it was through military power that the Inkas triumphed. However, it is quite another feat to make a cohesive and integrated empire out of the vanquished groups, particularly ones that were brought into the empire through warfare and bloodshed. The integration of an empire involves developing the means to both maintain control over the defeated and extract the resources or manpower that is desired without decimating them or making life so difficult as to lead to continuous revolts. The Inkas used institutions and policies that were both new and old, the policies probably vestiges of earlier systems employed by Wari and perhaps Tiwanaku. Road systems and khipus (knotted-string accounting devices) are two examples of such earlier practices that were adopted. The Inkas were in the process of consolidating their empire when the Spaniards arrived, and there is ample evidence that many groups, particularly in the central Andes, had adjusted to imperial control.

One of the Inkas' keys to success was their use of traditional systems of reciprocity but on a larger scale (Murra 1980). In Andean communities, reciprocal work, either between households or between the members of a community and its leaders, is a fundamental mechanism for completing projects for civic activities such as canal cleaning. Whoever organizes the activity supports the people who come to work with food, drink, and coca leaves. The Inkas expanded this to a state scale by requiring people to provide only labor and nothing from their own quantities of goods; the Inkas provided all the raw materials, food, and drink needed for the jobs to be done. In addition, local leaders were incorporated into the lower levels of the administration, so they were the ones in charge of organizing the labor. Thus, the system instituted by the Inkas was familiar to conquered people and conducted by local leaders.

The products of that labor, however, went to different places than the local community.

Morris (1998) has suggested that three factors were important in the development of the empire: an ideology of rule, the use of significant economic rewards, and the use of coercive military force. In contrast to most scholars, he argues that military force was actually less important than the first two factors and probably significant only late in the history of the empire. This somewhat surprising notion comes from there being remarkably little evidence of weapons at Inka sites, even at the administrative centers where we might expect such equipment to be stockpiled.

Since the 1990s, archaeological evidence of Inka expansionism has supported the idea that the "hallmark of Inka rule was the flexibility and variability with which Inka rulers governed their provinces" (Morris 1998, 295). Given the wide variety of societies that the Inkas faced, from state-level cultures such as the Chimú to simple fishing societies such as the Uru of Lake Titicaca, this flexibility was necessary. What determined the particular conditions of rule were the kinds of resources they wanted to control, the level of political authority already present in a region, and the amount of resistance that they faced.

Following Morris (1998), the main interest that the Inkas had in their conquered territories, and thus people, was economic. Thus, the Inka king claimed ownership of all lands, although he allowed his subjects the usufruct right to grow crops for themselves and to herd llamas and alpacas on his pastures. Bernabé Cobo ([1653] 1979) has an excellent account of the Inka policy regarding the lands of the conquered. He notes that both the agricultural land and animal herds were divided into three parts: one for the Sapa Inka, one for the state religion, and one for the use by local people. There is no information about the percentage of each part, but other statements suggest that sometimes the Sapa Inka received the greatest percentage and at other times the state religion did. Because many of the conquered groups grew few surpluses, this policy sounds like a recipe for mass

starvation. However, it is obvious that this tripartition was carried out over the course of several years and almost certainly involved not just the division of existing lands and pasture but the development of new ones. There was always sufficient land for the local people to be supported, probably the original field systems that existed at the time of their conquest by the Inkas. For example, research was conducted in the 1980s that studied the agricultural systems in the Colca Valley of southern Peru and found that the Inkas created new terrace systems with irrigation canals to supplement the existing rain-fed ones used prior to their arrival (see edited volume William Denevan, Kent Mathewson, and Gregory Knapp [1987]). In many regions of the Andes, this situation is repeated, indicating that the Inkas used the labor of their conquered subjects to expand food production so that it could be used for state and religious purposes.

Cobo is clear in indicating that the fields of the Inkas were worked prior to those of the local people, assuring the production of the food needed by the empire. These needs included feeding the armies as they expanded the empire, feeding those building the roads and administrative centers to keep the empire functioning, and feeding the local laborers who came to do other work for the empire. In addition, the enormous quantity of food produced was used as a buffer against environmental disasters, so that if a group lost its harvest to a late frost or summer hailstorm, the people would be provided for from the Inka storehouses. This sounds laudable; however, the chronicles also note that the people had to pay back the food that had been borrowed when production returned to normal.

In addition to the production of food, conquered people had to provide labor to the empire, which was called mit'a. This was a labor service that each household had to provide, each according to the skills of the inhabitants and the interests of the Inkas. The work was done in rotation, so different members of the community were gone at different times. All males between the ages of eighteen and fifty were subject to serving in the military if necessary

(D'Altroy 2003). Married men often brought their wives with them, and their children too. Other members of their villages were required to work their fields during their absence. Many of these did not return. Other individuals transported food to the Inka storehouses from the local fields or made crafts at regional administrative centers. The fleet of foot were put into service as *chaskis,* messengers who were stationed along the Inka highway to send messages back and forth.

The Inkas also required each family to provide a piece of clothing, but the state provided the wool or cotton to make it. The clothing they produced, which must have been in the hundreds of thousands of items, was used by the state for a wide variety of purposes: for the military, as gifts to conquered leaders, as sacrifices to the gods, and as basic clothing for some of the workers of the empire (Murra 1962).

Cloth was a fundamental part of the state finance system. D'Altroy and Earle (1985) define two distinct systems of production, staple finance and wealth finance. Staple finance "involves obligatory payments in kind to the state of subsistence goods such as grains, livestock, and clothing. . . . Staples are collected by the state as a share of commoner produce, as a specified levy, or as produce from land worked with corvée labor. This revenue in staples is then used to pay personnel attached to the state and others working for the state on a part-time basis" (D'Altroy and Earle 1985, 188). Cloth functioned in the staple finance system, as indicated by its uses. Staple finance was used primarily at the local or regional level.

Wealth finance involved producing goods of particular value, such as fine cloth and objects of gold, silver, or *Spondylus,* for the payment of officials and administrators. These goods were either produced directly by subjects for the empire or manufactured at the Inka administrative centers. The primary use of wealth finance was to support the managerial aspects of the empire (D'Altroy and Earle 1985). Such wealth was also used by the Inka elite and was one of the justifications for the Inka expansion.

To maintain both systems, the Inkas developed their famous infrastructure of roads and administra-tive centers (figure 10.7; Hyslop 1984, 1990). The road system was an expansion of existing roads, some of which had been constructed by the Wari state, but the Inkas upgraded them. There were two main trunk highways, one along the spine of the Andes and the other along the coast. Where the roads went through swampy areas, the roadway was built up. On steep terrain the roads might narrow, and they might widen in flatter areas. Suspension bridges were built to span the rivers. Along the coast, where the desert is relatively flat and uniform, the road might be marked only by borders of cobbles or wooden stakes (Hyslop 1984).

More important to the administration of the empire were the major and minor centers that were located along the roads. Major administrative centers were placed several days' walk from each other, with *tampus,* smaller centers with eating and sleeping facilities and storage, located about a day's walk from one another (Hyslop 1984). Hyslop notes that the actual distance between such structures varied widely, both in his archaeological survey of the Inka road system and in the ethnohistorical records.

As the empire expanded, it became necessary to develop a system to keep the king informed of developments at the far reaches of the empire. A system of runners called chaskis was used for this purpose. A message would be given to a chaski at the point of origin, and he would run as fast as possible to the next *chaskiwasi* (runner's house), probably located only a few kilometers (if that) away. As he approached, he would shout the message to the waiting chaski, who would then relay the message to the next runner along the route. We do not know how effective this system was, and we have to wonder how garbled the message might become as it was passed from runner to runner!

The best-known administrative center is Huánuco Pampa, located on the high puna of northern Peru. Located at 3,800 masl, the site has over 4,000 structures, including about 500 storehouses located on the hillside overlooking the site. Over a million bushels of produce could have been stored there if each storehouse were filled to the maximum at the

Figure 10.7. Inka road system. From Hyslop 1984, figure 1. Copyright 1984 by Elsevier.

same time. The storehouses are of two shapes, circular and rectangular, and both types are carefully constructed to maintain good conditions for the storage of agricultural produce (figures 10.8A and 10.8B). Excavations suggest the majority of the storerooms were for potatoes, with a smaller percentage devoted to maize and other goods (Morris 1992).

Huánuco Pampa is a good example of what Hyslop (1990) calls a radial-pattern Inka city. The huge main plaza includes an *usnu* (ceremonial platform). Streets and corridors radiate out from the plaza and

Figure 10.8. (A) Inka storehouse (collca*)* with circular plan at Huánuco Pampa. (B) Inka storehouse (collca*)* with square plan at Huánuco Pampa. Photos by Mahlon Barash, 1965. Reprinted by permission.

divide the city into four sections. Craft workshops, hospitality centers, royal accommodations and an *aqllawasi* (residence and workplaces of the Inka Chosen Women) were all found at the site. Although the estimates of the population of the city are between 12,000 and 15,000, it is difficult to know how much of the center was occupied at any one time. It is likely that much of the population consisted of mitayos, the mit'a workers who came to do various tasks for the empire.

To keep track of the flow of labor as well as the number of people, the Inkas used khipus as record-keeping and accounting devices (plate 8). Using the decimal system, each cord had knots tied into it in groups, each group representing a decimal unit. The cords might record the number of people, llamas, pots, or other objects. There was a special class of individuals, called khipu kamayuqs, whose job it was to maintain these records. Every year, a census was taken of the villages, and labor and land was reapportioned so that each household would receive adequate resources for the year. It has been suggested that khipus might also have served other functions, such as mnemonic devices for story-telling or as calendars.

Political Organization

The Inkas called their empire *Tawantinsuyu,* "the four parts together." The four parts were Chinchaysuyu, the northern part; Antisuyu, the eastern part; Qollasuyu to the south; and Kuntisuyu to the west (figure 10.1). Each was governed by an *apo,* who was usually a close family member of the king. The center of the empire was Cuzco, and the main roads leading out of it defined the boundaries among the four *suyus.* As can be seen in figure 10.1, the four parts were unequal in size and population. Within the suyus there were provinces, each being a grouping of 20,000 or 30,000 households. These round numbers were used to facilitate the administration of the empire. Conquered ayllus were organized into these provinces according to lower decimal units, each with a kuraka (leader) in charge. There were kurakas of 10,000 households, 5,000 households,

1,000 households, 500 households, and 100 households, with foremen of 50 households and 10 households below them. These kurakas were the former political and social leaders of conquered groups. In addition, there was a governor of each province who was a political appointee of the king and probably belonged to a royal lineage, although Inka de Privilegio might also have filled such positions.

One of the key features of Inka rule was the relationship between the Inka social class and the kurakas through whom the former ruled. As mentioned earlier, the Inka modeled their empire on traditional forms of reciprocity, so one of the principal aspects of rule was the display of generosity that befitted a reciprocal relationship. Indeed, Morris (1992, 1998) notes that the Inkas' interactions with their subjects were more akin to traditional forms of social interaction among less-complex societies. This is why the administrative centers such as Huánuco Pampa had such large areas for hospitality, and why the majority of ceramics found in such areas were serving vessels.

The hospitality involved was a complex interaction. For the Inkas, it involved not just feasting and drinking but the giving of gifts, such as textiles, high-status pottery and other objects, and even Chosen Women as wives. This was the traditional generosity offered by someone for services rendered. For the kurakas, these were gifts received but also symbolic evidence of submission to the Inka king. By taking them (which they had little choice to refuse), they accepted their responsibilities for doing the Inkas' bidding, including supplying and organizing the labor that was required.

In this sense, D'Altroy (2003) is correct in saying that calling the Inka administrative apparatus a bureaucracy is misleading. A bureaucracy is a hierarchical group of administrators who work full-time for the ruling group and are often members of the same ethnic group as the rulers. The Inka system was a veneer of ethnic Inkas who controlled the efforts of a vast number of local ethnic lords bound together by the reciprocal obligations just discussed. This system was hierarchical in that there were the different groups of households under the kurakas, but even these could probably belong to different ethnicities. For example, to organize a province of 20,000 households, different ethnic groups might be lumped together, such as in the Huánuco region (Grosboll 1993), and moved around to make up the appropriate decimal units.

Who were these kurakas? That is a question that is only now beginning to be answered by archaeological work. Because it was not simply households, but ayllus that were the focus of tribute and administration, the Inkas would use whatever existing social or political structure was present. We can imagine that ayllu heads would become leaders of one hundred or five hundred households, depending on the size of their ayllu. A political chief might be incorporated as a kuraka of a 1,000 households or perhaps one of 5,000 households. The highest position in the provinces, that of governor (*tokrikoq*), was usually an Inka noble, although others (rarely) were placed in that position (Rowe 1982).

Recent archaeological work is now revealing aspects of how the Inkas selected local people for service. At the site of La Paya/Guitián in the Calchaqúi Valley of northwestern Argentina, Felix Acuto (2010) has found evidence for the emergence of a new stratum of local elites as a result of the Inka conquest. There is little evidence of any hereditary status positions prior to the coming of the Inkas, so the Inkas had to create one. Who those people were is intriguing: Were they the people willing to work with the Inkas and thereby raise their own status, or were they local heads forced into the positions? A house made of Inka-style stonework and separated from the rest of the community suggests an individual receiving preferential treatment. The inclusion of quite a bit of wealth under the house also supports the idea that an important member of the administration lived there who benefited from his or her cooperation with the Inkas. Evidence for only some individuals having Inka prestige goods also supports this interpretation.

At other sites in the region, local resistance to Inka rule was manifest by the acceptance of Inka-style pottery, but only its use in domestic situations. In burials, the local ceramics were exclusively used. This resistance suggests that the individuals selected to be kurakas might indeed have been more cooperative than others.

With the majority of the administrative hierarchy being local ethnic kurakas, we can see the truth of D'Altroy's words: with approximately eighty provinces, the actual number of ethnic Inkas required to help in the administration was quite small. It is likely, however, that other positions were filled by members of the Cuzco nobility. For example, there were inspectors whose job it was to evaluate the activities of the provinces and to make sure that the provincial leaders conducted the affairs of state honestly. These people were the sons of rulers (D'Altroy 2003).

One of the most effective policies the Inkas implemented was to require the sons of high provincial leaders (to what level in the hierarchical order is not certain) to come to Cuzco to attend school. Rowe (1946) notes the training was formal, and the children learned Quechua, administrative skills, khipu use, and other knowledge, so they could return to their homelands upon the passing of their fathers to be good Inka administrators. This is also how the use of Quechua became the lingua franca of the Andes, a convenience for the Spaniards, who found it the most useful language for their purposes as well.

Another policy of conquest and subordination was to take the local *wak'as* (sacred idols) to Cuzco. Local leaders went to worship at these idols during their yearly sojourn in Cuzco. The effect this policy had was to keep the idols as hostages to reduce the chances of rebellion and to reinforce the Inka dominion over them.

As a result of Inka expansion, there were a number of special statuses that were created to do specific activities for the empire. These statuses, *aqllakuna, yanakuna, kamayuq,* and *mitmaqkuna,* were full-time workers for the empire and did no other service, such as mit'a. Probably the most famous of these were the aqllakuna, or Chosen Women. These women were selected from villages throughout the empire and had to be beautiful. They were brought to major centers, where they were taught religion, how to spin and weave, and how to make chicha (figure 10.9) (Rowe 1946). These women served in each administrative center, where they were in charge of the hospitality of the Inkas: making and serving food and drink and, perhaps, entertaining with musical instruments and dancing. The aqllakuna could also be given as wives to officials, especially kurakas, as a reward for exemplary service.

Yanakunas were males who provided personal services to particular high-status individuals or institutions. The word is often glossed as "servants," but Rowe (1982) cautions that they might have served more important roles than just that. Some, in fact, could have been high officials of the administration if they showed particular organizational abilities.

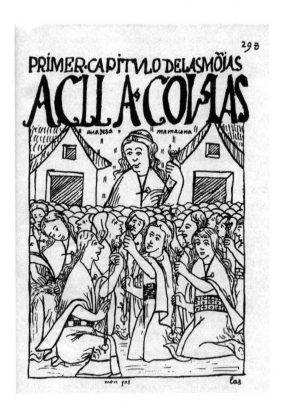

Figure 10.9. Aqllakuna. From Guaman Poma de Ayala (1584–1615) 1980.

Mostly, they served in a variety of capacities, such as in serving the Sapa Inka, cultivating fields, working for a temple, or even guarding royal mummies. The numbers of yanakuna who worked for the Inkas is unknown, but Rowe (1982, 101) notes that 230, or 5.6 percent of the individuals in service to the Inka from the Chupachu group, were of that status.

Kamayuqs were men with specific occupations, the particular occupation serving as the adjective for the term (e.g., khipu kamayuq). These individuals were often craftspeople before their conquest, so they were appointed to work for the king, state, or temples as their service. Like the previous two statuses, they were full-time and exempt from the mit'a. Also like the other two, the position was hereditary, passed down through the generations. Toward the end of the Inka Empire, there is evidence that the Inkas were moving toward a system of specialized communities of such kamayuqs, for example, the specialized pottery-making village near Cajamarca created by Thupa Inka (Espinoza Soriano 1970) or the 1,000 weavers and 100 potters installed at Milliraya near Lake Titicaca (Spurling 1992). The communities were provided with lands and herds to work for their own support in addition to the raw materials from which they fashioned their crafts.

D'Altroy (2003) notes that the Inkas probably allowed the demand for specific crafts to determine how many people would be put to work making them. Whereas some crafts were used for specific imperial tasks (e.g., weaving clothing for the army), others could be used for local consumption. Because these kamayuqs were full-time workers, often living away from their native communities, the effect this system had was to alienate the workers from their home villages and develop in them a greater loyalty to the empire.

Finally, the mitmaqkuna were individuals who were living away from their native lands. Rowe (1982) notes there were two kinds: one kind that served the local administration and one kind that was still under the jurisdiction of their native lords. The latter was largely restricted to the low-altitude food-producing farms of Qollasuyu. Generally, the Inkas moved entire villages and required the inhabitants to continue to wear their own ethnic clothing and speak their own language. The mitmaqkuna were provided food from the Inka storehouses until the land given to them was producing; thereafter, they produced the food they needed. Kamayuqs could also be mitmaqkuna, as should be evident from the previous discussion of Milliraya. The Inkas moved artisans from one region to another to produce the goods needed.

The principal rationale for the *mitmaq* policy was to deter rebellions by resistant groups such as the Chachapoyas and Kañaris. Uprooting people from their native lands and moving them across the empire to be settled among strangers must have had a profoundly pacifying effect. Given the critical ties native people had to their land, holding it sacred, and the importance of ancestors to their well-being, this policy must have been very effective.

Some mitmaqkuna resettlements were truly impressive, such as the system of state farms set up in the Cochabamba Valley, Bolivia, by Wayna Qhapaq (Wachtel 1982). Nathan Wachtel estimates that 14,000 workers came to work these fields from all over the empire. The fields were created to cultivate maize for the use of the army. But, not all the workers were mitmaqkuna; only a percentage was, and they were the people in charge of the granaries. The rest of the laborers were those who served their mit'a rotation, doing the hard labor of planting and harvesting.

In addition to the mitmaq policy, local people were often moved locally to increase crop production. As emphasized in chapter 9, in many regions of the Andes, the Late Intermediate Period was a time of local conflict, with many villages located on hilltops and agriculture limited to hill-slope terraced fields. After the Inka conquest, villages were relocated to lower elevations, where crops such as maize could be cultivated. In the Colca Valley, the system of irrigated terraces and lower-altitude broad fields that are still used by local people were constructed by the Inkas to increase productivity. They also constructed a reservoir and irrigation canal to feed a set of upper terraces that they rebuilt (Malpass 1987). The earlier terraces appear to have been rain-fed; therefore, their productivity was more subject to variations from year to year.

These new labor statuses provided dependable quantities of essential products that assured that the empire would function effectively. The aqllakuna provided both wealth finance and services essential to the generosity required of the state by its subjects. Kamayuqs and mitmaqkuna provided other important services, many in staple finance but also in administration, such as the role the khipu kamayuqs served in keeping records of the goods and services rendered to the state. Yanakunas were employed to assist the nobility and state institutions as they expanded. These new positions were maintained by the enormous productivity of the agricultural systems developed by the Inkas, in part by the new statuses themselves. Thus, the mutually reinforcing aspect of the state system allowed for its growth.

And who benefited from this system? Subject kurakas certainly did, and a large percentage of the goods produced went into the institutionalized reciprocity expected of the empire (D'Altroy and Earle 1985), but it did so only if the kurakas did their jobs in a way that provided the goods and services needed by the empire. The Inka nobility were the chief beneficiaries of the wealth finance system. Much of the wealth in luxury items produced by the state at its administrative centers was sent to Cuzco for the benefit of the elite. As mentioned in chapter 9, the finest craftspeople were also brought to Cuzco to work directly for the Inka nobility.

Unlike state-level societies elsewhere, however, there was no centralized bureaucracy for the distribution of the wealth. It is not clear how the wealth that came to Cuzco was distributed among the panaqas and other elite groups. That they had great wealth is indicated by the quantities of gold and silver that were produced in Cuzco to ransom Atawallpa from the Spaniards. Given that all the conquered lands and resources were claimed by the Sapa Inka, we can imagine that the goods produced became his, and he used them to reward those who worked for him as well as his family. But how non-royal ayllus and distantly related panaqas gained access to goods is less clear. Given the necessity of maintaining good relations among the nobility, it is likely that the king distributed a lot of the wealth as reciprocal gifts and received others in return. In addition, the corps and personal guard of the Sapa Inka were recruited from the sons of the nobility in Cuzco (D'Altroy 2003). Because these warriors were well-rewarded for their services, this could have been a key means by which wealth was spread around the aristocracy. Indeed, to maintain the enthusiasm for warfare and expansion, such a distribution system would have been required.

Another aspect of the wealth of the Inka nobility was the system of royal estates that were established throughout the later part of the empire, if not the earlier part as well. Inka kings could claim land for personal use and develop it into holdings with fields, craft production centers, and sometimes sizable numbers of tributaries. The land and resources were used to support the ruler and his family. A king's holdings reverted to his panaqa upon his death, and were used to provide the material means to support the king in death. The elaborate rituals required of both the agricultural calendar and mortuary services meant that substantial resources were needed. Many of the most famous archaeological sites in the Cuzco-Urubamba region were private estates, including Pisac, Ollantaytambo, and Machu Picchu (figure 10.10). Estates could also be given to other individuals, including non-Inkas, for services rendered. This, again, points out the importance of the reciprocal relations between the Inka state and its tributaries.

Cuzco, the Capital

At the heart of the empire or, as the Inkas called it, the Navel of the Universe, was Cuzco, their capital. We know from the discovery of Killke pottery under Inka buildings that the city predates the expansion of the empire. But we do not know

Figure 10.10. Machu Picchu. Photo by author.

much about its original layout due to four centuries of modifications by the colonial and modern governments, plus natural events such as earthquakes. Figure 10.11 is a generally accepted map of the city,[6] drawn from both historical sources and archaeological work. Two rivers, the Saphy and Tullumayo, were straightened to provide space for the city before they merged into the Huatanay River below the central sector of the city. Sarmiento de Gamboa ([1572] 1960) describes the city as being laid out in the image of a puma, with the Saqsawaman structure as the head and the confluence of the Tullumayo and Saphy rivers as the end of the tail. Others, however, dispute this literal translation and suggest the layout was more metaphorical (for a discussion of this debate, see Hyslop 1990, 50–51).

At the heart of the city was a great plaza divided into two parts by the Saphy River, which was covered over (Hyslop 1990). The two parts had separate names, *Awkaypata* and *Kusipata,* and probably uses. The former was modified by the Spaniards to become the current Plaza de Armas of the city. According to Polo (1916), the Awkaypata was covered by sand from the Pacific Ocean to a depth of two and one-half palms (perhaps 10 inches) to show reverence to the sea. The most important ceremonial activities were conducted in these plazas when the mummies of the past kings were brought there and provided with food and drink. Along the four sides

of these plazas were important buildings, including the palaces of some of the kings.

Cuzco was also divided into Hanan Cuzco and Hurin Cuzco sections, following the moiety division of the society. The Hanan Cuzco panaqas occupied the northwestern upper section of the city, and the Hurin Cuzco panaqas lived in the lower southeastern sector. The nonroyal ayllus lived outside this main sector of the city, separated from it by an area of agricultural fields for ceremonial uses. The residences of provincial lords, their families, and attendants were located in this region as well. Mitmaqkuna and other people, such as mitayos working in the capital, also lived in the vicinity of Cuzco but in a hinterland stretching out over a large area. Thus, Cuzco became a microcosm of the Inka Empire,

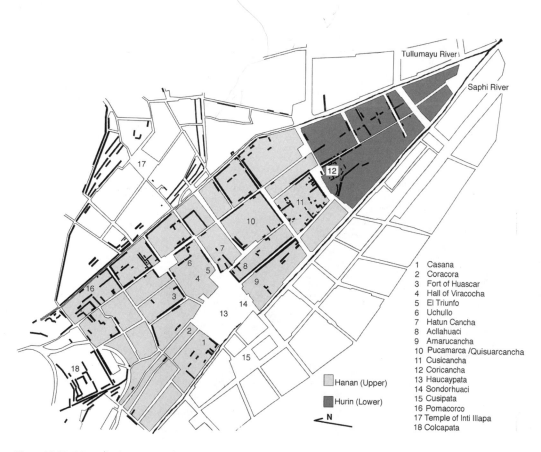

Figure 10.11. Map of Inka Cuzco. From Bauer 2004, map 10.1. Courtesy of University of Texas Press, copyright 2004.

with settlements of conquered peoples located in the geographical suyu of their homeland.

In addition to the residences of the royalty, an aqllawasi was located in a compound on the Awkaypata plaza. Many temples were also located in the city, notably the Qorikancha, or Sun Temple, the most sacred building in the realm. Today, the monastery of Santo Domingo is standing on the foundations of this temple, although some of the exquisite original temple walls remain (figure 10.12). The mummies of some kings, the sacred image of the Sun, called *Punchao,* and the sanctuaries of other gods were located within the Qorikancha.

Saqsawaman is the largest architectural complex ever built by the Inkas, and it is one of the most magnificent buildings in the Americas (figure 10.13). Although early Spanish writers referred to it as a fortress because of its impressive three-tiered set of zigzag walls, it is obvious from other chroniclers that it served several functions, including as a Sun Temple, storage depot, and stage for rituals (Hyslop 1990). Ironically, it never served a defensive function until the Spaniards used it to repel the Inka attacks during their siege in 1536. The building was constructed by

20,000 mitmaqkuna, according to Cieza de León ([1551] 1967) and was probably built during the reign of Pachakuti or Thupa Inka.

A final aspect of Inka architecture of note is its rectangularity. In many regions of the Andes, people lived in round or oval houses. In contrast, the Inkas preferred rectangular structures, although they employed trapezoids as windows, niches, and doorways. Therefore, rectangular structures that appear in settlements of round houses are often clues to the presence of Inka influence.

The basic unit of architecture was the *kancha,* an enclosed space with a group of rectangular structures within it (Hyslop 1990). The most common arrangement was three structures around an open patio. The enclosing wall typically had a single entrance, and the number of structures within could vary considerably. The kancha was the basis for both domestic structures and for religious and administrative structures.

Another distinctive architectural form of the empire was the *kallanka,* a long, single-room structure usually with more than one doorway (figure 10.5). Kallankas are often found in the centers of Inka set-

Figure 10.12. Inka stonework forming foundation of church of Santo Domingo in Cuzco. Photo by author.

Figure 10.13. Saqsawaman. Photo by author.

tlements, suggesting they had public functions, although what those functions were is not certain. They might have served as barracks or feasting areas.

Provincial Rule

It is fairly easy to characterize the Inka state as it existed when the Spaniards arrived in 1532 C.E. It is quite a bit more difficult to determine how it actually achieved the size and complexity it did. The enormous diversity of ethnic groups presented challenges to the Inka nobility in terms of how they could be incorporated into the empire. It is clear that there was no one system by which this happened. In addition, it is likely that the processes and mechanisms may have evolved as the empire expanded. A few examples of how incorporation was achieved serve to illustrate the dynamic nature of Inka provincial rule. Some regions, such as Xauxa and Huánuco, have been well described in the literature (D'Altroy 1992; Grosboll 1993; Morris and Thompson 1985). Therefore, I focus on some more recently described regions here.

PICHINCHA PROVINCE, ECUADOR The northern reaches of the Inka Empire were arguably the most difficult to subjugate due to the fierce resistance of the local ethnic groups. The conquest of Ecuador took over two decades, beginning perhaps with Pachakuti but certainly with Thupa Inka and extending into the reign of Wayna Qhapaq, the last king of the unified empire. Through the work of Frank Salomon (1986) and others, we know the Inkas used different mechanisms of interaction along this margin of the empire, including using local intermediate groups to obtain the resources they desired from more distant locations outside their control. Such was the case for the Yumbos, a group living to the west of Quito, in the montaña region between the highlands and the western lowlands (Lippi and Gudiño 2010; Salomon 1997).[7]

The Yumbos appear archaeologically around 700 C.E. and were an important group that provided lowland products such as cotton, tropical maize varieties, fruit, and salt, to the highland groups near Quito prior to the coming of the Inkas (Lippi 2004). They lived in small villages but built *tolas,* mounds that served as civic-ceremonial locations and possibly the residences of paramount chiefs. Two sites, Tulipa and Palmitopamba, located 12 km apart, are the largest settlements known. The former is an unusual set of monumental pools constructed for uncertain, but probably ceremonial, functions; the latter is both a domestic site and tola, and Lippi and Gudiño argue that it was the most important Yumbo site, given its size, location, and unique features.

The date of the Inkas' arrival in Yumbo territory is uncertain, but it is suggested as having been no earlier than 1490 C.E. and perhaps as late as 1534. Ethnohistorical accounts suggest the region was conquered late, but there is no evidence for Yumbo tribute, suggesting it was not incorporated in the traditional manner. After the Spanish conquest, the Inkas fled to the region and built forts to defend against the Spaniards. Other records make the intriguing suggestion that Rumiñawi, the captain of Atawallpa's personal guard, took the last Inka king's mummy, family members, and treasure to Yumbo territory to keep them safe from the Spaniards (Estupiñán Viteri 2003; cited in Lippi and Gudiño 2010).

Palmitopamba itself has little evidence for an Inka presence, although the ceramics and architecture indicate they did coexist at the site with the Yumbos (figure 10.14). Although the Inka presence is noted in some small stone features and on walkway borders approaching the tola at the top of the site, the total lack of Inka artifacts on the tola itself suggests the Inka respected the sacredness of the space to the Yumbos. This evidence, taken together, argues that the Inka simply maintained the special trading relationship that had existed prior to their arrival but coopted it to provide the goods they desired. The semi-autonomous nature of this relationship explains

Figure 10.14. Palmitopamba. The Yumbo tola is the flattened top of the hill. From Malpass and Alconini 2010, figure 10.3. Photo courtesy of Ronald Lippi.

why there are no records of actual tribute from the Yumbos.

CHIMOR As mentioned in chapter 9, the kingdom of Chimor (another name for the Chimú territory) was the most complex polity in South America at the end of the Late Intermediate Period. There is little in the ethnohistorical record about the specifics of how the Inkas were able to conquer the people here, and for a very long time there was little specific archaeological evidence to suggest the changes that the Inkas wrought on the Chimú political system. Work by Carol Mackey (2006, 2010) and William Sapp (2002) has begun to change this situation. Farfán, a regional capital of the Chimú, was thought to have been constructed after the conquest of the valley in 1300 C.E. Sapp (2002) has found, however, that the Sicán (Lambayeque) ethnicity had also used the site prior to the Chimú conquest, constructing the first of six major compounds that comprise the site. The Chimú constructed three others, and the Inkas built two after their conquest of the valley, probably around 1450 C.E. Mackey also found that the Inkas modified the four Chimú compounds to conduct new activities, such as craft production and additional storage. They also constructed an usnu in one of the compounds to conduct rituals of state.

Mackey (2010)[8] has identified a new form of architecture that the Inkas used in the construction of their compounds. The architecture is a blend of Chimú and Sicán traditions and does not follow Inka canons. She calls the resultant architectural style "conciliatory or diplomatic architecture" because it appears to be an effort to honor the local lords by continuing their traditions, although with modifications.

In addition to the architectural style, Mackey has identified three levels of elite residences at the compounds that corresponded to different statuses. Two residence types (A and B) in Compound VI were suggested as being the residences of Inka officials on the basis of the residences' sizes, construction features, offerings, and ceramics. The resident of the single Type A structure is considered to have been the most important person in the compound, based on the privacy and spaciousness of the structure. In addition, the Inkas buried their dead inside the compounds, in contrast to the burials of the locals, which were located in cemeteries away from the compounds.

The Wak'a Burial Platform located on the slopes of Cerro Faclo was a special mortuary complex that housed several different interments. Significantly, the only male burial at the site was an unusually tall individual who was buried at the top along with four females. All the other, approximately forty-five, individuals were females, but most if not all were clearly high status as indicated by their grave goods. They were probably aqlla, and were sacrificial offer-ings. Mackey interprets the Wak'a Burial Platform as the mortuary complex of an important local Chimú lord who was honored by the Inkas.

The site of Farfán was used for storage, probably of cloth manufactured at the site in new facilities in Compound IV. Storage was increased by constructing new storerooms in Compounds II and VI, and the security associated with it was increased. The Inka policy of showing hospitality was manifest in the construction of a workshop for making tinajas (large ceramic vessels used in brewing chicha). The distinctive form is found all over the site but especially in the several "hospitality mounds" located adjacent to four compounds. The large quantities of these tinajas, along with food preparation vessels and food, suggest these were for feasting.

In sum, the Inkas recognized that they must appease the local ethnic lords that they had conquered in this region to reduce the threat of rebellion by the formerly powerful Chimú. Thus, they developed a new architectural style that blended the local and imperial styles. They honored the Chimú dead by allowing them an exceptional burial platform. Yet they still required the labor of the local people in the manufacture of textiles and ceramics. Following Inka tradition, they hosted large parties outside the administrative compounds, where the local people (probably) were provided food and drink by their overlords. Whether any of these overlords were ethnic Inkas is uncertain; the skeletal remains of most individuals are of coastal origin, suggesting that the rule of Farfán was through local Chimú and Sicán elites.

YAMPARA The Yampara lived in the southeastern Bolivian highlands adjacent to where the Andes drop into the lower piedmont and Chaco regions. As such, they were on the border of the Inka Empire and experienced conflict with Chiriguano-Guaraní groups from the lower piedmont and Chaco regions. The conflicts probably predated the Inka conquest because there are records that suggest the Yampara allied themselves with the Inkas for protection from such incursions (Alconini 2010).

Excavations by Sonia Alconini (2010)[9] at the site of Yoroma have identified changes that occurred as a result of the Inka annexation of this region. Prior to the Inkas, during the Classic Yampara Period (800–1300 C.E.), a local elite began to emerge, based on the control of lithic production for export. These elites developed a cult of the ancestors, burying their dead in elaborate funerary urns typical of the period prior to this one. Areas of food production and consumption for workers at the lithic workshop indicate one means by which the elite used the reciprocal relationships of labor to differentiate themselves from others in the community. Nonetheless, status differences were not marked at this time, either architecturally or through artifacts.

With the arrival of the Inkas, significant changes occurred in some spheres of activity, although the overall pattern did not change. The size of the settlement increased and public architecture appeared. The latter is indicated by a large group of oblong rectangular conjoined rooms in the center of the site where some kind of public activities were performed. Grinding stones in one room suggest grain processing was one of these activities. The local architecture was circular, so the rectangular form of the structures suggests Inka influence as the source. In an adjacent circular compound, local high-status goods, such as star copper bells (figure 10.15), and Inka prestige items were discovered, suggesting the residents were important members of the local community but affiliated with the Inkas. A patio in this compound showed evidence of large-scale feasting associated with the continued production of lithic tools in a different part of the site. The evidence indicates that feasting was now restricted to a smaller group of individuals within a compound instead of in the open air (as in the earlier community) where more people could participate.

In a different part of the site, another feasting area was located near a funerary complex. The latter was located in the same place as the earlier elite burials. The lithic workshop from the previous period was expanded, and large-scale food and drink preparation was conducted in the same area. *Qollqas* (store-

Figure 10.15. Star copper bells from Yoroma. From Malpass and Alconini 2010, figure 4.7. Photo courtesy of Sonia Alconini.

rooms) were constructed nearby for storing the provisions necessary for this feasting. The feeding of the laborers was done here rather than in the elite residence to the north. The feasting in the residence was probably reserved for the local elite's reciprocal labor activities or for higher-status individuals, perhaps visiting Inka authorities when they came to visit. The evidence from the lithic workshop indicates that unfinished projectile points were the final product and that they were therefore destined for export. Given the presence of Inka forts to the east, whose function was to serve as buffers against the Chiriguano-Guaraní incursions, they were the likely destination for these points.

Placing Yoroma in its larger political context, note that two major Inka centers, Oroncota and Inqarry Moqo, are located near Yoroma. Oroncota had fine Inka architecture, a rarity in Qollasuyu, but it was neither large nor had impressive storage facilities. Still, it was more likely to have functioned as the residence of a higher kuraka than the site of Yoroma. Alconini suggests that the Inka did not modify the local Yampara political economy significantly; rather, they simply intensified the production of products such as projectile points through the incorporation of local lords who were in positions to assist in these activities. In turn, the assistance provided to the Inkas resulted in the increase in the local elite's status in their own communities. In contrast to the Calchaquí Valley discussed by Acuto (2010), it appears that there was less resistance to Inka incorporation in the Yampara territory, a conclusion that accords with the ethnohistorical records for the region.

NORTHERN CHILE The impact of the Inka state in the area of northern Chile and far southern Peru has been difficult to assess due to the paucity of ethnohistorical documents that pertain to it. Given that our comprehension of the Inka conquest has more often been based on such documents than on archaeology, the lack of knowledge is understandable. Calógero Santoro et al. (2010)[10] note that most researchers follow Murra's (1972) verticality model to suggest the indirect control of the Atacama region by ethnic groups from the Titicaca basin that were sent there by the Inkas. In turn, the coastal regions were controlled indirectly from highland centers. One reason for the assumption of indirect control of the coastal valleys has been the near absence of Inka architecture in this region.

Now, due to the volume of work that has been done on the Inkas and their impact in this region, a new model is emerging. There is more evidence (although not a lot) in the form of architecture for Inka intervention in the region. In addition, Inka prestige items such as colorful bird feathers, *Spondylus* shell fragments, copper *tumis* (ceremonial knives), and even khipu fragments have also been found, suggesting that local leaders were incorporated into the empire using the same mechanisms as in other regions. The Inkas were particularly interested in controlling guano deposits, and Covey (2000) has identified mitmaqkuna settlements along the coast. Finally, there is evidence of intensified maize and textile production at several sites in the region.

In contrast, in the highland zones of Arica, imperial infrastructure is much clearer, with the presence of Inka *tampus*, qollqas, *chullpas*, and usnus (platforms used for various purposes, such as rituals and viewing of activities) (see figure 10.16 for an usnu from Peru) and evidence for the Inka highway that passed through this region. Because this was the main locus of Inka control, the infrastructure was much more manifest in this region. The evidence that Inka-ized individuals from the Altiplano were used to control this region comes from the kinds of ceramics, which are more typical of those regions. The economic and political interactions that the Altiplano groups had with the Atacama and Arica ethnicities, some of which probably date back to Tiwanaku times, were simply converted to Inka uses after the conquest of the Altiplano. But the use of the Titicaca lords to rule this region is yet another aspect of the flexibility of Inka control of their empire.

INKA RELIGION

The religion of the Inkas had aspects unique to them as an ethnicity that developed in the Cuzco basin, but it also had more general aspects that were shared with the religions of other Andean peoples. There were several features that can be discerned: a group of deities of variable powers, ancestors who could influence the course of living humans, and an enormous diversity of sacred places called wak'as. D'Altroy (2003) defines the wak'a as any place that had transcendent power. The Inka world was suffused with such powers, many of which could be manipulated through the proper rituals.

It is a common misconception that the Inkas had a separation of religious and political power, one of the characteristics of a state level of sociopolitical complexity. Nothing could be further from the truth. It is true that there were distinct political and religious hierarchies that involved different individuals and that the two were separate. Nevertheless, Inka kings and nobility did little without consulting their dead ancestors and the priests and priestesses of the main temples to discern the proper course of action. A complex calendar of ritual activities defined

Figure 10.16. Usnu at Huánuco Pampa under reconstruction by a team of archaeologists, Peace Corps volunteers, and local farmers under the auspices of John Victor Murra. Photo by Mahlon Barash, 1965. Reprinted by permission.

when agricultural activities would commence and terminate. Sacrifices, including those of young boys and girls, were demanded on special occasions related to state activities. Religion was a pervasive force in Inka political and private life.

Major Deities

As mentioned in the section on their origins, the Inkas had a creator god called Wiraqocha, who was responsible for creating them. Nevertheless, except for a few appearances to certain kings, this god was not an important one. He is often, however, associated with *Inti*, the Sun, and *Illapa*, Thunder, and there is little doubt the three had overlapping powers that were not understood by the Spaniards. That all three were worshiped at the Qorikancha in Cuzco indicates their importance.

Inti, the Sun god, was the most important god to the Inkas, the one to which a third part of the products of all conquered lands and herds was dedicated. His main place of worship was the Qorikancha, but other Inka centers also had temples to his honor. He was created by Wiraqocha, and he was the father of Manqo Inka, the first king. Hence, all Inka kings were divine because they were descended from the Sun. This was the justification for their superior position in the social hierarchy, a fairly common practice in many ancient civilizations of the world. The High Priest of the Sun was the most important religious leader in the empire and was usually a brother or uncle of the king.

As in many other religions, the moon was considered the wife of the Sun, so *Mama-Quilla* was the wife of Inti. She had her own temple and was served by her own priestesses. The lunar calendar was as important as the solar one to the Inkas, and Mama-Quilla was an important deity in the agricultural cycle (Cobo [1653] 1990). Illapa, or *Inti-Illapa* as he is often called, reflecting the association with the Sun god, was the god of thunder but also other weather-related action, such as rainfall. Other celestial deities included many associated with the constellations, such as the Pleiades. Like other Andean people, the Inkas worshiped the gods of the earth and water, Pachamama and Mamaqocha, respectively. The former was important for crops, and even today, farmers make offerings to the Pachamama in gratitude for their crops.[11]

The Sacred Landscape of the Inkas

One of the most widespread beliefs in the Andes, long predating the Inka conquests, is that of wak'a. As previously mentioned, a wak'a is any place that has some kind of transcendent power. Rowe (1946) notes that wak'as seem to fall in the category of animatistic rather than animistic beliefs; that is, the object or location was the source of the power rather than the power being separate from, but residing in, the location. Just about anything could be a wak'a: a spring, a large rock, a hill, a tomb, a dead ancestor, the ancestor's tomb, even plants. Wak'as could be important to only a small group of people, such as a family or ayllu, or it could be more general and widespread, such as the wak'a Huanacauri, said to be the petrified brother of Manqo Inka. The power of a hill or mountain was proportional to its height: the snow-capped peaks of the Andes were considered to be the most powerful, and they are still venerated today (Allen 1988; Rowe 1948). It is thus no surprise that over the past decades, explorers and archaeologists have found a series of high-altitude Inka shrines at or near the summits of these peaks (Reinhard 1985; Reinhard and Ceruti 2010).

A very large number of wak'as were located around Cuzco. Cobo ([1653] 1990) is one of the best sources for a discussion of these sacred places. He noted that the wak'as were arranged in a radial pattern of lines, or *zeq'es*, that emanated from the vicinity of the Qorikancha in Cuzco (figure 10.17). There were at least 338 and perhaps as many as 400 wak'as located along the forty-two lines of the system. Bauer (1998), who has made a detailed study of these shrines using both ethnohistorical and archaeological information, has found that the wak'as represented many of the typical features of the landscape: caves, boulders, springs, mountaintops, houses, fountains, and canals. Each of these lines and wak'as was the responsibility of a particular kin group in Cuzco, which were required to conduct the proper rituals at the shrines each year.

More than a simple set of shrines, it is apparent that the zeq'e system was a symbolic map of the social relations of Cuzco as well. As mentioned, the region, and therefore people, around Cuzco were divided into two moieties, Hanan Cuzco and Hurin Cuzco, which, in turn, were divided into two further suyus (Bauer 1998). Chinchaysuyu and Antisuyu were part of Hanan Cuzco, and Qollasuyu and Kuntisuyu were the divisions of Hurin Cuzco. Chinchaysuyu, Antisuyu, and Qollasuyu each had nine zeq'es, but Kuntisuyu had fifteen. Each zeq'e, however, could have a different number of wak'as, which is why the total number is uncertain. The zeq'es were grouped in sets of three that were characterized as one of the Inka prestige categories of *kollana, payan,* and *kollao.* These prestige categories were also used in differentiating the panaqas, and Bauer (1998) interprets Cobo's descriptions to mean that different panaqas were responsible for different zeq'es according to these categories. A different model of this system suggests the ten nonroyal ayllus of Cuzco were paired with the panaqas, and maintained a line in the same zeq'e cluster. We can see that this system was incredibly complex and why there is so much variation in the descriptions of it by different chroniclers.

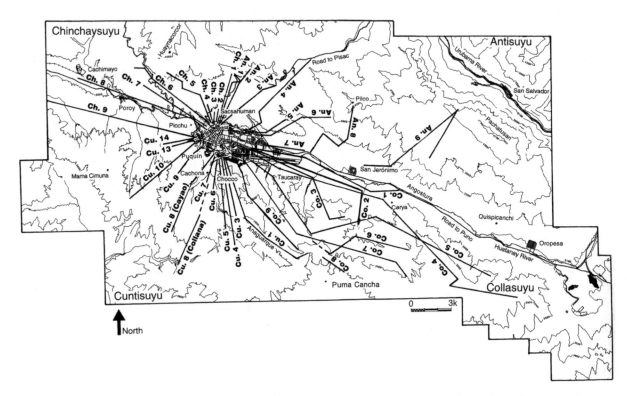

Figure 10.17. Cuzco zek'e system. From Bauer 1998, figure 11.1. Copyright 1998 by University of Texas Press. Courtesy of Brian Bauer and University of Texas Press.

Brian Bauer (1998) has made a careful archaeological study of the vicinity of Cuzco to locate the actual zeq'es and wak'as. Although the system is idealized as a series of straight lines radiating out from the Qorikancha, Bauer has found that in fact many of the lines were crooked, corresponding to variations in geography and the specific locations of the wak'as themselves. In addition, he found that not all the zeq'es originated at the Qorikancha; some began at some distance from it.

Bauer and David Dearborn (1995) have tested Tom Zuidema's (1977) hypothesis that the zeq'e system was an elaborate calendar and that each individual zeq'e corresponded to a single day, with some of them aligning to celestial events such as solstices. They have found little support for the concept, although they admit that the evidence is equivocal.

Practices and Practitioners

The Inka world was filled with rituals and practices that were required by the sacred powers, both deities and wak'as. Rowe (1946, 300–314)[12] provides an extensive list of the kinds of practices conducted by the Inkas. The Inkas typically consulted with religious practitioners before making any kinds of significant decisions. Divinations were conducted to learn the correct course of action. Any wak'a could answer questions (although the means by which it revealed an answer are uncertain), but oracles were used for the most important decisions. The two most famous oracles, and arguably the most powerful in the Inkas' eyes, were the Apo-Rimaq shrine along the Apurimac River near Cuzco and the Pachacamac shrine near Lima. Pachacamac was a shrine that dates at least to the Middle Horizon, and it was considered powerful enough that the Inkas left it in place and built a Sun Temple and other structures nearby.

All of the important wak'as had at least one attendant, and the ones dedicated to the major deities had a large staff. The Sun temples, both in Cuzco and the provinces, also had a group of *mamakunas,* a special group selected from among the Chosen Women. The main temples also maintained a hierarchy of practitioners, from a high priest down to assistants, which corresponded roughly to the administrative organization. It is this hierarchy of religious positions that is cited as evidence of a separation of church and state. It was the size of this hierarchy that required the second part of the agricultural tribute levied on conquered people.

The most common practices conducted for religious purposes were sacrifices. The most common sacrifices were of guinea pigs and llamas, which were offered in great quantities at major ceremonies. Cloth too formed a major sacrifice, with over one hundred textiles of the finest quality sacrificed at the Qorikancha every morning. Coca and *mullu* (*Spondylus* shell) were used for particular events. Food and chicha were offered to the mummies of the dead kings on ceremonial occasions as well. In addition to the sacrifices made, most ceremonies included dancing, singing, and consuming large quantities of chicha.

As previously noted, at the most important events, especially those pertaining to a king and to the most important wak'as, human sacrifices could be offered. These were usually children (figure 10.18). Also, when a king conquered a new territory, a few of the prisoners were brought to Cuzco to be sacrificed in his honor, although others merely had their throats trod on as a symbol of their submission.

The two major ceremonial events of the Inka year were *Qhapaq Raymi* and *Inti Raymi,* which took place on the December and June solstices, respectively. Qhapaq Raymi marked the beginning of the Inka year and was the most important festival. Among the several days of activities, the boys' puberty ceremonies were conducted as well as races

Figure 10.18. Inka *qhapaq cocha* child sacrifice. Photo by Johan Reinhard.

and contests. Due to the importance of this ceremony, all non-Inka residents of Cuzco were required to leave the city during it. Inti Raymi was the festival in honor of the Sun. At the end of this festival, the Inka king would conduct the ceremonial first plowing of the sacred fields in Cuzco, which marked the beginning of the planting season, although major planting was celebrated in August.

SUMMARY

The Inkas were successful in forging an empire through both their military and administrative policies. Using a cadre of professional warriors and generals drawn from the Inka people themselves and supplementing this with a much larger group of warriors from conquered groups, the Inka were able to expand their empire rapidly, starting sometime in the early fifteenth century, or a little before. Upon conquering a group, the Inkas organized them into decimal units, making an effort to keep ethnic groups together and minimizing changes to their lives. Land and herds were reapportioned, and local labor expanded the agricultural systems to provide the Inkas with the vast supplies of foods needed for imperial projects. The only thing required of local people was labor. Reciprocal relationships between the Inkas and conquered leaders were conducted using ancient practices familiar to most groups. Although conquered people could continue to worship their own deities and wak'as, they had to acknowledge the supremacy of Inka ones. The Inka Empire was being consolidated and was evolving throughout the rule of Wayna Qhapaq. With his untimely death, the empire faced a new threat: civil war. After that, the appearance of the Spanish conquistadores brought the empire to a dramatic end.

THE END OF THE EMPIRE: CIVIL WAR AND THE COMING OF THE SPANIARDS

With the death of Wayna Qhapaq, Atawallpa and Washkar, two sons by different mothers, both claimed to be the next legitimate king, although some sources suggest that Atawallpa might have originally claimed only to be ruler of the northern provinces. The Cuzco nobility accepted Washkar because he had been resident there during the long periods when his father was in Ecuador, although he had been a terrible ruler, alienating both kin and nonkin alike (D'Altroy 2003). It certainly did not help his case when he had the four honorary individuals killed who had accompanied Wayna Qhapaq's body back to Cuzco. Because he was Hanan Cuzco, the higher-status moiety of the Inkas, this was a serious breach of conduct. Washkar exacerbated the insult by revoking his Hanan Cuzco affiliation in favor of one to Hurin Cuzco.

When Washkar heard that his half-brother was challenging his rule, he sent an army north to defeat him. Depending on the source cited, this army either had some early successes or were turned back. Atawallpa had the significant advantage of having the most experienced army at his disposal, one that had been fighting in Ecuador for decades. He also had two excellent generals, Quizquiz and Challco-

chima. The forces of Atawallpa fought their way south, defeating the army of Washkar at every significant battle. This had the effect of lowering the morale of the southern army.

The final battles of the civil war were fought just outside Cuzco, and Washkar himself took leadership of his forces. He was captured in a battle, which effectively ended the war. He was taken as a hostage to Cuzco. Cusi Yupanki, Atawallpa's high priest of the Sun, arrived in Cuzco and arranged for the members of Washkar's lineage to be executed and his grandfather Thupa Inka's mummy to be burned. Washkar's own children and wives were killed before his eyes. The generals and high priest then supervised the execution of as many of the remaining members of Washkar's lineage as they could find (D'Altroy 2003). This effectively ended any threat to Atawallpa's claim to be king.

The news of his army's triumph reached Atawallpa as he was moving down the royal highway to be invested as Sapa Inka. It is a cruel fact of history that at virtually the same time, he heard news of the Spanish arrival on the north coast, and how they were burning and looting his subjects' villages. His confidence in his invincibility must have been at an all-time high, leading him to assume this ragtag band of strangers posed no significant threat to him. He could not have been more wrong.

Francisco Pizarro and his forces had been traveling south along the coast from his initial landfall at Coaque, Ecuador, in 1531 C.E. By November, 1532, he had gained sufficient reinforcements, to a force of 168 horsemen and foot soldiers, to ascend into the highlands to meet the Inka king, who was bivouacked in Cajamarca with a large force of his soldiers and personal guard. On his arrival in Cajamarca, Pizarro sent his lieutenant, Hernando de Soto, and fifteen horsemen to meet Atawallpa at his encampment outside the town. Through an interpreter they had brought, the Spaniards offered the king a ring of friendship, which was rejected, but the king then invited them to dine with him, which they rejected. After Atawallpa refused to go back to their camp (a wise choice!), they departed (D'Altroy 2003).

The next day, the Spaniards positioned themselves in the main square of Cajamarca, a perfect location for the surprise attack they had planned. There were relatively few exits from the square, and on the sides were probably kallankas, the long halls with multiple doorways where the Spanish soldiers and horsemen could hide. There they waited until nearly nightfall when Atawallpa arrived with a large contingent of his personal guard. They filled the square and awaited the arrival of the Spanish leadership. A priest and an interpreter advanced to the king's litter carrying a prayer book that was presented to Atawallpa as the word of God. When the king threw the book down, the priest ran for cover and Pizarro gave the order to attack. The roar of small cannons discharged directly into the massed Inka soldiers, plus the rush of the horsemen must have been a terrifying sight and sound to the Inkas. After two hours, the carnage ended, with perhaps 7,000 Inka soldiers killed but none of the Spaniards. Atawallpa was captured alive by Pizarro himself. The victory was so complete that Pizarro invited Atawallpa to dine with him that evening (D'Altroy 2003).

Recognizing the Spaniards' principal interest lay in the riches of his empire, Atawallpa made a bargain with them whereby he would fill a room 6 by 5 m half full of gold and the same room twice filled with silver for his freedom. This took several months, during which Pizarro sent expeditions to Cuzco and Pachacamac to learn more about the empire and to await reinforcements from Panama. John Hemming (1970) notes that the ransom resulted in each horsemen receiving about half a million dollars worth of gold and silver, with foot soldiers receiving about half that amount. Pizarro took approximately $3.5 million worth for his share.

In the end, the Spaniards decided that Atawallpa was more of a liability than an asset after the ransom was paid, so they tried him and executed him. He was saved from being burned, which would have destroyed his corpse and thus rendered moot the customary rituals and respect due the deceased king. In fact, Lippi and Gudiño (2010) note that Atawallpa's general, Rumiñawi, may have taken the corpse plus some of his treasure back to Ecuador and may have briefly stayed at Palmitopamba with them.

The Spaniards realized they needed a new ruler to use, so they installed a brother of Washkar as king. Unfortunately, he died en route to Cuzco, but another son, Manqo Inka, offered his services to the Spaniards in hopes of claiming his right to the kingship. When the Spanish forces arrived in Cuzco, they set about claiming the best palaces for themselves and continued the looting of the wealth of the Inkas.

After three years of uncomfortable co-rule, Manqo Inka realized he would never be rid of the Spaniards without armed conflict, so he escaped and set about raising an army to expel the foreigners. In 1536, coordinated attacks on Lima and Cuzco began. The attack on Lima collapsed after a single day when the Spaniards identified the leaders of the army and killed them. The siege of Cuzco, however, lasted for months, with repeated attacks and counterattacks by both sides. The siege ultimately failed because the Inka soldiers had to return to their homes to tend their fields as the agricultural cycle commenced.

Although the failure of this rebellion meant the end to the most serious challenge to Spanish rule, the Inkas continued their resistance from their new capital of Vilcabamba, located in the eastern forests north of Cuzco. There, the Inkas, under three kings, continued to attack Spanish outposts and the settlements of their allies until 1572, when Viceroy Toledo finally succeeded in defeating the last of the Inka resistance. The rule of the sons of the Sun was at an end.

THE LEGACY OF THE INKAS

Even though the Inka Empire collapsed at the hands of the Spaniards starting in 1532 C.E., testimony to their greatness and lasting impact can still be found in several aspects of western South American culture. Quechua, the language of the Inkas, is still spoken by many indigenous people from Ecuador to Chile. There are several dialects, but the basic language is the same. Its broad use started during Inka times when conquered leaders were required to learn it. It also owes its widespread character, however, to the fact the Spaniards found it the most useful language for interacting with their native subjects.

Many regions of the central Andes today have two different sets of agricultural terraces. One is an abandoned set that lies above a lower set of irrigated ones. The latter are used by local inhabitants for their livelihood. In places such as the Colca Valley, it is known that the abandoned terraces predate the Inkas and that the ones presently used were constructed under Inka authority (figure 10.19). Note also that of the roughly 1 million ha of terraced fields that exist in the Andes today, only about 40 percent are currently in use. The rest are abandoned, and the Inkas constructed many of those as well. They were abandoned as a result of colonial depopulation and resettlement practices (Denevan 1987).

In like fashion, one of the less appreciated aspects of Inka culture was their engineering skills. Research by civil engineers at the Inka sites of Tipón in the Cuzco Valley and at Machu Picchu have revealed that the Inkas understood the best ways and places for terraces and canals to be constructed (Wright 2006; Wright and Valencia Zegarra 2000). For example, it is evident that over 50 percent of the labor required to construct Machu Picchu went into the foundations for the main plaza alone (Wright and Valencia Zegarra 2000).

Much of the colonial architecture of Cuzco was constructed on the foundations of Inka buildings, many of which were destroyed during the siege of Cuzco in 1536. The magnificent stonework of the Inkas continues to impress all who see it, both because of its engineering aspects and because of its elegant aesthetics.

Figure 10.19. Abandoned terraces above ones in use near Coporaque in the Colca Valley. Photo by author.

The very fact the Inkas could form an empire as extensive as they did in less than a century, or perhaps a little more, ranks the Inka Empire as one of the great empires of the ancient world. It also speaks to their abilities as a people. Although most of this success was due to the skills of particular generals and the ambitions of the last kings, the ethnic Inka people of the Cuzco vicinity were as important in their support of their leaders.

Finally, John Rowe (1946) notes at the end of his treatise on Inka culture that an "Inka nation" exists in the minds and hearts of the modern people of Ecuador, Peru, and Bolivia which owe their roots to the unifying policies of the Inkas. Although such a shared sense of unity might be argued, there is no doubt that many modern people of these countries are proud to be the descendants of the Inkas and justly proud of the achievements of their ancestors. And so they should be.

NOTES

1. Learning about the Past

1. As mentioned in the preface and in conformance with new practices, I use B.C.E. (before the common era) and C.E. (common era) instead of B.C. (before Christ) and A.D. (*anno domini*, "in the year of our Lord"). This reflects a preference for using nonreligious terms in our dating procedures.

2. Geography of the Central and South Andes

1. As mentioned in chapter 1, all dates before about 1800 B.C.E. have been calibrated. If a single date is given rather than a range, it is the midpoint of the range of possible dates.

3. The Time before Temples

1. All ^{14}C dates were calibrated using Calib 7.0.0 (Stuiver and Paula Reimer 1993) and IntCal13, Marine13 (Reimer et al. 2013), or SHCal13 (Hogg et al. 2013), when appropriate. All calibrated ages are presented as one-sigma ranges, rounded to the nearest 100 cal year. For radiocarbon ages for which the standard errors were not available, a standard error of 100 years was used in Calib 7.0.0 to obtain an approximate calibrated age range. For radiocarbon age ranges, the one-sigma maximum and minimum values are presented. To convert the calibrated radiocarbon ages to B.C.E. dates, 1,950 years were subtracted.

2. These are the published dates. When the calibration program is used, the oldest dates of 12,280 ± 60 B.P. and 12,240 ± 50 B.P. calibrate to ~14,200–14,000 cal B.P., and the youngest age of 10,770 ± 340 B.P. calibrates to ~13,000–12,100 cal B.P.

3. Unfortunately, dates on marine shell along the Peruvian coast are difficult to calibrate due to strong upwelling, making a marine-reservoir correction impossible. For this reason, the Amotape date cannot be calibrated.

4.

4. Cesar Mendez has suggested that the site of Quereo is purely a paleontological site with no evidence of human activity (Kurt Rademaker pers. comm. 2014).

6. Of Masks and Monoliths

1. To call Chavín an *art style* is perhaps to give the wrong impression, that it was a monolithic way of producing and decorating pottery. The term as I use it here refers to a set of stylistic conventions of both form and decoration that are found across space. There is considerable variability in the way that these conventions were applied in different regions. That being said, the distinctive nature of the elements, given in Willey's description, make them readily identifiable.

7. Art and Power

1. The site of Huacas de Moche is also known as Cerro Blanco or simply Moche by other authors. Because Huacas de Moche is the accepted name used by scholars working at the site, I use it here. Doing this also reduces the confusion over the many meanings of the term *Moche*.

2. Paracas ceramics were originally defined from the Paracas Peninsula by Uhle in 1925. A more complete ten-phase sequence for this pottery was defined for the Ica Valley by Menzel, Rowe, and Dawson (1964), which I use here. Since these phases were originally defined, the first two have been discarded. Hence, the Paracas ceramics sequence begins with Ocucaje.

8. Clash of the Titans?

1. For the spellings of major structures, I follow Janusek (2008), who tends to combine terms into a single word (e.g., Pumapunku rather than Puma Punku).

2. Following current conventions, I restrict the term *Wari* to the culture that existed during this time period. I spell the name of the site that was the capital and probable source of the culture Huari.

3. In early publications, this site was called Netahaha, an error corrected in subsequent publications by the principal investigator, Justin Jennings.

4. Although only Moche IV forms are found at the Huacas de Moche, a suite of radiocarbon dates collected by Chapdelaine and reported in Lockard (2009) indicate that the site was still occupied into the eighth century, making the Moche IV ceramics there partially contemporary with the Moche V ceramics at Galindo, which also dates to that century. This points out one of the problems with using the Larco Hoyle sequence uncritically.

9. *Auca Runa, the Epoch of Warfare*

1. I use the term *Sicán* rather than *Lambayeque* following Shimada's (2000) rationale. The latter has been used inconsistently in the literature, and the detailed investigations of the Sicán by Shimada in the 1980s and 1990s provided a clearer sense of the temporal and spatial context of this culture. Note that there has been confusion between Lambayeque and Chimú in the literature as well (e.g., Donnan and Cock 1986) due to the lack of understanding of the differences between the two, which Shimada has clarified with the definition of the Sicán culture.

10. *Expansion and Empire*

1. The lists given in this paragraph are some of the most trusted and useful sources for our understanding of the Inka Empire. The lists are not exhaustive. For more complete discussions of these early sources, consult D'Altroy 2003, Pärssinen 1992, Pease 1995, Rowe 1946, Urton 1990, and Zuidema 1990. I have also used the English translations of the originals where available for the reader's consideration, although any of these sources have the citations for the originals.

2. A later version of this same myth states that Manqo and his sister/wife originated on two islands in Lake Titicaca and from there traveled north to Cuzco (Bauer and Stanish 2001). This myth accounts for the elaborate Inka shrine found on the Island of the Sun in that region.

3. This view is a generally accepted one, although there are others that are associated with different chroniclers and the scholars who use them.

4. After Wayna Qhapaq's death, two rival sons, Atawallpa and Washkar, both claimed the kingship, setting off a civil war that devastated the empire. As a result, neither expanded the size of the empire.

5. As noted in chapter 9, the power of these ethnicities may have been greatly overstated by the Inkas to make their conquests appear more impressive. For example, Betanzos (1996) notes that the Qolla fielded an army of 200,000 warriors against the Inkas and that both sides lost 100,000 warriors before the Inkas prevailed.

6. Many excellent descriptions of Inka Cuzco exist, so another detailed one here would be superfluous. See Hyslop 1990 and D'Altroy 2003 for good examples.

7. Unless otherwise noted, all information about the Yumbo comes from Lippi and Gudiño 2010.

8. The principal source for this section is Mackey 2010.

9. The principal source for this section is Sonia Alconini 2010.

10. The principal source for this section is Santoro et al. 2010.

11. It is not just crops that require veneration of Pachamama. On an excavation in the Colca Valley in the 1980s, our Peruvian workers asked us to provide an offering of alcohol to her before we removed a cache of ceramics left as an offering outside an ancient house. As we were making the libation, an eagle soared up over the ceremony, circled, and then disappeared. We had never seen it before and never saw it again afterward.

12. The principal source for this section is Rowe 1946, 300–314.

REFERENCES CITED

In addition to the references cited in the text, I have relied on the following works:

For general texts on Andean archaeology, see Isbell and Silverman 2002, 2006; Silverman 2004a; Silverman and Isbell 2002, 2008. In particular, the *Handbook of South American Archaeology* (Silverman and Isbell 2008) is a source of information about the entire continent, divided thematically. The journals *Latin American Antiquity*, *Andean Past*, and *Ñawpa Pacha* provide excellent articles on the region as well.

For books of particular utility for individual chapters, as well as newer volumes, see the following: For **chapters 5** and **6**, see Burger 1992; Conklin and Quilter 2008. For **chapter 7**, see Bawden 1996; Pillsbury 2001; Quilter and Castillo Butters 2010; Silverman and Proulx 2002. For **chapter 8**, see Isbell and McEwan 1991; Janusek 2008; Kolata 1993, 1996, 2003a; Stanish 2002; Tung 2012. For **chapter 9**, see Arkush 2011; Janusek 2008; Kolata 1993, 1996, 2003a; Stanish 2002; Vogel 2012. For **chapter 10**, see Bauer 1992, 2004; Burger, Morris, and Matos Mendieta 2007; D'Altroy 2003; Kolata 2013; Malpass 1993; Malpass and Alconini 2010; McEwan 2006.

Abbott, Mark, Michael Binford, Mark Brenner, and Kerry Kelts. 1997. "A 3500¹⁴C Yr High-Resolution Record of Water-Level Changes in Lake Titicaca, Bolivia/Peru." *Quaternary Research* 47(2): 169–180.

Acuto, Félix. 2010. "Living under the Imperial Thumb in the Northern Calchaquí Valley, Argentina." In Malpass and Alconini 2010, 108–150.

Alconini, Sonia. 2010. "Yampara Households and Communal Evolution in the Southeastern Inka Peripheries." In Malpass and Alconini 2010, 75–107.

Aldenderfer, Mark. 1998. *Montane Foragers: Asana and the South-Central Andean Archaic.* Iowa City: University of Iowa Press.

——. 2005. "Preludes to Power in the Highland Late Preceramic Period." In *Foundations of Power in the Prehispanic Andes,* edited by Kevin J. Vaughn, Dennis Ogburn, and Christina A. Conlee, 14–35. Archaeological Papers of the American Anthropological Association 14. Washington, DC: American Anthropological Association.

Aldenderfer, Mark, Nathan Craig, Robert Speakman, and Rachel Popelka-Filcoff. 2008. "Four-Thousand-Year-Old Gold Artifacts from the Lake Titicaca Basin, Southern Peru." *Proceedings of the National Academy of Sciences* 105(3): 5002–5005.

Allen, Catherine. 1988. *The Hold Life Has: Coca and Cultural Identity in an Andean Community.* Washington, DC: Smithsonian Institution Press.

Alva, Walter, and Christopher Donnan. 1993. *Royal Tombs of Sipán.* Los Angeles: Fowler Museum of Cultural History, University of California.

Anders, Martha. 1986. "Dual Organization and Calendars Inferred from the Planned Site of Azángaro—Wari Administrative Strategies." PhD diss., Cornell University.

——. 1991. "Structure and Function at the Planned Site of Azángaro: Cautionary Notes for the Model of Huari as a Centralized Secular State." In Isbell and McEwan 1991, 165–197.

Arkush, Elizabeth. 2006. "Collapse, Conflict, Conquest: The Transformation of Warfare in the Late Prehispanic Andean Highlands." In *The Archaeology of Warfare: Prehistories of Raiding and Conquest,* edited by Elizabeth Arkush and Mark Allen, 286–335. Gainesville: University Press of Florida.

——. 2008. "War, Chronology, and Causality in the Titicaca Basin." *Latin American Antiquity* 19(4): 339–373.

——. 2011. *Hillforts of the Ancient Andes: Colla Warfare, Society, and Landscape*. Gainesville: University Press of Florida.

Arriaza, Bernardo, Matthew Doubrava, Vivien G. Standen, and Herbert Haas. 2005. "Differential Mortuary Treatment among the Andean Chinchorro Fishers: Social Inequalities or In Situ Regional Cultural Evolution?" *Current Anthropology* 46(4): 662–671.

Arriaza, Bernardo, Vivien G. Standen, Vicki Cassman, and Calogero Santoro. 2008. "Chinchorro Culture: Pioneers of the Coast of the Atacama Desert." In Silverman and Isbell 2008, 45–58.

Aveni, Anthony. 2000. *Between the Lines: The Mystery of the Giant Ground Drawings of Ancient Nasca, Peru*. Austin: University of Texas Press.

Azami, Eri, and Oliver Velásquez. 2010. "Procesos Sociales en la Cultura Chancay: Estudio del Patrón Arquitectónico del Sitio Arqueológico de Pisquillo Chico." In Romero Velarde and Svendsen 2010, 249–262.

Bandy, Matthew. 2006. "Early Village Society in the Formative Period in the Southern Lake Titicaca Basin." In Isbell and Silverman 2006, 210–236.

Bauer, Brian. 1992. *The Development of the Inca State*. Austin: University of Texas Press.

——. 1996. "The Legitimation of the Inca State in Myth and Ritual." *American Anthropologist* 98(2): 327–337.

——. 1998. *The Sacred Landscape of the Inka: The Cuzco Ceque System*. Austin: University of Texas Press.

——. 2004. *Ancient Cuzco: Heartland of the Inca*. Austin: University of Texas Press.

——, ed. 2007. *Kasapata and the Archaic Period of the Cuzco Valley*. Cotsen Institute of Archaeology Monograph 57. Los Angeles: University of California.

Bauer, Brian, and Miriam Aráoz. 2010. "La Fase Qasawirka en la Región de Andahuaylas." In Romero Velarde and Svendsen 2010, 151–174.

Bauer, Brian, and R. Alan Covey. 2002. "Processes of State Formation in the Inca Heartland (Cuzco, Peru)." *American Anthropologist* 104(3): 846–874.

Bauer, Brian, and David Dearborn. 1995. *Astronomy and Empire in the Ancient Andes*. Austin: University of Texas Press.

Bauer, Brian, Lucas Kellett, and Miriam Aráoz Silva. 2010. *The Chanka: Archaeological Research in Andahuaylas (Apurimac), Peru*. Cotsen Institute of Archaeology Monograph 68. Los Angeles: University of California.

Bauer, Brian, and Charles Stanish. 2001. *Ritual and Pilgrimage in the Ancient Andes: The Islands of the Sun and the Moon*. Austin: University of Texas Press.

Bawden, Garth. 1991. "Cheqo Wasi, Huari." In Isbell and McEwan 1991, 55–70.

——. 1996. *The Moche*. Cambridge, MA: Blackwell.

——. 2001. "The Symbols of Late Moche Social Transformation." In Pillsbury 2001, 285–306.

——. 2004. "The Art of Moche Politics." In Silverman 2004a, 116–129.

Benfer, Robert. 1986. "Holocene Coastal Adaptations: Changing Demography and Health at the Fog Oasis of Paloma, Peru, 5000–7800 BP." In *Andean Archaeology: Papers in Memory of Clifford Evans*, edited by Ramiro Matos Mendieta, Solveig A. Turpin, and Herbert H. Eling, 45–64. Institute of Archaeology Monograph 27. Los Angeles: University of California.

Benitez, Leonard. 2009. "Descendants of the Sun: Calendars, Myth, and the Tiwanaku State." In Young-Sánchez 2009, 49–82.

Bennett, Wendell Clark. 1936. "Excavations in Bolivia." *Anthropological Papers of the American Museum of Natural History* 35.

——. 1953. *Excavations at Wari, Ayacucho, Peru*. Yale University Publications in Anthropology 49. New Haven: Yale University Press.

Bennett, Wendell Clark, and Junius Bird. 1965. *Andean Culture History*. 2nd and rev. ed. Garden City, NY: Natural History Press.

Bermann, Marc. 1994. *Lukurmata: Household Archaeology in Prehispanic Bolivia*. Princeton: Princeton University Press.

Bermann, Marc, Paul Goldstein, Charles Stanish, and Luis Watanabe. 1989. "The Collapse of the Tiwanaku State: A View from the Osmore Drainage." In Rice, Stanish, and Scarr 1989, 269–285.

Betanzos, Juan de. 1996. *Narrative of the Incas*. Translated by Roland Hamilton and Dana Buchanan. Austin: University of Texas Press.

Billman, Brian. 2010. "How Moche Rulers Came to Power. Investigating the Emergence of the Moche Political Economy." In Quilter and Castillo Butters 2010, 181–200.

Bird, Junius. 1963. "Pre-Ceramic Art from Huaca Prieta, Chicama Valley." *Ñawpa Pacha* 1: 29–34.

Bird, Junius, John Hyslop, and M. D. Skinner. 1985. "The Preceramic Excavations at the Huaca Prieta, Chicama Valley, Peru." *Anthropological Papers of the American Museum of Natural History* 62: 1. New York: American Museum of Natural History.

Blom, Deborah. 2005. "Embodying Borders: Human Body Modification and Diversity in Tiwanaku Society." *Journal of Anthropological Archaeology* 24(1): 1–24.

Blom, Deborah, Benedikt Hallgrimsson, Linda Keng, Maria Lozada, and Jane Buikstra. 1998. "Tiwanaku 'Colonization': Bioarchaeological Implications for Migration in the Moquegua Valley, Peru." *World Archaeology* 30(2): 238–261.

Blom, Deborah, John Janusek, and Jane Buikstra. 2003. "A Reevaluation of Human Remains from Tiwanaku." In Kolata 2003a, 435–446.

Borrero, Luis. 2008. "Early Occupations in the Southern Cone." In Silverman and Isbell 2008, 59–78.

Bourget, Steve. 2001. "Rituals of Sacrifice: Its Practice at Huaca de la Luna and Its Representation in Moche Iconography." In Pillsbury 2001, 89–110.

———. 2010. "Cultural Assignations during the Early Intermediate Period. The Case of Huancaco, Virú Valley." In Quilter and Castillo Butters 2010, 201–222.

Bragayrac, Enrique. 1991. "Archaeological Excavations in the Vegachayoq Moqo Sector of Huari." In Isbell and McEwan 1991, 71–80.

Brennan, Curtiss. 1980. "Cerro Arena: Early Cultural Complexity and Nucleation in North Coastal Peru." *Journal of Field Archaeology* 7(1): 1–22.

Briceño, Jesus. 1995. "El Recurso Agua y el Establecimiento de los Cazadores Recolectores en el Valle de Chicama." *Revista del Museo de Arqueología, Antropología e Historia* [Trujillo, Perú] No.5: 143–162.

———. 1999. "Quebrada Santa María: Las Puntas en Cola de Pescado y la Antigüedad del Hombre en Sudamerica." In *El Período Arcaico en el Perú: Hacia una Definición de los Origenes*, edited by Peter Kaulicke, Special issue of *Boletín de Arqueología PUCP* no. 3: 19–30.

Brooks, Sarah. 1998. "Prehistoric Agricultural Terraces in the Rio Japo Basin, Colca Valley, Peru." PhD diss., University of Wisconsin, Madison.

Browman, David. 1970. "Early Peruvian Peasants: The Culture History of a Central Highlands Valley." PhD diss., Harvard University.

———. 1981. "New Light on Andean Tiwanaku: A Detailed Reconstruction of Tiwanaku's Early Commercial and Religious Empire Illuminates the Processes by Which States Evolve." *American Scientist* 69(4): 408–419.

Brush, Stephen B. 1977. *Mountain, Field, and Family: The Economy and Human Ecology of an Andean Valley*. Philadelphia: University of Pennsylvania Press.

Bryan, Alan, and Ruth Gruhn. 2003. "Some Difficulties in Modeling the Original Peopling of the Americas." *Quaternary International* 109–110: 175–179.

Bueno Mendoza, Alberto. 1982. "El Antiguo Valle de Pachacamac: Espacio, Tiempo, y Cultura." *Separata de Boletín de Lima* 5: 3–52.

Burger, Richard. 1984. *The Prehistoric Occupation of Chavín de Huántar, Peru*. Publications in Anthropology 14. Berkeley: University of California Press.

———. 1988. "Unity and Heterogeneity within the Chavín Horizon." In *Peruvian Prehistory*, edited by Richard Keatinge, 99–144. Cambridge, UK: Cambridge University Press.

———. 1992. *Chavín and the Origins of Andean Civilization*. New York: Thames and Hudson.

———. 2008. "Chavín de Huántar and Its Sphere of Influence." In Silverman and Isbell 2008, 681–703.

Burger, Richard, Karen Mohr Chávez, and Sergio Chávez. 2000. "Through the Glass Darkly: Prehispanic Obsidian Procurement and Exchange in Southern Peru and Northern Bolivia." *Journal of World Prehistory* 14(3): 267–362.

Burger, Richard, and Michael Glascock. 2000. "Locating the Quispisisa Obsidian Source in the Department of Ayacucho, Peru." *Latin American Antiquity* 11(3): 258–268.

Burger, Richard, and Ramiro Matos Mendieta. 2002. "Atalla: A Center on the Periphery of the Chavín Horizon." *Latin American Antiquity* 13(2): 153–177.

Burger, Richard, Craig Morris, and Ramiro Matos Mendieta, eds. 2007. *Variations in the Expression of Inka Power*. Washington, DC: Dumbarton Oaks Research Library and Collection.

Burger, Richard, and Lucy Salazar. 2008. "The Manchay Culture and the Coastal Inspiration for Highland Chavín Civilization." In Conklin and Quilter 2008, 85–105.

———. 2010. "La Cultura Manchay y la Inspiración Costeña para la Civilización Altoandina de Chavín." In Romero Velarde and Svendsen 2010, 13–38.

Burger, Richard, and Lucy Salazar-Burger. 1980. "Ritual and Religion at Huaricoto." *Archaeology* 33(6): 26–32.

———. 1985. "The Early Ceremonial Center at Huaricoto." In *Early Ceremonial Architecture in the Andes*, edited by Christopher B. Donnan, 111–138. Washington, DC: Dumbarton Oaks Research Library and Collection.

———. 1991. "The Second Season of Investigations at the Initial Period Site of Cardal, Peru." *Journal of Field Archaeology* 18(3): 275–296.

Cabello Balboa, Miguel. 1951. *Miscelánea Antárctica*. Lima: Universidad Nacional Mayor de San Marcos.

Calancha, Antonio de la. 1638. *Crónica Moralizada del Ordén de San Agustín en el Perú con Sucesos Ejemplares en Esta Monarquía*. Barcelona: Pedro Lacavalleria.

Calaway, Michael. 2005. "Ice-Cores, Sediments and Civilization Collapse: A Cautionary Tale from Lake Titicaca." *Antiquity* 79(306): 778–790.

Canziani A., José. 1992. "Patrones de Asentamiento en el Valle de Chincha, Peru." *II Curso de Prehistoria de América Hispánica, Comisión V Centenario, Universidad de* Murcia, 87–123.

Cardona Rosas, Augusto. 2002. *Arqueología de Arequipa: De Sus Albores a los Incas*. Arequipa: Centro de Investigaciones Arqueológicas de Arequipa.

Carmichael, Patrick. 1991. "Prehistoric Settlement of the Ica-Grande Littoral, Southern Peru." Research report, Social Sciences and Humanities Research Council of Canada, Ottawa.

Castillo Butters, Luis Jaime. 2001. "The Last of the Mochicas: A View from the Jequetepeque Valley." In Pillsbury 2001, 307–332.

———. 2010. "Moche Politics in the Jequetepeque Valley: A Case for Political Opportunism." In Quilter and Castillo Butters 2010, 83–109.

Castillo Butters, Luis Jaime, and Jeffrey Quilter. 2010. "Many Moche Models. An Overview of Past and Current Theories and Research on Moche Political Organization." In Quilter and Castillo Butters 2010, 1–16.

Castillo Butters, Luis Jaime, and Santiago Uceda Castillo. 2008. "The Mochicas." In Silverman and Isbell 2008, 707–730.

Cavallaro, Rafael. 1991. *Large-Site Methodology: Architectural Analysis and Dual Organization in the Andes.* Department of Archaeology, Occasional Papers No. 5. Calgary: University of Calgary.

Chapdelaine, Claude. 2006. "Looking for Moche Palaces at the Huacas de Moche Site." In *Palaces and Power in the Americas: From Peru to the Northwest Coast,* edited by Jessica Joyce Christie and Patricia Joan Sarro, 23–43. Austin: University of Texas Press.

———. 2009. "Domestic Life in and around the Urban Sector of the Huacas of Moche Site, Northern Peru." In *Domestic Life in Prehispanic Capitals: A Study of Specialization, Hierarchy, and Ethnicity,* edited by Linda Manzanilla and Claude Chapdelaine, 181–196. Memoirs of the Museum of Anthropology 46. Ann Arbor: University of Michigan Museum of Anthropology.

———. 2010. "Moche and Wari during the Middle Horizon on the North Coast of Peru." In *Beyond Wari Walls: Regional Perspectives on the Middle Horizon Peru,* edited by Justin Jennings, 213–232. Albuquerque: University of New Mexico Press.

Chatfield, Melissa. 1998. "Ceramics from the Site of Choquepukio, Cuzco, Peru." Paper delivered at the 63rd annual meeting of the Society for American Archaeology, Seattle, March 25–29.

Chávez, Karen Lynne Mohr. 1977. "Marcavalle: The Ceramics from an Early Horizon Site in the Valley of Cusco, Peru, and the Implications for South Highland Socio-Economic Interactions." PhD diss., University of Pennsylvania.

———. 1980. *The Archaeology of Marcavalle, an Early Horizon Site in the Valley of Cuzco, Peru.* Berlin: D. Reimer.

———. 1988. "The Significance of Chiripa in Lake Titicaca Basin Developments." *Expedition* 30(3): 17–26.

Chepstow-Lusty, Alex, Michael Frogley, Brian Bauer, Mark Bush, and Alfredo Tupayachi Herrera. 2003. "A Late Holocene Record of Arid Events from the Cuzco Region, Peru." *Journal of Quaternary Science* 18(6): 491–502.

Chu Barrera, Alejandro. 2008. *Bandurria: Arena, Mar y Humedal en el Surgimiento de la Civilización Andina.* Huacho: Proyecto Arqueológico Bandurria.

Church, Warren B., and Adriana von Hagen. 2008. "Chachapoyas: Cultural Development at an Andean Cloud Forest Crossroads." In Silverman and Isbell 2008, 903–926.

Cieza de León, Pedro. (1551) 1967. *El Señorio de los Incas; 2a Parte de la Crónica del Perú.* Lima: Instituto de Estudios Peruanos.

Clarkson, Persis. 1990. "The Archaeology of the Nazca Pampa: Environmental and Cultural Parameters." In *The Lines of Nazca,* edited by Anthony F. Aveni, 117–172. Memoirs of the American Philosophical Society 183. Philadelphia: American Philosophical Society.

Cobo, Bernabé. (1653) 1979. *History of the Inca Empire: An Account of the Indians' Customs and Their Origin, Together with a Treatise on Inca Legends, History and Social Customs.* Translated by Roland Hamilton. Austin: University of Texas Press.

———. 1990. *Inca Religion and Customs.* Translated by Roland Hamilton. Austin: University of Texas Press.

Cohen, Mark. 1977. "Population Pressure and the Origins of Agriculture: An Archaeological Example from the Coast of Peru." In *The Origins of Agriculture,* edited by Charles Reed, 135–177. The Hague: Mouton.

Conklin, William. 1978. "The Revolutionary Weaving Inventions of the Early Horizon." *Ñawpa Pacha* 16: 1–12.

———. 1985. "The Architecture of Huaca de Los Reyes." In *Early Ceremonial Architecture in the Andes,* edited by Christopher Donnan, 139–164. Washington, DC: Dumbarton Oaks Research Library and Collection.

———. 2008. "Introduction." In Conklin and Quilter 2008, xxvii–xxxii.

Conklin, William, and Jeffrey Quilter, eds. 2008. *Chavin: Art, Architecture, and Culture.* Cotsen Institute of Archaeology Monograph 61. Los Angeles: University of California.

Conlee, Christina. 2005. "The Expansion, Diversification, and Segmentation of Power in Late Prehispanic Nasca." In *Foundations of Power in the Prehispanic Andes,* edited by Kevin Vaughn, Dennis Ogburn, and Christina Conlee, 121–233. Archaeological Papers of the American Anthropological Association 14. Arlington, VA: American Anthropological Association.

Conrad, Geoffrey, and Arthur Demarest. 1984. *Religion and Empire. The Dynamics of Aztec and Inca Expansionism.* New York: Cambridge University Press.

Cordy-Collins, Alana. 1992. "Archaism or Tradition?: The Decapitation Theme in Cupisnique and Moche Iconography." *Latin American Antiquity* 3(3): 206–220.

Couture, Nicole, and Kathryn Sampeck. 2003. "Putuni: A History of Palace Architecture at Tiwanaku." In Kolata 2003a, 226–263.

Covey, R. Alan. 2000. "Inka Administration along the Far South Coast of Peru." *Latin American Antiquity* 11: 119–138.

———. 2006. *How the Incas Built Their Heartland: State Formation and Innovation of Imperial Strategies in the Sacred Valley, Peru.* Ann Arbor: University of Michigan Press.

———. 2011. "Landscapes and Languages of Power in the Inca Imperial Heartland (Cuzco, Peru)." *SAA Archaeological Record* 11(4): 29–32, 47.

Cowen, Ron. 2007. "Peru's Sunny View." *Science News* 171(18): 280–281.

Daggett, Richard. 1984. "The Early Horizon Occupation of the Nepeña Valley, North Central Coast of Peru." PhD diss., University of Massachusetts, Amherst.

———. 1987. "Toward the Development of the State on the North Central Coast of Peru." In Haas, Pozorski, and Pozorski 1987, 70–82.

D'Altroy, Terence. 1992. *Provincial Power in the Inka Empire.* Washington, DC: Smithsonian Institution Press.

———. 2003. *The Incas.* Malden, MA: Blackwell.

D'Altroy, Terence, and Timothy Earle. 1985. "Staple Finance, Wealth Finance, and Storage in the Inka Political Economy [with Comments and Reply]." *Current Anthropology* 26(2): 187–206.

D'Altroy, Terence, Verónica Williams, and Ana María Lorandi. 2007. "The Inkas in the Southlands." In Burger, Morris, and Matos Mendieta 2007, 85–134.

de la Vega, Garcilaso. (1609) 1966. *Royal Commentaries of the Incas and General History of Peru.* Translated by Harold Livermore. Austin: University of Texas Press.

de la Vera Cruz, Pablo. 1987. "Cambio en el Patrón de Asentamiento y el Uso y Abandono de los Andenes en Cabanaconde, Valle de Colca, Peru." In Denevan, Mathewson, and Knapp 1987, 89–128.

Denevan, William. 1987. "Terrace Abandonment in the Colca Valley, Peru." In Denevan, Mathewson, and Knapp 1987, 1–44.

Denevan, William, Kent Mathewson, and Gregory Knapp, eds. 1987. *Pre-Hispanic Agricultural Fields in the Andean Region, Part I.* BAR International Series, 359(i). Oxford: British Archaeological Reports.

Dillehay, Thomas. 1989. *Monte Verde: A Late Pleistocene Settlement in Chile,* vol. 1: *Paleoenvironment and Site Context.* Smithsonian Series in Archaeological Inquiry. Washington, DC: Smithsonian Institution Press.

———. 1992. "Widening the Socio-Economic Foundations of Andean Civilization: Proto-Types of Early Monumental Architecture." *Andean Past* 3:55–66.

———. 1997. *Monte Verde: A Late Pleistocene Settlement in Chile.* vol. 2: *The Archaeological Context and Interpretation.* Washington, DC: Smithsonian Institution Press.

———. 2001. "Town and Country in Late Moche Times: A View from Two Northern Valleys." In Pillsbury 2001, 259–283.

———. 2008. "Profiles in Pleistocene History." In Silverman and Isbell 2008, 29–43.

———, ed. 2011a. *From Farming to Foraging in the Andes: New Perspectives on Food Production and Social Organization.* New York: Cambridge University Press.

———. 2011b. "Conclusions." In Dillehay 2011a, 285–310.

Dillehay, Thomas, Duccio Bonavia, Steven Goodbred, Mario Pino, Victor Vasquez, Teresa Rosales Tham, William Conklin, Jeff Splitstoser, Delores Piperno, José Iriarte, Alexander Grobman, Gerson Levi-Lazzaris, Daniel Moreira, Marilaura López, Tiffiny Tung, Anne Titelbaum, John Verano, James Adovasio, Linda Scott Cummings, Phillipe Bearéz, Elise Dufour, Olivier Tombret, Michael Ramirez, Rachel Beavins, Larisa DeSantis, Isabel Rey, Philip Mink, Greg Maggard, and Teresa Franco. 2012. "Chronology, Mound-Building and Environment at Huaca Prieta, Coastal Peru, from 13700 to 4000 Years Ago." *Antiquity* 86: 48–70.

Dillehay, Thomas, and Alan Kolata. 2004. "Long-Term Human Response to Uncertain Environmental Conditions in the Andes." *Proceedings of the National Academy of Sciences* 101(12): 4325–4330.

Dillehay, Thomas, Gregory Maggard, Jack Rossen, and Kary Stackelbeck. 2011. "Technologies and Material Culture." In Dillehay 2011a, 205–228.

Dillehay, Thomas, Claudio Ramírez, Mario Pino, Meghan B. Collins, James Rossen, and J.D. Pino-Navarro. 2008. "Monte Verde: Seaweed, Food, Medicine, and the Peopling of South America." *Science* 320: 784–786.

Dillehay, Thomas, Jack Rossen, Thomas C. Andres, and David E. Williams. 2007. "Preceramic Adoption of Peanut, Squash, and Cotton in Northern Peru." *Science* 316(5833): 1890–1893.

Dillehay, Thomas, Jack Rossen, Greg Maggard, Kary Stackelbeck, and Patricia Netherly. 2003. "Localization and Possible Social Aggregation in the Late Pleistocene and Early Holocene on the North Coast of Perú." *Quaternary International* 109–110: 3–11.

Dillehay, Thomas, Jack Rossen, and Patricia Netherly. 1999. "Middle Preceramic Household, Ritual, and Technology in Northern Peru." *Chungará* 30(2): 111–124.

Donnan, Christopher. 1976. *Moche Art and Iconography.* UCLA Latin American Studies No. 33. Los Angeles: UCLA Latin American Center.

———. 1978. *Moche Art of Peru: Pre-Columbian Symbolic Communication.* Los Angeles: Museum of Cultural History.

———. 1990. "An Assessment of the Validity of the Naymlap Dynasty." In *The Northern Dynasties: Kingship and Statecraft in Chimor,* edited by Michael Moseley and Alana Cordy-Collins, 243–274. Washington, DC: Dumbarton Oaks Research Library and Collection.

———. 2001. "Moche Ceramic Portraits." In Pillsbury 2001, 127–40.

———. 2010. "Moche State Religion. A Unifying Force in Moche Political Organization." In Quilter and Castillo Butters 2010, 47–69.

Donnan, Christopher, and Luis Jaime Castillo Butters. 1992. "Finding the Tomb of a Moche Priestess." *Archaeology* 45: 38–42.

Donnan, Christopher, and Guillermo Cock, eds. 1986. *The Pacatnamú Papers.* Vol. 1. Los Angeles: Museum of Cultural History, University of California.

———, eds. 1997. *The Pacatnamú Papers,* vol. 2: *The Moche Occupation.* Los Angeles: Fowler Museum of Cultural History, University of California.

Donnan, Christopher, and Sharon Donnan. 1997. "Moche Textiles from Pacatnamú." In *The Pacatnamú Papers,* Vol. 2, edited by Christopher Donnan and Guillermo Cock, 215–242. Los

Angeles: Fowler Museum of Cultural History, University of California.

Donnan, Christopher, and Carol Mackey. 1978. *Ancient Burial Patterns of the Moche Valley, Peru*. Austin: University of Texas Press.

Druc, Isabelle. 1998. *Ceramic Production and Distribution in the Chavín Sphere of Influence*. British Archaeological Reports International Series No. 731. London: J. and E. Hedges.

Dulanto, Jalh. 2008. "Between Horizons: Diverse Configurations of Society and Power in the Late Pre-Hispanic Central Andes." In Silverman and Isbell 2008, 761–782.

Duviols, Pierre. 1980. "La Guerra entre el Cuzco y los Chankas: Historia o Mito?" *Revista de la Universidad Complutense* 28(117): 363–372.

Dwyer, Edward. 1971. "The Early Inca Occupation of the Valley of Cuzco, Peru." PhD diss., University of California, Berkeley.

Earle, Timothy, Terence D'Altroy, Christine Hastorf, Catherine Scott, Cathy Costin, Glenn Russell, and Elsie Sandefur. 1983. *Archaeological Field Research in the Upper Mantaro, Peru, 1982–1983: Investigations of Inka Expansion and Exchange*. Institute of Archaeology Monograph 28, Los Angeles: University of California.

Edwards, Matthew. 2010. "Archaeological Investigations at Pataraya: A Wari Outpost in the Nazca Valley of Southern Peru." PhD diss., University of California, Santa Barbara.

Eeckhout, Peter. 2003. "Ancient Monuments and Patterns of Power at Pachacamac, Central Coast of Peru." *Beitrage zur Allgemeine und Vorleichenden Archaeologie* 23: 139–182.

———. 2004. "La Sombra de Ychsma: Ensayo Introductorio Sobre la Arqueología de la Costa Central del Perú en los Períodos Tardíos." In *Arqueología de La Costa Central del Peru en los Períodos Tardíos*, edited by Peter. Eeckhout, 403–424. Special issue of the *Bulletin de l'Institut Français d'Etudes Andines* 33(3).

Engel, Frédéric. 1957. "Sites et Établissements Sans Céramique de la Côte Péruvienne." *Journal de la Société des Américanistes* 46: 67–156.

———. 1973. "New Facts about Pre-Columbian Life in the Andean Lomas." *Current Anthropology* 14(3): 271–280.

Erickson, Clark. 1985. "Applications of Prehistoric Andean Technology: Experiments in Raised Field Agriculture, Huatta, Lake Titicaca." In *Prehistoric Intensive Agriculture in the Tropics*, edited by Ian Farrington. BAR International Series, 232(1). Oxford: British Archaeological Press.

———. 1999. "Neo-Environmental Determinism and Agrarian 'Collapse' in Andean Prehistory." *Antiquity* 73: 634–642.

Erickson, David, Bruce Smith, Andrew Clarke, Daniel Sandweiss, and Noreen Tuross. 2005. "An Asian Origin for a 10,000-Year-Old Domesticated Plant in the Americas." *Proceedings of the National Academy of Sciences of the United States of America* 102(51): 18315–18320.

Espinoza, Pedro. 2010. "Arquitectura y Procesos Sociales Tardíos en Maranga, Valley Bajo de Rímac, Lima." In Romero Velarde and Svendsen 2010, 263–309.

Espinoza Soriano, Waldemar, ed. 1964. *Visita Hecha a la Provincia de Chucuito por Garci Díez de San Miguel en el Año 1567*. Lima: Casa de la Cultura.

———. 1970. "Los Mitmas Yungas de Collique en Cajamarca, Siglos XV, XVI, y XVII." *Revista del Museo Nacional* 36(1969–1970): 9–57.

Estupiñán Viteri, Tamara. 2003. *Tras las Huellas de Rumiñahui*. Quito: Auspicio del Banco General Rumiñahui.

Feldman, Robert. 1987. "Architectural Evidence for the Development of Nonegalitarian Social Systems in Coastal Peru." In Haas, Pozorski, and Pozorski 1987, 9–14.

———. 1992. "Preceramic Architecture and Subsistence Traditions." *Andean Past* 3: 67–86.

———. 2009. "Talking Dogs and New Clothes, or the Maritime Hypothesis Revisited." In Marcus and Williams 2009, 89–98.

Finucane, Brian. 2009. "Maize and Socio-Political Complexity in the Ayacucho Valley, Peru." *Current Anthropology* 50: 535–545.

Finucane, Brian, Patricio Maita Agurto, and William Isbell. 2006. "Human and Animal Diet at Conchopata, Peru: Stable Isotope Evidence for Maize Agriculture and Animal Management Practices during the Middle Horizon." *Journal of Archaeological Science* 33: 1766–1776.

Finucane, Brian, J. Ernesto Valdez, Ismael Pérez Calderon, Cirilo Vivanco Pomacanchari, Lidio Valdez, and Tamsin O'Connell. 2007. "The End of Empire: New Radiocarbon Dates from the Ayacucho Valley and Their Implications for the Collapse of the Wari State." *Radiocarbon* 49(2): 579–592.

Fladmark, Knut. 1978. "The Feasibility of the Northwest Coast as a Migration Route for Early Man." In *Early Man in America from a Circum-Pacific Perspective*, edited by Alan Lyle Bryan, 19–28. Occasional Papers of the Department of Anthropology 1, University of Alberta. Edmonton, Canada: Archaeological Researches International.

Flannery, Kent. 1972. "The Cultural Evolution of Civilization." *Annual Review of Ecology and Systematics* 3: 399–426.

Fontugne, Michel, Pierre Usselmann, Danièle Lavallée, Michèle Julien, and Christine Hatté. 1999. "El Niño Variability in the Coastal Desert of Southern Peru during the Mid-Holocene." *Quaternary Research* 52: 171–179.

Fogel, Heidy. 1993. "Settlements in Time: A Study of Social and Political Development during the Gallinazo Occupation of the North Coast of Peru." PhD diss., Yale University.

Franco Jordan, Régulo, Cesar Gálvez Mora, and Segundo Vásquez Sánchez.1994. "Arquitectura y Decoración Mochica en la Huaca Cao Viejo, Complejo El Brujo: Resultados Preliminares." In *Moche: Propuestas y Perspectivas: Actas del Primer Coloquio sobre la Cultura Moche,* edited by Santiago Uceda and Elias Mujica, 147–180. Lima: Asociación Peruana para el Fomento de las Ciencias Sociales.

———. 2010. "Moche Power and Ideology at the El Brujo Complex and in the Chicama Valley." In Quilter and Castillo Butters 2010, 110–131.

Frye, Kirk, and Edmundo de la Vega. 2005. "The Altiplano Period in the Titicaca Basin." In Stanish, Cohen, and Aldenderfer 2005, 173–184.

Gálvez Mora, Cesar. 1992. "Evaluación de Evidencias Paijanenses en Tres Zonas de Ascope, Valle de Chicama." In *Revista del Museo de Arqueología* [Trujillo] No.3: 31–50.

Gálvez Mora, Cesar, and Jesús Briceño Rosario. 2001. "The Moche in the Chicama Valley." In Pillsbury 2001, 141–158.

Geisso, Martin. 2003. "Stone Tool Production in the Tiwanaku Heartland." In Kolata 2003a, 363–383.

Ghezzi, Ivan. 2006. "Religious Warfare at Chankillo." In Isbell and Silverman 2006, 67–87.

Ghezzi, Ivan, and Clive Ruggles. 2007. "Chankillo: A 2300-Year-Old Solar Observatory in Coastal Peru." *Science* 315(5816): 1239–1243.

Glowacki, Mary. 1996. "The Wari Occupation of the Southern Highlands of Peru: A Ceramic Perspective from the Site of Pikillacta." PhD diss., Brandeis University.

———. 2002. "The Huaro Archaeological Site Complex: Rethinking the Huari Occupation of Cuzco." In Isbell and Silverman 2002, 267–286.

Glowacki, Mary, and Michael Malpass. 2003. "Water, Huacas, and Ancestor Worship: Traces of a Sacred Wari Landscape." *Latin American Antiquity* 14(4): 431–448.

Glowacki, Mary, and Gordon McEwan. 2001. "Pikillacta, Huaro y la Gran Región del Cuzco: Nuevas Interpretaciones de la Ocupación Wari de la Sierra Sur." In *Huari y Tiwanaku: Modelos vs. Evidencias. Segunda Parte,* edited by Peter Kaulicke and William H. Isbell. Special issue of *Boletín de Arqueología PUCP* no. 5: 31–49.

Goldstein, Paul. 2005. *Andean Diaspora: The Tiwanaku Colonies and the Origins of South American Empire.* Gainesville: University Press of Florida.

———. 2009. "Diasporas within the Ancient State: Tiwanaku as Ayllus in Motion." In Marcus and Williams 2009, 277–302.

Grieder, Terence. 1978. *The Art and Archaeology of Pashash.* Austin: University of Texas Press.

Greider, Terence, and Alberto Bueno Mendoza. 1985. "Ceremonial Architecture at La Galgada." In *Early Ceremonial Architecture in the Andes,* edited by Christopher Donnan, 93–109. Washington, DC: Dumbarton Oaks Research Library and Collection.

Grieder, Terence, Alberto Bueno Mendoza, C. Earle Smith Jr., and Robert Molina. 1988. *La Galgada, Perú: A Preceramic Culture in Transition.* Austin: University of Texas Press.

Grosboll, Sue. 1993. ". . . And He Said in the Time of the Ynga, They Paid Tribute and Served the Ynga." In Malpass 1993, 44–76.

Grossman, Joel. 1972. "An Ancient Gold Worker's Tool Kit: The Earliest Metal Technology in Peru." *Archaeology* 25(4): 270–275.

Guaman Poma de Ayala, Felipe. (1584–1615) 1980. *El Primer Corónica y Buen Gobierno.* Edited by John Murra, Rolena Adorno, and Jorge Urioste. Translated by Jorge Urioste. Mexico City: Siglo Ventiuno.

Guffroy, Jean. 1989. "Un Centro Ceremonial Formativo en el Alto Piura." *Bulletin de l'Institut Francais d'Etudes Andines* 18(2): 161–208.

Haas, Jonathan, and Winifred Creamer. 2004. "Cultural Transformations in the Central Andean Late Archaic." In Silverman 2004a, 35–50.

Haas, Jonathan, Shelia Pozorski, and Thomas Pozorski, eds. 1987. *The Origins and Development of the Andean State.* Cambridge, UK: Cambridge University Press.

Haeberli, Joerg. 2006. "Where and When Did the Nasca Proliferous Style Emerge?" In Isbell and Silverman 2006, 401–434.

Hastings, Charles, and Michael Moseley. 1975. "The Adobes of Huaca del Sol and Huaca de la Luna." *American Antiquity* 40(2): 196–203.

Hastorf, Christine, ed. 1999. *Early Settlement at Chiripa, Bolivia: Research of the Taraco Archaeological Project.* Contributions of the University of California Archaeological Research Facility No. 57. Berkeley: Archaeological Research Facility, University of California.

———. 2005. "The Upper (Middle and Late) Formative in the Titicaca Region." In Stanish, Cohen, and Aldenderfer 2005, 65–94.

———. 2008. "The Formative Period in the Titicaca Basin." In Silverman and Isbell 2008, 545–562.

Haun, Susan, and Guillermo Cock Carrasco. 2010. "A Bioarchaelogical Approach to the Search for Mitmaqkuna." In Malpass and Alconini 2010, 193–220.

Hayden, Brian. 1995. "Pathways to Power: Principles for Creating Socioeconomic Inequalities." In *Foundations of Social Inequality,* edited by Douglas T. Price and Gary Feinman, 15–86. New York: Plenum.

Heffernan, Kenneth. 1989. "Limatambo in Late Prehistory: Landscape Archaeology and Documentary Images of Inca

Presence in the Periphery of Cuzco." PhD diss., Australian National University, Canberra.

Hemming, John. 1970. *The Conquest of the Incas*. London: Macmillan.

Heyerdahl, Thor, Daniel Sandweiss, and Alfredo Narváez. 1995. *The Pyramids of Túcume: The Quest for Peru's Forgotten City*. New York: Thames and Hudson.

Hogg, Alan, Quan Hua, Paul Blackwell, Mu Niu, Caitlin Buck, Thomas Guilderson, Timothy Heaton, Johnathan Palmer, Paula Reimer, Ron Reimer, Christian Turney, and Susan Zimmerman. 2013. "SHCal13 Southern Hemisphere Calibration, 0–50,000 Years Cal BP" *Radiocarbon* 55(4): 1889–1903.

Hyslop, John. 1984. *The Inka Road System*. New York: Academic Press.

———. 1990. *Inka Settlement Planning*. Austin: University of Texas Press.

Isbell, Billie Jean. 1978. *To Defend Ourselves: Ecology and Ritual in an Andean Village*. Latin American Monographs No. 47. Austin: Institute of Latin American Studies, University of Texas.

Isbell, William. 1977. *The Rural Foundation for Urbanism. Economic and Stylistic Interaction between Rural and Urban Communities in Eighth-Century Peru*. Illinois Studies in Anthropology No. 10. Urbana: Uiversity of Illinois Press.

———. 1983. "Shared Ideology and Parallel Political Development: Huari and Tiwanaku." In *Investigations of the Andean Past: Papers from the First Annual Northeast Conference on Andean Archaeology and Ethnohistory,* edited by Daniel Sandweiss, 186–208. Ithaca: Cornell University Latin American Studies Program.

———. 1989. "Honcopampa: Was It a Huari Administrative Centre?" In *The Nature of Wari: A Reappraisal of the Middle Horizon Period in Peru,* edited by R. Michael Czwarno, Frank Meddens, and Alexandra Morgan. BAR International Series 525. Oxford: British Archaeological Reports.

———. 1991. "Conclusion: Huari Administration and the Orthogonal Cellular Architectural Horizon." In Isbell and McEwan 1991, 293–316.

———. 1997a. *Mummies and Mortuary Monuments: A Postprocessual Prehistory of Central Andean Social Organization*. Austin: University of Texas Press.

———. 1997b. "Reconstructing Huari: A Cultural Chronology of the Capital City." In *Emergence and Change in Early Urban Societies*, edited by Linda Manzanilla, 181–228. New York: Plenum.

———. 2004. "Mortuary Preferences: A Wari Culture Case Study from Middle Horizon Peru." *Latin American Antiquity* 15(1): 3–32.

———. 2008. "Wari and Tiwanaku: International Identities in the Central Andean Middle Horizon." In Silverman and Isbell 2008, 731–759.

Isbell, William, Christine Brewster-Wray, and Lynda Spickard. 1991. "Architecture and Spatial Organization at Huari." In Isbell and McEwan 1991, 19–54.

Isbell, William, and Anita Cook. 2002. "A New Perspective on Conchopata and the Andean Middle Horizon." In Silverman and Isbell 2002, 249–305.

Isbell, William, and Gordon McEwan, eds. 1991. *Huari Administrative Structure: Prehistoric Monumental Architecture and State Government*. Washington, DC: Dumbarton Oaks Research Library and Collection.

Isbell, William, Jean-Pierre Protzen, and Stella Nair. 2002. "The Gateways of Tiwanaku: Symbols or Passages?" In Silverman and Isbell 2002, 189–224.

Isbell, William, and Katharina J. Schreiber. 1978. "Was Huari a State?" *American Antiquity* 43(3): 372–389.

Isbell, William, and Helaine Silverman, eds. 2002. *Andean Archaeology I: Variations in Sociopolitical Organization*. New York: Kluwer Academic/Plenum.

———, eds. 2006. *Andean Archaeology III: North and South*. New York: Springer.

Isbell, William, and Alexei Vranich. 2004. "Experiencing the Cities of Wari and Tiwanaku." In Silverman 2004a, 167–182.

Isla, Elizabeth, and Daniel Guerrero. 1987. "Socos: Un Sitio Wari en el Valle de Chillón." *Gaceta Arqueológica Andina* 14(4): 23–28.

Isla, Johny. 2001. "Wari en Palpa y Nasca: Perspectivas desde el Punto de Vista Funerario." In *Huari y Tiwanaku: Modelos vs. Evidencias. Segunda Parte,* edited by Peter Kaulicke and William H. Isbell. Special issue of *Boletín de Arqueología PUCP* no. 5: 555–583.

Isla, Johny, and Markus Reindel. 2006. "Burial Patterns and Sociopolitical Organization in Nasca 5 Society." In Isbell and Silverman 2006, 374–400.

Izumi, Seiichi, Pedro Cuculiza, and Chiaki Kano. 1972. Excavations at Shillacoto, Huánuco, Peru. *The University Museum Bulletin No. 3*. Tokyo: University of Tokyo.

Izumi, Seiichi, and Toshihiko Sono. 1963. *Andes 2: Excavations at Kotosh, Peru, 1960*. Tokyo: Kadokawa Publishing Company.

Jackson, Donald, César Méndez, Roxana Seguel, Antonio Maldonado, and Gabriel Vargas. 2007. "Initial Occupation of the Pacific Coast of Chile during Late Pleistocene Times." *Current Anthropology* 48(5): 725–731.

Janusek, John. 2003. "Vessels, Time, and Society: Toward a Chronology of Ceramic Style in the Tiwanaku Heartland." In Kolata 2003a, 264–295.

———. 2004a. "Household and City in Tiwanaku." In Silverman 2004a, 183–208.

———. 2004b. *Identity and Power in the Ancient Andes: Tiwanaku Cities through Time*. New York: Routledge.

———. 2005. "Collapse as Cultural Revolution: Power and Identity in the Tiwanaku to Pacajes Transition." In *Foundations of*

Power in the Prehispanic Andes, edited by Kevin Vaughn, Dennis Ogburn, and Christina Conlee, 175–210. Archaeological Papers of the American Anthropological Association No. 14. Arlington, VA: American Anthropological Association.

———. 2008. *Ancient Tiwanaku.* Case Studies in Early Societies. New York: Cambridge University Press.

Jennings, Justin. 2006. "Understanding Middle Horizon Peru: Hermeneutic Spirals, Interpretive Traditions, and Wari Administrative Centers." *Latin American Antiquity* 17(3): 265–286.

———. 2010. "Becoming Wari: Globalization and the Role of the Wari State in the Cotahuasi Valley of Southern Peru." In *Beyond Wari Walls: Regional Perspectives on Middle Horizon Peru,* edited by Justin Jennings, 37–56. Albuquerque: University of New Mexico Press.

Jennings, Justin, and Nathan Craig. 2001. "Politywide Analysis and Imperial Political Economy: The Relationship between Valley Political Complexity and Administrative Centers in the Wari Empire of the Central Andes." *Journal of Anthropological Archaeology* 20(4): 479–502.

Jennings, Justin, and Willy Yépez. 2001. "Collota, Netahaha y el Desarollo del Poder Wari en el Valle de Cotahuasi, Arequipa, Peru." In *Huari y Tiwanaku: Modelos vs. Evidencias. Segunda Parte,* edited by Peter Kaulicke and William H. Isbell. Special issue of *Boletín de Arqueología PUCP* no. 5: 13–29.

Johnson, David, Donald Proulx, and Stephen Bourget. 2006. "The Correlation between Geoglyphs and Subterranean Water Resources in the Río Grande de Nazca Drainage." In Isbell and Silverman 2006, 307–332.

Jolie, Edward A., Thomas F. Lynch, Phil R. Geib, and James M. Adovasio. 2011. "Cordage, Textiles, and the Late Pleistocene Peopling of the Andes." *Current Anthropology* 52(2): 285–296.

Julien, Catherine. 1993. "Finding a Fit: Archaeology and Ethnohistory of the Incas." In Malpass 1993, 177–233.

———. 2000. *Reading Inca History.* Iowa City: University of Iowa Press.

Julien, Daniel. 1993. "Late Pre-Inkaic Ethnic Groups in Highland Peru: An Archaeological-Ethnohistorical Model of the Political Geography of the Cajamarca Region." *Latin American Antiquity* 4(3): 246–273.

Kaulicke, Peter. 1993. "Evidencias Paleoclimáticas en Asentamientos del Alto Piura durante el Período Intermedio Temprano." In *Registro de Fenómeno El Niño y de Eventos ENSO en América del Sur,* edited by José Macharé and Luc Ortlieb, 283–311. Lima: *Bulletin de l'Institut Francais d'Etudes Andines* 22.

———. 1994. *Los Origines de la Civilizacion Andina. Historia General del Perú,* vol. 1: *Arqueología del Perú.* Lima: Editorial Brasa.

Keefer, David, Susan DeFrance, Michael Moseley, James Richardson III, Dennis Satterlee, and Amy Day-Lewis. 1998. "Early Maritime Economy and El Niño Events at Quebrada Tacahuay, Peru." *Science* 281: 1833–1835.

Kembel, Silvia. 2001. "Archaeological Sequence and Chronology at Chavín de Huantar, Peru." PhD diss., Stanford University.

———. 2008. "The Architecture of the Monumental Center of Chavín de Huantar: Sequence Transformations, and Chronology." In Conklin and Quilter 2008, 35–81.

Kembel, Silvia Rodriguez, and Herbert Haas. 2013. "Radiocarbon Dates from the Monumental Architecture at Chavín de Huántar, Peru." *Journal of Archaeological Method and Theory* 22(2): 345–427.

Kembel, Silvia, and John Rick. 2004. "Building Authority at Chavín de Huantar: Models of Social Organization and Development in the Initial Period and Early Horizon." In Silverman 2004a, 77–115.

Klink, Cynthia. 2005. "Archaic Period Research in the Rio Huenque Valley, Peru." In Stanish, Cohen, and Aldenderfer 2005, 13–24.

Klink, Cynthia, and Mark Aldenderfer. 2005. "A Projectile Point Chronology for the South-Central Andean Highlands." In Stanish, Cohen, and Aldenderfer 2005, 25–54.

Klymyshyn, A. Ulana. 1982. "Elite Compounds in Chan Chan." In Moseley and Day 1982, 119–143.

———. 1987. The Development of Chimú Administration in Chan Chan." In Haas, Pozorski, and Pozorski 1987, 97–110.

Knobloch, Patricia. 1991. "Stylistic Date of Ceramics from the Huari Centers." In Isbell and McEwan 1991, 247–258.

Knudson, Kelly, T. Douglas Price, Jane E. Buikstra, and Deborah E. Blom. 2004. "The Use of Strontium Isotope Analysis to Investigate Tiwanaku Migration and Mortuary Ritual in Bolivia and Peru." *Archaeometry* 46(1): 5–18.

Kolar, Miriam, with John Rick, Perry Cook, and Jonathan Abel. 2012. "Ancient Pututus Contextualized: Integrative Archaeoacoustics at Chavín de Huántar, Peru." In *Flower World: Music Archaeology of the Americas,* edited by Matthias Stöckli and Arnt Adje Both, 223–254. Berlin: Ekho Verlag.

Kolata, Alan. 1982. "Chronology and Settlement Growth at Chan Chan." In *Chan Chan Andean Desert City,* edited by Michael Moseley and Kent Day, 67–85. Albuquerque: University of New Mexico Press.

———. 1990. "The Urban Concept of Chan Chan." In Moseley and Cordy-Collins 1990, 107–144.

———. 1993. *The Tiwanaku: Portrait of an Andean Civilization.* Cambridge, MA: Blackwell.

———, ed. 1996. *Tiwanaku and Its Hinterland: Archaeology and Paleoecology of an Andean Civilization,* vol. 1: *Agroecology and Paleoecology of an Andean Civilization.* Washington, DC: Smithsonian Institution Press.

———, ed. 2003a. *Tiwanaku and Its Hinterland: Archaeology and Paleoecology of an Andean Civilization,* vol. 2: *Urban and Rural Archaeology.* Washington, DC: Smithsonian Institution Press.

———. 2003b. "Tiwanaku Ceremonial Architecture and Urban Organization." In Kolata 2003a, 175–201.

———. 2013. *Ancient Inca*. New York: Cambridge University Press.

Kolata, Alan, Michael Binford, Mark Brenner, John Janusek, and Charles Ortloff. 2000. "Environmental Thresholds and the Empirical Reality of State Collapse: A Response to Erickson (1999)." *Antiquity* 74: 424–426.

Kolata, Alan, and Charles Ortloff. 1996. "Agroecological Perspectives on the Decline of the Tiwanaku State." In Kolata 1996, 181–201.

Kolata, Alan, Oswaldo Rivera, Juan Carlos Ramírez, and Evelyn Gemio. 1996. "Rehabilitating Raised-Field Agriculture in the Southern Lake Titicaca Basin of Bolivia: Theory, Practice, and Results." In Kolata 1996, 203–230.

Krzanowski, Andrzej. 1991a. "Chancay: Una Cultura Desconocida?" In *Estudios sobre la Cultura Chancay, Perú*, edited by Andrzej Krzanowski, 19–35. Krakow: Uniwersytet Jagiellonski.

———. 1991b. "Observaciones sobre la Arquitectura y Patrón de Asentamiento de la Cultura Chancay." In *Estudios sobre la Cultura Chancay, Perú*, edited by Andzej Krzanowski, 37–56. Krakow: Uniwersytet Jagiellonski.

Lambert, Patricia, Celeste Marie Gagnon, Brian Billman, M. Anne Katzenberg, José Carcelén, and Robert Tykot. 2012. "Bone Chemistry at Cerro Oreja: A Stable Isotope Perspective on a Regional Economy in the the Moche Valley, Peru during the Early Intermediate Period." *Latin American Antiquity* 23(2): 144–166.

Lanning, Edward. 1967. *Peru before the Incas*. Englewood Cliffs: Prentice-Hall.

Larco Hoyle, Rafael. 1948. *Cronología Arqueológica del Norte del Perú*. Buenos Aires: Sociedad Geográfica Americana.

Lathrap, Donald. 1973. "Gifts of the Cayman: Some Thoughts on the Subsistence Base of Chavín." In *Variation in Anthropology: Essays in Honor of John C. McGregor*, edited by Donald Lathrap and Jody Douglas, 91–103. Urbana: Illinois Archaeological Survey.

———. 1977. "Our Father the Cayman, Our Mother the Gourd: Spinden Revisited, or a Unitary Model for the Emergence of Agriculture in the New World." In *Origins of Agriculture*, edited by Charles Reed, 713–751. The Hague: Mouton.

Lathrap, Donald, Donald Collier, and Helen Chandra. 1975. *Ancient Ecuador—Culture, Clay and Creativity 3000–300 B.C.* Chicago: Field Museum of Natural History.

Lau, George. 2002a. "The Ancient Community of Chinchawas: Economy and Ceremony in the North Highlands of Peru." PhD diss., Yale University.

———. 2002b. "Feasting and Ancestor Veneration at Chinchawas, North Highlands of Ancash, Peru." *Latin American Antiquity* 13: 279–304.

———. 2006. "Northern Exposures: Recuay-Cajamarca Boundaries and Interaction." In Isbell and Silverman 2006, 143–170.

———. 2008. "Ancestor Images in the Andes." In Silverman and Isbell 2008, 1027–1045.

Lavallée, Daniele. 1979. "Telarmachay. Campamento de Pastores en la Puna de Junín del Período Formativo." *Revista del Museo Nacional* 43: 61–109.

Lavallée, Daniele, Michele Julien, Philippe Béarez, Pierre Usselmann, Michel Fortugne, and Aldo Bolaños. 1999. "Pescadores-Recolectores Arcaicos del Extremo Sur Peruano: Excavaciones en la Quebrada de los Burros (Tacna, Peru) Primeros Resultados 1995–1997." *Bulletin de l'Institut Français d'Etúdes Andines* 28: 13–52.

Lechtman, Heather. 1980. "The Central Andes: Metallurgy without Iron." In *The Coming of the Age of Iron*, edited by Theodore Wertime and James Muhly, 267–334. New Haven: Yale University Press.

———. 2003. "Tiwanaku Period (Middle Horizon) Bronze Metallurgy in the Lake Titicaca Basin." In Kolata 2003a, vol. 2, 404–431.

Lemon, Roy, and Charles Churcher. 1961. "Pleistocene Geology and Paleontology of the Talara Region, Northwest Peru." *American Journal of Science* 259(6): 410–429.

Leoni, Juan. 2006. "Ritual and Society in Early Intermediate Period Ayacucho: A View from the Site of Ñawimpukyo." In Isbell and Silverman 2006, 279–304.

Lettau, Heinz, and Katharina Lettau. 1978. *Exploring the World's Driest Climate*. Institute for Environmental Studies Report 101. Madison: Center for Climatic Research, Institute for Environmental Studies, University of Wisconsin-Madison.

Lippi, Ronald. 2004. *Tropical Forest Archaeology in Western Pichincha, Ecuador*. Case Studies in Archaeology. Belmont, CA: Thomson/Wadsworth.

Lippi, Ronald, and Alejandra Gudiño. 2010. "Inkas and Yumbos at Palmitopamba in Northwestern Ecuador." In Malpass and Alconini 2010, 260–278.

Llagostera Martinez, Agustín. 1979. "9,700 Years of Maritime Subsistence on the Pacific: An Analysis by Means of Bio-indicators in the North of Chile." *American Antiquity* 44(2): 309–324.

Lockard, Gregory. 2008. "A New View of Galindo: Results of the Galindo Archaeological Project." In *Arqueología Mochica: Nuevos Enfoques*, edited by Luis Jaime Castillo Butters, Hélene Berniere, Gregory Lockard, and Julio Rucabaldo, 275–291. Lima: Institut Français d'Etudes Andines and Fondo Editorial de la Pontificia Universidad Católica del Peru.

———. 2009. "The Occupational History of Galindo, Moche Valley, Peru." *Latin American Antiquity* 20(2): 279–302.

López Hurtado, Enrique. 2010. "Pachacamac y Panquilma: Relaciones de Poder en la Costa Central durante los Períodos Tardíos." In Romero Velarde and Svendsen 2010, 311–326.

Lorenz, Bernhard, and Peter Fuchs. 2009. "Sechin Bajo: The Origin of Sunken Circular Courts in Coastal Peru?" Paper presented at the 28th Northeast Conference on Andean and Amazonian Archaeology, New Paltz, NY, October 10–11.

Lozada, Maria, Jane Buikstra, Gordon Rakita, and Jane Wheeler. 2009. "Camelid Herders: The Forgotten Specialists in the Coastal Señorío of Chiribaya, Southern Peru." In Marcus and Williams 2009, 351–364.

Lumbreras, Luis Guillermo. 1960. "La Cultura de Wari, Ayacucho." *Etnología y Arqueología* 1: 130–226.

———. 1974. *The Peoples and Cultures of Ancient Peru*. Translated by Betty Meggars. Washington, DC: Smithsonian Institution Press.

———. 1993. *Chavín de Huántar: Excavaciones en la Galería de las Ofrendas*. Materialien zur Allgemeinen und Vergleichenden Archäologie No. 51. Mainz am Rhein: Philipp von Zabern.

Lynch, Thomas. 1971. "Preceramic Transhumance in the Callejón de Huaylas, Peru." *American Antiquity* 36(2): 139–148.

———. 1974. "The Antiquity of Man in South America." *Quaternary Research* 4: 356–377.

———, ed. 1980. *Guitarerro Cave. Early Man in the Andes*. New York: Academic Press.

———. 1983. "The Paleo-Indians." In *Ancient South Americans*, edited by Jesse Jennings, 87–138. San Francisco: Freeman.

Mackey, Carol. 1987. "Chimú Administration in the Provinces." In Haas, Pozorski, and Pozorski 1987, 121–129.

———. 2006. "Elite Residences at Farfán: A Comparison of the Chimú and Inca Occupations." In *Palaces and Power in the Americas: From Peru to the Northwest Coast*, edited by Jessica Joyce Christie and Patricia Joan Sarro, 313–352. Austin: University of Texas Press.

———. 2009. "Chimú Statecraft in the Provinces." In Marcus and Williams 2009, 325–349.

———. 2010. "The Sociological and Ideological Transformation of Farfán under Inka Rule." In Malpass and Alconini 2010, 221–259.

Mackey, Carol, and A. Ulana Klymyshyn. 1990. "The Southern Frontier of the Chimú Empire." In *The Northern Dynasties: Kingship and Statecraft in Chimor*, edited by Michael Moseley and Alana Cordy-Collins, 195–226. Washington, DC: Dumbarton Oaks Research Library and Collection.

MacNeish, Richard, Thomas Paterson, and David Browman. 1975. *The Central Peruvian Prehistoric Interaction Sphere*. Papers of the Robert S. Peabody Foundation for Archaeology No. 7. Andover, MA: Robert S. Peabody Foundation for Archaeology.

Maggard, Gregory. 2010. "Late Pleistocene Colonization and Regionalization in South America: Early Preceramic Fishtail and Paiján Settlement Patterns on the North Coast of Perú." PhD diss., University of Kentucky, Lexington.

Maggard, Gregory, and Thomas Dillehay. 2011. "El Palto Phase (13800–9800 BP)." In Dillehay 2011a, 77–94.

Makowski, Krzysztof. 2008. "Andean Urbanism." In Silverman and Isbell 2008, 633–657.

———. 2010. "Religion, Ethnic Identity, and Power in the Moche World: A View from the Frontiers." In Quilter and Castillo Butters 2010, 280–305.

Malpass, Michael. 1983. "The Paiján Occupation of the Casma Valley, Peru." In *Investigations of the Andean Past: Papers from the First Annual Northeast Conference on Andean Archaeology and Ethnohistory,* edited by Daniel Sandweiss, 1–20. Ithaca: Cornell University Latin American Studies Program.

———. 1985. "Two Preceramic and Formative Period Occupations in the Cordillera Negra, Peru." In *Recent Studies in Andean Archaeology and Ethnohistory,* edited by D. Peter Kvietok and Daniel Sandweiss, 15–40. Ithaca: Cornell University Latin American Studies Program.

———. 1987. "Prehistoric Agricultural Terracing at Chijra in the Colca Valley, Peru: Preliminary Report II." In Denevan, Mathewson, and Knapp 1987, 45–66.

———, ed. 1993. *Provincial Inca: Archaeological and Ethnohistorical Assessment of the Impact of the Inca State*. Iowa City: University of Iowa Press.

———. 2001. "Sonay: Un Centro Wari Celular Orthogonal en el Valle de Camaná." In *Huari y Tiwanaku: Modelos vs. Evidencias. Segunda Parte,* edited by Peter Kaulicke and William H. Isbell. Special issue of *Boletín de Arqueología PUCP* no. 5: 51–67.

Malpass, Michael, and Sonia Alconini, eds. 2010. *Distant Provinces in the Inka Empire: Toward a Deeper Understanding of Inka Imperialism*. Iowa City: University of Iowa Press.

Malpass, Michael, and Pablo de la Vera Cruz. n.d. "Occupation of the Lomas Zone East of Camaná, Southern Peru." Unpublished manuscript, 2001, Ithaca College.

Malpass, Michael, and Karen Stothert. 1992. "Evidence for Preceramic Houses and Household Organization in Western South America." *Andean Past* 3: 137–163.

Marcus, Joyce. 1987. *Late Intermediate Period Occupation at Cerro Azúl, Perú*. University of Michigan Museum of Anthropology Technical Report No. 20. Ann Arbor: University of Michigan Museum of Anthropology.

Massey, Sarah. 1991. "Social and Political Leadership in the Lower Ica Valley. Ocucaje Phases 8 and 9." In *Paracas Art & Architecture: Object and Context in South Coastal Peru,* edited by Anne Paul, 315–348. Iowa City: University of Iowa Press.

Matos Mendieta, Ramiro. 1959. "Los Wankas, Datos Históricos y Arqueológicos." *Actas y Trabajos del II Congreso Nacional de Historia del Perú: Epoca Prehispánica* 1: 187–210.

———. 1975. "Prehistoria y Ecología Humana en las Punas de Junín." *Revista del Museo Nacional* 41: 37–80.

———. 1978. "The Cultural and Ecological Context of the Mantaro Valley during the Formative Period." In *Advances in Andean Archaeology*, edited by David Browman, 307–325. The Hague: Mouton.

———. 2000. "The 'Señoríos' in the Sierra and Central Coast." In Minelli 2001, 37–48.

Matos Mendieta, Ramiro, Solvin Turpin, and Herbert Eling Jr., eds. 1986. *Andean Archaeology, Papers in Memory of Clifford Evans*. Monograph 27, Institute of Archaeology. Los Angeles: University of California.

McAndrews, Timothy L. 2005. *Wankarani Settlement Systems in Evolutionary Perspective: A Study in Early Village-Based Society and Long-Term Cultural Evolution in the South-Central Andean Altiplano*. University of Pittsburgh Memoirs in Latin American Archaeology No. 15. Pittsburgh: University of Pittsburgh Department of Anthropology.

McEwan, Gordon. 1991. "Investigations at the Pikillacta Site: A Provincial Huari Center in the Valley of Cuzco." In Isbell and McEwan 1991, 93–119.

———. 1996. "Archaeological Investigations at Pikillacta, a Wari Site in Peru." *Journal of Field Archaeology* 23(2): 169–186.

———, ed. 2005. *Pikillacta: The Wari Empire in Cuzco*. Iowa City: University of Iowa Press.

———. 2006. *The Incas: New Perspectives*. Santa Barbara: ABC-CLIO.

McEwan, Gordon, Melissa Chatfield, and Arminda Gibaja. 2002. "The Archaeology of Inca Origins: Excavations at Choquepukio, Cuzco, Peru." In Isbell and Silverman 2002, 287–302.

McInnis, Heather. 2006. "Middle Holocene Culture and Climate on the South Coast of Peru: Archaeological Investigation of the Pampa Colorada." PhD diss., University of Oregon.

Means, Philip. 1931. *Ancient Civilizations of the Andes*. New York: Charles Scribner and Sons.

Meggers, Betty Jane, Clifford Evans, and Emilio Estrada. 1965. *Early Formative Period of Coastal Ecuador: The Valdivia and Machalilla Phases*. Smithsonian Contributions to Anthropology 1. Washington, DC: Smithsonian Institution Press.

Meltzer, David, Donald Grayson, Gerardo Ardila, Alex Barker, Dena Dincauze, C. Vance Haynes, Francisco Mena, Lautaro Nuñez, and Thomas Dillehay. 1997. "On the Pleistocene Antiquity of Monte Verde, Southern Chile." *American Antiquity* 62(4): 659–663.

Mengoni Goñalons, Guillermo Luis. 2008. "Camelids in Ancient Andean Societies: A Review of the Zooarchaeological Evidence." *Quaternary International* 185(1): 59–68.

Menzel, Dorothy. 1959. "The Inca Occupation of the South Coast of Peru." *Southwestern Journal of Archaeology* 15(2): 125–142.

———. 1964. "Style and Time in the Middle Horizon." *Ñawpa Pacha* 2: 1–106.

———. 1968. "New Data on Middle Horizon Epoch 2A." *Ñawpa Pacha* 6: 47–114.

———. 1977. *The Archaeology of Ancient Peru and the Work of Max Uhle*. Berkeley: R. H. Lowie Museum of Anthropology, University of California.

Menzel, Dorothy, John Rowe, and Lawrence Dawson. 1964. *The Paracas Pottery of Ica; a Study in Style and Time*. University of California Publications in American Archaeology and Ethnology Vol. 50. Berkeley: University of California Press.

Millaire, Christopher. 2010. "Moche Political Expansionism as Viewed from Virú. Recent Archaeological Work in the Close Periphery of a Hegemonic City-State System." In Quilter and Castillo Butters 2010, 223–251.

Minelli, Laura Laurencich, ed. 2000. *The Inca World: The Development of Pre-Columbian Peru, A.D. 1000–1534*. Norman: University of Oklahoma Press.

Montané, Julio. 1968. "Paleo-Indian Remains from Laguna de Tagua Tagua, Central Chile." *Science* 161: 1137–1138.

Montesinos, Fernando de. 1882. *Ophir de España. Memorias Antiguas Historiales y Políticas del Peru*. Edited by Marcos Jiménez de la Espada. Madrid: Imprenta de Miguel Ginesta.

Moore, Jerry, and Carol Mackey. 2008. "The Chimú Empire." In Silverman and Isbell 2008, 783–807.

Morris, Craig. 1992. "Huánuco Pampa and Tunsukancha: Major and Minor Nodes in the Inka Storage Network." In *Inka Storage Systems*, edited by Terry LeVine, 151–175. Norman: University of Oklahoma Press.

———. 1998. "Inka Strategies of Incorporation and Governance." In *Archaic States*, edited by Gary Feinman and Joyce Marcus, 293–310. Santa Fe: School of American Research Press.

Morris, Craig, and Julián Idilio Santillana. 2007. "The Inka Transformation of the Chincha Capital." In Burger, Morris, and Matos Mendieta 2007, 135–164.

Morris, Craig, and Donald Thompson. 1985. *Huánuco Pampa: An Inka City and Its Hinterland*. London: Thames and Hudson.

Morris, Craig, and Adriana von Hagen. 1993. *The Inka Empire and Its Andean Origins*. New York: Abbeville Press.

Moseley, Michael. 1975. *The Maritime Foundations of Andean Civilization*. Menlo Park, CA: Cummings.

———. 1987. "Punctuated Equilibrium: Searching the Ancient Record for El Niño." *Quarterly Review of Anthropology* 8(3): 7–10.

———. 1992. "Maritime Foundations and Multilinear Evolution: Retrospect and Prospect." *Andean Past* 3: 5–42.

———. 1997. "Climate, Culture, and Punctuated Change: New Data, New Challenges." *Review of Archaeology* 18(1): 19–28.

———. 2001. *The Incas and Their Ancestors: The Archaeology of Peru.* Rev. ed. New York: Thames & Hudson.

Moseley, Michael, and Alana Cordy-Collins. 1990. *The Northern Dynasties: Kingship and Statecraft in Chimor.* Washington, DC: Dumbarton Oaks Research Library and Collection.

Moseley, Michael, and Kent C. Day, eds. 1982. *Chan Chan: Andean Desert City.* Albuquerque: University of New Mexico Press.

Moseley, Michael, and Eric Deeds. 1982. "The Land in Front of Chan Chan: Agrarian Expansion, Reform, and Collapse in the Moche Valley." In Moseley and Day 1982, 22–53.

Moseley, Michael, Robert Feldman, Paul Goldstein, and Luis Watanabe. 1991. "Colonies and Conquest: Tiahuanaco and Huari in Moquegua." In Isbell and McEwan 1991, 121–140.

Moseley, Michael, Donna Nash, Patrick Ryan Williams, Susan DeFrance, Ana Miranda, and Mario Ruales. 2005. "Burning Down the Brewery: Establishing and Evacuating an Ancient Imperial Colony at Cerro Baúl, Peru." *Proceedings of the National Academy of Sciences* 102(48): 17264–17271.

Murra, John. 1962. "Cloth and Its Functions in the Inca State." *American Anthropologist* 64(4): 710–728.

———. 1972. "El 'Control Vertical' de un Máximo de Pisos Ecológicos en la Economía de las Sociedades Andinas." In *Visita de la Provincia de León de Huánuco en 1562,* by Iñigo Ortíz de Zúñiga, edited by John Murra, 429–476. Huánuco, Perú: Universidad Nacional Hermilio Valdizán.

———. 1980. *The Economic Organization of the Inka State.* Greenwich, CT: JAI Press.

Nash, Donna, and Patrick Ryan Williams. 2009. "Wari Political Organization: The Southern Periphery." In Marcus and Williams 2009, 257–276.

Netherley, Patricia. 1990. "Out of Many, One: The Organization of Rule in the North Coast Polities." In Moseley and Cordy-Collins 1990, 461–488.

Noller, Jay. 1993. "Late Cenozoic Stratigraphy and Soil Geomorphology of the Peruvian Desert, 3–18°S: A Long-Term Record of Hyperaridity and El Niño." PhD diss., University of Colorado, Boulder.

Nuñez, Lautaro, Juan Varela, and Rodolfo Casamiquela. 1987. "Ocupación Paleoindia en el Centro Norte de Chile: Adaptación Circumlacustre en las Tierras Bajas." *Estudios Atacameños* 8: 142–185.

Ortloff, Charles, Robert Feldman, and Michael Moseley. 1985. Hydraulic Engineering and Historical Aspects of the pre-Columbian Intravalley Canal Systems of the Moche Valley, Peru." *Journal of Field Archaeology* 12(1): 77–98.

Owen, Bruce. 2005. "Distant Colonies and Explosive Collapse: The Two Stages of the Tiwanaku Diaspora in the Osmore Drainage." *Latin American Antiquity* 16(1): 45–80.

———. 2009. "Early Agriculture in the Coastal Osmore Valley, Peru: Synchronous Events and Macroregional Processes in the Formation of Andean Civilization." In Marcus and Williams 2009, 121–144.

Pachacuti Yamqui Salcamayhua, Juan de Santa Cruz. (1613) 1950. "Relación de Antigüedades desde Reyno del Perú." In *Tres Relaciones de Antigüedades Peruanas,* edited by Marcos Jiménez de la Espada, 207–281. Asunción: Editora Guaranía.

Pärrsinen, Martti. 1992. *Tawantinsuyu: The Inca State and Its Political Organization.* Helsinki: Societas Historica Finlandiae.

Parsons, Jeffrey, Charles Hastings, and Ramiro Matos Mendieta. 1997. "Rebuilding the State in Highland Peru: Herder-Cultivator Interaction during the Late Intermediate Period in the Tarama-Chinchaycocha Region." *Latin American Antiquity* 8(4): 317–341.

Patterson, Thomas. 1971. "Chavín: An Interpretation of Its Spread and Influence." In *Dumbarton Oaks Conference on Chavín,* edited by Elizabeth Benson, 29–48. Washington, DC: Dumbarton Oaks Research Library and Collection.

———. 1983. "The Historical Development of a Coastal Andean Social Formation in Central Peru, 6000–500 BC." In *Investigations of the Andean Past: Papers from the First Annual Northeast Conference on Andean Archaeology and Ethnohistory,* edited by Daniel Sandweiss, 21–37. Ithaca: Cornell University Latin American Studies Program.

Patterson, Thomas, and Edward Lanning. 1964. "Changing Settlement Patterns on the Central Peruvian Coast." *Ñawpa Pacha* 2: 113–123.

Paul, Anne. 1990. *Paracas Ritual Attire: Symbols of Authority in Ancient Peru.* Norman: University of Oklahoma Press.

———. 1991. "Paracas: An Ancient Cultural Tradition on the South Coast of Peru." In *Paracas Art & Architecture: Object and Context in South Coastal Peru,* edited by Anne Paul, 1–34. Iowa City: University of Iowa Press.

Paulsen, Allison. 1976. "Environment and Empire: Climatic Factors in Prehistoric Andean Culture Change." *World Archaeology* 8: 121–132.

Pearsall, Deborah. 1988. "An Overview of Formative Period Subsistence in Ecuador: Paleoethnobotanical Data and Perspectives." In *Diet and Subsistence: Current Archaeological Perspectives,* edited by Brenda Kennedy and Genevieve Le-Moine, 149–159. Edmonton: University of Calgary, Archaeological Association.

———. 2008. "Plant Domestication and the Shift to Agriculture in the Andes." In Silverman and Isbell 2008, 105–120.

Pease, Franklin. 1995. *Las Crónicas y los Andes.* Lima: Pontificia Universidad Católica del Perú, Fondo Editorial.

Peréz Calderón, Ismael, and José Ochatoma Paravicino. 1998. "Viviendas, Talleres, y Hornos de Producción Alfarera Huari en Conchopata *Conchopata: Revista de Arqueología* 1: 72–92.

Perry, Linda, Ruth Dickau, Sonia Zarillo, Irene Holst, Deborah Pearsall, Dolores Piperno, Mary Jane Berman, Richard Cooke, Kurt Rademaker, Anthony Ranere, J. Scott Raymond, Daniel Sandweiss, Franz Scaramelli, Kay Tarble, and James Zeidler. 2007. "Starch Fossils and the Domestication and Dispersal of Chili Peppers (Capsicum spp. L.) in the Americas." *Science* 315(5814): 986–988.

Perry, Linda, Daniel Sandweiss, Dolores Piperno, Kurt Rademaker, Michael Malpass, Adán Umire, and Pablo de la Vera. 2006. "Early Maize Agriculture and Interzonal Interaction in Southern Peru." *Nature* 440(7080): 76–79.

Pillsbury, Joanne, ed. 2001. *Moche Art and Archaeology in Ancient Peru.* Studies in the History of Art 63, Center for Advanced Study in the Visual Arts. Washington, DC: National Gallery of Art.

Piperno, Dolores. 1988. *Phytolith Analysis: An Archaeological and Geological Analysis.* New York: Academic Press.

——. 2009. "The Origins of Plant Cultivation and Domestication in the New World Tropics: Patterns, Process, and New Developments." *Current Anthropology* 52(S4): S453–S470.

——. 2011. "Northern Peruvian Early and Middle Preceramic Agriculture in Central and South American Contexts." In Dillehay 2011a, 275–284.

Piperno, Dolores, and Deborah Pearsall. 1998. *The Origins of Agriculture in the Lowland Neotropics.* San Diego: Academic Press.

Plourde, Aimée, and Charles Stanish. 2006. "The Emergence of Complex Society in the Titicaca Basin: The View from the North." In Isbell and Silverman 2006, 237–257.

Polo de Ondegardo, Juan, 1916 [1571]. "Relación de los fundamentos acerca del notable daño que resulta de no guarder a los Indios sus fueros." In *Colección de Libros y Documentos Referentes a la Historia del Perú,* edited by Horacio Urteaga, vol. 3, 45–188. Sammartí, Lima.

Ponce Sanginés, Carlos. 1970. *Las Culturas Wankarani y Chiripa y su Relación con Tiwanaku.* La Paz, Bolivia: Academia Nacional de Ciencias de Bolivia.

——. 1981. *Tiwanaku, Espacio, Tiempo y Cultura: Ensayo de Síntesis Arqueológica.* La Paz: Los Amigos del Libro.

——. 1995. *Tiwanaku, 200 Años de Investigaciones Arqueológicas.* La Paz: Producciones CIMA.

Portugal Ortiz, Max. *Escultura Prehispánica Boliviana.* La Paz: UMSA, 1998.

Pozorski, Shelia, and Thomas Pozorski. 1979. An Early Subsistence Exchange System in the Moche Valley, Peru. *Journal of Field Archaeology* 6: 413–432.

——. 1987. *Early Settlement and Subsistence in the Casma Valley, Peru.* Iowa City: University of Iowa Press.

——. 1992. "Early Civilization in the Casma Valley, Peru." *Antiquity* 66(253): 845–870.

——. 2002. "The Sechín Alto Complex and Its Place within Casma Valley Initial Period Development." In Isbell and Silverman 2002, 21–51.

——. 2006. "Las Haldas: An Expanding Initial Period Polity of Coastal Peru." *Journal of Anthropological Research* 62(1): 27–52.

——. 2008. "Early Cultural Complexity on the Coast of Peru." In Silverman and Isbell 2008, 607–631.

——. 2011. "The Square-Room Unit as an Emblem of Power and Authority within the Initial Period Sechín Alto Polity, Casma Valley, Peru." *Latin American Antiquity* 22: 1–25.

Pozorski, Thomas. 1975. "El Complejo de Caballo Muerto: Los Frisos de Barro de La Huaca de Los Reyes." *Revista del Museo Nacional* 41: 211–251.

——. 1980. "The Early Horizon Site of Huaca de Los Reyes: Societal Implications." *American Antiquity* 45(1): 100–110.

——. 1982. "Early Social Stratification and Subsistence Systems: The Caballo Muerto Complex." In Moseley and Day 1982, 225–254.

——. 1987. "Changing Priorities within the Chimú State: The Role of Irrigation Agriculture." In Haas, Pozorski, and Pozorski 1987, 111–120.

Pozorski, Thomas, and Shelia Pozorski. 1990. "Huaynuná, a Late Cotton Preceramic Site on the North Coast of Peru." *Journal of Field Archaeology* 17: 17–26.

——. 2005. "Architecture and Chronology at the Site of Sechin Alto, Casma Valley, Peru." *Journal of Field Archaeology* 30: 143–161.

Pozzi-Escot, Denise. 1991. "Conchopata: A Community of Potters." In Isbell and McEwan 1991, 81–92.

Price, T. Douglas, and Gary Feinman. 2010. *Images of the Past.* 7th ed. New York: McGraw-Hill Higher Education.

Pringle, Heather. 1998. "The Slow Birth of Agriculture." *Science* 282(5393): 1446–1450.

Proulx, Donald. 1994. "Stylistic Variation in Proliferous Nasca Pottery." *Andean Past* 4: 91–107.

——. 2001. "The Ritual Use of Trophy Heads in Ancient Nasca Society." In *Ritual Sacrifice in Ancient Peru,* edited by Elizabeth P. Benson and Anita Cook, 119–123. Austin: University of Texas Press.

——. 2008. "Paracas and Nasca: Regional Cultures on the South Coast of Peru." In Silverman and Isbell 2008, 563–586.

Quilter, Jeffrey. 1989. *Life and Death at Paloma: Society and Mortuary Practices in a Preceramic Peruvian Village.* Iowa City: University of Iowa Press.

——. 1991. "Late Preceramic Peru." *Journal of World Prehistory* 5(4): 387–438.

——. 1992. "To Fish in the Afternoon: Beyond Subsistence Economies in the Study of Early Andean Civilization." *Andean Past* 3: 111–125.

Quilter, Jeffrey, and Luis Jaine Castillo Butters, eds. 2010. *New Perspectives on Moche Political Organization.* Washington, DC: Dumbarton Oaks Research Library and Collection.

Quilter, Jeffrey, and Michele Koons. 2012. "The Fall of Moche: A Critique of Claims for South America's First State." *Latin American Antiquity* 23(2): 127–143.

Quilter, Jeffrey, Bernardino Ojeda E., Deborah Pearsall, Daniel Sandweiss, John Jones, and Elizabeth Wing. 1991. "Subsistence Economy of El Paraíso, an Early Peruvian Site." *Science* 251: 277–283.

Rademaker, Kurt. 2012. "Early Human Settlement of the High-Altitude Pucuncho Basin, Peruvian Andes." PhD diss., University of Maine at Orono.

Ranere, Anthony, and Richard G. Cooke. 2003. "Late Glacial and Early Holocene Occupation of Central American Tropical Forests." In *Under the Canopy: The Archaeology of Tropical Rain Forests,* edited by Julio Mercader, 219–248. Piscataway, NJ: Rutgers University Press.

Reimer, Paula, Edouard Bard, Alex Bayliss, J. Warren Beck, Paul Blackwell, Christopher Bronk Ramsey, Caitlin Buck, Hai Cheng, R. Lawrence Edwards, Michael Friedrich, Pieter Grootes, Thomas Guilderson, Haflidi Haflidason, Irka Hajdas, Christine Hatté, Timothy Heaton, Dirk Hoffmann, Alan Hogg, Konrad Hughen, K. Felix Kaiser, Bernd Kromer, Sturt Manning, Mu Niu, Ron Reimer, David Richards, E. Marian Scott, John Southon, Richard Staff, Christian Turney, and Johannes van der Plicht. 2013. "IntCal13 and Marine13 Radiocarbon Age Calibration Curves 0–50,000 Years Cal BP." *Radiocarbon* 55(4): 1869–1887.

Reindel, Markus, and Johny Isla. 1999. "Das Palpa-Tal: Ein Archiv des Vorgeschicte Peru." In *Nasca: Geheimnisvolle Zeichen im Alten Peru,* edited by Judith Rickenback, 177–198. Zurich: Museum Rietberg.

Reinhard, Johan. 1985. "Sacred Mountains: An Ethno-Archaeological Study of High Andean Ruins." *Mountain Research and Development* 5(4): 299–317.

——. 1988. *The Nazca Lines: A New Perspective on Their Origin and Meaning.* 4th ed. Lima: Editorial Los Pinos.

Reinhard, Johan, and Maria Constanza Ceruti. 2010. *Inca Rituals and Sacred Mountains. A Study of the World's Highest Archaeological Sites.* Cotsen Institute for Archaeology Monograph No. 67. Los Angeles: University of California.

Renfrew, Colin, and Paul Bahn. 2004. *Archaeology: Theories, Methods, and Practice.* 4th ed. New York: Thames & Hudson.

Rice, Don, Charles Stanish, and Phillip Scarr. 1989. *Ecology, Settlement, and History in the Osmore Drainage, Peru. Part I.* BAR International Series 545(i). Oxford: British Archaeological Reports.

Richardson, James, III. 1978. "Early Man on the Peruvian North Coast. Early Maritime Exploitation and Pleistocene and Holocene Environment." In *Early Man in America from a Circum-Pacific Perspective,* edited by Alan Bryan, 274–289. Occasional Papers of the Department of Anthropology 1. University of Alberta. Edmonton, Canada: Archaeological Researches International.

——. 1981. "Modeling the Development of Sedentary Maritime Economies on the Coast of Peru: A Preliminary Statement." *Annals of the Carnegie Museum* 50(5): 139–150.

——. 1994. *People of the Andes.* Montreal: St. Remy Press, and Washington, DC: Smithsonian Books.

Rick, John. 1980. *Prehistoric Hunters of the High Andes.* New York: Academic Press.

——. 2005. "The Evolution of Authority and Power at Chavín de Huántar, Peru." In *Foundations of Power in the Prehispanic Andes,* edited by Kevin Vaughn, Dennis Ogburn, and Christine Conlee, 71–89. Archeological Papers of the American Anthropological Association No. 14. Washington, DC: American Anthropological Association.

——. 2008. "Context, Construction, and Ritual in the Development of Authority at Chavín de Huántar." In Conklin and Quilter 2008, 3–34.

Rick, John, Christian Mesia, Daniel Contreras, Silvia R. Kembel, Rosa Rick, Matthew Sayre, and John Wolf. 2009. "La Cronología de Chavín de Huántar y Sus Implicancias para el Período Formativo." In *El Período Formativo: Enfoques y Evidencias Recientes. Cincuenta Años de la Misión Arqueológica Japonesa y Su Vigencia. Segunda Parte,* edited by Peter Kaulicke and Yoshio Onuki. Special issue of *Boletín de Arqueología PUCP* no. 13: 87–132.

Riddell, Fritz, and Lidio Valdéz. 1988. "Hacha y la Ocupación Temprana de Acarí." *Gaceta Arqueológica Andina* 16: 6–10.

Rivera, Mario. 2008. "The Archaeology of Northern Chile." In Silverman and Isbell 2008, 963–977.

Rivera Casanovas, Claudia. 2003. "Ch'iji Jawira, a Case Study of Ceramic Specialization in the Tiwanaku Urban Periphery." In Kolata 2003a, 296–315.

Roark, Richard. 1965. "From Monumental to Proliferous in Nasca Pottery." *Ñawpa Pacha* 3: 1–92.

Rollins, Harold, James Richardson, and Daniel Sandweiss. 1986. "The Birth of ENSO: Geoarchaeological Evidence and Implications." *Geoarchaeology* 1(1): 3–16.

Romero Velarde, Rubén, and Trine Pavel Svendsen, eds. 2010. *Arqueología en el Perú: Nuevos Aportes para el Estudio de las Sociedades Andinas Prehispánicas.* Lima: Anheb Impresiones.

Roosevelt, Anna Curtenius, M. Lima da Costa, C. Lopes Machado, Michel Michab, Norbert Mercier, Helene Vallados, James Feathers, William Barnett, M. Imazio da Silvieria, A. Henderson, J. Silva, B. Chernoff, D. Reese, J.A. Holman, Nicholas Toth, and Kathy Schick. 1996. "Paleoindian Cave Dwellers in the Amazon: The Peopling of the Americas." *Science* 272(5260): 373–384.

Rosas, Hermilio, and Ruth Shady. 1970. *Pacopampa: Un Centro Formativo en la Sierra Nor-Peruano.* Lima: Seminario de Historia Rural Andino, Universidad Nacional Mayor de San Marcos.

Rose, Courtney Elizabeth. 2001. "Household and Community Organization of a Formative Period Bolivian Settlement." PhD diss., University of Pittsburgh.

Rossen, Jack. 1991. "Ecotones and Low-Risk Intensification: The Middle Preceramic Habitation of Nanchoc, Northern Peru." PhD diss., University of Kentucky, Lexington.

——. 2011. "The Las Pircas Phase (9800–7800 B.P.)." In Dillehay 2011a, 95–116.

Rossen, Jack, Thomas Dillehay, and Donald Ugent. 1996. "Ancient Cultigens or Modern Intrusions? Evaluating Botanical Remains in an Andean Case Study." *Journal of Archaeological Science* 23: 391–407.

Rossen, Jack, Maria Teresa Planella, and Rubén Stehberg. 2010. "Archaeobotany of Cerro El Inga, Chile, at the Southern Inka Frontier." In Malpass and Alconini 2010, 14–43.

Rostworowski de Diez Canseco, Maria. 1977. *Etnia y Sociedad. Costa Peruana Prehispánica.* Lima: Instituto de Estudios Peruanos.

——. 1977a. "Breve Ensayo sobre el Señorío de Ychma." In Rostworowski 1977, 197–210.

——. 1977b. "Mercaderes del Valle de Chincha en la Época Prehispánica: Un Documento y unos Comentarios." In Rostworowski 1977, 97–140.

——. 1977c. "Pescadores Artesanos, y Mercaderos Costeños en el Perú Prehispánico." In Rostworowski 1977, 211–264.

——. 1977d. "El Señorío de Collique." In Rostworowski 1977, 21–96.

——. 1978–1980. "Guarco y Lunahuaná: Dos Señorios Prehispánicos de la Costa Sur Central del Peru." *Revista del Museo Nacional* 44: 135–214.

Rowe, John. 1944. *An Introduction to the Archaeology of Cuzco.* Papers of the Peabody Museum of American Archaeology and Ethnology 27, No. 2. Cambridge, MA: Harvard University.

——. 1946. "Inca Culture at the Time of the Spanish Conquest." In *Handbook of South American Indians,* edited by Julian Steward, 183–330. Bureau of American Ethnography Bulletin No. 143. Washington, DC: U.S. Government Printing Office.

——. 1948. "The Kingdom of Chimor." *Acta Americana* 6(1–2): 26–59.

——. 1956. "Archaeological Explorations in Southern Peru, 1954–1955." *American Antiquity* 22(2): 135–151.

——. 1962. *Chavín Art, an Inquiry into Its Form and Meaning.* New York: Museum of Primitive Art.

——. 1963. "Urban Settlements in Ancient Peru." *Ñawpa Pacha* 1: 1–28.

——. 1982. "Inca Policies and Institutions Relating to the Cultural Unification of the Empire." In *The Inca and Aztec States, 1400–1800: Anthropology and History*, edited by Goerge Collier, Renato Rosaldo, and John Wirth, 93–118. New York: Academic Press.

Rundel, Philip, and Michael Dillon. 1998. "Ecological Patterns in the Bromeliaceae of the Lomas Formations of Coastal Chile and Peru." *Plant Systematics and Evolution* 212: 261–278.

Salomon, Frank. 1985. "The Dynamic Potential of the Complementarity Concept." In *Andean Ecology and Civilization*, edited by Yoshio Masuda, Izumi Shimada, and Craig Morris, 511–532. Tokyo: University of Tokyo Press.

——. 1986. *Native Lords of Quito in the Age of the Incas.* Cambridge, UK: Cambridge University Press.

——. 1997. *Los Yumbos, Niguas, y Tsáchila o Colorados durante la Colonia Española: Etnohistoria del Noroccidente de Pichincha, Ecuador.* Quito: Ediciones Abya-Yal.

Sandweiss, Daniel. 1992. *The Archaeology of Chincha Fishermen: Specialization and Status in Inka Peru.* Bulletin of the Carnegie Museum of Natural History No. 29. Pittsburgh: Carnegie Museum of Natural History.

——. 2009. "Early Fishing and Inland Monuments: Challenging the Maritime Foundations of Andean Civilization?" In Marcus and Williams 2009, 39–54.

Sandweiss, Daniel, Alice Kelley, Daniel Belknap, Joseph Kelley, Kurt Rademaker, and David Reid. 2010. "GPR Identification of an Early Monument at Los Morteros in the Peruvian Coastal Desert." *Quaternary Research* 73: 439–448.

Sandweiss, Daniel, Heather MacInnis, Richard Burger, Asunción Cano, Bernardino Ojeda, Rolando Paredes, María del Carmen Sandweiss, and Michael Glasscock. 1998. "Quebrada Jaguay: Early South American Maritime Adaptations." *Science* 281: 1830–1832.

Sandweiss, Daniel, James Richardson III, Elizabeth J. Reitz, Jeffrey T. Hsu, and Robert Feldman. 1989. "Early Maritime Adaptations in the Andes: Preliminary Studies at the Ring Site, Peru." In Rice, Stanish, and Scarr 1989, 35–84.

Sandweiss, Daniel, James Richardson III, Elizabeth J. Reitz, Harold B. Rollins, and Kirk A. Maasch. 1996. "Geoarchaeological Evidence from Peru for a 5000 Years B.P. Onset of El Niño." *Science* 273: 1531–1533.

——. 1997. "Determining the Early History of El Niño. Response [to T.J. DeVries, L. Ortleib, A. Diaz, L. Wells, Cl. Hillaire-Marcel, L.E. Wells, and J. Noller]." *Science* 276: 965–967.

Sandweiss, Daniel, Ruth Shady Solís, Michael Moseley, David Keefer, and Charles Ortloff. 2009. "Environmental Change and Economic Development in Coastal Peru between 5,800 and 3,600 Years Ago." *Proceedings of the National Academy of Science* 106(5): 1359–1363.

Santoro, Calógero, Verónica Williams, Daniela Valenzuela, Álvaro Romero, and Vivien Standen. 2010. "An Archaeological Perspective on the Inka Provincial Administration of the South-Central Andes." In Malpass and Alconini 2010, 44–74.

Sapp, William, III. 2002. "The Impact of Imperial Conquest at the Palace of a Local Lord in the Jequetepeque Valley, Northern Peru." PhD diss., University of California, Los Angeles.

Sarmiento de Gamboa, Pedro. (1572) 1960. *Historia de los Incas.* Biblioteca de Autores Españoles (continuación) 135. Madrid: Ediciones Atlas.

Schreiber, Katharina. 1991. "Jincamocco: A Huari Administrative Center in the South Highlands of Peru." In Isbell and McEwan 1991, 199–213.

———. 1992. *Wari Imperialism in Middle Horizon Peru.* Anthropological Papers of the Museum of Anthropology 87. Ann Arbor: University of Michigan Press.

Schreiber, Katharina, and Josué Lancho Rojas. 1995. "The Puquios of Nasca." *Latin American Antiquity* 6(3): 229–254.

———. 2003. *Irrigation and Society in the Peruvian Desert: The Puquios of Nasca.* Lanham: Lexington Books.

Seddon, Matthew. 2005. "The Tiwanaku Period Occupation on the Island of the Sun." In Stanish, Cohen, and Aldenderfer 2005, 135–142.

Service, Elman. 1975. *Origins of the State and Civilization: The Process of Cultural Evolution.* New York: W. W. Norton.

Shady Solís, Ruth. 1997. *La Ciudad Sagrada de Caral: Supe en los Albores de la Civilización en el Perú.* Lima: Universidad Nacional Mayor de San Marcos.

———. 2006a. "America's First City? The Case of Late Archaic Caral." In Isbell and Silverman 2006, 28–66.

———. 2006b. "Caral-Supe and the North-Central Area of Peru: The History of Maize in the Andes and Where Civilization Came into Being." In *Histories of Maize: Multidisciplinary Approaches to the Prehistory, Linguistics, Biogeography, Domestication, and Evolution of Maize,* edited by John Staller, Robert Tykot, and Bruce Benz, 381–402. New York: Elsevier/Academic Press.

———. 2009. "Caral-Supe y su Entorno Natural y Social en los Orígenes de la Civilización." In Marcus and Williams 2009, 99–120.

Shady Solís, Ruth, Camilo Dolorier, Fanny Montesinos, and Lyda Casas. 2000. "Los Orígenes de la Civilización en el Perú: El Área Norcentral y el Valle de Supe durante el Arcaico Tardío." *Arqueología y Sociedad* 13: 13–48.

Shady Solís, Ruth, Jonathan Haas, and Winifred Creamer. 2001. "Dating Caral, a Preceramic Site in the Supe Valley on the Central Coast of Peru." *Science* 292: 723–726.

Shady Solís, Ruth, and Arturo Ruiz. 1979. "Evidence for Interregional Relationships during the Middle Horizon on the North-Central Coast of Peru." *American Antiquity* 44(4): 676–684.

Shimada, Izumi. 1990. "Cultural Continuities and Discontinuities on the North Coast of Peru, Middle-Late Horizons." In *The Northern Dynasties: Kingship and Statecraft in Chimor,* edited by Michael Moseley and Alana Cordy-Collins, 297–392. Washington, DC: Dumbarton Oaks Research Library and Collection.

———. 1991. "Pachacamac Archaeology: Retrospect and Prospect." In *Pachacamac: A Reprint of the 1903 Edition,* by Max Uhle, edited by Izumi Shimada, xvi–lxvi. University Museum of Archaeology and Anthropology Monograph No. 62. Philadelphia: University of Pennsylvania Press.

———. 1994. *Pampa Grande and the Mochica Culture.* Austin: University of Texas Press.

———. 1995. *Cultura Sicán: Dioses, Riqueza, y Poder en la Costa Norte del Perú.* Lima: Banco Continental.

———. 2000. "The Late Prehispanic Coastal States." In Minelli 2000, 49–110.

———. 2010. "Moche Sociopolitical Organization. Rethinking the Data, Approaches, and Models." In Quilter and Castillo Butters 2010, 70–82.

Shimada, Izumi, Robert Corruccini, Julie Farnum, Kazuharu Mine, Rafael Vega-Centeno, and Victor Curay. 1998. "Sicán Population and Mortuary Practice: A Multi-Dimensional Perspective." Paper presented at the 63rd annual meeting of the Society for American Archeology, Seattle, March 25–29.

Shimada, Izumi, Crystal Barker Schaaf, Lonnie Thompson, and Ellen Mosley-Thompson. 1991. "Cultural Impacts of Severe Droughts in the Prehispanic Andes: Application of a 1500-Year Ice Core Precipitation Record." *World Archaeology* 22(3): 247–270.

Silverman, Helaine. 1990. "The Early Pilgrimage Center at Cahuachi: Archaeological and Anthropological Perspectives." In *The Lines of Nazca,* edited by Anthony F. Aveni, 207–244. Memoirs of the American Philosophical Society 183. Philadelphia: American Philosophical Society.

———. 1993. *Cahuachi in the Ancient Nasca World.* Iowa City: University of Iowa Press.

———. 2002. "Nasca Settlement and Society on the Hundredth Anniversary of Uhle's Discovery of the Nasca Style." In Isbell and Silverman 2002, 121–158.

———, ed. 2004a. *Andean Archaeology.* Malden, MA: Blackwell.

———. 2004b. "Introduction: Space and Time in the Central Andes." In Silverman 2004a, 1–15.

Silverman, Helaine, and William Isbell, eds. 2002. *Andean Archaeology II: Art, Landscape, and Society.* New York: Kluwer Academic/Plenum Publishers.

———, eds. 2008. *Handbook of South American Archaeology.* New York: Springer.

Silverman, Helaine, and Donald Proulx. 2002. *The Nasca*. Malden, MA: Blackwell.

Slovak, Nicole, Adina Paytan, and Bettina Wiegand. 2009. "Reconstructing Middle Horizon Mobility Patterns on the Coast of Peru through Strontium Isotope Analysis." *Journal of Archaeological Science* 36: 157–165.

Spurling, Geoffrey. 1992. "The Organization of Craft Production in the Inca State: The Potters and Weavers of Milliraya." PhD diss., Cornell University.

Stackelbeck, Kary. 2008. "Adaptational Flexibility and Processes of Emerging Complexity: Early to Mid-Holocene Foragers in the Lower Jequetepeque Valley, Northern Peru." PhD diss., University of Kentucky, Lexington.

Stackelbeck, Kary, and Thomas Dillehay. 2011. "The Tierra Blanca Phase (7800–5000 BP)." In Dillehay 2011a, 117–134.

Stahl, Peter. 2008. "Animal Domestication in South America." In Silverman and Isbell 2008, 121–130.

Standen, Vivien G., Bernardo T. Arriaza, and Calógero M. Santoro. "Chinchorro Mortuary Practices on Infants: Northern Chile Archaic Period (BP 7000–3600)." In *Tracing Childhood: Bioarchaeological Investigations of Early Lives in Antiquity,* edited by Jennifer L. Thompson, Marta P. Alfonso-Durruty, and John J. Crandall, 58–74. Gainseville: University Press of Florida.

Standen, Vivien, and Bernardo Arriaza. 2000. "Trauma in the Preceramic Coastal Populations of Northern Chile: Violence or Occupational Hazards?" *American Journal of Physical Anthropology* 112: 239–249.

Stanish, Charles. 1989. "An Archaeological Evaluation of an Ethnohistorical Model in Moquegua." In Rice, Stanish, and Scarr 1989, 303–320.

———. 1992. *Ancient Andean Political Economy*. Austin: University of Texas Press.

———. 2002. *Ancient Titicaca: The Evolution of Complex Society in Southern Peru and Northern Bolivia*. Berkeley: University of California Press.

———. 2009. "The Tiwanaku Occupation of the Northern Titicaca Basin." In Marcus and Williams 2009, 145–164.

Stanish, Charles, Amanda Cohen, and Mark Aldenderfer, eds. 2005. *Advances In Titicaca Basin Archaeology 1*. Cotsen Institute of Archaeology Monograph No. 54. Los Angeles: University of California.

Stanish, Charles, Kirk Frye, Edmundo de la Vega, and Matthew Seddon. 2005. "Tiwanaku Expansion into the Western Titicaca Basin, Peru." In Stanish, Cohen, and Aldenderfer 2005, 103–114.

Stothert, Karen. 1988. *La Prehistoria Temprana de la Península de Santa Elena, Ecuador: Cultura las Vegas*. Miscelánea Antropológica Ecuatoriana Monográfica No. 10. Guayaquil: Museos del Banco Central del Ecuador.

———. 1992. "Early Economies of Coastal Ecuador and the Foundations of Andean Civilization." *Andean Past* 3: 43–54.

Stothert, Karen, Dolores Piperno, and Thomas Andres. 2003. "Terminal Pleistocene/Early Holocene Human Adaptation in Coastal Ecuador." *Quaternary International* 109–110: 23–43.

Stuiver, Minze, and Paula Reimer. 1993. "Extended ^{14}C Data Base and Revised CALIB 3.0 ^{14}C Age Calibration Program." *Radiocarbon* 35: 215–230.

Sutter, Richard. 2009. "Prehistoric Population Dynamics in the Andes." In Marcus and Williams 2009, 9–38.

Sutter, Richard, and Rosa Cortez. 2005. "The Nature of Human Sacrifice (with Comments and Reply)." *Current Anthropology* 46(4): 521–549.

Tantalean, Henry. 2010. "Del Espacio Inclusivo al Espacio Exclusivo: Las Primeras Sociedades Sedentarias (1400 A.N.C.–400 D.N.C.) del Valle Quilcamaya-Tintiri, Azángaro, Puno." In Romero Velarde and Svendsen 2010, 39–70.

Tello, Julio C. 1959. *Paracas: Primera Parte*. Lima: Empresa Gráfica T. Scheuch.

———. 1960. *Chavín: Cultura Matríz de la Civilizacion Andina*. Publicación Antropológica del Archivo "Julio C. Tello" de la Universidad Nacional Mayor de San Marcos No. 2. Lima: Universidad Nacional Mayor de San Marcos Press.

Tello, Julio César, and Toribio Mejía Xesspe. 1979. *Paracas: Segunda Parte, Cavernas y Necrópolis*. Lima: Universidad Nacional Mayor de San Marcos.

Terada, Kazuo. 1985. "Early Ceremonial Architecture in the Cajamarca Valley." In *Early Ceremonial Architecture in the Andes*, edited by Christopher Donnan, 191–208. Washington, DC: Dumbarton Oaks Research Library and Collection.

Terada, Kazuo, and Yoshio Onuki. 1982. *Excavations at Huacaloma in the Cajamarca Valley, Peru, 1979*. Report 2 of the Japanese Scientific Expedition to Nuclear America. Tokyo: University of Tokyo Press.

———. 1985. *The Formative Period in the Cajamarca Basin, Peru: Excavations at Huacaloma and Layzón, 1982*. Report 3 of the Japanese Scientific Expedition to Nuclear America. Tokyo: University of Tokyo Press.

———. 1988. *Las Excavaciones en Cerro Blanco y Huacaloma, Cajamarca, Peru, 1985*. Tokyo: University of Tokyo Press.

Thompson, Lonnie, Ellen Mosley-Thompson, John F. Bolzan, and Bruce R. Koci. 1985. "A 1500-Year Record of Tropical Precipitation in Ice Cores from the Quelccaya Ice Cap, Peru." *Science* 229(4717): 971–973.

Thompson, Lonnie, Ellen Mosley-Thompson, Mary. E. Davis, Ping-Nan Lin, Keith Henderson, J. Cole-Dai, John Bozan, and Kam-Biu Liu. 1995. "Late Glacial Stage and Holocene Tropical Ice Core Records from Huascarán, Peru." *Science* 269: 46–50.

Toohey, Jason. 2011. "Formal and Stylistic Variation in the Ceramic Assemblage at the Late Intermediate Period Site of Yanaorco in the Cajamarca Highlands of Northern Peru." *Ñawpa Pacha* 31(2): 171–200.

Topic, John. 1982. "Lower-Class Social and Economic Organization at Chan Chan." In Moseley and Day 1982, 145–176.

———. 1986. "A Sequence of Monumental Architecture from Huamachuco." In *Perspectives on Andean Prehistory and Protohistory: Papers from the Third Annual Northeast Conference on Andean Archaeology and Ethnohistory,* edited by Daniel Sandweiss and D. Peter Kvietok, 63–83. Ithaca: Cornell University Latin American Studies Program.

———. 1990. "Craft Production in the Kingdom of Chimor." In *The Northern Dynasties, Kingship and Statecraft in Chimor,* edited by Michael Moseley and Alana Cordy-Collins, 145–176. Washington, DC: Dumbarton Oaks Research Library and Collection.

———. 1991. "Huari and Huamachuco." In Isbell and McEwan 1991, 141–164.

———. 2009. "Settlement Patterns in the Huamachuco Area." In Marcus and Williams 2009, 211–240.

Topic, John, and Theresa Lange Topic. 1992. "The Rise and Decline of Cerro Amaru: An Andean Shrine during the Early Intermediate Period and Middle Horizon." In *Ancient Images, Ancient Thought: The Archaeology of Ideology: Proceedings of the Twenty-third Annual Conference of the Archaeological Association of the University of Calgary,* edited by A. Sean Goldsmith, Sandra Garvie, David Selin, and Jeanette Smith, 167–180. Edmonton: University of Calgary Archaeological Association.

Topic, Theresa Lange. 1991. "The Middle Horizon in Northern Peru." In Isbell and McEwan 1991, 233–246.

———. 2009. "The Meaning of Monuments at Marcahuamachuco." In Marcus and Williams 2009, 241–256.

Tung, Tiffiny. 2012. *Violence, Ritual, and the Wari Empire: A Social Bioarchaeology of Imperialism in the Ancient Andes.* Gainseville: University Press of Florida.

Uceda, Santiago. 2001. "Investigations in the Huaca de la Luna, Moche Valley: An Example of Moche Religious Architecture." In Pillsbury 2001, 47–68.

———. 2010. "Theocracy and Secularism: Relationships between the Temple and Urban Nucleus and Political Change at the Huacas de Moche." In Quilter and Castillo Butters 2010, 132–158.

Uhle, Max. 1991. *Pachacamac: A Reprint of the 1903 Edition.* Edited by Izumi Shimada, University Museum of Archaeology and Anthropology Monograph No. 62. Philadelphia: University of Pennsylvania Press.

Urton, Gary. 1990. *The History of a Myth: Pacariqtambo and the Origins of the Incas.* Austin: University of Texas Press.

———. 2001. "A Calendrical and Demographic Tomb Text from Northern Peru." *Latin American Antiquity* 12(2): 127–147.

Vallejo, Francisco. 2010. "Evidencias Arqueológicas de un Nuevo Estilo Cerámico en el Valle de Huaura para el Período Intermedio Tardío: El Paso del Horizonte Medio al Intermedio Tardío." In Romero Velarde and Svendsen 2010, 229–248.

Vargas Ugarte, Rubén. 1936. "La Fecha de la Fundación de Trujillo." *Revista Histórica* 10: 229–239.

Verano, John. 2001. "War and Death in the Moche World: Osteological Evidence and Visual Discourse." In Pillsbury 2001, 111–126.

Verano, John, and Jack Rossen. 2011. "Human Remains." In Dillehay 2011a, 163–176.

Vogel, Melissa. 2003. "Life on the Frontier: Identity and Sociopolitical Change at the Site of Cerro La Cruz, Peru." PhD diss., University of Pennsylvania.

———. 2011. "Style and Interregional Interaction: Ceramics from the Casma Capital of El Purgatorio." *Ñawpa Pacha* 31(2): 201–224.

———. 2012. *Frontier Life in Ancient Peru: The Archaeology of Cerro la Cruz.* Gainesville: University Press of Florida.

Vranich, Alexei. 2009. "The Development of the Ritual Core of Tiwanaku." In Young-Sánchez 2009, 11–34.

Wachtel, Nathan. 1982. "The Mitimas of the Cochabamba Valley: The Colonization Policy of Huayna Capac." In *The Inca and Aztec States, 1400–1800: Anthropology and History,* edited by George Collier, Renato Rosaldo, and John Wirth, 199–235. New York: Academic Press.

Wallace, Dwight. 1991. "The Chincha Roads: Economics and Symbolism." In *Ancient Road Networks and Settlement Hierarchies in the New World,* edited by Charles Trumbold, 253–263. Cambridge, UK: Cambridge University Press.

Watanabe, Shinya. 2001. "Wari y Cajamarca." In *Huari y Tiwanaku: Modelos vs. Evidencias. Segunda Parte,* edited by Peter Kaulicke and William H. Isbell. Special issue of *Boletín de Arqueología PUCP* no. 5: 531–542.

Webster, Demuth, and John Janusek. 2003. "Tiwanaku Camelids. Subsistence, Sacrifice, and Social Reproduction." In Kolata 2003a, 343–362.

Weir, Glendon, and J. Phillip Dering. 1986. "The Lomas of Paloma: Human Environmental Relations in a Central

Peruvian Fog Oasis: Archaeobotany and Palynology." In Matos Mendieta, Turpin, and Eling 1986, 18–44.

Wernke, Steven. 2003. "An Archaeo-History of Andean Community and Landscape: The Late Prehispanic and Early Colonial Colca Valley." PhD diss., University of Wisconsin, Madison.

Wheeler, Jane. 1995. "Evolution and Present Situation of the South American Camelids." *Biological Journal of the Linnean Society* 54: 271–295.

Wheeler, Jane, Edgardo Pires-Ferreira, and Peter Kaulicke. 1976. "Preceramic Animal Utilization in the Central Peruvian Andes." *Science* 194: 483–490.

Whitehead, William. 2006. "Redefining Plant Use at the Formative Site of Chiripa in the Southern Titicaca Basin." In Isbell and Silverman 2006, 258–279.

Willey, Gordon. 1971. *An Introduction to American Archaeology,* vol. 2: *South America.* Englewood Cliffs: Prentice-Hall.

Williams, Carlos. 1985. "A Scheme for the Early Monumental Architecture of the Central Coast of Peru." In *Early Ceremonial Architecture in the Andes,* edited by Christopher Donnan, 227–240. Washington, DC: Dumbarton Oaks Research Library and Collection.

Williams, Patrick Ryan. 2001. "Cerro Baúl: A Wari Center on the Tiwanaku Frontier." *Latin American Antiquity* 12(1): 67–83.

Williams, Patrick Ryan, and Donna Nash. 2002. "Imperial Interaction in the Andes: Huari and Tiwanaku at Cerro Baúl." In Isbell and Silverman 2002, 243–265.

Wilson, David John. 1988. *Prehispanic Settlement Patterns in the Lower Santa Valley, Peru: A Regional Perspective on the Origins and Development of Complex North Coast Society.* Washington, DC: Smithsonian Institution Press.

Wirrmann, Denis, Philippe Mourguiart, and L. Fernando de Oliviera Almeida. 1988. "Holocene Sedimentology and Ostracod Distribution in Lake Titicaca: Paleohydrological Interpretations." In *Quaternary of South America and Antarctic Peninsula,* Vol. 6, edited by Jorge Rabassa, 89–127. Rotterdam: A. A. Balkema.

Wise, Karen. 1997. "The Late Archaic Period Occupation at Carrizal, Perú." *Contributions in Science* 467: 1–16.

———. 1999. "Kilómetro 4 y la Ocupación del Período Arcaico en el Area de Ilo, al Sur del Perú." *El Período Arcaico en el Perú: Hacia una Definición de los Origenes,* edited by Peter Kaulicke. Special issue of *Boletín de Arqueología PUCP* no. 3: 335–363.

Wright, Henry. 1984. "Prehistoric Political Formations." In *On the Evolution of Complex Societies,* edited by Timothy Earle, 41–77. Malibu: Undena Press.

Wright, Kenneth. 2006. *Tipón: Water Engineering Masterpiece of the Inca Empire.* Reston, VA: ASCE Press.

Wright, Kenneth, and Alfredo Valencia Zegarra. 2000. *Machu Picchu: A Civil Engineering Marvel.* Reston, VA: ASCE Press.

Wright, Melanie, Christine Hastorf, and Heidi Lennstrom. 2003. "Prehispanic Agriculture and Plant Use at Tiwanaku: Social and Political Implications." In Kolata 2003a, 384–403.

Young-Sánchez, Margaret, ed. 2009. *Tiwanaku: Papers from the 2005 Mayer Center Symposium at the Denver Art Museum.* Frederick and Jan Meyer Center for Pre-Columbian and Spanish Colonial Art at the Denver Art Museum. Denver: Denver Art Museum.

Zeidler, James. 2008. "The Ecuadorian Formative." In Silverman and Isbell 2008, 459–488.

Zuidema, R. Tom 1964. *The Ceque System of Cuzco: The Social Organization of the Capital of the Inca.* International Archives of Ethnography No. 50. Leiden: E. J. Brill.

———. 1977. "The Inca Calendar." In *Native American Astronomy,* edited by Anthony Aveni, 219–259. Austin: University of Texas Press.

———. 1982. "Myth and History in Ancient Peru." In *The Logic of Culture: Advances in Structural Theory and Methods,* edited by Ino Rossi, 150–175. South Hadley, MA: J. F. Bergin.

———. 1990. *Inca Civilization in Cuzco.* Austin: University of Texas Press.

———. 2009. "Tiwanaku Iconography and the Calendar." In Young-Sánchez 2009, 83–100.

INDEX

Page numbers in italics refer to figures and tables.